# THE CULTURAL WORK OF EMPIRE

*Lord Clive (1725–1774) receiving from the Nawab* by Edward Penny.

# THE CULTURAL WORK OF EMPIRE

## THE SEVEN YEARS' WAR AND THE IMAGINING OF THE SHANDEAN STATE

◆ ◆ ◆

CAROL WATTS

Edinburgh University Press

For John and Harry

© Carol Watts, 2007

Edinburgh University Press Ltd
22 George Square, Edinburgh

Typeset in 10.25/12.5 Sabon by
Servis Filmsetting Ltd, Manchester, and
printed and bound in Great Britain by
Antony Rowe Ltd, Chippenham, Wilts

A CIP record for this book is available from the British Library

ISBN 978 0 7486 2564 2 (hardback)

# CONTENTS

# ACKNOWLEDGEMENTS

Writing a book always seems a Shandean enterprise, and the making of this one has lived up to its subject more than most. It began with the formative wit and critical inspiration of Terry Eagleton at Oxford many years ago, and has been shaped by the remarkable environment of the School of English and Humanities at Birkbeck, University of London, where my colleagues and students past and present have generously informed my thinking more than they know. The book has been given time to come to fruition, and I want to thank Isobel Armstrong and Tom Healy especially for that. I am grateful to John Barrell, Markman Ellis, Harriet Guest, Doug Hamilton, Bill Schwarz, David Wootton and Brian Young, for the chance to test my ideas, and parts of chapters, in their company, including papers at Queen Mary, Sussex, York, the Institute for Historical Research and the National Maritime Museum; to Peter Osborne, for the space to experiment with eighteenth-century material on women's time and Blair's Britain in the pages of *Radical Philosophy*; to Susanna Rustin for commissioning pages on Sterne and war in the *Guardian*; to Caroline Bergvall, Catherine Boyle, Rod Mengham and Denise Riley for underlining the creative possibilities of new kinds of writing even as this project came into the light of day; and to the members of the travelling Duke University research colloquium on *Subjectivity and Subjectivation*, where the present day urgencies of a global war for empire were made more than theoretically evident. Particular warm (and wine-filled) thanks are due to Ian Higgins for his close and enlightening reading of an early draft of the manuscript, to Vivien Jones and David Wootton for supporting what became a crucial period of AHRC-funded leave, ensuring the book's completion, and to John Barrell and Alberto Moreiras for their hugely reinforcing readings, and interrogations, of the proposal and final manuscript.

John and Harry Kraniauskas have lived alongside this sprawl of papers and ideas for more years than we care to remember, and have made it what it is. They continually remind me of the pleasures, and the necessity, in the Shandean 'lesson to the world, "*to let people tell their stories their own way*" '. This book is for them, with love.

Grateful thanks to the University Press of Florida for permission to reprint from *The Works of Laurence Sterne*, edited by Melvyn New; to the Burghley House Collection for the reproduction of Angelica Kauffman's 'Maria'; to Derby Museums and Art Gallery for the reproduction of Joseph Wright of Derby's 'Maria and her Dog Silvio'; to the Massachusetts Historical Society for permission to use the detail from 'A Prospective Plan of the Battle fought near Lake George' which can be viewed in its entirety at their online archive. The British Library kindly gave permission to reproduce 'View of the Forts on the Hills of Veloor' from Orme's three volume history, and also Edward Penny's 'Lord Clive and the Nawab of Bengal'. Sections on Voltaire in Chapter 1 have appeared previously in my 'A Comedy of Terrors: *Candide* and the Jus Publicum Europaeum', *South Atlantic Quarterly* 104:2 (2005), 337–47; and those on Mary Collier in Chapter 5 were first briefly explored in my 'Time and the Working Mother: Kristeva's "Women's Time" Revisited', *Radical Philosophy* 91 (1998), 6–18.

# ILLUSTRATIONS

# ABBREVIATIONS

*BJ*      Laurence Sterne, *Continuation of the Bramine's Journal*, in *A Sentimental Journey through France and Italy and Continuation of the Bramine's Journal: The Text and Notes*, The Florida Edition of the Works of Laurence Sterne, vol. 6, ed. Melvyn New and W. G. Day (Gainesville, FL: University Press of Florida, 2002).

*Sermons*   *The Sermons of Laurence Sterne*, The Florida Edition of the Works of Laurence Sterne, vols 4–5; ed. Melvyn New (Gainesville, FL: University Press of Florida, 1996). References are to the sermon number, followed by the page number in the Florida edition.

*SJ*      Laurence Sterne, *A Sentimental Journey through France and Italy*, collected with *Continuation of the Bramine's Journal: The Text and Notes*, The Florida Edition of the Works of Laurence Sterne, vol. 6 (ed.), Melvyn New and W. G. Day (Gainesville, FL: University Press of Florida, 2002).

*TS*      Laurence Sterne, *The Life and Opinions of Tristram Shandy, Gentleman: The Text*, The Florida Edition of the Works of Laurence Sterne, vols 1–2, ed. Melvyn New and Joan New (Gainesville, FL: University Presses of Florida, 1984). References are to Sterne's original volume and chapter numbers, followed by the page number in the Florida edition.

# INTRODUCTION

## THE CULTURAL WORK OF EMPIRE

We do not pretend to give the name of history to what we have written.
*Annual Register* (1758)[1]

Tuesday, 14 September 1762. In the small Sussex village of East Hoathly, a shopkeeper and parish officer, Thomas Turner, sat down to write an entry into his journal. He was an assiduous man, and his diary is full of the detailed transactions of daily life, from his household ledgers to the composition of his dinners, a recipe for leftovers, important in a time of scarcity, saved from the monthly magazines. Despite his concern for self-improvement, voiced with a certain shamefaced regularity after each Sunday sermon, he liked a sociable drink. On this particular evening he had been visited by a close friend, Mr Tipper, who in addition to knowing 'immortal Hudibras by heart' (as his tombstone records) was also a Newhaven brewer, and excise officer during the hop harvest. Turner's record was to the point. 'At home all day and pretty busy. In the afternoon employed myself a-writing. In the even Mr Tipper read to me part of a – I know not what to call it but *Tristram Shandy*.'[2]

Mr Tipper had brought along Laurence Sterne's comic novel a little after its first volumes had made such an impact on the circles of fashionable literary life. And if we put aside for a moment that briefest tremor of typographical consternation in Turner's entry at quite what it was that his guest was reading aloud, we might note that his hesitation was not attributable to ignorance. Sterne's was one of a range of books that Turner records encountering in the pages of his journal. He liked Shakespeare, shared with many of his contemporaries a familiarity with sermons (Sterne's among them), and was keen to keep up with the matter of the monthly magazines and the news from the *London Gazette* and the *Sussex Weekly Advertiser*. He was interested in politics (the Wilkite *North Briton*: 'an extreme good paper'[3]), and his consumption of geographical grammars suggests an interest in the world beyond the confines of his parish. He was as likely to spend an evening sketching out the royal family tree, having enjoyed Arthur Collins's *The Peerage of England*, as he was a convivial time with his friend.

In short, Thomas Turner liked being part of the ebb and flow of a wider literate culture, and had a sense of the formation of his own opinion to which the self-authorship of the diary is testimony. Reflecting on the pieces collected in the *London Magazine* in 1764, Turner remarked, 'perhaps I may be partial in my opinion, and only think them excellent as they agree with my own sentiments, for we are apt to be partial in our judgement of men and books as they agree and are similar to our own thoughts, few having so sound a judgement as to think and act impartial when their interests or sentiments are the topic.'[4] What Turner's thoughts were on the nature of *The Life and Opinions of Tristram Shandy, Gentleman* we will never know. Yet the telling break in his sentence, marked in Shandean style by a hyphen ('part of a – I know not what to call it'[5]) will nonetheless prove an unexpected entry point into the sentiments of British culture in the mid-eighteenth century, for which Laurence Sterne's writing will provide the key. For the moment we will keep its prospect hanging, like Mrs Shandy suspended at the keyhole in the pages of the most extraordinary novel of the day.

Turner had good cause to exercise his opinions over the period of the journal, which he began in 1754 and managed to keep up for almost a decade. In 1756 Britain went to war with France over territories in North America and Canada, and conflict ignited around the globe, also breaking out in India, on the coast of West Africa and in the Caribbean. The Seven Years' War (otherwise known in its American theatre as the French and Indian Wars) would move Britain's imperial fortunes into a new phase. In the September of Mr Tipper's visit, victory seemed certain, though the Spanish had also recently entered the fray. British soldiers had taken Havana a month earlier, while on another flank a motley force (largely made up of French deserters and Indian recruits) was then approaching Manila in the Spanish Philippines.[6] It was a global war, if the word 'global' is not quite to be understood in its modern, instrumentally exhaustive, sense: British power, though not yet an empire in systemic terms, was extending through capillaries of trade and conquest further than ever before. 'Ministers in this country, where every part of the World affects us, in some way or other, should consider the *whole Globe*', noted the Duke of Newcastle, in the thick of it as prime minister in the 1750s.[7]

If that understated 'consideration' of the globe meant aggression, at the hub of village life in East Hoathly (where Newcastle was Lord of the Manor), it was weighed sometimes quite literally as a cost. The inhabitants of the south coast and its environs saw the ships and reported rumours of impressment, feared invasion and worried like their more landbound compatriots over the wartime privations of money, food and trade, the loss of friends and relatives. They might turn away from 'the World' to local business – and references to the war in Turner's journal, if mentioned at all, increasingly take second place to provincial affairs – but even in that turning away was a registering of a newfound reach: sensed in the shifting market for commodities, patterns of credit, and far-flung lives. Alongside Turner's reports of marital disquiet and cricket games, what he called the 'little circle of my knowledge'[8] was shaped by a wider world; not only by the repercussions of the events taking place in 'Europe, Asia, Africa and America',[9] but also by forms of national imagining that had been generated in the face of such a global prospect.

What is interesting about the account of wartime fortunes in Turner's journal is how far his views ventriloquate the saws of wider public opinion. Despite his sense of partiality, these are not singular, private sentiments. The language of the journal at key points is indistinguishable from rhetoric found in the jeremiads and pamphlets of the time, assumed sometimes with a certain self-conscious oratory. The early anxieties at military failure are expressed in characteristically gendered terms as a concern at 'a spirit of effeminacy and self-interest' which seems 'almost to over-spread the whole face of this kingdom': phrases which had found powerful expression in one of the most widely read tracts of the period, John Brown's *An Estimate of the Manners and Principles of the Times*.[10] In 1759 Turner celebrates the turning point of the war on the occasion of a national thanksgiving, with language that seems quite distinct from his own everyday observations:

> For I think that no nation had ever greater occasion to adore the Almighty Disposer of all events than Albion, whose forces meet with success in almost all quarters of the world, and where plenty once more rears her pleasing aspect. The pestilential distemper is now no more among our herds; and there now seems to reign a spirit of unity in our national councils, [and] a king sitting on the British throne whose whole intention seems to be that of making the happiness of every individual of his subjects the same as his own. Oh, let Britain think on these blessings and adore the giver of them! Let us with all sincerity and pure devotion in one voice continue to supplicate the blessing of the Almighty on this happy isle![11]

Fresh from his visit to the village church, it was evidently religious doctrine that shaped Turner's anticipation of national unity, 'Albion' synonymous with the Jerusalem of the lesson ('The text is Psalm 122: 6: "Pray for the peace of Jerusalem: they shall prosper that love thee".')[12] The coincidence of good harvests and military success was evidently interpreted as providential by design, and a sign of the unity of a specifically Protestant imperial purpose which else-where was celebrated in more intensely millennial terms.[13] But if it was the 'practical divinity' of the sermon, in Samuel Johnson's words,[14] which provided the rhetorical dynamic of Turner's opinion and his sense of connection with the 'one voice' of the nation, his patriotism reveals something of the anatomy of identifying with the purpose of the state at this time. On the one hand it entailed a giving over of private opinion to the interests of higher authority, and paradoxically through the abnegation of one's own will the accruing of a certain individuated rhetorical power and ownership in the process. And on the other, it involved the expression of *love*: here an affection for king and country, in a posited equality with the monarch that anticipated a mutual exchange of 'happiness'. This was *consent* in the making, but in its affirmation of imperial successes 'in almost all quarters of the world' such consent carried with it another kind of fashioning that this book explores as the *cultural work* of empire: the generation and renewal of the lineaments of the state.

## State Stories

To conjure up the 'cold monster'[15] of the state as a privileged term here might seem to interrupt a mid-century scene more appropriate to the explanatory logics of the nation and its narrations; logics which can perhaps more evi-dently be deciphered in the cultural (and literary) life of a historical moment, given the potency of the 'pulsation of the national sign'.[16] Turner clearly felt the rhetorical heat of belonging to the nation and its church at the height of wartime, and his daily labour as an instrument of the more abstract determi-nations of the state – as a parish officer carrying out the law, as a tradesman negotiating local taxation with excise officers, as a subject supporting the war (and thus the state's monopoly of the use of violence) – provided a particular syntax for the rhythms of his life which was undoubtedly less expressive (though carefully noted in his journal even so). Yet the intense personal individuation and paradoxical alienation of Turner's private sentiments, and the celebration of his own part in the sovereign dissemination of 'happiness', are testimony to the political rationality of the time,[17] and to a wider social body denoted by the state, one no less concerned with the collective partici-pation and the identifications which animated the 'nation', if its lexicon was of another order.

   The state is often conceptualised in highly reified terms as a 'kind of natural object',[18] a 'mythified abstraction';[19] or in apparatuses which locate political power in largely unified institutions, exercising authority over a given territory. I want to think of it more performatively as the political form of social life, one that despite such a tendency towards hypostatisation is also registered and constituted in fluid and capillary practices of administration, in regimes of knowledge and activity, in modes of writing (surveying, mapping, quantifying, narrativising), and as a utopian and imaginary limit. As such, it was increasingly woven through the fabric of ordinary eighteenth-century British lives: not just in terms of individual encounters with the law, but in questions of conduct, welfare, livelihood, health, trade, the discipline and freedoms of time.

If there is a drama addressed in this book, it concerns the making of 'modern' subjectivity in such an environment, the *experience* of encountering, sometimes testing, the self's imagined and practical limits, in both private and collective terms. In the 1760s, I will suggest, individual subjectivities were revealed as suddenly intensified, freed unevenly, though never absolutely, from the rituals of traditional ties, in ways that produced thought, new fields of action, and answering kinds of conformity reinvesting in those ties anew. The reach of the self could seem, for some, disorientatingly extensive and enhanced by circumstance, even as it was brought to make sense in newly abstracted and morally dutiful ways.

If such deracination is central to modernity, it contributes to a familiar state story, one that might be described (in Hegelian terms) as a growing secularisation of the values through which life was held to be meaningful. This secular story would doubtless have been news to the Sunday faithful in 1759, Thomas Turner among them, or to the Yorkshire vicar whose writing (sermons included), with its wayward trajectories and sentimental toleration, animates my account. Yet in commenting – in confessional or fictional form – on the world in which they find themselves, both men inhabit in highly personal ways the tensions and possibilities of their time: the religious and national/political values which defined their belonging, and also their sense of freedom; values generating what Étienne Balibar has termed a 'fictive universality'. Such universality, or universalities, imply not that 'the idea that the common nature of individuals is given or already there, but, rather, the fact that it is produced inasmuch as particular identities are relativized, and become mediations for the realization of a superior and more abstract goal'[20]. The pressures of imperial expansion might find universalising explanation in the values of the protestant Church, or in the rolling out of 'English' liberty and power across the globe; both working in the 1760s to produce and reinforce the sense of empire as a providential and civilisational birthright that might be lived internally, whatever (for many) its sacrificial costs and posthumous rewards.

It seems important to keep the human contradictions, and historical indeterminacies, of such state imagining alive, its potential for failure, the heterogeneous and sometimes recalcitrant object of its disciplines. It is precisely at the place where the uncertainties of individual autonomy – the local warmth of private life and affiliations of kinship, the messiness of opinions, desires, freedoms, investments, securities – meet the complex imbrications of social life that 'the price to be paid for the universalistic liberation of the individual', in Balibar's words, is weighed.[21] What brought its cost into relief in the 1760s, I want to suggest, was the living out of this everyday drama as it was shaped and brought into being by the impact of 'global' imperial war, a war which demanded its own universalising narratives of legitimation, even as the 'relativisation of identity' Balibar describes was visited on the population in the most powerful terms.

One aspect of the 'price' of this exchange – liberation, in return for subjection – is already evident in the rhetoric of Turner's diary. On the one hand is the registering of a personally styled sense of individuation, such that it seemed to him impossible 'to think and act impartial'. A self might experience his or herself as sometimes radically free to form views distinct from tradition or authority (and consequent unease, euphoria, and crises of conscience). And on the other, in the same breath, as subject to a structural marginality or insignificance, one's 'opinion' given over to the judgement of others. For the philosopher David Hume there was 'wonder' in such a double bind. He noted how curious it was 'to observe the implicit submission with which men resign their own sentiments and passions to those of their leaders':

> When we enquire by what means this wonder is brought about, we shall find that as FORCE is always on the side of the governed, the governors have nothing to support them except opinion. 'Tis therefore, on opinion only that government is founded; and this maxim extends to the most despotic and most military governments, as well as to the freest and most popular.[22]

In the circulation of opinion was a form of governance: Turner's private crafting of opinion was a measure of his participation in wider forms of consent. Yet Hume's statement takes on a particular inflection in the climate of the war and its aftermath, one that has the scent of political potentiality. Consent to the will of the imperial state brought about contradictions, a consciousness of what it meant to sacrifice one's own passions and sentiments, and more than that – a livelihood, a life even – for the wider ambitions of the nation; contradictions which had to be made safe if 'the governed' were to remain so. The populous presence of 'the governed', a sense of their *number*, was a 'force' that had to be defused in the 1760s, sometimes on the streets. Consent had to be won, and if that meant for some the comforts of the abstract recognition conferred by public culture, others 'gave' their consent, as John Barrell has discussed, by simply walking down the king's highway (from where they might be press-ganged into service).[23] The considerable armoury of state activities, from the stark and ubiquitous reminder of the gallows to the promotion of social 'happiness' that had begun to figure in early utilitarian arguments and the establishing of welfare institutions, might suggest that the governors had more at their disposal than mere opinion. But Hume grasps, to a degree, the *reactive* nature of such a repertoire. As if, like the opening of Pandora's box, energies had been released which proved not so easy to contain. What if the price of such liberation was refused? Or what if its terms admitted new kinds of social subjects, whose very inclusion would transform the nature of the exchange? How far, given Britain's extension around the globe, should such 'opinion' reach?

## Pedagogies of Consent

As the Seven Years' War entered the realms of domestic 'common conversation',[24] charted in journals and quantified in newspapers, the matter of theatrical jokes and financial rumour, it dragged in its wake a long-established vision of the 'imagined community' of the nation, in Benedict Anderson's widely used phrase,[25] a vision which would have been familiar to generations of British subjects accustomed to a fight with the traditional enemy across the Channel. Identification with such a national community, for all its seeming capaciousness, was an uneven and sometimes conflicted experience, defined as it was through the centralised power of England – Turner's 'Albion' – and permeated by paternal forms of authority. It was a community founded on the sacrifice of those whose belief began and often ended with bread in their stomach rather than any abstract allegiance to a cause, or marked by an instrumental hope invested in the better life that the expanding economies of empire might bring – economies which could strengthen local and regional ties rather than echoing the supposed 'one voice' of the nation. Such an imagining was an ideological fiction, a horizon of seeming communal desires, but it was lived, sometimes brutally. Often aggressively xenophobic, it could be accompanied by riots and victimisation in its policing of the boundaries of the familiar and the foreign.[26]

Yet, as David Garrick's Christmas pantomime of 1759, *The Harlequin's Invasion*, reveals, nationalist spectacle could also work in pedagogic ways. His play marked the high point of the war by pressing 'King Shakespeare' into service, drawing on the most jingoistic of sentiments, complete with cod-French accents and stock national characters ('Bog' and 'Taffy'), and belting out the most anthemic of sea songs, 'Heart of Oak'. At the same time it reflected upon its own reception. Despite the patriotic fervour of the drama, and its rousing special effects, the final song declared 'Ye Britons may fancy ne'er lead you astray, / Nor e'er through your senses your reason betray'. In this invocation of rational control over the passions Garrick was appealing to his public to exhibit their 'wisdom' by honouring their national poet ('Ye sons of Taste adore him'), while offering a way of rising above the violence of nationalistic feeling which had often erupted to wreck his auditorium.[27]

The realm of taste operated just as exclusive a vision as the chauvinism which still rampages through British tabloids today, since not everyone was to be included in such a sharing out of cultural capital (daughters of Taste often among them). Yet taste was significant not simply because it represented a measured and peculiarly British common sense (one that maintained, on one level at least, the illusion that it might be available to all[28]), but because its task was thereby the production of political subjects who might be seen to build community beyond the fragmented forms and baser passions of civil society. Whatever the competing interests invested in the war, and the burdens it imposed, claims were made for its greater good as a contribution to the 'universal' happiness of the nation, as if it might begin to represent those capacities for reason and harmony that were summed up in the contemporary notion of the perfectability of mankind. And it was, in turn, the aggressive dissemination of this 'happiness' abroad that would underwrite British imperial expansion (and with it an imagined internal unity), as another invasion drama from 1759 underlined:

> Here shall fair liberty erect her throne,
> And foe to Tyrants, rule un-aw'd by none:
> The vital heat, to distant realms convey'd,
> Shall cherish nations, happy in her aid,
> A warlike race, by gracious heav'n design'd
> To save, and guard the rights of griev'd mankind.[29]

There were diverse ways of belonging to the imagined community of the nation, whether in the playhouses, at the pulpit, or forming opinion by the fireside. At its most idealised such a vision of community could be found replicated in the numerous clubs and societies that circulated opinion, and devised projects and forms of organising in its light. As Jonas Hanway described in the late 1750s, the philanthropic work of the mid-century had produced 'a Society . . . composed . . . of *all parties* and complexions; triumphing over all *little passions*, and *private animosities*, actuated by *one common spirit* . . . for the common interest'.[30]

At stake here is not simply a sense of commonality in the nation, but the outlines of 'an *idea* of the state', in the words of David Lloyd and Paul Thomas, one that could claim to reconcile contesting interests by rising rationally and disinterestedly above them. An idea, moreover, that had in mind the 'proper subjects' who would people such a polity.[31] The revocation of passions and personal sentiments that Hume had noted was a form of discipline that guaranteed a limited enfranchisement. 'Remember', wrote Sir William

Jones in 1783, 'that a free state is only a more numerous and more powerful club, and that he only is a free man, who is a member of such a state.'[32] Freedom entailed the ceding of individual autonomy to a more impersonal and representative political order, and to a formal equality the mid-eighteenth century was not yet able to countenance, but which had begun to haunt and pressure the imagining of what freedom might bring. What did it mean to belong, and how extensive was its community to be? As Thomas Turner sat down to listen to *Tristram Shandy* and write his journal, he was already a member of the 'club', which was widening to include 'true-born Englishmen' like him: independent, property-owning tradesmen, invested in the fortunes of empire, suspicious of paternalism but in love with authority, their interpellation by the state returning as if generated in their very sinews, articulated as if from the heart. In the years of the war and its aftermath, what then might be the import of *Tristram Shandy*'s 'lesson to the world *"to let people tell their stories their own way"* '(TS 9.25.785)?

## Cultural Work and the Imperial State

The Seven Years' War is generally considered a conflict in which domestic consent was easily won, not least because it was the only war of the century in which overseas trade expanded. As Kathleen Wilson has argued, 'there were strong material reasons . . . for ordinary English people to be avidly interested in imperial affairs', caught up as they were in diverse ways, 'from the financing of ships and investments in cargoes to money lending to merchants and ship owners and colonial land speculation as well as the distribution, consumption and population patterns which spread colonial and British goods across regions, oceans and nations'.[33] In the 1760s it was the Scots, in particular, who were seen to ride and administer these commercial and imperial energies, held to be more 'curious' than their English counterparts (a 'curiosity' in part driven by the underdevelopment and expropriation of their land). Yet even those who could turn away from the harsher exigencies of war and expansion to the local peace of private life tasted the fruits of empire in their tea, spoke its encounters with new words daily entering the language, or made out its outlines in their dreams. It was common to demand more as governments brought conflicts to a close, and the Seven Years' War was no exception. For some the peace came prematurely in 1763 with the Treaty of Paris. Though global supremacy seemed assured, some of the territorial and thus commercial gains taken in the complex economic endgame of which William Pitt appeared the chessmaster were given up; mindful of the historical lessons of the Treaty of Utrecht fifty years earlier, after which France and Spain had quickly recovered as imperial competitors, many (like Thomas Turner) saw the conclusion of the war as 'inglorious'.[34]

As Michael Mann describes, the Seven Years' War was a 'traditional' conflict:

> Unlike later wars, it involved no divisive political ideologies. The instrumental rationality of the participants made it a 'limited war'. In Britain the propertied 'people' generally supported the war; the 'populace' still lacked more than local organization. Politics concerned only strategy and whether peace was being too hurriedly sought and burdens were reluctantly accepted until after war ended.[35]

While accurate enough in its confirmation of a picture of the mid-century domestic political climate in which partisan conflict had much reduced, Mann's description nonetheless neglects a number of factors that make an image of consensus more uneasy. These concern what I am calling the *cultural work* of the state, part of the process of legitimation for a polity seeking to accommodate the demands of empire by forms of consolidation and centralisation at home. It is this notion of cultural work which cements the different strategies of this book, and which here needs brief explanation, not least because through its gaps and contradictions are the traces of wider kinds of struggle to define political and social being at this time, which have reverberations long after the Seven Years' War had come to an end.

In their book *The Great Arch*, Philip Corrigan and Derek Sayer argue that the process of English state formation is a continual cultural revolution. 'The repertoire of activities and institutions conventionally identified as "The State" are cultural forms, and cultural forms, moreover, of particular centrality to bourgeois civilization', they write. And continue:

> Marx, who did not reduce the state to 'bodies of armed men', grasped this when he wrote in an early essay that the 'abstraction of the *state as such* belongs only to modern times, because the abstraction of private life belongs only to modern times. The abstraction of the *political state* is a modern product.' States, if the pun may be forgiven, *state*; the arcane rituals of a court of law, the formulae of royal assent to an Act of Parliament, visits of school inspectors, are all statements. They define, in great detail, acceptable forms and images of social activity and individual and collective identity; they regulate, in empirically specifiable ways, much . . . of social life. Indeed, in this sense 'the State' never stops talking.[36]

This is to acknowledge the mediated nature of legitimation, what Corrigan and Sayer term the 'constitutive regulation' of subjectivity orchestrated by state forms. The manufacture of consent is a means of determining what counts as meaningful social being, and the circulation of opinion, as we have seen, can be an interpellative mode of state 'talk' even as it takes on the most private character. Indeed the articulation of opinion as an expression of a 'prior' private sentiment (to which the world might be held to conform, as Turner ruefully reflected) could be seen as a measure of its success. That the state 'states' in the 1760s, writing itself rhetorically into being, is part of my contention here; it has, moreover, a performativity about it which generated, sometimes despite its own efforts, a Shandean repertoire.

It is my view that the long process of the abstraction of the modern state takes an intense cultural turn at the mid-point in the eighteenth century, which is not to say that its forms were not already moulding the regulation of social life before this point.[37] Rather it is to emphasise that the conjuncture[38] of this particular war for empire demanded forms of state imagining in which the abstraction of the political state and private life reached a new phase. A disabling hypostatisation of terms – a reified State, a separate private sphere – can derive from such an abstraction, but it is to be avoided here. Not only does it tend to corrall those inhabiting the geographies of social life in ways that take such an ideological division, for all its material effects, at its word (not least in ascribing agency along rigidly conceived gender lines), but it also can play down the ongoing dynamic of such an abstraction. It risks taking such a separation as a given, thereby naturalising the social order it describes, rather than regarding such an order as something forged, inscribed, and *worked*.

Such an imagining was immediately geopolitical, concerned with the metaphorical mastery of space. One consequence of winning the war was the need to make sense of an extraordinary extension of territorial boundaries that troubled the limits of the state understood as a delimited arena. This was undoubtedly an imperative of the political imagination for those occupied, like Edmund Burke, with the question of what it might mean 'to govern a Large Empire upon a plan of Liberty'.[39] But while such spatial projection set cartographers and surveyors to work, and company writers to their ledgers to calibrate the flows of commodities, people and revenues involved in the 'tentacular'[40] spread of British markets, it also involved a reimagining of the polity itself – and the subjective lives of those comprising it – which animated the literature and culture of the time. An older notion of a body politic persisted, as if the socius might simply assume gigantist proportions and thus arrogate expansion to the machinic balance of its organs and limbs. 'Cato' captures something of this pressure in 1765, in a tract anxious about the taking of territories that 'probably never will be perambulated':

> The Territory acquired is so immense, that it must make the Time of Acquisition a remarkable Aera of this Government, and produce a great Change in our Situation and Circumstances as a Society. As the smallest

Member of a Natural Body affects the whole in some Degree; so every one Circumstance with regard to a Political Body has some Influence upon every other. A Nation must accomodate [sic] itself some way or other, well or ill, to the whole extent of its Territory.[41]

For Cato this question of 'accommodation' entailed concerns about depopulation that might irretrievably weaken the body politic – or, as in the words of Sterne's Walter Shandy, produce a form of 'state-apoplexy' (*TS* 1.18.53) – a kind of geopolitical instability in which, it was feared, there would be 'nobody at home' to work or trade.[42] There was a note of incredulity in Burke's analysis of what it would mean to incorporate 'a great a growing People spread over a vast quarter of the Globe, almost from the Polar Circle to the Equator seperated (sic) from us by a mighty Ocean' into 'the weight [of a] gross dead body'.[43] I want to note this moment of potential deterritorialisation in the experience of empire, in which the question of quite what it was that would bind person to person across the massively extended nation – was it sympathy, trade, utility, friendship, custom, mechanism, subjection? – was suddenly in question. In which the universalising abstractions – fictions – of British power might seem no more than the thinnest of wish-fulfilments when measured against the brutal realities of conflict and encounter, and the ignorance and misprision that accompanied them. A moment too in which new kinds of subjects might emerge, loosed in messy and uncertainly provisional ways from the ties that had traditionally defined their place in the world. If there was 'work' needed to make the challenges of empire palatable, to suture individuals nonetheless into the imperial story of their time, it sometimes took fantastical forms. It could also fail.

One answer to the risk of such a voyage out was the consolidation of boundaries at 'home'. Private life appeared a retreat from a wider theatre of commercial and imperial action, though its very abstraction was a symptom of the same process. Its values also informed new kinds of social administration. It was as if with increasing abstraction and extension the 'idea of the state' was to take more palpable form. The bricks and mortar of new kinds of disciplinary institutions such as the magdalen and foundling hospitals, workhouses and early factories could mark the limits of inclusion by defining what lay outside. These were the visible tip of the iceberg, one might argue, of an administrative rationality that had long begun to transform the governance of population, and which would produce in mid-eighteenth-century Britain, in the words of Edward Thompson, 'new disciplines, new incentives, and a new human nature upon which these incentives could bite effectively'.[44] There was, in short, an internal colonisation taking place alongside the reach of imperial conquest abroad, one that was in the process of redefining 'the political form of the relation between sovereignty and dependence', in Marx's terms.[45] And if these 'incentives' appeared in charitable form as a sign of state love – traced in this book in the sentimental fantasies of the period – its calculus was never far behind. As Oliver Goldsmith's *Vicar of Wakefield* discussed, it was time for 'power' to try the 'utility' of its people in subtler and gentler ways: 'if properly treated' they might 'serve to sinew the state in times of danger'.[46]

John Brewer's powerful account of the British 'fiscal–military state' in the eighteenth century points out the centrality of administration to its maintenance and formation, a state whose 'key technology was not derived from the arts of war but from the counting house'.[47] As he details in *The Sinews of Power*, taxation entailed surveillance, and a legal uniformity across the nation whose efficiency was unmatched by imperial competitors.[48] Combined with the operation of a public debt, it was a 'dangerous financial power' as Immanuel Kant later described it,[49] that bore fruit on the battlefield in the Seven Years' War, but which had resulted, Brewer argues, from the pens of transcribers and ledger keepers, clerks and excise officers, as much as from the actions of military men. If the 'arts of war' depended on it, so it seemed did the peace that followed. This administrative rationality was intensified in the American colonies with disastrous effects, and in India too, where the East India Company applied itself to writing the state into being after 1765 as if nothing had preceded it. It was a quantitative vision that testified to the mastery of circumstances (a belief in calculation that Brewer's account explores); but if on the one hand it conveyed a humdrum deliberation that might translate into the 'Silent, Steady Policy'[50] of government, on the other, it was evidence of a fantastic wish-fulfilment, and no less the stuff of state imagining as such. It would set in train the postcolonial unravelling of empire in the thirteen colonies, and find itself underwritten by direct coercion and violence in Bengal. A vision of control, then, that projected across the continents, and also into the private affinities of home. Thomas Turner's trust in ledgers and calculation extends to the ideal qualities of his future spouse: someone who will guarantee his affairs, such that 'I can be assured in their management will be sustained no loss'.[51]

By 'cultural work' I am referring to this general process of subject formation, and to a broader penetration of an instrumental rationality connecting governance and the flows of public culture, which Hume had noted with a certain astonishment. 'Whoever speaks of culture speaks of administration as well': if this is a technocratic truth lived out in modern times, Theodor Adorno's account has its roots (like Weber's) in the eighteenth century, at a moment when 'culture' – not least in the formulations of taste itself – is being torn away from everyday praxis.[52] Its 'work' enters subjective realms of fantasy and identification, whereby the state arguably assumes a monopoly of *symbolic* violence – articulating what might stand for common sense, what constitutes an intelligible life – alongside the direct coercion which is its province.

'Community understood as a work or through its works would presuppose that common being, as such, be objectifiable and producible (in sites, persons, buildings, discourses, institutions, symbols: in short, in subjects)', writes Jean-Luc Nancy. If eighteenth-century war – and the disorientating challenges of empire – intensified just such a production of 'common being', it also exposed its logic, the *containment* of the meaning of political community which such a work implied. As Nancy argues, 'the political, if this word may serve to designate not the organisation of society but the disposition of community as such, the destination of its sharing, must not be the assumption or the *work* of love or of death'.[53] There were intimations in the 1760s about what such a 'disposition of community' might mean – not least in the acknowledgement of a 'future where there may be no more inequality', in Sarah Scott's words[54] – but it seemed almost unintelligible, an impossible and sometimes obscene prospect. The cultural work of empire was indeed a work of both love and death – a sacrificial identification with the common being of the nation – but at times in the 1760s, in its contradictions and fracturing, it was possible to glimpse the calculus that held it in place, and beyond that, perhaps, the impossible horizon of the political itself. It is for this reason that we might see intimations in this decade of a potential for radicalism normally associated with the post-revolutionary 1790s.

At this point in the mid-eighteenth century there emerge multiple 'ideas of the state' in images of bounded communities, through which the contradictions of the violence inherent in the cultural work I've been sketching are raised and defused, and which expand and contract as they negotiate the limits of belonging with the '*whole Globe*'[55] in view. Ideas that are tested in literature and philosophy, played out in parliamentary debates, and in the formation of social groups and communities at this time. Ideas that are under pressure, and which often reveal unspoken exclusions even as they test the communality of social belonging. The image of the family is an instance of cultural work of this kind: as a metaphor for the state with a long history, it returns powerfully in the 1760s, as we will see, sometimes in the most seemingly anachronistic and 'residual' form, both as an ideal model for patriarchal domestic order, set out by William Blackstone in his influential codification of English law,[56] and as a sometimes sentimentalised place of solidarity and retreat in a harsh world. It is a construction that can stretch across the Atlantic to include the colonial progeny of the 'mother country' – a way of thinking domination as an inclusiveness without representation – or serve to emphasise the local as a kind of national imagining. Its vision of community can also provide a way of expelling the visible paraphenalia of state violence – prisons, wars, excisemen, the gallows – to the distant horizon, while paradoxically reinventing its regulation at home. The domestic household takes its place in this sense alongside other images of community, such as the improved country estate, the asylum institution, and sentimental friendships, as a *work of administration*: understood as a symbolic imagining, in which seemingly natural modes of affective fellowship (feelings of trust, reciprocity, familial care for others) are both invoked, and yet form in the same breath what Corrigan and Sayer term 'impositional claims'.[57]

Such a 'cultural work' was not all-pervasive, though to function in ideological terms, it increasingly had to appear so. Indeed for all its instrumental intensities, there was no guarantee that people's lives and predilections would answer its subtler forms of regulation in predictable ways. As Kathleen Wilson has richly shown, in the political realm consent to the burden imposed by the war – at great material cost to the lives of the populace – was itself often articulated through a consciousness of rights and liberties, that might be mobilised in a nationalistic defence of the commercial and territorial 'birthright of Englishmen' across the globe, but equally might be diverted into forms of political radicalism and resistance that would prove more difficult to contain.[58] Some forms of popular struggle, notably the furore over John Wilkes, took the juridico-political state to task and thereby as their defining horizon, strengthening it in the process. Yet there were other kinds of community defined by local affiliations and contingent encounters, from motley shipboard crews to mutual associations, whose very *combining* might appear an insurrectionary threat.[59] The cultural work I have been describing addresses this fear at one level, by substituting its own visions of (political) community. And by seeing off claims which paradoxically emerge from the formal promise inherent in the state as such: a democratic potential that might burst through the clubbish confines of 'freedom' to demand an unimaginable equality.

Edmund Burke was having none of it. As he reflected in 1768, thinking back on the aftermath of the Seven Years' War in a year marked by 'tumults':

> In the complicated oeconomy of great kingdoms, and immense revenues, which in a length of time, and by a variety of accidents, have coalesced into a sort of body, an attempt towards a compulsory equality in all circumstances, and an exact practical definition of the supreme rights in every case, is the most dangerous and chimerical of all enterprizes. The old building stands well enough, though part Gothic, part Grecian and part Chinese, until an attempt is made to square it into uniformity. Then it may come down on our heads all together in much uniformity of ruin; and great will be the fall thereof.[60]

With the expansion of all great empires comes the possibility of collapse, as mid-eighteenth-century Britain was reminded in the story of Rome. The fissures that opened up in the 'old building' were not easily to be papered over. And the acute inequalities exposed by the war – from the conspicuous consumption of the nabobs to the shoddy recompense of numerous others – were particularly persistent, leaching away faith in the paternalist certainties that held the edifice together. The sheer calculus of empire was at its most naked, not just as it was visited upon the populations of distant territories, but also on the lives and bodies of those who had made it possible. It was a 'strange absurdity', as Goldsmith's Citizen of the World described in a phrase that will reverberate through my book, which had brought the nation to exchange 'her best and bravest subjects for raw silk, hemp and tobacco . . . her hardy veterans and honest tradesmen . . . for a box of snuff or a silk petticoat'.[61]

Alongside the vision of consensus around this major imperial war, then, is another version of events, which acknowledges the social and political weight of this sense of 'absurdity'. For Giovanni Arrighi, the Seven Years' War inaugurates a phase of rebellion stretching to 1848: 'the deeper origins of this wave of rebelliousness can be traced to the previous struggle for the Atlantic because its agents were precisely the social forces that had been brought into being and forged into new communities by that struggle: the colonial settlers, the plantation slaves, the metropolitan middle classes'.[62] If the aim of the cultural work I have been sketching is the generation of 'proper subjects' for the state, there were other 'improper' and unexpected voices emerging from the contradictions and interstices of empire at home and abroad who told another story. Belonging could appear the most iconoclastic of enterprises when huge numbers of new Britons now inhabited territories across the globe. Some of the most concerted challenges would come in the aftermath of the war from the prospect of inclusion, and with it the legal extension of rights to those who were not properly speaking subjects at all, such as slaves; or from those like the American colonists whose membership of the club could suddenly feel counterfeit, less a matter of freedom than expropriation. Often these claims took the universalising pretensions of state at their literal word. There were also many differing examples of resistance across the empire beyond the reach, or in direct refusal, of state 'opinion', from the Indian uprisings across North America, the revolts in Jamaica and the actions of Irish Whiteboys, to conflict in India, and the 'combinations' of the poor taking part in the tumults on London streets. If they brought home the question of governance, and with it a palpable sense of *number* – these were also signs of alternative forms of communal social being, different economies, which were not so easily corralled. This was, for many, no 'limited war', and its 'success' exposed the limits, and at times the failure, of state imagining. If there was something truly chimerical it did not lie with impossible dreams of equality, as Burke had argued, but in the sometimes fantastical managing of what had become 'a great and difficult object'.[63]

### Empire and the Cock-and-Bull Tale

We have kept Mrs Shandy waiting at the keyhole for long enough, as Laurence Sterne might say. This is a book about the work of Laurence Sterne. It is Sterne's writing – from *The Life and Opinions of Tristram Shandy, Gentleman*, published in intermittent volumes between 1759 and 1767, and his *Sermons of Mr Yorick* (1761), to the later *A Sentimental Journey* (1768) and his final 'journal to Eliza', *Continuation of the Bramine's Journal*, kept in 1767–8 – which will provide a perhaps unlikely key to the moment of the Seven Years' War and the years which follow; unlikely because such mercurial work might seem a long way from the weighty issues of the day. Indeed in their ironic flight from the identifiable panoramas of eighteenth-century life, which writers like Fielding and Smollett had reproduced with a detail corroborated by coach timetables, Sterne's narratives have a more aleatory relation to their time that posed a conundrum to readers and critics alike. Thomas Turner was not alone in his uncertainty about a novel that could be named only by itself: 'I know not what to call it—except *Tristram Shandy*.'[64] If Sterne's work remained to many 'a *riddle*, without an *object*',[65] I will argue that his writing provides an extraordinary register of the processes I have been describing, and moreover that the *non-knowledge* that often accompanies its reception is a paradoxical symptom of this.

Recent work on Sterne has noted the connections in his writing to the moment of the Seven Years' War, picking up most often on the figure of the military veteran, uncle Toby, and his reprise of war games on the bowling green in *Tristram Shandy*.[66] The novel's paralleling of the moment of Utrecht in 1713 with the Treaty of Paris concluding the Seven Years' War fifty years on was a common point of comparison in mid-century public debate, as I've argued elsewhere, and Sterne was not averse to turning to his advantage satirical games with the possible literal applications of his 'compleat system of modern politics'[67] to the 'militiating' mid-century.[68] For all the difficulty of assessing with clarity Sterne's definitive position on the war, or indeed finally on any topical matter of the day, he was, after all, a child of military barracks, losing his soldier father to sickness in an earlier campaign in Jamaica. Sterne knew the human cost of war, the consequences – death, infant mortality, poverty, dependence – of living in what we might see as an eighteenth-century risk society. It was an awareness that found its way into his letters and sermons, as well as the dramas of his narratives.[69]

If Sterne's work functions like a 'cultural barometer', in Thomas Keymer's terms,[70] we might want to think carefully about what it entails to recover this. One route has proved to be a rich intertextuality, acknowledging, as Melvyn New's sustained scholarship has shown, that the 'community' of *Tristram Shandy* (and by extension Sterne's writings as a whole) 'is represented by all the authors and books, all their documents and cultures and artifacts' animating its engagement with the world.[71] An attentively worked sense of the literary landscape of the mid-century reveals that characteristics commonly ascribed to Sterne's seeming protomodernism are alive and anticipated in a wider field of writing, as Keymer has perceptively revealed in his analysis of the practices of serial fiction in particular, such that it becomes possible to track the development of a 'mode of writing able to absorb and respond to new texts, trends and tastes as they emerged, holding its position at this culture's cutting edge with a kind of self-renewing fashionability'.[72] This is valuable critical work. If it begs questions, they involve the use of a more attentuated literary notion of culture that I would argue inevitably reduces cultural and historical pressures to the notion of a running context or 'backdrop', or to kinds of authorial network or intertextual contact. And with them, crucially, for all its literary carefulness, a narrowness in conceptual understanding of the modernity animating Sterne's writing – quite why and how it might be that its formal self-consciousness, its novelty, and its registering of the abstraction attendant on the book market, powerfully connect with the historical constitution of subjectivity at this particular time. However illuminating and productive the immersion of Sterne's writing in mid-century culture, such that its practices might be revealed as 'typical' of the times, it seems important also to retain a critical sense of the horizon of its modernity, its grasp (and reflexive cognition) of a mutating present, that was and is not so easily explained (or tamed) into intelligibility.[73]

My path then is a different and speculative one. Sterne's work testifies, I will suggest, to what it meant to be sutured into the cultural work of empire. To state this is to take a risk: what does it mean to appear to reduce this writing – its sensual pathos and ironic lightness of touch, its moral economies, its formal play and not least its humour – to the business of state imagining, scratching away at its meaning, like Walter Shandy defacing the words of Erasmus in the text? Critical readings of Sterne's work, as Eve Kosofsky Sedgwick remarks, can often sound 'plonking, churlish, literal-minded',[74] and it is often when the critic is at her most literal that Sterne's writing has its comic revenge. There is undoubtedly a moment of reduction in my account, which argues that there is a passage in Sterne's writing which resembles something like a story of incorporation: from the serious comic play and protest of *Tristram Shandy*, when the contradictions between strands of opinion seem at their most generative and critical, through the ironic collusions and sentiment of the *Journey*, and finally to the last text, written as Sterne was dying, where his fantasy of impossible freedom and love has internalised the very scene of empire for its theatre. To acknowledge this is not to close down the tensions and ambiguities of the work (as any student of Sterne's knows who has tried it, these are not narratives that smooth out easily into a coherent sense of 'story'). But it is at times to play out a literalism that I see less as a reduction, than as varying kinds of *proximity* to the writing: sometimes staying close up, to work away at the specific constellations of meanings and material which have not yet been fully elaborated in Sterne criticism, and which throw new light on the period; and elsewhere to come at it obliquely, as if (to continue the timely cinematic metaphor) swooping down with a crane shot, in order to take in other writing, newer critical angles, and thus what makes his writing in all its idiosyncrasy typical of the time.

I want in this way to do justice to the digressive energies of Sterne's narratives, while also showing the matter of their connection to the broader formation of domestic imperial culture. If this is a book on Laurence Sterne, then, it will also involve us with the work of others – Samuel Johnson, Voltaire, Oliver Goldsmith, Sarah Scott, Phillis Wheatley, Charles Churchill, Ignatius Sancho, Tobias Smollett, Jean-Jacques Rousseau and Mary Wollstonecraft – with the labour of moral philosophers, philanthropists, grammarians and letter writers – with economic and political tracts, not least by Edmund Burke – with paintings by Francis Hayman, Angelica Kauffman and Joseph Wright of Derby – and with the material life of 'things', like the wandering of an image from the page, through drawing rooms and on to the surface of a watch case. It will take us on global trajectories flowing from El Dorado to Abyssinia, Boston to Surat, Ireland to France and four miles in diameter of a Yorkshire parish. It will reach back to seventeeth-century arguments over sovereignty, and forward into a future where Karl Marx will struggle with the Prussian censor in Shandean terms. It will involve the historical anatomy of jokes. It will also offer us a gendered tale – surprisingly enough perhaps for this of all writers – in which what proves most incomprehensible about Sterne's work for its time is its intimation of a certain imperial truth both underlying and also contesting the cultural work I have begun to describe: that in the last instance the subject of empire in mid-eighteenth-century Britain is, constitutively, *feminine*.

My book thus begins in Chapter 1 with an exploration of the global trajectories of empire at work in three novels from the war's *annus mirabilis*, 1759: Voltaire's *Candide*, Johnson's *Rasselas* and Sterne's *Tristram Shandy*. Chapters 2 and 3 focus in more detail on the masculine economies of the conflict and its aftermath. They look closely at the climate of the Seven Years' War and the Shandean text, examining the way the symbolic figure of the benevolent military veteran comes to manage the calculus behind the imperial system, how patriarchal familialism returns as a way of imagining the state, and the mid-century birth of the 'true-born Englishman' as a 'BEING . . . circumscribed with rights' (*TS* 1.2.3). The discussion of friendship in Chapter 4 takes a more winding conceptual path, exploring the sentimentalism of the period and its relation to a notion of 'imperial recoil', in which a projected love for others becomes a question of utility; testing its concerns with the place of friendship in the poetics of Phillis Wheatley and the state imagining of Sarah Scott. The following two chapters then take forward the relation of women to the cultural work of imperial state, firstly, in Chapter 5, by tracing the wandering of Sterne's potent figure of 'poor Maria' through paintings, drawing rooms and watchcases, as a sign of the disciplinary production of 'women's time' and the violence of primitive accumulation. Chapter 6 addresses Sterne's relations with Eliza Draper in India, and the way in which the connection between love and femininity tames the imagining of the 'difficult object' of empire in Burke's terms, and yet in its perceived obscenity offers a sometimes 'Brahminical' intimation of an impossible freedom.

Throughout I am testing a critical wager: that the digressive 'Shandean' momentum of Sterne's writing relates in unspoken ways to the notation of imperial experience, and thus to the specific conditions of the modernity of mid-century life. If there was something that unknowingly bound Sterne's writing to Thomas Turner, as he earnestly and deliberately wrote himself into the pages of his journal that September evening, it was the invisible horizon of the historical present, one that as yet, in the words of the *Annual Register*, could not yet be given 'the name of history' at all.[75] 'I defy the best cabbage planter that ever existed . . . to go on coolly, critically, and canonically, planting his cabbages one by one, in straight lines, and stoical distances, especially if slits in petticoats are unsew'd up—without ever and anon straddling out, or sidling into some bastardly digression—'(*TS* 8.1.655), writes Sterne's narrator. If Thomas Turner's hyphenated consternation represents for me just such a seam (and undoubtedly a seduction too far for the parish officer), beyond it lay a devastating cock-and-bull tale in which the state would be constituted in no less Shandean terms.

## Notes

1  [Edmund Burke], 'History of the War', *Annual Register* 1 (1758), p. 77.

2  Thomas Turner, 14 September 1762, *The Diary of Thomas Turner 1754–1765*, ed. David Vaisey (Oxford: Oxford University Press, 1984), p. 258.

3  Ibid. 13 July 1763, p. 275.

4  Ibid. 3 August 1764, p. 299.

5  Turner may possibly be echoing the title of John Gay's first play *The What d'ye Call it* (1715), which is interchangeable with the idea of generic uncertainty in the period.

6  I am indebted to Fred Anderson's brilliant *Crucible of War: The Seven Years' War and the Fate of Empire in British North America 1754–1766* (London: Faber and

Faber, 2000) for a sense of the shifting fortunes and causes of the conflict, and to Bill Schwarz for its recommendation.

7 Thomas Pelham-Holles, Duke of Newcastle, quoted in Richard Middleton, *Bells of Victory* (Cambridge: Cambridge University Press, 1986), p. 77.

8 Turner, *Diary*, 30 August 1762, p. 256. Turner's knowledge of the war was informed by the reports of friends and acquaintances, including his cousin, a surgeon on the ship that witnessed the execution of Admiral Byng.

9 Ibid. 20 October 1759, p. 191. Turner is recording the news of the surrender of Quebec and the death of General Wolfe: 'Oh what pleasure it is to every true Briton to see with what success it pleases Almighty God to bless His Majesty's arms with, they having success at this time in Europe, Asia, Africa and America.'

10 John Brown, *An Estimate of the Manners and Principles of the Times* (London: L. Davis and C. Reymers, 1757). Brown's jeremiad went through seven official and unauthorised editions in 1757 alone and was widely reviewed. For its influence see John Sekora, *Luxury: The Concept in Western Thought, Eden to Smollett* (Baltimore and London: Johns Hopkins University Press, 1977).

11 Turner, *Diary*, 16 February 1759, p. 175.

12 Ibid. p. 174.

13 See for example Samuel Langdon's *Joy and Gratitude to God For the Long Life of a Good King and the Conquest of Quebec* (Portsmouth, NH: Daniel Fowle, 1760): 'when we recollect all our conquests in *Africa*, the *West-Indies*, and these northern parts of *America*; – when we consider how greatly the war has embarrassed and weaken'd *France* and *Austria*, the two main pillars of the *Papacy*; – we may see very evident tokens of God's favour to his Church' (p. 42). The implied servitude of catholic empires in the narrativisation of imperial competition (not least in the form of the Spanish black legend) was a familiar strategy. Langdon's evangelical 'joy and gratitude' is infused however with a patriotic concern for the British defence of the 'natural rights of mankind' (p. 22) which played out in complex ways in the thirteen colonies. As Murray Pittock has discussed, in Britain, such an assertion of Protestant unity belied the ongoing tensions and conflicts between Anglicanism and Nonconformism, by no means as homogeneous a picture as Turner's eulogy suggests. Nonetheless, 'it may have been the Seven Years' War and still more the French Revolution which served to unite a Protestant Britain pursuing imperial aims'. See Murray G. H. Pittock, *Inventing and Resisting Britain: Cultural Identities in Britain and Ireland 1685–1789* (London: Macmillan, 1997), pp. 128–9.

14 'Of morality little is necessary to be said because it is comprehended in practical divinity, and is perhaps better taught in English sermons than in any other books ancient or modern'. Samuel Johnson, *The Idler* 91 (12 January 1760) in W. J. Bate, John M. Bullitt, and L. F. Powell (eds), *The Yale Edition of the Works of Samuel Johnson: The Idler and The Adventurer* (New Haven and London: Yale University Press, 1963), II, 283. Henceforth noted by date and page number.

15 Michel Foucault, 'The Political Technology of Individuals', in Luther H. Martin, Huck Gutman, Patrick H. Hutton (eds), *Technologies of the Self: A Seminar with Michel Foucault* (London: Tavistock Press, 1988), p. 161.

16 Homi K. Bhabha, 'DissemiNation: time, narrative, and the margins of the modern nation', in Homi K. Bhabha, ed., *Nation and Narration* (London and New York: Routledge, 1990), p. 299.

17 'Happiness' was not only a classical ideal for a political society, writes Foucault of the biopolitics developing in the eighteenth century, 'but a requirement for the survival and development of the state. It is a condition, it is an instrument, and not simply a consequence. People's happiness becomes an element of state strength.' Foucault, 'The Political Technology of Individuals', p. 158.

18 Ibid. p. 151.

19 Michel Foucault, 'Governmentality', in G. Burchell, C. Gordon, and P. Miller (eds), *The Foucault Effect: Studies in Governmentality* (London: Harvester Wheatsheaf, 1991), p. 103.

20 Étienne Balibar, 'Ambiguous Universality', in his *Politics and the Other Scene* (London and New York: Verso Books, 2002), p. 157.

21 Ibid. pp. 161–3.

22 David Hume, 'On the First Principles of Government', in his *Essays and Treatises on Several Subjects* (London: A Millar; Edinburgh: A. Kincaid and A. Donaldson, 1758), p. 20.

23 John Barrell, *English Literature in History 1730–80: An Equal Wide Survey* (London: Hutchinson, 1983), p. 118. Barrell is discussing the 'tendentiously capacious' nature of consent as understood by John Locke in his *Two Treatises of Civil Government*: 'It seems hard therefore to see how the people as a whole can ever have the right to dissent (except by emigration) from a government.'

24 The new *Annual Register*, for example, saw its combination of historical matter and lighter material that might more easily enter into 'common conversation' as more likely to insinuate a general 'taste of knowledge'; in the case of the war, 'we are of the opinion, that the reader will find some entertainment, as well as some help to his memory, from reading a connected sense of those very remarkable and interesting events which this war has produced, and which he has hitherto no where seen but in a loose detached manner.' [Burke], 'History of the War', p. 77.

25 'It is imagined as a *community*, because, regardless of the actual inequality and exploitation that may prevail in each, the nation is always conceived as a deep, horizontal comradeship. Ultimately it is this fraternity that makes it possible, over the past two centuries, for so many millions of people, not so much to kill, as willingly to die for such limited imaginings'. Benedict Anderson, *Imagined Communities: Reflections on the Origin and Spread of Nationalism* (London: Verso, 1991), p. 7.

26 As such this reaction remains part of the populist arsenal of governance in Britain. One of the slogans of the Labour government in the run up to the 2005 election was the pledge to 'protect our borders'.

27 David Garrick, *Harlequin's Invasion; or, A Christmas Gambol*, in Harry William Pedicord and Frederick Louis Bergmann (eds), *The Plays of David Garrick* (Carbondale and Edwardsville: Southern Illinois University Press, 1980), I, I.i.49; III.ii.131–2; II.ii.16. The pantomime opened on 31 December 1959, achieving 25 performances, and was adapted for the following seasons, running for 18 performances in 1760–61, and 13 in 1761–2.

28 The intricacies of this debate can be seen in Edmund Burke's 'Introduction on Taste', added to the second edition of his *A Philosophical Enquiry into the Origin of our Ideas of the Sublime and the Beautiful* in 1759. There Taste is regarded as a sensual 'ground-work' common to all, and yet a form of cultivation produced in the interaction of the imagination, sensibility and judgement which is radically uneven, a quality that has to be learned through exercise and skill, and not therefore within the purview of everyone.

29 Anon., Prologue to *The Invasion, A Farce* (London: L. Davis and C. Reymers, 1759), p. iii. The play is dedicated to the Antigallican Society.

30 [Jonas Hanway], *A Letter from a Member of the Marine Society Shewing the Piety, Generosity and Utility of their Design, with respect to the Sea-Service, at this Important Crisis*, 4th edn (London: J. Waugh; W. Fenner; C. Say, 1757), p. 30. See Kathleen Wilson, *The Sense of the People: Politics, Culture and Imperialism, 1715–1785* (Cambridge: Cambridge University Press, 1995), p. 78.

31 David Lloyd and Paul Thomas, *Culture and the State* (New York and London: Routledge, 1998), p. 4.

32 Sir William Jones, *The Principles of Government; In a Dialogue Between a Scholar and a Peasant, Written by a Member of the Society for Constitutional Information* (London: printed and distributed gratis by the Society for Constitutional Information, 1783), p. 14. Quoted in John Brewer, Neil McKendrick and J. H. Plumb, *The Birth of a Consumer Society: The Commercialization of Eighteenth-Century England* (London: Europa, 1982), p. 231.

33 Kathleen Wilson, 'Empire of Virtue: The Imperial Project and Hanoverian Culture 1720–1785', in Lawrence Stone (ed.), *An Imperial State at War: Britain from 1689 to 1815* (London and New York: Routledge, 1994), p. 129.

34 Turner, 5 May 1763, p. 270. It was a view that fuelled the controversy over Wilkes's *North Briton* no. 45 in the same year. Others saw the peace brokered by Bute's government as overdue, particularly when those arguing for its prolongation were also held to be those making financial gains from the conflict at the expense of the costs in lives and the rising public debt.

35 Michael Mann, *The Sources of Social Power, Volume II: The Rise of Classes and Nation-States 1760–1914* (Cambridge: Cambridge University Press, 1993), p. 116. Mann goes on to point out that in the post-war mid-1760s the 'outs' and 'excludeds' nonetheless called government to account, accusing it of corruption, only to be met by 'escalating patronage and coercion', a 'despotism' countered in Wilkite popular unrest.

36 Philip Corrigan and Derek Sayer, *The Great Arch: English State Formation as Cultural Revolution* (Oxford: Basil Blackwell, 1985), p. 3.

37 Nor is it to suggest with a kind of culturalist functionalism, that all forms of political and economic activity were cultural without remainder: the state monopoly of violence, the expropriation of common land, the legal defence of property which had people hanged for stealing spoons, the obligations of the parish officer, all were shaped by and shaped in turn the meaning of social life, without being reducible to 'culture' per se. This is simply to acknowledge that the object of cultural analysis is not culture as such, and at the same time to refuse (with Corrigan and Sayer) its superstructural construction as somehow distinct from the practices of material life.

38 The stress on *conjuncture* is important here, since it provides a specific focus for what might otherwise appear a generalised picture of disciplinary pressures and determinations: it names a point of temporal heterogeneity, capturing, in the words of Louis Althusser and Étienne Balibar, 'these so-called backwardnesses, forwardnesses, survivals and unevennesses of development which *co-exist* in the structure of the real historical present', and which Raymond Williams termed the dominant, residual and emergent forms at work in any cultural formation. See Louis Althusser and Étienne Balibar, *Reading Capital*, trans. Ben Brewster (London: Verso, 1979), p. 106; Raymond Williams, *Marxism and Literature* (Oxford: Oxford University Press, 1977), pp. 121–7. War, it might be argued, brings those forces and contradictions into conjunctural relief. I have in mind here Lukács's discussion of the emergence of the mass army and its perceived connection with the historical experience of the 'inner life of the nation'. While the Seven Years' War is not a mass event in this modern sense, I would argue that the extension of the conflict through the capillaries of economic and cultural life, in a war arena stretching across the globe, produced 'concrete possibilities' for the emergence of a historical consciousness in the 1760s that may suggest an earlier tentative phase of Lukács's thesis. See Georg Lukács, *The Historical Novel*, trans. Hannah and Stanley Mitchell (Harmondsworth: Pelican Books, 1981), pp. 21–3.

39 Edmund Burke, 'Speech on the Declaratory Resolution' (3 February 1766), in Paul Langford (ed.), *The Writings and Speeches of Edmund Burke: Party, Parliament and the American Crisis 1766–1774* (Oxford: Clarendon Press, 1981), II, 47. Burke's speeches henceforth noted by text and page number from this edition.

40 The term is John Brewer's. See his *The Sinews of Power: War, Money and the English State* (London: Unwin Hyman, 1989), p. 185.

41 'Cato', *Thoughts on a Question of Importance Proposed to the Public, whether is it probable that the Immense Extent of Territory acquired by this Nation at the late Peace, will operate towards the Prosperity or the Ruin of the Island of Great Britain?* (London: J. Dixwell, 1765), p. 11.

42  Ibid. p. 21.

43  Burke, 'Speech on the Declaratory Resolution', p. 49. Burke is addressing the governing of America, which some had seen to parallel the governing of an English Corporation without representation in Parliament. 'Are Gentlemen really serious when they propose this?'

44  E. P. Thompson, 'Time, Work-Discipline and Industrial Capitalism', in his *Customs in Common* (Harmondsworth: Penguin, 1991), p. 354.

45  Karl Marx, 'Labour Rent', *Capital Volume Three*, trans. David Fernbach (Harmondsworth: Penguin Books, 1991), p. 927. The 'expropriation of the mass of the people from the land' (p. 724), which Marx terms 'so-called primitive accumulation', is central to this process of internal colonisation and intensifies in the 1760s. I address it more detail in Chapter 5.

46  Oliver Goldsmith, *The Vicar of Wakefield*, in Arthur Friedman (ed.), *The Collected Works of Oliver Goldsmith* (Oxford: Clarendon Press, 1966), IV, 151.

47  John Brewer, 'The Eighteenth-Century British State: Contexts and Issues', in Stone, p. 52.

48  Brewer, *The Sinews of Power*, pp. 126–34.

49  Immanuel Kant, *Perpetual Peace and Other Essays on Politics, History, and Morals*, trans. Ted Humphrey (Indianapolis and Cambridge: Hackett Publishing Company, 1983), p. 109. Kant's essay on perpetual peace was responding in part to the significant moment of the Treaty of Utrecht in 1713, as does *Tristram Shandy*.

50  Burke, 'Speech on Townshend Duties' (15 May 1767), p. 64.

51  Turner, *Diary*, 14 April 1765, p. 319.

52  Theodor Adorno, 'Culture and Administration', in his *The Culture Industry: Selected Essays on Mass Culture*, ed. Jay Bernstein, trans. Wes Blomster (London: Routledge, 1991), p. 93.

53  Jean-Luc Nancy, *The Inoperative Community*, trans. Peter Connor et al. (Minneapolis and Oxford: Minnesota University Press, 1991), pp. 31, 40. My italics.

54  Sarah Scott, *A Description of Millenium Hall*, ed. Gary Kelly (Peterborough, Ont.: Broadview Press, 1995), p. 245.

55  Duke of Newcastle, quoted in Middleton, *Bells of Victory*, p. 77.

56  'The individuals of the state, like members of a well-governed family, are bound to conform their general behaviour to the rules of propriety, good neighbourhood, and good manners; and to be decent, industrious, and inoffensive in their respective stations,' William Blackstone, *Commentaries on the Laws of England*, 3rd edn, 4 vols (Oxford: Clarendon Press, 1765–9), IV, 162.

57  Corrigan and Sayer, *The Great Arch*, p. 7.

58  Wilson, *Sense of the People*, pp. 198–205.

59  On this point see Peter Linebaugh, *The London Hanged* (Harmondsworth: Penguin, 1993) and with Marcus Rediker, *The Many-Headed Hydra: The Hidden History of the Revolutionary Atlantic* (London: Verso Books, 2000).

60 Burke, 'Observations on a Late State of the Nation' (1768), p. 175.

61 Oliver Goldsmith, Letter XVII, *The Citizen of the World*, in Arthur Friedman (ed.), *The Collected Works of Oliver Goldsmith* (Oxford: Clarendon, 1966), II, 75.

62 Giovanni Arrighi, *The Long Twentieth Century: Money, Power, and the Origins of Our Times* (London: Verso, 1994), p. 52.

63 Burke, 'Observations on a Late State of the Nation', p. 194.

64 Turner, *Diary*, 14 September 1762, p. 258.

65 A review of a French account of the two most recent volumes of *Tristram Shandy*, *London Chronicle* (16 April 1765), 373.

66 See David McNeil on Sterne's 'cultural sense of war memory' in his *The Grotesque Depiction of War and the Military in Eighteenth-Century English Fiction* (Newark, Delaware: University of Delaware Press; London: Associated University Presses, 1990), p. 158; Mark Loveridge, 'Stories of COCKS and BULLS: The Ending of *Tristram Shandy*', *Eighteenth-Century Fiction*, 5 (1992), 42; the chapter 'The Literature of Whiggism and the Politics of War' in Thomas Keymer, *Sterne, The Moderns, and the Novel* (Oxford: Oxford University Press, 2002), 184–214. See also Frank McLynn, *1759: The Year that Britain Became Master of the World* (London: Jonathan Cape, 2004), pp. 254–6 which uses *Tristram Shandy* to introduce a chapter on Frederick of Prussia's new techniques in warfare and their use in the battle of Minden in 1759. Simon During's 'Transports of the Imagination: Some Relations between Globalization and Literature' relates Sterne's sentimental travelling and the moment of the war to the forging of a subjectivity that permitted the English to transport themselves around the globe, and is thus closer to my interests here. See *Arena Journal* 20 (2002–3), 123–39.

67 Anon., *Explanatory Remarks Upon the Life and Opinions of Tristram Shandy, Wherein the Morals and Politics of this Piece are clearly laid open*, by Jeremiah Kunastrokius MD (London: E. Cabe, 1760), p. 44.

68 As the narrator of *Tristram Shandy* playfully 'beseeches' the reader to believe, he has 'no thoughts' 'in the character of my uncle *Toby*—of characterizing the militiating spirits of my country—the wound upon his groin, is a wound to every comparison of that kind,—nor by *Trim*, that I meant the duke of *Ormond*—or that my book is wrote against predestination, or free will, or taxes—If 'tis wrote against any thing,——'tis wrote, an' please your worships, against the spleen'. Laurence Sterne, *The Life and Opinions of Tristram Shandy, Gentleman: The Text*, The Florida Edition of the Works of Laurence Sterne, vols 1–2, ed. Melvyn New and Joan New (Gainesville, FL: University Presses of Florida, 1984), 4.22.360. Further references to *Tristram Shandy* cited in my text are to Sterne's original volume and chapter numbers, followed by the page number in the Florida edition.

69 See for example the sermon preached in 1761 to celebrate the accession of George III, where the lesson from *Chronicles* is framed by Sterne's blunt sense of the

human cost of imperial expansion: 'enlargement of empire, by the destruction of its people (the natural and only valuable source of strength and riches) was a dishonest and miserable exchange'. Laurence Sterne, *The Sermons of Laurence Sterne*, The Florida Edition of the Works of Laurence Sterne, vols 4–5; ed. Melvyn New (Gainesville, FL: University Press of Florida, 1996), 40.376. Further references to the *Sermons* are cited in my text by sermon number, followed by the page number in the Florida edition.

70 Keymer, *Sterne*, p. 86.

71 Melvyn New, 'Sterne and the Narrative of Determinateness', *Eighteenth-Century Fiction* 4:4 (1992), 329. New is relating this 'community' specifically to Sterne's ontological experience of writing, reflecting on the curiousness of his positioning as a 'rural Anglican clergyman, in the indeterminate, existential, absurd, phenomenological, solipsistic universe where we nowadays seem to find him' (322).

72 Keymer, *Sterne*, p. 149.

73 I am then far from regarding Sterne as a 'stranded Modern', or concluding that the formal qualities of his work 'do indeed lift it clear of the culture in which it was written', as Keymer (p. 4) surmises of my earlier article 'The Modernity of Sterne', in David Pierce and Peter de Voogd (eds), *Laurence Sterne in Modernism and Postmodernism* (Amsterdam: Rodopi, 1996), pp. 19–38. Rather, I have been suggesting that modernity is itself a historical and temporal condition, in which such distanciation is internal to the social experience of abstraction and historical self-definition in mid-eighteenth-century Britain; and here, that such a condition has specific co-ordinates in a 'globalising' war for empire.

74 Eve Kosofsky Sedgwick, *Between Men: English Literature and Male Homosocial Desire* (New York: Columbia University Press, 1985), p. 79. Sedgwick is considering *A Sentimental Journey* in particular.

75 [Burke], 'History of the War', p. 77.

# LUNACY IN THE COSMOPOLIS (1759): EXPANSION AND IMPERIAL RECOIL

Whatever interest we take in the fortune of those with whom we have no acquaintance or connexion, and who are placed altogether out of the sphere of our activity, can produce only anxiety to ourselves, without any manner of advantage to them. To what purpose should we trouble ourselves about the world in the moon?

Adam Smith, *The Theory of Moral Sentiments* (1759)[1]

The rest I dedicate to the MOON, who, by the bye, of all the PATRONS or MATRONS I can think of, has most power to set my book a-going, and make the world run mad after it.

Laurence Sterne, *Tristram Shandy* (1759)

The errant trajectories of people and things that shape the Shandean universe testify to a widespread form of 'lunacy' characteristic of the imperial project in mid-century Britain. It was not only philosophers who reflected on the troubling presence of the 'world in the moon', and the potential affiliations with the fortunes of unknown others who inhabited it.[2] These were flows which traversed the globe, connecting lives and territories in previously unimaginable and accidental ways. If the experience of empire itself was not new in the 1760s, though the reach of British power was unparalleled, its administration and governance now required new forms of cultural labour which in their imaginative projection began to unsettle the boundaries of 'home' in distinctive ways. For all the craziness of attempting to chart and understand the 'tentacular' movement of conquest and commerce, it proved a sober enterprise in orientation even in the most domestic of circumstances. Its tremors were felt in the security of a man's credit, shopkeepers' transactions, failed harvests and the marriage market. A hand on a loom in Bengal had its impact in Spitalfields. The husbandry of 'imperial cane' in St Kitts had reverberations for the livelihood of a village grocer in East Sussex. However distant 'the world in the moon', it would have its sway on the tides of social life. And while it was possible to hymn the vast network of connections as a machine whose wheels turned harmoniously in 'Leeds, or Cairo, Lima or Bombay', in the words of John Dyer, 'though all, unconscious of the union, act',[3] it also generated a palpable uncertainty. Was this then a new form of anxiety? A modern madness, that demanded adaptation to global kinds of extension, and thus a transformation in the very form of social subjectivity itself?

Adam Smith's *The Theory of Moral Sentiments* is a book which commits itself to thinking the limits of ethical feeling in such a climate. The question it poses in 1759 – 'to what purpose should we trouble ourselves about the world in the moon?' – is arguably one prompted by the 'purpose' of empire. And it is shared by the three literary works that emerge in the same year, which respond in different ways to the geopolitics of this particular 'global' war, and thus to the universalising tendencies of empire at the mid-century. Three works which weigh the deterritorialising flows of people and things, desires and anxieties, against the founding of community. Narratives which seem in impossible dialogue in 1759, and which are the subject of this chapter: Voltaire's *Candide*, Samuel Johnson's *Rasselas*, and the first volumes of Sterne's *Tristram Shandy*.

### Candide and the Cosmopolis

'What sort of world is this?' said Candide, on board the Dutch ship. 'A quite mad world, and a quite dreadful one,' replied Martin. 'You know England; are they as mad there as in France?' 'It's a different type of madness,' said Martin. 'You know that these two nations are at war over some acres of snow on the Canadian border; and that they are spending much more than the whole of Canada is worth on this fine war. To tell you precisely if there are more people who ought to be locked up in one country or in the other, that's something of which my limited intellect isn't capable. All I know is that the people we are going to see are very splenetic.'[4]

When Candide arrives on the shores of England the first thing he witnesses is the execution of Admiral Byng, whose failure to win Minorca for the British had become symptomatic of a wider loss of nerve. He promptly refuses to 'put a foot on English soil'. 'In this country', he is informed, 'it is thought a good idea to kill an admiral from time to time in order to encourage the others' (p. 59). The death of Byng at the outset of the Seven Years'

War, within the cockpit of England's national politics an exorcism of military failure, becomes in Voltaire's narrative one more instance of the ubiquity of state-sponsored imperial violence. If there is something 'mad' and inexplicable about events, which have a way of working their bloody and remorseless way through the lives and bodies of the citizens of the world, there is nonetheless an immanent and distributive logic to their absurdity. All suffer, in this Panglossian best of all possible worlds, and it is in the cheerfully stated credo that 'nothing is susceptible to improvement' (p. 2) that the real horror lies.

Voltaire's sense of the lunacy of the Seven Years' War was informed by intimate knowledge. As one time lover of Frederick the Great, Prussian ally of the British, who had precipitated the conflict in 1756, Voltaire was aware of the complexities of personality contributing to the war as well as the diplomatic strategy in which he had been a participant since the 1740s. Convinced of the disaster that faced the French in their struggle for North America if they were to continue to be sucked into defending Austria against the Prussians, he had operated as a go-between to try and restore peace. 'We are in a labyrinth from which we cannot emerge except in rivers of blood and over dead bodies', he wrote in 1758: 'it is a very sad thing to have to uphold a ruinous war on sea for several acres of ice in Acadia and to see armies of one hundred thousand men melting away in Germany without being able to claim one acre of land there'.[5] His sense of the human cost of this war was no exaggeration: the French army would lose about a fifth of its number every year for the duration.[6] But Voltaire's proximity to the diplomatic machinations of the period, and his disillusion with the Prussian 'philosopher king', confirmed his view that international relations were synonymous with the cynical endgames of the powerful. As his entry on 'War' in the *Pocket Philosophical Dictionary* reflected in 1764:

> Famine, plague and war are the three most famous ingredients of this wretched world. You can include in the famine category all the bad food to which scarcity reduces us to eat with the effect of shortening our lives in the hope of keeping them going.
>
> Under plague I include all the contagious diseases, which number two to three thousand. These two gifts come to us from Providence. But war, which combines all these gifts, comes to us from the imaginations of three or four hundred people scattered across the world with the name of princes or ministers; and it is perhaps for that reason that in several dedications they are called the living images of the Divinity.[7]

The spectacle of 'heroic butchery' that greets Candide in the battle between the Bulgars and the Abars (the Prussians and the French) takes place in 'conformity with international law' (p. 6). The black absurdity of the narrative, with its slapstick reduction of conflict to a gestics of flesh and technologies of slaughter, punctures the notion of heroic sacrifice central to eighteenth-century patriotic accounts of war. It also troubles the forms of cosmopolitanism that emerge as an ethical antidote to such imperial violence in the 1760s, whether in the revisiting of international projects for perpetual peace,[8] or that explored in Smith's *The Theory of Moral Sentiments* as the potential for a universalised sympathy.[9] 'What does the future of humanity, benevolence, modesty, temperance, gentleness, wisdom and piety matter to me', ventriloquates Voltaire's dictionary entry, 'when half a pound of leadshot fired from six hundred feet shatters my body, and I die at twenty years of age in unspeakable torment with five or six thousand other dying men, when my eyes, opening for the last time, see the town where I was born destroyed by sword and fire, and the last sounds in my ears are the cries of women and children dying in the ruins, the whole thing for the alleged benefit of a man we do not know?'[10]

### The Time of War

The Seven Years' War was for Voltaire one more instance of a deathly history animated by the interests of the powerful and the intolerant, the latest of a series of wars contesting universal monarchy or dominion. As David Wootton notes, in the early 1750s Voltaire was writing his *Essai sur les moeurs*, and had reached a moment in the history of the seventeenth century that he characterised as 'the age of usurpers from almost one end of the earth to the other': 'the whole universe is a vast panorama of brigandage abandoned to fortune'.[11] It was a vision coloured by the imperial adventurism of his own time. If seventeenth-century philosophy and history provided a key, it was nevertheless not quite the panorama of a Hobbesian war of all against all, which Voltaire regarded as a 'prison', since certain societies demonstrated to his eyes that the state of nature could be peaceable. But it was a vision of war and brigandage as a state of culture, naturalised as the way of particular worlds or, in the words of *Candide*, 'globules'; one, moreover, in which *time* had come, in Hobbesian fashion, 'to be considered in the nature of Warre; as it is in the nature of Weather'. 'The nature of War', wrote Thomas Hobbes, 'consisteth not in actuall fighting; but in the known disposition thereto, during all the time there is no assurance to the contrary. All other time is PEACE'.[12]

The events of the mid-century appeared to mark a transformation in the time of war such that the distinction made by Hobbes between a 'known disposition' for war and peace was more ambiguous. Montesquieu's account of *le doux commerce* was widely circulated: the view that 'Peace is the natural effect of trade' codified in his *The Spirit of the Laws*.[13] The liberty of English culture had long seemed synonymous with its commercial spirit to the anglophile Voltaire. But peace was not necessarily its corollary. Such was the scramble for imperial dominance that peace itself could appear to be war by other means. Voltaire tackles one aspect of this transformation in his dictionary entry on war, when he notes the paradoxical logic at work in Montesquieu's notion of the 'right of natural defence', when peace may entail attacking another state who may otherwise become too powerful: 'If there was ever a clearly unjust war, the one that you propose is it. It amounts to killing your neighbour for fear that your neighbour (who is not attacking you) might be in a position to attack you; in other words, you risk ruining your country in the hope of ruining for no good reason someone else's'.[14]

A clear demarcation between the sublime violence of war, and the feminising and thus weakening commercial culture of peace was an explanatory fiction in the eighteenth century, one that Kant rehearses in his *Critique of Judgement*:

> War itself, provided it is conducted with order and a sacred respect for the rights of civilians, has something sublime about it, and gives nations that carry it on in such a manner a stamp of mind only the more sublime the more numerous the dangers to which they are exposed, and which they are able to meet with fortitude. On the other hand, a prolonged peace favours the predominance of a mere commercial spirit, and with it a debasing self-interest, cowardice, and effeminacy, and tends to degrade the character of the nation.[15]

This is a view we meet repeatedly in the British jeremiads of the mid-century, which often saw war as a necessary purgative. Yet the two states – of war and commercial peace – could also be imagined in a more symbiotic exchange in this of all wars. As the British poet laureate William Whitehead versified in 1758:

> If protected Commerce keep
> Her tenor o'er yon heaving Deep
> What have we from War to fear?
> Commerce steels the nerves of War;
> Heals the havoc Rapine makes,
> And new strength from Conquest takes.[16]

The moment of the Seven Years' War underlines a fundamental shift in what Hobbes had called the 'known disposition' to war, and thus its temporality. Britain's system of public debt had provided a potentially limitless war chest. As Allen W. Wood has discussed, Kant acknowledged in his later project on perpetual peace that it had now become necessary to confront 'the economic effect of the international arms race as a historical *novum*'.[17] The moment of the Seven Years' War makes this transformation evident, not least through a renewed orientation to the future which the ideology of the British imperial state would attempt to make its own, backed by resources like no other. Voltaire's work captures this shift in part because it grasps the particular significance of British imperial power at this conjunctural moment. The competition for empire between states was nothing new, but the readiness to wage war, generated by an extraordinary financial engine, had shifted a gear across the Channel, and found, it seemed, a political form.

In his collapsing of the times of peace and war, and scalpel-like scepticism about the 'rights of citizens' in any putative global order, Voltaire examines the 'brigandage' of imperial reason. *Candide* tests the symbiosis of war and economy, described here by the scholar and Manichean, Martin:

> Everywhere the weak loathe the powerful, while cringing before them, and the powerful treat them like sheep whose wool and meat go to market. A thousand assassins organized in regiments run from one end of Europe to another, carrying out murder and robbery to feed themselves while never disobeying orders, for there is no more respectable occupation. And in those towns that seem to be enjoying peace, where commerce and the arts flourish, people are so eaten up with envy, anxiety and disquiet that they would be less miserable in a city under siege. (p. 47)

If Voltaire's writing traces the numerous historical circuits of conquest, his characters caught up in the often violent movement across borders, cultures and systems of belief like pieces of flotsam, it sees these circuits in terms of the flows and violences of *accumulation*. It is this, I would argue, that makes his work a deeply engaged reaction to its time; the awareness that imperial power entailed not just conquest of territory and subjection abroad, nor only the piling up of booty in the coffers of a few, but widespread forms of expropriation and governance *internal* to the boundaries of the state. Thus in his radical work of 1768, *The ABC, or Dialogues between ABC, translated from the English by Mr Huet*, interlocutor B, a Frenchman, lists the self-inflicted abuses than 'run' the world:

> leaving aside the art of regularly murdering the human race through war . . . we have the art of snatching the food and clothing from those who sow the corn and process the wool; the art of amassing the whole nation's treasure in the money coffers of five or six hundred people; the art of killing in public with full ceremony, on the authority of half a sheet of paper, people who displease . . .[18]

Internal forms of discipline and coercion accompany the amassing of the wealth of the state; inextricable, for Voltaire, with a long history of religious persecution that had surfaced in the Calas affair in the early 1760s. And while the Englishman, A, declares that 'most of these horrible abuses have been abolished in England', the impact of imperial accumulation there was just as uncompromising: rapid enclosure of common land, draconian penal laws, widespread impressment, rigorous taxation, food and money shortages, and the conspicuous consumption of those, like the 'nabobs', who found themselves at the top of the pile. Even Adam Smith saw the 'tumults' of the 1760s in terms of a fundamental antagonism between 'combinations' of the rich and poor, which the rich could not afford to lose.[19] If religious toleration was more widespread there than in France, it had its flashpoints, as the furore around the naturalisation of Jews in the 1750s, and the later Gordon riots, testified. Voltaire nonetheless admired England, which at times approximated the best of possible worlds in key respects, even confessing 'jealousy' towards the close of the war at its particular combination of liberty, toleration and success: 'they now have no monks nor convents, but they have victorious fleets; their clergy produces good books and begets children; their peasants have made infertile lands fertile; their commerce encircles the globe, and their philosophers have taught us truths we did not suspect'.[20] It was perhaps for the hubris of others to take such government to task, he noted dryly. 'God forbid I should educate kings, their esteemed ministers, their esteemed manservants, their esteemed confessors, and their esteemed tax-collectors! I understand nothing about it, I respect them all. It is only for Mr Wilkes to weigh in the balance of his English scales those at the head of the human race'.[21]

### Universal Brigandage and Belonging

Candide's search for the best of all possible worlds is an attempt to find resources for happiness in the midst of universal brigandage. Like all the wandering storytellers of the book, he continually discovers himself to be an instrument of competing forces, on one side and then another, meting out punishment and being carved up in turn. The times of war and peace concertina in the narrative, as if the tables might be turned at any time, alternating between servitude and the power conferred by money, friend and 'foreigner'. This is an arresting vision of historical contingency that conveys something of the instability of imperial experience, against the progressivist narratives which even before their nineteenth-century canonisation equated empire with the rolling out of civilisation across the globe. It dovetails with the accounts of historians who acknowledge that captivity and subjection, and indeed, unexpected forms of assimilation, were also the lot of 'metropolitan' subjects: Linda Colley's *Captives*, for example, which recovers individual stories from the circuits of empire, and sees 'the bodies of English, Welsh, Scottish and Irish men and women, seized in successive captivity crises overseas, mark out the changing boundaries over time of Britain's imperial aggression, and the frontiers of its inhabitants' fears, insecurities, and deficiencies'.[22]

But in Voltaire's sharply comic absurdities of transformation and servitude there is also a political work. This constant series of reversals emphasises the contingency of belonging to any particular world, the seeming impossibility of inhabiting a community or nation that is not subject to radical forms of dislocation, deracination, even in the most domestic of theatres. Thus the apprentice pastry-cook of Voltaire's dictionary entry on 'Patrie' is 'preening himself on loving his homeland', in Ciceronian style, only to be interrogated:

> 'What do you mean by your homeland?' asked a neighbour, 'is it your oven? Is it the village where you were born, and which you have never again seen since? Is it the street where your mother and father lived, who were ruined and who have reduced you to stuffing little pies for a living? Is it the Town Hall where you will never be a quarter-master's clerk? Is it the church of Our Lady where you have never been able to make it as a choirboy, while a ridiculous fool is archbishop and duke, with an income of twenty thousand gold *louis*?'
>
> The apprentice pastry-cook did not know what to say in reply. A thinker, listening to this conversation, concluded that in a country spread over a fairly large area there were often several million people with no homeland.[23]

The effect of empire, I want to suggest, was just such a testing of ties: the weighing of what it meant to identify with an imagined community of home or nation when it had become necessary, in the words of one British minister, to consider the *'whole Globe'*.[24] What were the limits of domestic belonging? Would expansion weaken the love for home, like a large family grown too extensive to know? In the realm of the apprentice pastry-cook, the question of calculus begins to creep in, as if feeling at home also involves a just balance, the banishing of *ressentiment*. 'Home' telescopes: no bigger than a patch of land, or a bed from which no-one can remove you in the dead of night. Voltaire's writing defamiliarises an affective nationalism by calling attention to the arbitrariness of identification, and the production of multiple 'worlds'. In the process it exposes the cultural work of empire.

'It is sad', Voltaire observes ironically, that 'in order to be a good patriot one is very often the enemy of the rest of mankind'.[25] If his work is uncompromisingly political it is because he holds on to the presence of antagonism, the language of friends and enemies, rather than take refuge in an overarching concept of 'humanity' or 'mankind'. Wars fought in the name of humanity often impute an extreme barbarism to their adversaries, as the British imperial project reveals; Voltaire's refusal to take on such an ideological fiction is also a resistance to the flight from the political that such a notion of 'humanity' might imply. In this sense he would seem wholly anticosmopolitan in his stance. However, the short story 'The History of the Travels of Scarmentado', a dry run for the later *Candide* set in the seventeenth century, provides a scenario which might test such a conclusion. On his travels from empire to empire, approaching Africa, the wandering narrator is captured by African pirates:

> Our captain complained bitterly to them. He asked them why they violated the law of nations in this way. The African captain replied, 'You have long noses, and we have flat noses. You have straight hair and we have curly hair. You have skin that is the color of ash, and we have skin the color of ebony. As a consequence my people and your people must, according to the sacred laws of nature, always be enemies. You buy us at markets on the Guinea coast as if we were beasts of burden, and make us do any work that is both backbreaking and humiliating. You have us beaten with whips in the mountains in order to force us to extract a type of yellow earth, which in itself is useless and which isn't worth anything like as much as a good Egyptian onion. So, when we meet up with you and find ourselves the stronger, we enslave you, we make you labor in our fields, and if you don't we slice off your noses and your ears.
>
> There was nothing I could say in reply to so wise a speech. I went and labored in the field of an old African woman in order to preserve my nose and ears. After a year my freedom was purchased.[26]

The actions of the pirates may appear to be against the 'laws of nations', but they are legitimated by a natural law that enshrines racial difference as a fundamental antagonism, one indeed, that appears to underwrite forms of bondage and forced labour. There is, then, paradoxically, a certain reciprocity in the encounter, and the weighing of value systems – the extraction of gold contrasted with the cultivation of crops – which Scarmentado meets with equanimity, unable to answer 'so wise a speech'. While the logic of this reasoning is deliberately perverse, it also captures a truth: while the physical characteristics of noses and hair are pointedly arbitrary, they are also naturalised within the racist discourse of the period and within the slave system itself.

What makes this encounter then at once vertiginous and incontrovertible is that the African captain makes its terms of domination his own, assuming the right to reverse the status of participants according to his own literal appropriation of a seemingly natural law. He, rather than the European captives, assumes the place of the enunciative subject of empire. His repetition of the law of imperial reason offers no contradiction to its logic, but it nonetheless dislodges it, as if through a catachresis or misnaming, and thus calls attention to a certain reflexivity in the narrative which Scarmentado's response disavows. If there are resources for agency and happiness in Voltaire's world, they may lie here in the *action* of his narrative; in the acknowledgement, sometimes registered in the unease surrounding a seeming non-knowledge – 'nothing I could say in reply' – that against the naturalising grain and symbolic maintenance of universal empire, histories of the most violent and traumatic kind involved states of *culture*, not nature, and might be questioned, retold, occupied. It is not just that the experience of empire was uncertain, as the imperial 'true stories' of captivity and metamorphosis reveal. It is that there is also a universalising, systemic thought at work here, parodied in Voltaire's satire which like Swift's, pushes its rationality to the limit. A systemic thought which reveals the instrumental connections underlying the random encounters between people who inhabit different parts of global circuits of power. And if a cosmopolitan international order is here out of the question, 'interrupted' by a brigandage which is a mirror of the way of the world, there is nonetheless a perverse form of recognition – an impossible equality – posited here between friends and enemies, to which I want to return.

It is no accident that this reversal takes place on a pirate ship, belonging to the corsairs whom Francis Bacon may have had in mind when he described pirates as 'the common enemy of human society'.[27] From classical times there was a certain 'tang of brine' about the shipboard community, as Jacques Rancière describes it, which evoked a 'maritime enterprise governed entirely by profit and survival', and moreover, the scent of democracy that might indeed register as a threat to a landbound social order.[28] Yet that terrestrial order required the energies of such enterprise. In *Candide* the actions of pirates are integral to the global flows of people and wealth, not easily differentiated from legal forms of accumulation. Like the Dutch merchant who makes off with Candide's booty from El Dorado, a plantation owner who has customarily cut off the limbs of his African slave – 'the price that has to be paid so that you can eat sugar in Europe' (p. 43) – only to meet a watery fate when his ship is destroyed by a Spanish adversary, mercantile capital rides the vagaries of a world 'abandoned to fortune'. Fortune understood in a Machiavellian sense, perhaps: 'she shows her potency where there is no well regulated power to resist her, and her impetus is felt where she knows there are no embankments and dykes built to restrain her'.[29] In such a deterritorialised space, fortune suggests a particular relation to temporality, which the buccaneering economy can make its own; not the calculation and governance of the future, but a constant adapting of policy to the 'demands of the times'.[30]

In its contrast of the plenitude of the golden city of colonial fantasy, where exchange is unnecessary, with the rampant energies of commercial life, *Candide* draws on a tradition of utopian imagining. El Dorado is a small monarchical state, without prisons or law courts, which values knowledge more than the precious stones that collect like pebbles in the street, and where the king greets his foreign guests with a hug and kiss on both cheeks. Surrounded by mountains, it is 'sheltered from the rapacity of the European nations, who have an incredible mania for the pebbles and mud of our land, and who, in order to get their hands on them, would kill every last one of us and leave not a single survivor' (p. 39). Its inhabitants can never leave. Yet Candide is restless, and impelled to renounce the happiness of this 'human' place, knowing that the wealth he can take with him will aid his search for Cunégonde. The structure of the colonial quest is unravelled by global flows and trajectories, governed by fortune. The perambulations of each storyteller result in a litany of suffering, which may nonetheless be better, the old woman suggests, than standing still. Martin's conclusion, 'that human beings are born to live either in convulsions of restlessness or in the lethargy of boredom', is an observation about the impetus of metaphysical and economic life that Samuel Johnson also addresses in *Rasselas*. 'Candide did not agree, but he had no alternative to propose' (p. 77).

However, the small community that assembles on Candide's farm in Turkey at the end of the tale is an 'alternative' of a kind. In Voltaire's plea for toleration in the affair of the Calas and Sirven families, he imagines 'the human race resembles a crowd of passengers on board a ship':

> Some are at the stern, others at the prow, many in the hold and in the bilges. The ship leaks on every side, the storm does not abate: the wretched passengers will all be swallowed up! Instead of giving each other the necessary assistance which would make the passage less arduous, should we make the voyage still more dreadful? . . . what does it matter to which sect they belong? They should work together to stop the ship from leaking, so that each one, by securing his neighbour's life, also secures his own. Yet they quarrel with one another and perish.[31]

The distinctly inorganic community beached up on Candide's farm knows the value of this lesson, each working for their neighbour: from the princess turned pastry chef, the former prostitute who takes up embroidery, and a philosopher who digs the land, to the monk who has converted to Islam and discovers carpentry. Theirs is an equality of suffering, and the very eccentricity of their coming together suggests something of the abstract and unthinkable global system that Voltaire's work unravels: the parity, for example, imagined between the subjection of the slave and the soldier;[32] or the distribution of violence that might connect mutilation in Surinam and the sugar in a European cup of tea. Just as the telling of their stories is a form of self-constitution – sometimes of the most geographically extra-vagant kind – the collectivity is itself a form of self-making that they can call home. And while they reject metaphysical reflection in favour of labour, in that famous phrase 'il faut cultiver le jardin', this motley group do not choose physiocratic self-sufficiency as a retreat from social life, à la Rousseau, nor even quite like their Turkish neighbour, as an acknowledgement that power and knowledge lie elsewhere. The conclusion is haunted by a 'tang' of political imagining, a republican potential. The order suggested in property is an antidote to the rage of accumulation: by working their own land they may find a means of voicing their relation to the world. As Voltaire's dictionary entry on 'Patrie' suggests, the owner of a cultivated field 'could say': 'I am part of the whole, part of the community, a part of the sovereign power: that is my country.'[33]

Candide and his friends significantly can't find the words to say it. But the world has crucially passed through them. In this sense a cosmopolitan 'alternative' is acted out by *Candide* after all, like an unconscious lunacy that the bourgeois order can only countenance in a slip of the tongue. One in which a love for mankind is made answerable to the specific, local conditions in which people find themselves. One that acknowledges the parity of friend and enemy. And one actively shaped by the ethical recognition of the stranger (who is also oneself), and his or her story, as the only route to the constituting of home as the best of all possible worlds.

### *Rasselas*: Imperial Recoil

1759. In Britain the taking of Quebec from the French was celebrated in the streets with bell ringing and fireworks. In the pages of his journal *The Idler*, Samuel Johnson was more circumspect, imagining the scene as it might have been viewed by an Indian chief contemplating 'the art and regularity of European war'. Its panorama suggests a 'brigandage' worthy of *Candide*:

> Those invaders ranged over the continent, slaughtering in their rage those that resisted, and those that submitted, in their mirth. Of those that remained, some were buried in caverns, and condemned to dig metals for their masters; some were employed in tilling the ground, of which foreign tyrants devour the produce; and when the sword and the mines have destroyed the natives, they supply their place by human beings of another colour, brought from some distant country to perish here under toil and torture.[34]

This is a general scene of expropriation, marked by the extraction of wealth from the land, forced labour, and a human traffic which continually replenishes its stock. By invoking the chief as a spectator, a story told through the eyes of a stranger, Johnson draws on a rhetorical tradition exemplified by the figure of the 'noble savage', an exotic vantage point that provides the opportunity for a critique of European ways. But this is an observer who inhabits his own land, unlike the numerous fictional visitors to Britain's shores, and it is the invaders who are the strangers. His opinion works against the grain of the representative 'untutor'd' Indian who was portrayed welcoming a civilising subjection in Pope's *Windsor-Forest*, his soul 'never taught to stray', in the words of *An Essay on Man*.[35] The figure of the Indian was undergoing a form of tropological migration at the mid-century. It is possible to see in Johnson's vignette not only the outlines of the contemplative spectators who people the history painting of the period – not least in Benjamin West's vision of the death of General Wolfe – but also perhaps the briefest shadowing of a romantic melancholy that would come to be embodied in the image of the sorrowing Indian, mourning the loss of life and land.

Yet however potentially affecting the romantic tableau, it was at the mid-century premature. Johnson's construction of his 'petty chief' is informed by the politics of alliance that had brought Indian visitors to London and their councils to the attention of the press: as interlocutors in the transactions of empire, playing off the interests of the English and the French. These are the specific lineaments of what for Johnson is a bigger picture of the role of virtue in the imposition of imperial sovereignty. The treaty-breaking his spectator perceives on the part of these 'sons of rapacity' who have taken his land is part of a wider moral violation of 'written law', laws which the invaders do not 'communicate': 'For how can they preach it to an Indian nation, when I am told that one of its first precepts forbids them to do to others what they would not that others should do to them'. This is an imperial war not fought for reasons of Christian conversion or 'humanity', but for the 'empty dignity of dominion' over territory they can neither people nor traverse.[36] If the French had dealt with the Indians with a certain equality in North America, exemplified for Johnson in their frequent intermarriages, the British had not learned the importance of such colonial management: treating the Indians as 'mere animals', rather than recognising the value of communicating the language and the '*natural, civil,* and *religious*' principles of British society along with it.[37] Peace would entail their translation. It is a point repeatedly made in his political writing at the outset of the Seven Years' War.

Johnson's Indian observer decides to wait for his moment of revenge, when his nation has mastered the methods of the Europeans: the competing invaders will be driven back to their ships and the land recovered. If this imagined resistance to the sovereignty of a 'new race of men' seems no more than a fable suited to a frontier romance, it did not appear so in the last years of the Seven Years' War, when the Indian nations were united by religious and prophetic means in an uprising that stretched across a swathe of land from the Great Lakes basin to the Mississippi and the Ohio Valley. But in Johnson's work the particularity of this story resolves itself at a more general and geometric level. One of the universalising tropes of empire, which we have already seen in the reversals at work in Voltaire, is that it can come back at you: a form of *imperial recoil*, which at times can look like the operation of justice, and at others like the revelation of a deeper instrumental logic that turns without mercy on those who attempt to wield it.

The moment of Quebec was held in the streets of Britain to be the antithesis of the failure at Minorca, exemplified in the mythic death of General Wolfe, as we will see in Chapter 2. But its realities were far from those of heroic self-sacrifice. Not only was the settler landscape devastated, as Fred Anderson describes in his magisterial history of the war, but scalping, a widespread practice among some New England regiments, was also sanctioned by Wolfe himself 'when the enemy are Indians, or Canads. dressed as Indians'.[38] Massacres were commonplace, and the British would later resort to the use of biological warfare, in the form of smallpox-impregnated blankets, to see off the pan-Indian threat. Johnson's sense of the barbarity of warfare, and the mad 'rage' and 'mirth' of the aggressors, is a comment on the 'art and order of European war', undermining the moral justification for its prosecution. It is probably more rooted in particular truth than he knew. But the gap between the patriotic vision and the instrumental realities of war leads in his work to an acute sense of the different ways in which history might be experienced and represented by 'contending nations', like the earlier acquisition of Louisbourg, which Johnson had described from the position of the English, and then the French.[39] At stake for him was war's first casualty, truth; and what challenged it in part was news: the appetite at home for patriotic stories of victory and sensational tales of cruelty: 'the writer of news never fails in the intermission of action to tell how the enemies murdered children and ravished virgins; and if the scene of action be somewhat distant, scalps half the inhabitants of a province'.[40] This assault on truth was more than a responsibility for historians. [41] It represented for Johnson a potential breaking of the very bonds of human society which required belief in the words of others. Another kind of treaty breaking, and one that would lead 'every man . . . [to] disunite himself from others, inhabit his own cave, and seek prey only for himself'.[42]

## Turning East

Johnson's writing attempts to work against such a catastrophic loss of faith and the feared primitive reversion that might accompany it. His is a constant battle to find forms of philosophical and moral truth that prevent a retreat into the 'cave' of private interests, which seemed at once a lunacy tolerated by the age, and a characteristic of his own demon, melancholia. In *The History of Rasselas, Prince of Abissinia*, the oriental tale published in 1759 a few weeks after the emergence of *Candide*, Johnson explores the conditions for this struggle, but he does so, I would argue, in a narrative which is no less engaged in charting questions posed by the pressures and energies of empire than its absurdist counterpart. According to James Boswell, Johnson was himself aware of the parallels: 'I have heard Johnson say, that if they had not been published so closely one after the other that there was not time for imitation, it would have been in vain to deny that the scheme of that which came latest was taken from the other'.[43] In Voltaire's novel the violence of accumulation cuts a material path through histories and lives like a blade through meat. *Rasselas* in contrast is about a travelling spectatorship and a sense of metaphysical crisis. It attempts to find a philosophical and aesthetic position from which the logics of accumulation, and the gnawing discontent and instability they give rise to, can be observed with recourse to an 'impartial' higher law; and which it is the role of the poet to communicate as a 'legislator of mankind'.[44] Turning east, Johnson avails himself of an imaginative remove, which lifts contemporary history into the long temporal reach of antiquity. At the same time it allows him to speak in abstract rather than directly political ways from the site of empire and governance, in a story about escaping from and returning to its citadel. In this sense Johnson's Happy Valley reflects a defensive view of an imperial Britain that was opening its borders to the 'whole *Globe*', but anxious about what such extension might bring in return. An empire that needed, moreover, to reflect on lessons from the ruins of the past.

    *Rasselas* famously shares the concerns of Johnson's earlier poem *The Vanity of Human Wishes*, where the nature of human desire is charted around the globe:

> Let Observation with extensive View,
> Survey Mankind, from *China* to *Peru*;
> Remark each anxious Toil, each eager Strife,
> And watch the busy Scenes of crouded Life;
> Then say how Hope and Fear, Desire and Hate,
> O'erspread with Snares the clouded Maze of Fate,
> Where wav'ring Man, betray'd by vent'rous Pride,
> To tread the dreary Paths without a guide;
> As treach'rous Phantoms in the Mist delude,
> Shuns fancied Ills, or chases airy Good.[45]

Like Juvenal's tenth satire, of which it is perhaps the most famous version, Johnson's poem routes the trajectories of human desire through individual examples of statecraft, from the internal machinations of Wolsey to the imperial ambition of Alexander and Charles XII of Sweden. *Rasselas* investigates this confluence of desire and power in the form of an Abyssinian prince, potential inheritor of an absolutist monarchy, who is beset by 'Phantoms' even in the 'Happy Valley' where he lives: a utopian place surrounded by impassable mountains where all wants and needs are satisfied. Rasselas suffers from boredom – a condition that was just finding a name in mid-century Europe – needing variety to alleviate his life, and the proximity of misery to underline his own freedom and happiness. Rasselas loses himself in a 'visionary bustle' in which he saves orphaned virgins and defeats oppression, fantasies which take him beyond the 'boundary of [his] life' to find a means of escape. The novel is a philosophical meditation on 'the choice of life' and the necessary presence of pain and death in the search for happiness. What interests me is the extent to which it is a parable fitted to the times.

## State Imagining

If the Happy Valley connotes an Edenic perfection, it also suggests a condition of plenitude which represents an ur-state in the utopian thinking of the period, whether in the natural gift economy of the Tahiti of Bougainville and Diderot, or in the monarchical society of *Candide*'s El Dorado, where precious stones litter the streets. Johnson's version is more statist: the Valley is both a holding place for future rulers of empire, and a security environment which is exemplified in the architecture of the palace itself:

> This house, which was so large as to be fully known to none but some ancient officers who successively inherited the secrets of the place, was built as if suspicion herself had dictated the plan. To every room there was an open and secret passage, every square had a communication with the rest, either from the upper stories by private galleries, or by subterranean passages from lower apartments. Many of the columns had unsuspected cavities, in which a long race of monarchs had reposited their treasures. They then closed up the opening with marble, which was never to be removed but in the utmost exigencies of the kingdom; and recorded their accumulations in a book which was itself concealed in a tower not entered but by the emperour, attended by the prince who stood next in succession. (p. 41)

This view of the mystery associated with an eastern empire is undoubtedly coloured by contemporary antiquarian accounts of Egypt in particular, themselves part of a long tradition of interest in hermetic philosophy that had revived in the mid-eighteenth century. Stored in the vaults of the Happy Valley is a secret history of accumulation known to a few initiates. If this treasure house has bought the state a 'fortress' like security, it also suggests a labyrinthine strategy, 'as if suspicion herself had dictated the plan'. It is not secrecy itself that is necessarily to be feared here; Johnson may have agreed with William Warburton, author of *The Divine Legation of Moses*, that awe at the mysteries of power – and crucially at the transcendence of law – maintained respect for the order of the state.[46] But the combination of secrecy and a certain accumulative inertia and unfreedom does seem to be at issue in *Rasselas*. 'Wealth heap'd on Wealth, nor Truth nor Safety buys,/ the Dangers gather as the Treasures rise', as Johnson's poem reminded.[47] Wealth, like knowledge, needs to circulate; Rasselas, as a fourth son, has to cope with his curiosity, and choose, like Candide, to enter a world of pain. The dangers to the protected realm of the happy valley involve the revelation, on the one hand, of the uneasy truth of unfreedom in this impossible 'blissful captivity'(p. 40), where there 'is neither labour to be endured nor danger to be dreaded, yet . . . all that labour and danger can procure or purchase' (p. 44). And on the other hand the threat that disclosure might bring from outside: the possibility of invasion.

In his 1756 review of Lewis Evans's *Geographical, Historical, Political . . . Essays*, which included cartographical details of North America, Johnson had connected the ability to wander imaginatively over the region with the surveying of the 'immense wastes of the western continent' prompted 'by stronger motives than science or curiosity could ever have supplied', that is, by war.[48] The technology that might deliver the security of an olympian vision over the globe is also imagined in *Rasselas* as a philosophical vantage point provided by the art of flying:

> How must it amuse the pendent spectator to see the moving scene of land and ocean, cities and deserts! To survey with equal security the marts of trade, and the fields of battle; mountains infested by barbarians, and fruitful regions gladdened by plenty, and lulled by peace! How easily shall we then trace the Nile through all his passage; pass over to distant regions, and examine the face of nature from one extremity of the earth to the other! (pp. 51–2)

Yet such spectatorship has a cost. Even if it were possible (and the Icarus-like pretensions of the flying mechanist are underlined), the knowledge would have to remain a secret if security were to be maintained. 'A flight of northern savages' might arrive with 'irresistible violence' by the same means, and 'even this valley, the retreat of princes, the abode of happiness, might be violated by the sudden descent of some of the naked nations that swarm on the coast of the southern sea' (p. 52). Imperial recoil haunts the most abstract of expansionist fantasies. At the same time the relation between imagination and dominion itself is continually exposed. One manifestation of imperial competition was an awareness of the link between spectatorship and surveillance. As the traveller Carsten Niebuhr had observed with a certain incredulity in the Indian city of Surat, the English governor would not allow him to make a plan of the town, nor a 'Frenchman to live in a high apartment from which he had a view of the citadel'.[49] The madness of the eccentrics Rasselas meets involves their perspectival elevation, like the astronomer who is convinced he has the authority to mete out universal justice in his supposed controlling of the climate. Such madness is present for Johnson in a general human propensity to let the imagination 'tyrannise' reason. Ascent to a universalising vision thus has to be mediated by a knowledge that has passed along the byways of practical experience, and which knows the stakes. It is only their God-given greater knowledge, Imlac the poet argues, which prevents the powerful Europeans being invaded and colonised in turn by the 'Asiaticks and Africans' whom they 'easily visit' for 'trade and conquest' (p. 63).

It is no accident then that it is Imlac who guides Rasselas on his pilgrimage beyond the Happy Valley. As a philosopher who knows the nature of 'traffick',[50] and indeed who has proved himself someone who can make accumulated wealth circulate and grow, he is the ideal companion to the contemplative prince. Rasselas discovers the currency of money, and the fluency of social movement that communication with strangers allows; the stock that accrues to him is knowledge. Johnson's very language for the acquisition of knowledge and experience is shaped by the circulating desires and energies of worldly life, and by the 'print' of empire, as if, despite its protest, it cannot be imagined distinctly from them.[51] To take one example: 'curiosity', a word that repeats throughout the tale, is a commitment to finding truth and happiness, a willingness to keep on the move, and at once a form of instrumentalism, in which the desire to discover new things echoes the 'universal knowledge' of expanding dominion.[52] At the end of the tale, Rasselas's curious travels culminate in the desire for his own 'little kingdom, in which he might administer justice in his own person, and see all the parts with his own eyes; but he could never fix the limits of his dominion, and was always adding to the number of his subjects' (p. 150). Fulfilment of his dream is impossible, so he returns with the others to Abyssinia.

## Returning Home

'The man who would want his homeland never to be larger, or smaller, or richer or poorer would be a citizen of the world', wrote Voltaire in his definition of 'Patrie'.[53] If Rasselas, like Candide, concludes that what is given can only be the best of all possible worlds, he is not a citizen in this sense. In *Candide* there is a delinking of people from their seeming organic connections to place, community and nation: fighting for men they do not know, for reasons they do not understand, suffering chameleon-like transformations which leave their violent imprint on the stories they tell and the communities they assemble. Voltaire's narrative asks what it means to be an agent in such a history, and to ride the vanities of competing 'worlds' in a universe where the devil may already have won. 'Citizenship' is thus what Candide potentially realises in constructing a homeland from Turkish soil, benefiting from the participation and tolerance of others. Contentment with working what is given is the same as not wishing your neighbours ill: this is, in the words of Johnson's novel, a 'choice of life', but one marked by equality. In contrast with this ethical position, it is not clear how far Rasselas is transformed by his perambulations. He returns home to a realm already established by imperial accumulation, having learned perhaps that he is a subject of a higher, providential law, which is as wrapped in mystery, and more deserving of awe for its divine architect than the truths secreted in the palace of the Happy Valley.

If *Rasselas* is indeed a negotiation of the meaning of home, it reveals dimensions of the cultural work of empire internal to Britain at this time. It is a work that looks both inward and outward, consolidating on the one hand a domestic vision of the state in a commonly used analogy with the family, and on the other managing anxiety at expansion with recourse to theodicean debate. Just as the family experiences discord of a generational or marital kind, the kingdom can also be riven by discontent, Rasselas explains to his sister Nekayah, however 'just or vigilant' the 'administration of public affairs'. Indeed such discontent may not be 'without reason', since it is a concomitant of increasingly expansive authority: 'as any man acts in a wider compass, he must be more exposed to opposition from enmity or miscarriage from chance; whoever has many to please or to govern, must use the ministry of many agents, some of whom will be wicked, and some ignorant, by some he will be misled, and by others betrayed' (p. 96). Fortune begins to leach away security, and discontent surface, the more the 'world' extends.

Yet the prospect is not uniformly bleak. Even in times of war, 'universal distress', the experience of calamity is uneven:

> thousands and ten thousands flourish in youth, and wither in age, without the knowledge of any other than domestick evils, and share the same pleasures and vexations whether their kings are mild or cruel, whether the armies of their country pursue their enemies, or retreat before them. While courts are disturbed with intestine competitions, and ambassadours are negotiating in foreign countries, the smith still plies his anvil, and the husbandman drives his plow forward; the necessaries of life are required and obtained, and the successive business of the seasons continues to make its wonted revolutions. (p. 98)

The rhythms of natural life go on: Johnson's vision might appear to counter Voltaire in its arguing against the total penetration of 'universal distress'. Voltaire both acknowledged the dislocation of ordinary lives from the actions of the powerful and yet also registered the traumatic reverberations of those actions: the safe zone of private life shrinking to the size of a bed from which no-one can remove you in the dead of night. Yet *Rasselas* also poses the same question here as *Candide*: to what extent do national – global – events impact on everyday life? In what ways can people far removed from the theatres of action and decision be seen as *subjects* of imperial history in the making?

The domestic focus of this discussion in the pages of *Rasselas* is significant in 1759, as is the role of women in the weighing of private life. Nekayah is a proto-bluestocking, whose final fantasy is the building of 'models of prudence, and patterns of piety' for the future (p. 150). In her debate about the necessity of marriage, and emphasis on virtue as providing 'quietness of conscience' and 'a steady prospect of a happier state', Johnson has her articulate moral values of which women were held to be custodians. As she says to her brother at the prospect of 'unreasonable' discontent, 'I hope that I shall always have spirit to despise, and you, power to repress' (p. 96). This gendered division between moral and political agency has a powerfully material effect on life in mid-eighteenth-century Britain. It was an explanatory fiction, before which women in particular felt they had to genuflect. The writer Frances Brooke, arriving in Quebec in the early 1760s shortly after Wolfe's victory, writes a shrewd political assessment of the time ventriloquated through the men in her novel *The History of Emily Montague*, even as her women characters deny any interest: 'I think no politics worth attending to but those of the little commonwealth of women: if I can maintain my empire over hearts, I leave the men to quarrel for every thing else'.[54]

In wartime this ideological divide underlined the separation of private life from the clash of armies and nations taking place elsewhere. As Harriet Guest has discussed, in 1757 Elizabeth Carter reported news of failure in North America, and the build up of troops she had seen with her own eyes on the coast of Kent, with a certain detachment: 'Our present national prospects may be bad . . . [but] at all events, beyond good wishes and prayers, what need have people in private life to think at all about them?' Her correspondent Catherine Talbot concurs: what is needed is a 'quiet acquiescence' on the part of 'private persons . . . in the fate of nations'.[55] This imagining of the local and familial as a form of retreat can be interpreted on a number of levels. It was, after all, literally the case that thousands went about their business according to patterns of daily life that were seemingly unaffected by 'global' conflict. Yet leaving aside the numerous ways in which the war shaped rhythms of life – in the movement of population, taxation, kinds of scarcity, impressment and the vagaries of commerce and credit – the question of consent or 'acquiescence' here also suggests a level of disavowal. Turning away from the world is also a way of constituting it. The sense of separation from the 'fate of nations' also marks a work of community, the exclusive making of 'home', replete with tropes and metaphors like the pastoral vision of the purposeful husbandman working the land, or the quiet regulation of the household. In the anonymous 1762 poem 'Corydon's Farewell, on Sailing in the Late Expedition Fleet', a seaman's elegiac generation of 'homefelt joys' has woodmen sawing to the perfect anthemic rhythms of 'Heart of Oak', while the 'tender, watchful mother' sits knitting, her children's play presaging the future: the boys building houses from wood chips, the girls making mud pies.[56]

The private, domestic realm of feeling was a means of grasping the universal, as Carter writes to Mrs Vesey: 'Universal and remote consequences would operate very faintly on our reason, if the heart was not by infinite wisdom formed to feel the private and immediate stroke.'[57] Guest argues illuminatingly that it is precisely such local and sympathetic attachments that 'make national identity a matter of customary second nature', and moreover, led to a refashioning of patriotism in the light of feminine sensibility that had a greater universalising claim in the 1770s and 1780s than the realm of masculine politics, which could seem tawdry and partisan by comparison.[58]

The imagining of home, then, is a way of actively producing subjects for a universal history it appears to hold at arm's length. In the period of the Seven Years' War and its aftermath the affirmation of domestic life did do more than produce a comforting sense of the solidarity of what we might now see as a 'home front', answering those jeremiads which saw 'effeminate' weakness at home leading to disaster abroad. A perceived separation from, and yet consent to, the actions of the state was a means of its reimagining at this time, not just an opportunity for its critique; no less a work of empire than learning to manage the Indians in the western continent. The state, in this sense, is not that entity distinguished from privatised social life (as the powerful ideological story of separate spheres might have it), but a political formulation of the social: a relation, rather than a thing. State power is sometimes brutally experienced in all its hypostatised force (a repressive apparatus), and elsewhere, at the same time, as a fluid assemblage of modes of administration and recognition, which took a number of idealised and fantasised forms: the transcendent, transparent order imagined as a virtuous disinterest by patriot ideology, the localised, familial order of regulated community, forms which shaped the institutions, societies, and the very subjecthood, of mid-eighteenth-century British life. If imperial expansion revealed the very constitution of state sovereignty by stretching these fantasies to their limits, it required a level of imaginative risk in the 1760s which somehow had to be made secure.

The fashioning of home was a domestic work demanded by empire because in its quiet images of bounded belonging it defused the seriousness of what it would mean for the social order if the dislocation from the purpose of the state were really the case. What if, as in *Candide*, there were indeed no allegiances at stake nor barriers in the wandering across borders and cultures, along the curious circuits of trade? Or if it were possible to join without guilt or betrayal the motley communities forged, against the grain of the naturalised identifications of race and culture, amongst the collisions of the 'fate of nations'? Or, most significantly, if 'discontent' in the context of a sudden, and to some, apocalyptic, imperial expansion, had to be countered by the 'power to repress'? These were demonstrable realities. The domestic realm becomes the first line of defence, not simply against threats of invasion from without and the cacophony of distant conflict, but from the deterritorialisations of empire within.

In Johnson's *Rasselas* retreat is not a solution as such. The pastoral life is shown to be 'cankered with discontent', its inhabitants 'condemned to labour for the luxury of the rich'. The hermit, a military veteran, is bored and 'distracted' in his remove from the world, and decides to return to society (pp. 85–6). The restlessness of every sector of life suggests something of what I termed earlier the general time of war: envy, competition, subjection, chance. Without guarantee of justice, but also not lacking in hope. However, if the inhabitants of the Happy Valley are to learn what it means to inhabit the best of all possible worlds, it is through the rearticulation of the 'stream of life' in a different temporal economy altogether: eternity. Contemplation of Egyptian ruins functions like a philosophical *memento mori* of the decline of past civilisations: mummified bodies the signs of former tenderness for 'relations and friends' (p. 146) and the pyramids inscrutable evidence of 'fabricks raised before the time of history' (p. 105). Ultimately the novel's concern at a world undergoing 'extension' finds a solution in Imlac's discussion of 'immateriality' and the soul:

> 'I know not, said Rasselas, how to conceive of anything without extension: what is extended must have parts, and you allow, that whatever has parts may be destroyed.' 'Consider your own conceptions, replied Imlac, and the difficulty will be less. You will find substance without extension. An ideal form is no less real than material bulk: yet an ideal form has no extension. It is no less certain, when you think on a pyramid, that your mind possesses the idea of a pyramid, than that the pyramid itself is standing. What space does the idea of a pyramid occupy more than the idea of a grain of corn? Or how can either idea suffer laceration? As is the effect such is the cause; as thought is, such is the power that thinks; a power impassive and indiscerptible. (p. 148)

Imlac's lesson on the nature of substance and thought is the abstract culmination of the book. Drawing on a tradition of scholastic thought that Descartes had transformed into the very thinking of the subject, it is a way of finding an answer to the conundrum described by Nekayah in which 'to the mind, as to the eye, it is difficult to compare with exactness objects vast in their extent, and various in their parts . . . We differ from ourselves just as we differ from each other, when we only see part of the question, as in the multifarious relations of politicks and morality: but when we perceive the whole at once, as in numerical computations, all agree in one judgement, and none ever varies his opinion' (p. 99). The finitude of the world, its mutability and tendency to destruction, is counterposed with the existence of the self-constituting 'power that thinks', an intimation of the infinite which can only be annihilated by the will of 'higher authority'. The proper 'choice of life' is thus obedience to a divine sovereignty, which is conceived, in the words of Étienne Balibar, not in the terms 'of an external or revealed dogma, but to an internal structure of thought whose structure is that of a sovereign decision, an absent presence, or a source of intelligibility that as such is incomprehensible'.[59]

At the heart of this philosophical vision is a fantasy of impossible permanence that also concerns the theological underpinnings of the state. Alongside an image of a defensively bounded world, fortress of security, emerges the utopian prospect of an imperial state *without extension* that Johnson can only countenance in absolutist terms: the 'incomprehensible' subject position from which universal thought might be imagined. It was after all the biblical story of Daniel that came to Johnson at the outset of the Seven Years' War, as his imagination wandered over the lakes and mountains of North America. A place, he reported, that some had 'marked as the seat destined by Providence for the fifth empire':[60] the final kingdom that 'filled the whole earth', as Nebuchadnezzar's dream had revealed, and that God intended should 'stand forever'.[61]

### The Shandean Subject of Empire

Have you read Tristram Shandi? T'is a very unaccountable book; an original one. They run mad about it in England.

Voltaire[62]

Not English, Sir.
Johnson[63]

This is not an exchange that ever took place, though the comments are true enough. It is difficult to think of a novel that might appear less concerned with its moment than *Tristram Shandy*, seemingly far removed in its formal play and self-reflexive wit from the weighty matters of the times, and in its definition of the '*world*' as 'four *English* miles diameter' of a Yorkshire parish (*TS* 1.7.10), as emphatically local as *Rasselas* appeared universal in its pretensions. The word 'Shandy' is a Yorkshire dialect word for 'crazy'; the novel's lunacy seemed peculiarly homegrown, its comic vernacular drawn – as the text itself reminds you – from the 'copious store-house of original materials' (*TS* 1.21.71) that John Dryden had long before argued was as whimsical as the English climate. A comic climate fully grasped, perhaps, by those who were in key respects outsiders, the Scots and Irish: Swift, Sterne, Smollett, Goldsmith, Congreve, Sheridan.[64] For some early reviewers it was oddly anachronistic. The *Lloyd's Evening Post* could not make sense of what Voltaire termed an 'unaccountable book': 'This is not an age for wit and humour', it reported. 'Arms and military achievements engross the attention of one part of the public; pleasure and luxury occupy the minds of the other'.[65]

Yet Sterne's novel begins as a book of the war, no less than *Candide* and *Rasselas*. It is belatedly dedicated (twice) to William Pitt, architect of the conflict and Secretary of State, just as Voltaire's opening reference to French failure at the battle of Minden ties his narrative to the times. Its juxtaposition of the moment of writing in the 1750s with memories of the military campaigns of forty and more years before, points to a commonly made series of comparisons during the Seven Years' War with Marlborough's battles and the golden age of Queen Anne. *Tristram Shandy* could indeed be read as a 'masterpiece of allegory', suggested one pamphlet, in which the baffling juxtapositions of its wit in fact dealt in the current fate of nations:

> What is the Siege of *Namur*, which he often mentions, but the Siege of Fort St. Philip's in Minorca?—or, the wound his uncle Toby received there but the distress the nation was thrown into thereupon? His application to the study of fortification, and knowledge therein gained, means nothing else but the rectitude and clear sightedness of the administration which afterwards took up the reins of government.[66]

Such a literal reading of the novel as a particular gloss on the Byng affair, was unique, and somewhat tongue-in-cheek. But if such literalism has its uses in exposing the topicality of Sterne's work, it is not the only route to understanding what made this 'unaccountable' work testimony to its time.

## Nothing odd will do for long . . .

Johnson's *Rasselas* constructs its statist vision of empire, I suggested, by invoking in a divine sovereignty whose presence can be read in the ruins of past civilisations, an impossible permanence. If *Tristram Shandy* represented the opposite, tied as it was to the vagaries of the present moment, and unashamedly out of kilter in its storytelling, it nevertheless makes comic capital out of the very material that is cause for melancholic contemplation in Johnson's parable. Sterne continually stages different kinds of hermeneutic failure where Johnson hopes for the stability of universalising thought. The crisis in naming the Shandean baby is an instance of this failure. 'Tristmegistus' is the paternal choice, in an allusion to the all-encompassing encyclopaedic abilities of the hermetic philosopher; the name 'Tristram' the accidental result and a kind of fall from grace, a name synonymous with sadness, the accident itself a sign of impregnable mysteries which the novel reproduces in its 'motley emblem', the marbled page.

Naming, as we will see in Chapter 3, is about paternal control, and it brings with it a history of state fantasy that haunted the mid-eighteenth century, put to work anew. But its failure suggests that Sterne's writing and Johnson's numerous projects share common concerns, for all their pronounced differences. It is failure that marks 'Dictionary' Johnson's attempt to fix the English language in the early 1750s according to the best usage of his forefathers, consigned instead to endless digressive journeys around the kingdom if he is to register its mutability.[67] Imperial visionary turned itinerant, he is a Shandean figure despite his best intentions. The words of Sterne's narrator aptly describe his condition, trammelled up in 'rolls, records, documents and endless genealogies, which justice ever and anon calls him back to stay the reading of' (*TS* 1.14.41–2). There are resonances between the melancholic plight of Doctor Johnson and the paternal principle in *Tristram Shandy*, attempting to establish order in a life which comes to resemble a 'state of *warfare*' (*TS* 5.16.447), brought ultimately to contemplate the 'maze' of social existence as Walter Shandy does his fishpond. However strong the desire to establish an overarching vision and thus control, the reality is that events collapse into contingency, 'errors' which rebound on lives and philosophies in incontrovertible ways; both *Rasselas* and *Tristram Shandy* are in their own ways about coming to terms with this fact.

The failure to name the world in your own image is a sign of modernity, to which both texts are responding. It also marks an imperial conundrum. The political consequences of such a failure are part of the matter of Sterne's textual jokes. In one, Francis the First, king of France, decides to strengthen his links with Switzerland (to whom he is in debt) by asking 'her' to be godmother to his next child. Switzerland reciprocates by claiming the traditional right of the godmother to name the child. Instead of a name acceptable to the French throne such as Francis or Henry, the Swiss republic decides on 'Shadrach, Mesech and Abed-nego'. The king declares he will have nothing more to do with the Swiss, but unable to find the funds to pay them off, he decides to 'go to war with 'em' (*TS* 4.21.358–9). In this naming is a form of subjection, which is to be met by force. The joke underlines the point exploited in Sterne's novel as a whole: that naming involves both power and 'jeopardy'. Language is a zone of risk and transformation, which is often conveyed, like the circumcision of the sash window, through a form of anti-semitic shock. But there is more to the allusion to the biblical book of Daniel than this. If Johnson sees in Daniel's prophecy an image of lasting empire, Sterne draws on a vertiginous form of cultural (mis)naming: Shadrach, Mesech and Abed-nego, like Daniel, are Jews who are given new names by the conquering Babylonians, an acculturation which results in their gaining power over affairs of state, but whose limits are tested when the king discovers they will not worship false gods. Amidst a story about competing powers, is a complex brokerage of position, an image of imperial transculturation that ultimately keeps its virtue intact and unchanged. Such a fantasy of metamorphosis *without* an attendant loss of identity returns repeatedly in the culture of the time, as we will see, often marked not just by xenophobic dismissal of, but also an ambivalent identification with, the figure of the stranger.

## CANDID and Miss CUNEGUND's Affairs

*Bright Goddess,*
    If thou art not too busy with CANDID and Miss CUNEGUND'S affairs,—
take *Tristram Shandy*'s under thy protection also. (*TS* 1.9.16–17)

Sterne had both *Rasselas* and *Candide* in mind as he completed the first two volumes of *Tristram Shandy* in the autumn of 1759. He modelled the size and paper quality of the first York edition of this book on the feel and shape of Johnson's text.[68] It was, however, the extraordinary success of the then anonymous *Candide* that he hoped to emulate, as his address to the moon jokingly underlines. But the book seems present in the early pages of *Tristram Shandy* in other ways, not least in the self-conscious constitution of the 'world' of the novel, like one of Voltaire's 'globules': communities constructed with their own laws and customs, their own hobbyhorsical definitions of belonging, sometimes against the grain of a wider universe which might threaten them at any moment.

    In British sentimental writing from the period retreat to a familial community of this kind is often a defensive measure, as we will see, shutting out the harsh inequalities of a system it can do little about. Voltaire offers no such comfort. Yet if *Tristram Shandy* underlines its provincial distance from London in the drama of Mrs Shandy's 'lying-in', and the story of uncle Toby's war games on the bowling green echoes this tactic of retreat, the novel also shares with *Candide* a sense of the sometimes violent flows and forces that course through the local boundaries of home. For all its familial security, this is also a community subject to contingency: to unexpected death and accident, to intimations of bastardy, to a bombardment of *things*, and to a constant flow of imaginative associations and desires that unpick its certainties. Later chapters of this book explore what it means to construct the Shandean familial 'world', with its genealogies and networks of friendship, in mid-eighteenth-century Britain. How, indeed, such a worlding relates to the cultural work of the state at this time, part of the 'purpose' of public culture shared by other literary, legal and political texts. At the close of this chapter, however, I want to grasp more specifically the way the novel's crazy (Shandean) particularity becomes a means of restaging what constitutes the universal, the local as a means of reading the wider world.

### A small circle described upon the circle of the great world . . .

The lunacy of *Tristram Shandy* charts the caprices of a world of risk and fortune, which the newly born protagonist appears destined to ride wherever they might lead. But it is also comment on the eccentric private languages through which individuals negotiate that world. If this private madness is the stuff of Swiftian satire, and a fear that dogged Samuel Johnson, what makes it distinctive in Sterne's work is its ironic and sometimes sympathetic generalisation. The small world within a world is emphatically provincial, shrinking and shifting with the idiosyncrasies of its cast of characters, but it is also curiously representative. The condition of incommunicability between characters caught up in separate hobbyhorsical universes raises a fundamental question about the bonds of social life: what it is that cements relations between people, even in the most intimate of circumstances, when their motives and inner worlds seem impossible to decipher. The novel shares, then, a testing of social ties that is analogous to that of Voltaire and his pastry-cook.

One effect of this 'retreat' is critical: to expose the universalising pretensions of the powerful as yet one more privatised game, but one with serious cost. The gravity and sententiousness that Yorick describes as a 'taught trick to gain credit of the world for more sense and knowledge than a man was worth' (*TS* 1.11.28) – in a passage regarded by Mikhail Bakhtin as an 'epigraph to the whole history of the European novel'[69] – are answered by the novel's own 'law of gravity', in which everything that elevates itself must answer to its material – sexual, physical, scatalogical – ground. This is a time-honoured satirical method, one that has political force in *Candide*, where the telescoping from the saws of imperial reason and law to the brute reality of flesh and bone makes its point: the cost of being sacrificed to the strategies of the powerful. If *Tristram Shandy* differs in important respects from Voltaire's relentless satiric exposure of the mechanics of a universe animated by conflict, it shares his sceptical understanding of the 'natural' way of the world as a state of culture, one legitimating the authority of those with 'employments of dignity or power' (*TS* 1.5.8). And like *Candide* it demonstrates a belief in the significance of storytelling, not simply as a means of coping with a threatening world, but as a self-fashioning that suggests the seizing of a certain cultural capital and thereby a form of freedom: 'A lesson to the world "*to let people tell their stories their own way*"'(*TS* 9.25.785).

The reduction to 'four *English* miles diameter of a Yorkshire parish' is thus no retreat, wholly distinct from the 'circle of the great world' (*TS* 1.7.11), but rather a means of its negotiation and imagining. There is undoubtedly a defensiveness in the setting of boundaries that, at a time of emergent nationalism, serves to sketch what might be seen as a counter-modernity: in the novel's returning to a past, traditional way of life, for example, among those who attempt to relegate the deterritorialising flows and conflicts of the social order busily concerned with 'the whole *globe*' to an elsewhere beyond the borders of the familiar 'world'. If this counter-modernity echoes certain trends in mid-eighteenth-century culture which we have already seen in the brief outline of a 'home front', it is informed perhaps by an outsider's grasp of the cost and meaning of exclusion, in its 'tale of . . . impotence and disfigurement, of lives of quiet desperation conducted far from the centres of power and prestige', in Terry Eagleton's words.[70] However, it is a gesture deliberately ironised in Sterne's narrative, where boundaries are always porous, and subject to seduction. The particularity of the local community is connected to the eccentric byways and circuits that shape cosmopolitan knowledge, histories of transmission: '—from *Greece* it got to *Rome*,—from *Rome* to *France*,—and from *France* to *England*:——So things come round.——' (*TS* 5.12.441). Desires run riot, opinions are traded, things 'crowd in so thick'. *Tristram Shandy*, like *Rasselas*, grasps that knowledge of the 'world' requires commerce with it; and unlike in Johnson's parable, this digressive passage becomes a question of *form*. If this is closer to the satirical realm of *Candide*, with its picaresque routeing of encounters along the international road, and paratactical stringing together of anecdotes and episodes, the radical contingency of Sterne's novel is distinctive in key respects.

## Wit: The Montage Effect

What explodes into the pages of *Tristram Shandy* is not the brutal slapstick of the best of all possible worlds, but a formal play that marks a newly *interiorised* sense of time and experience. The traditional community of the Shandy household and its environs of the late seventeen teens is cut through by the present moment of writing in 1759; cut through not simply to dramatise a moment of psychological immediacy (as Samuel Richardson's writing had already achieved in the 1740s), nor just as a dramatic device, though in the early volumes in particular it does resemble Henry Fielding's armchair theatre, with curtains rising and falling on the imagined past, and suspense created at will.[71] Rather, the juxtaposition of temporal zones resembles a form of montage, calling attention to its medium, an effect underlined by the pasting together of what Bakhtin saw as images of social discourse: the sermon, the legal tract, and fragments of other literary works. Montage produces variations in pace, and also, in its manipulation of time, a spatialisation of the narrative which the author discusses with his 'hypercritic':

> it is but poor eight miles from *Shandy-Hall* to Dr. *Slop*, the man-midwife's house;—and that whilst *Obadiah* has been going those said miles and back, I have brought my uncle *Toby* from *Namur*, quite across all *Flanders*, into *England*:—That I have had him ill upon my hands near four years;—and have since travelled him and Corporal *Trim* in a chariot and four, a journey of near two hundred miles down into *Yorkshire*;—all which put together, must have prepared the reader's imagination for the entrance of Dr. *Slop* upon the stage,——as much, at least (I hope) as a dance, a song, or a concerto between the acts. (*TS* 2.8.120)

This novel's delight in the ruse of duration is a sign of something more than the literary self-consciousness that proved fodder to modernist writers in the twentieth century. The writerly experience of what it might mean to be in several places at once feeds into the generation of an immense subjective theatre for which Sterne has been labelled a proto-Romantic, but which has, I want to suggest, a historical particularity about it. The dialectic between a myopic concentration in the immediate moment and yet a boundless expansiveness that threatens to collapse at any time, might be seen as the plight of the 'modern' eighteenth-century writer, as Swift lampooned in the *Battle of the Books*, trapped in the exigencies of each passing moment. If Sterne knows his Swift, lamenting the shrinking compass of the writer in the 'great harvest of our learning' with his narrator's wish to have been born 'when a man in the literary world might have stood some chance' (*TS* 1.21.72), this formal conundrum is symptomatic of the mid-century moment in ways that Swift could not have anticipated.

The practice of montage, Sergei Eisenstein reminds us, is about the production of new knowledge which sparks from the juxtaposition of previously unconnected images.[72] Later we might want to consider how this resembles the 'wit' of Sterne's narratives, and the way such wit discovers in irony a form of historical duration. Here, however, an archaeology is now required, one that sees in the formal 'lunacy' of Sterne's writing the lineaments of mid-century experience. The cutting together of the 'militiating' 1750s and

1760s with the life of forty years and more before is, as Chapters 2 and 3 will reveal, an act of historical cognition, one that reveals the pressure of the future on the Shandean 'world' of 'four *English* miles diameter', and the pace of change in the present. If the novel tests what Sheldon Pollack has termed 'affective attachments to old structures of belonging',[73] it does so in order to discover what belonging might mean when the 'whole *Globe*' is to be considered, and the universalising forces that attempt to constitute it. 'To what purpose should we trouble ourselves about the world in the moon?', asked Adam Smith in 1759. In Sterne's response to this question throughout the Seven Years' War and its aftermath is a Shandean route to the understanding of the formation of imperial subjectivity in eighteenth-century Britain. It was a story that writers, poets and pamphleteers, and the state itself, undertook to imagine.

## Notes

1 Adam Smith, *The Theory of Moral Sentiments*, ed. D. D. Raphael and A. L. Macfie (Oxford: Clarendon Press, 1976), p. 140.

2 The belief that the moon was an inhabited country, or contained another parallel earth 'inhabited by a race of men, who live in the same manner, as we do here', had classical roots, as Pierre Bayle reminded in the entry on Xenophanes in his *Dictionary*. It was a philosophical fantasy that addressed a planetary relativism – a Copernican shift – also allegorised influentially by Fontenelle. It fed into the genre of 'strange but true' tales that registered the wider encounters of imperial experience. Bayle notes Bishop Wilkins's treatise *The World in the Moon*, translated by Montaigne, which concerned the discovery of a 'new world'. See *The Dictionary Historical and Critical of Mr. Peter Bayle*, trans. P. Desmaizeaux, 2nd edn (5 vols, 1734; reprinted New York and London: Garland, 1984), p. 576. Elkanah Settle's opera *The World in the Moon* took on the same theme in 1697, and Daniel Defoe picked up on its ramifications as an allegory of imperial competition (referring to the Wilkins text) in his *The Consolidator: Or, Memoirs of Sundry Transactions from the World in the Moon. Translated from the Lunar Language. By the Author of the True-Born English Man* (London: Benjamin Bragg, 1705), where he considers the power and superior technological proficiency of the Chinese empire to have lunar origins: 'all was exactly as it is here, an Elementary world, peopled with Folks, as like us as if they were only Inhabitants of the same Continent, but in a remote Climate' (p. 56). Voltaire's sense of alternative globes or 'globules' – and thus the contemporaneity of multiple empires – is clearly informed by the reflection on parallel universes, and it finds its way in to *Tristram Shandy*, when the man in the moon, impressed by the advanced learning of 'a man in the earth', exclaims 'What have we MOONITES done!' (*TS* 5.33.472).

3 John Dyer, *The Fleece: A Poem in Four Books* (London: R. and J. Dodsley, 1757), IV, 135, ll.304, 306.

4 Voltaire [François Marie Arouet], *Candide and Related Texts*, trans. David Wootton (Indianapolis/Cambridge: Hackett Publishing Co., 2000), p. 58. All further references to *Candide* are cited by page number in the text.

5 Voltaire to J. R. Tronchin, 12 February 1758, quoted in Merle L. Perkins. 'European Politics', *Studies on Voltaire and the Eighteenth Century* 36 (1965), 62. This account offers a useful overview of Voltaire's involvement in diplomacy from the 1740s on.

6 Brewer, *Sinews of Power*, p. 41. It was not just the continental armies who bore the cost of the conflict. The battle over Acadia, French-speaking, Catholic Nova Scotia (protected under the terms of the Treaty of Utrecht), resembles modern 'ethnic cleansing' in its forcible removal of an indigenous population by British and New England forces, as Fred Anderson discusses in *Crucible of War*, pp. 113–14.

7 Voltaire, 'Guerre. War', in *Political Writings*, ed. and trans. David Williams (Cambridge: Cambridge University Press, 2000), p. 7.

8 See for example the discussion of the Abbé de Saint-Pierre's *Projet pour rendre la paix perpétuelle en Europe* (1713), and Rousseau's edition, *Paix perpétuelle* (1761), which represented forms of utopianism that Voltaire contested. For the complexity of Voltaire's response to both, including his correspondence with Frederick II in the topic, see Merle L. Perkins, 'Voltaire and the Abbé de Saint-Pierre on World Peace', *Studies on Voltaire and the Eighteenth Century* 18 (1961), 9–34; and her 'Peace Projects of Saint-Pierre and Rousseau', *Studies on Voltaire and the Eighteenth Century* 36 (1965), 92–111. One of the many limitations of the project for a supranational government was its European exclusivity, which was subject to a certain ridicule. The elimination of slave-owning, says C in *The ABC, or, Dialogues between ABC, translated from the English by Mr Huet*, 'will follow as sure as night follows day when *abbé* Saint-Pierre's perpetual peace is signed up by the Great Turk and all the powers . . .' *Political Writings*, p. 137.

9 Though Smith is clear that sympathy alone is not sufficient to underwrite such humanitarianism, preferring in his account of the 'impartial spectator' to develop a stoical form of conscience which self-reflexively recognises one's duty as a 'citizen of the world', and at the same time one's conformity to a greater systemic harmony governed not by sympathy, nor public spirit, but by utility.

10 Voltaire, 'Guerre. War', *Political Writings*, pp. 10–11. On the representation of international law in *Candide*, and Carl Schmitt's account of the British maritime balance of power in the period, see my 'A Comedy of Terrors: *Candide* and the Jus Publicum Europaeum', *South Atlantic Quarterly* 104:2 (2005), 337–47.

11 Quoted in Voltaire, *Candide and Related Texts*, p. 123 n1.

12 Thomas Hobbes, *Leviathan*, ed. C. B. Macpherson (Harmondsworth: Penguin Books, 1968), p. 186.

13  C. L. de S. Baron de Montesquieu, *The Spirit of the Laws*, trans. T. Nugent (New York: Hafner Publishing Company, 1949), xx: 2. The work was first published in 1748.

14  Voltaire, 'Guerre. War', *Political Writings*, p. 11.

15  Immanuel Kant, *The Critique of Judgement*, trans. James Creed Meredith (Oxford: Clarendon Press, 1986), pp. 112–13.

16  W. Whitehead, 'Verses to the People of England', *Annual Register* 1(1758), p. 398. It is interesting to explore the way in which tropes of such a symbiosis are present in the literature of the period, such as the moment in Dyer's *The Fleece* when the 'long ranks' of bales of wool 'Like war's bright files, beyond the sight extend'. Dyer, III, p. 101, ll.343–4.

17  Allen W. Wood, 'Kant's Project for Perpetual Peace', in *Cosmopolitics: Thinking and Feeling beyond the Nation*, ed. Pheng Cheah and Bruce Robbins (Minneapolis: University of Minnesota Press, 1998), p. 75 n6.

18  Voltaire, *The ABC, or, Dialogues between ABC, translated from the English by Mr Huet*, in *Political Writings*, p. 177.

19  Adam Smith, *Lectures on Jurisprudence*, ed. R. L. Meek, D. D. Raphael, P. G. Stein (Oxford: Clarendon Press, 1978), p. 83: 'Laws and governments may be considered in this and indeed in every case as a combination of the rich to oppress the poor and preserve to themselves the inequality of the goods which would otherwise be soon destroyed by the attacks of the poor, who if not hindered by the government would soon reduce the others to an equality with themselves by open violence.' The language of 'combinations' is characteristic of the 1760s, in which early forms of unionism were beginning to emerge and would make their grievances known on the streets. Smith's lectures date from this period.

20  Voltaire to La Chalotais, 6 November 1762, quoted in Perkins, 'European Politics', p. 70.

21  Voltaire, 'Gouvernement. Government', *Political Writings*, p. 49.

22  Linda Colley, *Captives: Britain, Empire and the World 1600–1850* (London: Jonathan Cape, 2002), p. 12.

23  Voltaire, 'Patrie. Homeland', *Political Writings*, p. 27.

24  Brewer, *Sinews of Power*, p. 175.

25  Voltaire, 'Patrie. Homeland', *Political Writings*, p. 29.

26  Voltaire, 'The History of the Travels of Scarmentado', in *Candide and Related Texts*, p. 129.

27  Quoted in Peter Linebaugh and Marcus Rediker, *The Many-Headed Hydra: Sailors, Slaves, Commoners and the Hidden History of the Revolutionary Atlantic* (New York and London: Verso Books, 2000), p. 62. The chapter on the maritime 'Hydrarchy' is particularly pertinent here.

28  Jacques Rancière, *On the Shores of Politics*, trans. Liz Heron (London and New York: Verso Books), pp. 2, 1.

29 Niccolò Machiavelli, *The Prince*, trans. George Bull (Harmondsworth: Penguin Books, 1961), pp. 130–1.

30 Ibid. As Linebaugh and Rediker discuss, the 'war' against piracy intensified in Britain in the 1720s after the awarding of the *asiento*, the running of the slave trade, to British merchants in 1713. 'Pirates had ruptured the middle passage . . . By 1726 the maritime state had removed a major obstacle to the accumulation of capital in its ever-growing Atlantic system.' See Linebaugh and Rediker, *The Many-Headed Hydra*, pp. 171–3. The suppression of piracy by the state undoubtedly reinforced the distinction between legal and illegal forms of maritime capital which Voltaire confounds.

31 Voltaire, 'An address to the public concerning the parricides imputed to the Calas and Sirven families', in *Treatise on Tolerance and Other Writings*, ed. and trans. Simon Harvey (Cambridge: Cambridge University Press, 2000), p. 134.

32 See the conversation 'On Physical Serfdom' in The ABC, where the Englishman argues controversially that 'the only difference between a negro and the soldier is that the soldier costs a lot less'. *Political Writings*, p. 135.

33 Voltaire, 'Patrie. Homeland', *Political Writings*, p. 26.

34 Johnson, *The Idler* 81 (3 November 1759), p. 253.

35 Alexander Pope, *Windsor-Forest*, in E. Audra and Aubrey Williams (eds), *The Twickenham Edition of the Poems of Alexander Pope* (London and New Haven: 1961), I, 191–2, ll.401–406.; Alexander Pope, *An Essay on Man*, in Maynard Mack (ed.), *The Twickenham Edition of the Poems of Alexander Pope* (London and New York: Methuen and Yale University Press, 1951), IIIi, 27, ll.99–102.

36 Johnson, *Idler* 81, p. 254.

37 Samuel Johnson, 'Observation on a Letter from a French Refugee in America to his Friend a Gentleman in England, in *The Literary Magazine, Or Universal Review* 2 (May–June 1756), Donald J. Greene (ed.), *The Yale Edition of the Works of Samuel Johnson: Political Writings* (New Haven and London: Yale University Press, 1977), X, 171.

38 Anderson, *Crucible of* War, pp. 788–9 n1. Anderson notes that Wolfe's 'terrorism' laid waste to the area, destroying 1,400 farms, according to a conservative estimate of the time. See his detailed account of the taking of Quebec in the chapter 'Dubious Battle', pp. 344–68.

39 This was a significant event to choose, as Anderson's account makes clear. While Louisbourg seemed to present a classic case of siege warfare, as detailed by Vauban, the French attempt to claim the honours of war in defeat according to the rules fell on deaf ears. Jeffrey Amherst refused, insisting that everyone who had taken up arms would be sent to England and the civilian population deported to France. It may have been this that leads Johnson's account to weigh differing views of honour, in which the 'French' version of events notes the barbarity of the English: 'A trader always makes war with the cruelty of a pirate'. Johnson, *The Idler* 20 (26 August 1758), p. 65.

40 Johnson, *The Idler* 31(11 November 1758), p. 95.

41 Boswell records Johnson's unfulfilled intention in 1760 'of writing a history of the recent and wonderful successes of British arms in all quarters of the globe', noting that Johnson recorded a resolution to obtain 'books for Hist. of War'. Boswell adds: 'he would have been under no intention to deviate from the truth, which he held very sacred, or to take a licence which a learned divine told me he once seemed . . . jocularly to allow to historians'. James Boswell, *Life of Samuel Johnson* (London: Everyman, 1992), p. 180. The editors of his diaries note that Johnson may have been intending a history of war in general, and not of the progress of the conflict in particular, though in my view the impulse to assess the current moment in historiographical terms is undoubtedly present in his journalism and fictional writing at this time. See Samuel Johnson, in E. L. McAdam, Jr., with Donald and Mary Hyde (eds), *The Yale Edition of the Works of Samuel Johnson: Diaries, Prayers and Annals* (New Haven and London: Yale University Press, 1958), I, 72.

42 Johnson, *The Idler* 20 (26 August 1758), p. 62.

43 What makes them similar in Boswell's view is their refutation of optimism, though he also makes clear their differences: 'Voltaire, I am afraid, meant only by wanton profaneness to obtain a sportive victory over religion, and to discredit belief of a superintending Providence: Johnson meant, by shewing the unsatisfactory nature of things temporal, to direct the hopes of man to things eternal.' Boswell, *Life of Samuel Johnson*, p. 215.

44 Samuel Johnson, *The History of Rasselas, Prince of Abissinia*, ed. D. J. Enright (Harmondsworth: Penguin Books, 1985), p. 62. All further references cited by page number in the text.

45 Samuel Johnson, 'The Vanity of Human Wishes', in *Juvenal in English*, ed. Martin M. Winkler (Harmondsworth: Penguin, 2001), p. 220, ll.1–10.

46 See William Warburton's discussion of the role and degeneration of the 'mysteries' in pagan and classical societies, and thus a history of relations between religion and the evolution of the 'civil policy' of the state, in his *The Divine Legation of Moses Demonstrated, on the Principles of a Religious Deist, From the Omission of the Doctrine of a Future State of Rewards and Punishments in the Jewish Dispensation* (London: Fletcher Gyles, 1738), especially Book Two, Section IV, 133–231.

47 Johnson, 'Vanity of Human Wishes', p. 221, ll.27–8.

48 Johnson, 'Review of Lewis Evans, *Analysis of a General Map of the Middle British Colonies in America*', in Donald J. Greene (ed.), *The Yale Edition of the Works of Samuel Johnson: Political Writings* (New Haven and London: Yale University Press, 1977), X, 200. The review was published in *The Literary Magazine, Or Universal Review* 1:6 (15 Sept–15 Oct 1756), 293–9.

49 Carsten Niebuhr, *Travels through Arabia, and Other Countries in the East. Performed by M. Niebuhr, now a Captain of Engineers in the Service of the King of Denmark*, trans. Robert Heron, 2 vols (Edinburgh: R. Morison, G. Mudie, T. Vernor, 1792), II, 406.

50 This symbiosis of philosophy and commerce is ideal for Johnson, combining 'extensive views' with the particularity of trading interest in the way he later argued Adam Smith had achieved in his *The Wealth of Nations* (which was in manuscript in the 1760s, though not published until 1776). See Boswell, *Life of Samuel Johnson*, p. 482.

51 See John Barrell's discussion of Johnson's imperial fantasising in the Plan to his *Dictionary*, where Johnson compares his vision of the English language to the civilising perspective of a Roman soldier surveying the shores of England, ready to bring them under subjection and 'settle them under laws'. Barrell, *Equal Wide Survey*, pp. 148–9.

52 Thus in tracts such as the anonymous *A Letter on the Nature and State of Curiosity* (London: J. Roberts, 1736) curiosity is linked both with the accumulation of wealth and knowledge and with conquest: 'I persuade myself that a Man who is truly curious, even in his own way, will consequently have a natural Curiosity to know most things . . . since our Desires are unbounded as well as the Curiosity of the Curious; so all are for universal Conquest, etc. and still more especially in Knowledge' (p. 63).

53 Voltaire, 'Patrie. Homeland', *Political Writings*, p. 29.

54 Frances Brooke, *The History of Emily Montague* (Toronto: McClelland and Stewart, 1983), p. 87. Brooke's novel was published in 1769, and offers an account of French and English methods of conquest and the liberty of Indian culture. She has Edward Rivers note that 'the sex we have so unjustly excluded from power in Europe have a great share in Huron government', concluding 'In the true sense of the word, *we* are the savages, who so impolitely deprive you of the common rights of citizenship, and leave you no power but that of which we cannot deprive you, the resistless power of your charms', pp. 39–40. Brooke's journal *The Old Maid* had similarly played up the feminine figure of the spinster, while using the opportunity to comment on the early years of the war.

55 Montagu Pennington (ed.), *A Series of Letters between Mrs. Elizabeth Carter and Miss Catherine Talbot, from the year 1741 to 1770. To which are added, Letters from Mrs. Carter to Mrs. Vesey, between the years 1763 and 1787; published from the original manuscripts*, 2 vols (London: F. C. and J. Rivington, 1808), II, 410–11, Deal, 16 July 1757. The first volume is cited hereafter as *Carter and Talbot*, the second *Carter to Vesey*. See Harriet Guest, *Small Change: Women, Learning, Patriotism* (Chicago: Chicago University Press, 2000), p. 176. Guest's excellent account, and in particular the chapter 'This Sentiment of Home', pp. 176–219, informs my thinking here.

56 Anonymous, 'Corydon's Farewell, on Sailing in the Late Expedition Fleet', published in the *Gentleman's Magazine* 32 (April 1762); anthologised in Roger Lonsdale (ed.), *The New Oxford Book of Eighteenth-Century Verse* (Oxford: Oxford University Press, 1984), pp. 504–5. Lonsdale suggests that the 'expedition

fleet' may have been that which sailed for Havana from Spithead in the previous month. (p. 849)

57 Carter to Vesey, 30 October 1763, 2.96.

58 Guest, *Small Change*, p. 187.

59 Étienne Balibar, 'Citizen Subject', in Eduardo Cadava, Peter Connor and Jean-Luc Nancy (eds), *Who Comes After the Subject?* (London and New York: Routledge, 1991), p. 35.

60 Johnson, 'Review of Lewis Evans', p. 200. Johnson's review of this major work of cartography includes a verse from Bishop Berkeley's 'America or the Muse's Refuge: A Prophecy' which appears to have been cited from memory: 'Westward the seat of empire takes its way,/The four first acts already past,/The fifth shall end the drama with the day,/Time's noblest product is the last' (p. 201). Johnson is not convinced by Evans's attempt to promote English settlement nor the policy that underwrites such expansion: 'it will very little advance the power of the English to plant colonies on the Ohio by dispeopling their native country' (p. 211).

61 Daniel's interpretation of the Babylonian king's dream in Daniel 2 describes the 'fifth empire' established by God as a kingdom that 'shall never be destroyed' and 'break into pieces and consume' all the others (2.44). Scholars had established the four others as Babylon, Medo-Persia, Greece and Rome and the contemporary willingness to assign the fifth to North America catches a sense of the millennial sentiments of the time.

62 Voltaire to Francesco Algarotti, September 1760, in Theodore Besterman (ed.), *Les Oeuvres Complètes de Voltaire* (Banbury, Oxon.: The Voltaire Foundation, 1972), xxii, 119.

63 Samuel Johnson, from 'An Account of Dr. Johnson's Visit to Cambridge in 1765', *New Monthly Magazine* 10 (1818), 389. See Howes, p. 138.

64 On this point see Terry Eagleton, 'The Good-Natured Gael', in his *Crazy John and the Bishop and other Essays on Irish Culture* (Cork: Cork University Press/Field Day, 1998), 68–139; I have speculated on Sterne's relation to Ireland in my 'Sterne's Politicks, Ireland and the Nature of Evil-Speaking', in Thomas Keymer (ed.), *The Cambridge Companion to Sterne* (Cambridge: Cambridge University Press, forthcoming, 2008).

65 Anonymous letter reviewing first two volumes of *Tristram Shandy*, *Lloyd's Evening Post* 6 (May 1760), 539.

66 Anon., *Explanatory Remarks Upon the Life and Opinions of Tristram Shandy*, pp. 44–5.

67 See Barrell, *An Equal Wide Survey*, on this point.

68 See Keymer, *Sterne*, pp. 61–2.

69 Mikhail Bakhtin, 'Discourse and the Novel', in *The Dialogic Imagination*, ed. Michael Holquist, trans. Caryl Emerson and Michael Holquist (Austin, TX: 1981), p. 310.

70 Eagleton, 'The Good-Natural Gael', p. 133.

71  Which is how George Eliot saw Fielding's novelistic practice: 'he seems to bring his arm-chair to the proscenium and chat with us in all the lusty ease of his fine English. But Fielding lived when the days were longer (for time, like money, is measured by our needs), when summer afternoons were spacious, and the clock ticked slowly in the winter evenings'. George Eliot, *Middlemarch* (Harmondsworth: Penguin Books, 1965), p. 170.

72  See, for example, Eisenstein's discussion of wit and the tropes of montage in 'Dickens, Griffith and the Film Today', in his *Film Form: Essays in Film Theory*, ed. and trans. Jay Leyda (London: Dennis Dobson, 1951), pp. 195–255.

73  Sheldon Pollack, 'Cosmopolitan and Vernacular in History', *Public Culture* 12:3 (2000), 624.

# PATRIOT GAMES: MILITARY MASCULINITY
# AND THE RECOMPENSE OF VIRTUE

In late 1761 the first of a series of four large history paintings by Francis Hayman was exhibited at Vauxhall Gardens. It commemorated the taking of Montreal by General Amherst in the previous year, an event which had effectively secured Canada for the British following Wolfe's success in Quebec. *The Surrender of Montreal to General Amherst* portrayed a humanitarian act of relief, in which the General was shown extending his arms compassionately to the kneeling population of the city – both French and Indian – who had starved under siege. The painting was inscribed, according to a guidebook, with the words: 'POWER EXERTED, CONQUEST OBTAINED, MERCY SHOWN! MDCCLX'. It testified to the fact, as the account put it, that 'clemency is the genius of the British nation':[1] and thus to a seemingly just economy of military power, the eighteenth-century equivalent of 'precision' warfare. The minimum of expenditure obtains the rightful end, and the remainder is mercy.[2] This equation provided the kernel of the ideological justification for British imperial conquest as simultaneously expedient and improving, a conquest that subjugated peoples might eventually come to be grateful for. Hayman's painting exhibited the iconic density of such a belief, invoking classical models of victorious magnanimity – the figures of Scipio Africanus and Alexander – melded with Christian charity. It also captured the centrality of a particular mid-century construction of masculinity, in which the man of feeling was put to work in the interests of the state: a cultural work which is the focus of my interest here.

Hayman's paintings were enormously popular.[3] Among the numerous pictures exhibited in the pleasure gardens, including scenes from Shakespeare and Richardson, the fashionable ruins of Palmyra and earlier moments of victory, Hayman's history paintings were showcased in a newly built saloon to the

Rotunda, entered through a 'gothic portal' and lit in the evening by candles. By 1764, after the conclusion of the war, Hayman's picture of Amherst was flanked by his two allegorical treatments of Britannia paying homage to the victory. *The Triumph of Britannia* (1762) marked Admiral Hawke's earlier naval success at Quiberon Bay with an image of Neptune driving Britannia through the waves, replete with a medallion portrait of George III and sea nymphs carrying those of his seven admirals. *Britannia Distributing Laurels* (1764) portrayed the military generals in full Roman robes, including General Wolfe, whose death Benjamin West would later famously represent.[4] The crisis of national confidence that had accompanied the execution of Admiral Byng – to Candide's alarm – at the outset of the war, had evidently been eclipsed.

In equally triumphalist form a fourth painting was hung opposite the picture of Amherst, representing *Lord Clive Receiving the Homage of the Nabob* (1762). At stake here was a different kind of transaction: less a vision of clemency than an encounter predicated on the meaning of the exchange that would take place beneath the British standard after the Battle of Plassey. It was a subject 'of the most interesting nature to every Briton' which the guide-book undertook to explain. Clive is shown extending the hand of friendship to the Nabob's principal general, who is shortly to be placed by the British in the stead of his former master:

> Meer Jaffer wears on his face strong remains of the emotions already mentioned, but his dejection seems to be faintly alleviated by the General's manner of receiving him. The extension of his arms and the inclination of his body is most movingly expressive of doubt, submission and resignation, which is heightened by an Indian officer laying the Subbah's standard at his feet. The future Subah or Nabob is attended by his son, a youth of about eighteen years of age, bewitchingly handsome, and painted with a masterly propriety.[5]

Read into the bodily expression of the Nabob is a complex story of defeat and reinstatement, rendered with a certain orientalist pleasure. His encounter with Clive's 'attitude of Friendship' presages the moment when the British began to assume the role of the state in Bengal, which would culminate in the East India Company's taking on of the *Diwani* – the right to organise and collect taxes – in 1765.

Contained within these four enormous canvases, invoking territories from North America to India, was thus a diffuse field of meaning that comprised the imperial world of mid-century domestic patriotism. A complex, affective field, in which concepts of law, duty and justice encountered a realm of feeling, both benevolent and violent. If the vision of Amherst giving succour to the rightfully vanquished was a potent one, of a piece with the much-touted self-sacrifice associated with the death of Wolfe,[6] the image of Clive was perhaps more equivocal, connoting as it did the vast booty stripped from Bengal, and state strategy. The former occludes the violence associated with imperial conquest in the name of duty and compassion, the second rationalises it into a colonial act of 'exchange' (which is no exchange at all), limited power for subjection. Both offer in different ways, within their triumphalism, a spectacle of apology for imperial conflict. For some foreign spectators, notably the vilified French, it was hard to stomach. Visiting London at the time, Pierre Grosley noted the immense investment in the memorialization of imperial conquest, from friends working on sculptures of Wolfe to the anti-gallican feeling on the streets and the stage. While Hayman's painting of Amherst ably conveyed 'a tender and noble compassion',[7] it was not one he cared to linger on: 'a glance was enough for these monuments: I cut short my examination of them as soon as it was possible, but often came across French people stopped by the charitable English, who gave them an explanation of all their details and all their charms'.[8]

Grosley had been relieved to find that the inhabitants of London did not match up to the bloodthirstiness of their reputation; their taste for battle and 'these spectacles of carnage and blood, which all other nations have banished from their theatres' were renowned.[9] His account nonetheless captures the complexity of patriotic spectacle. It could be aggressively xenophobic, and triumphalist in the extreme. As Horace Walpole reported in 1761, 'the generality are not struck with anything under a complete victory – if you have a mind to be well with the mob of England, you must be knocked on the head like Wolfe, or bring home as many diamonds as Clive'.[10] Josiah Tucker, the Dean of Gloucester, reflected that pacifism could only appear a madness in the climate that had been whipped up by newspapers, which were conducting a '*trade in blood*'.[11] Yet the effects of patriotic spectacle could take a 'charitably' pedagogic form, as suggested by Grosley's ironic description of the English spectators' drive to explain. The domestic script of empire was taught as much as felt and seemingly instinctive; there were complex interpellations at work. Not least, in the generation of a *new* discourse of humanitarianism, in which the British imperial project might be equated with the exporting of a realm of universal benevolence, even as it engaged in expansionism of a brutal and universalising kind. And if Hayman's history paintings participated in this generation of equivalences, there were other forms of street and cultural spectacle from below that rendered the contradictions and their cost more palpable, no less theatricalised through the 'inclination' of the body.

### *Alas! poor* Bates

The military veteran was a recurrent figure in mid-century culture, and a familiar spectacle in London streets, for the maimed and infirm who did not receive pensions were allowed to beg in public as a reward for their sacrifice to king and country. Such begging often involved the display of appalling campaign injuries. As an earlier ballad sang, to the tune of Lillabullero:

> THE Soldier disbanded, and forc'd for to beg,
> May talk of his Wars, and his Suff'rings so hard;
> But tho' seamed o'er with Scars, and with never a Leg,
> His Wants we neglect, nor his Courage regard;
>     And the Lass that is poor
>     Is sent for a Whore,
> With Hemp and with Hammer to make her Complaint;
>     But if you have Money
>     All Honours are done ye,
> A Coward's a Hero, a Whore is a Saint.[12]

It is clear that the treatment of veterans and the dereliction of those in power who had, after all, set about raising a militia and press-ganging men into service, had long been felt to be a powerful injustice, which intensified at the mid-century with a new Militia Act and the awareness that some were netting untold riches from the sacrifice of others.[13] Moreover it was exacerbated by the bad press both the army and navy had received in the early years of the war. In one such instance, prompted by a series of alarms and defeats, Samuel Johnson (himself a militia man) had registered the perceived lack of military mettle in the *Idler* in 1758, conjuring a scenario in which, tempted by the scent of roast meat and tobacco, the army might be brought to 'bear at once the grimaces of the Gauls, and the howl of the Americans' and 'look an enemy in the face'.[14]

Even as the tide in the war began to turn, the acute sense of misrepresentation remained. Writing a detailed account of the taking of Martinique and Guadeloupe from the French, one Richard Gardiner, Captain of Marines on the ship *Rippon*, expressed his frustration at the Caribbean plantation owners' complaint at the local economic consequences of military action, and the lack of recognition from home. The losses had been huge. The troops had been 'exposed to Dangers they had never known, to Disorders they had never felt, to a Climate more fatal than the Enemy, and to a Method of fighting they had never seen'.[15] 'Half-broiled to Death at one Time, and half-starved at another', they had nonetheless dutifully proved that 'Conquest' was the 'Recompense of Virtue'. Gardiner's aim was evidently to set the record straight.

> Surely some Allowance is to be made for those, who so often sacrifice their
> Lives, and always their Ease, for the service of the Nation and the Benefit of

the Publick, and who fight for them, bleed and starve for them, whenever they are called upon.[16]

Yet if Gardiner's pamphlet ends with the patriotic declaration that 'ROYAL Approbation is the most GLORIOUS Reward a Soldier can acquire', the question of recompense is left subtly unanswered, and the notion of 'Allowance' takes on the form of a more material demand.[17] What was the particular nature of this sacrifice and its proper reward, the true 'Recompense of Virtue'?

This was a question widely considered in the culture at large, and graphically posed by the bodies of the men who begged on the streets. Hogarth's engraving *The Times, Plate II* of 1762 portrayed a group of grotesquely injured men who did not benefit from a misdirected fountain of state assistance.[18] In the literature of the period the veteran – as a 'poor', 'wounded', or 'broken-hearted' soldier – became the object of sentimental concern in a way that generated much more than an occasion for sympathy. In the 1763 poem 'The Pluralist and Old Soldier', a soldier 'maimed and in the beggars' list' makes the case for recompense to a 'well-fed' parson, as his right:

> *Sol.*  At Guadeloupe my leg and thigh I lost,
>         No pension have I, though its right I boast;
>         Your reverence, please some charity bestow,
>         Heav'n will pay double—when you're there, you know.
> *Plu.*  Heav'n pay me double! Vagrant—know that I
>         Ne'er give to strollers, they're so apt to lie:
>         Your parish and some work would you become,
>         So haste away—or constable's your doom.[19]

David McNeil has rightly argued that Trim's rationalisation of his knee wound in *Tristram Shandy* – 'the shot which disabled me at the battle of Landen, was pointed at my knee for no other purpose, but to take me out of his [King William's] service, and place me in your honour's [uncle Toby's], where I should be taken so much better care of in my old age' (*TS* 8.19.693) – is 'Sterne's way of subtly satirising the inadequate pensions awarded to veterans, especially the disabled'.[20] In Smollett's *Humphry Clinker* Lieutenant Lismahago is similarly seen to have risked his 'youth', 'blood' and 'constitution' in the recent campaigns in Canada, 'amidst the dangers, the difficulties, the horrors and hardships of a war, for the consideration of three or four shillings a-day'.[21] As Smollett had earlier acknowledged in the *Critical Review*, 'there are, both in army and navy neglected, and consequently broken-hearted men of merit; too many we fear, whom our miscarriages may at length teach us to prefer'.[22]

The anonymous work that Smollett was reviewing here, and which bears an uncanny resemblance to *Tristram Shandy* in 'militiating' content if not delivery, suggests the complexity of this sense of miscarriage. *The Life and Memoirs of Mr Ephraim Tristram Bates, Commonly Called Tristram Bates, a Broken-Hearted Soldier* emerged in 1756, three years before Sterne began to publish his novel.[23] Tristram Bates is born to be a soldier, acting out Marlborough's campaigns in his parish, his head full of military jargon, like Sterne's uncle Toby. He names his hapless son after a string of commanders: 'Marlborough-Eugene-Turenne-Peterborough-Saxe-Cumberland'. Despite his dedication to the reputation of these men of rank, Tristram never achieves the status of officer, something his mother ascribes to 'the many Shocks the Fortunes of her Family met with the very Year she bore him'. His family remain in a state of illegitimacy. Strangers sob over his tomb with a line cleverly reworked in *Tristram Shandy*: 'Alas! poor Bates'.[24]

Whether Sterne was aware of this text is unclear. The number of coincidences make it seem likely.[25] What is certain is that both novels draw on a current sense of unease at the human cost of what Smollett, in his *Continuation of the Complete History of England*, saw as the people's 'savage appetite for war and carnage which they had for some time avowed'.[26] Such a vision of the atavistic 'appetite' for conflict was a convenient fiction, which drummed up patriotic fervour at home, and, as Pierre Grosley's memoir attests, fear abroad. Yet as the story of Tristram Bates reveals, it was well known that cooler, economic endgames were being played out on the international stage. The narrative works through a series of sentimental encounters, central to which are military veterans themselves, conscious of their status as pawns in the strategies of others. Bates conducts a kind of vox pop:

> 'Well! but, says *Bates*, what think you of the present Times?' 'Bad enough, says *Timbertoe*,—I would not begin the World again! Every Body are for themselves—No-body thinks of *Old England*. – Patriots bully for their Country, now, as Prostitutes talk of Love; but they have Money always in *View*. I have been in 18 pitched Battles, and nine Sieges, Skirmishes I never mention, this is all I have to shew, a Bed and a little plain Food; I don't despise or slight it: But am Sorry I have no Companions—Scarce a Comrade to talk with – Fellows whose Brothers *voted* for my Lord \*\*\*, here eating the Bread of Hundreds, who are *limping* about the Country, and wanting even these Rascals *Leavings*. – But you are young; I should not dishearten you; perhaps the Times may mend.'[27]

Emerging from these vignettes is a sense of dislocation, in a world driven by money and corruption. And an acute feeling of class inequality, conveyed in the following encounter with a deserving sailor:

A *Sailor* past by about this Time with a Wooden Leg, and tho' he did not sollicit Charity, *Bates* knew the *Asking Eye* too well, to let him pass unassisted;
'There's *Sixpence*, cries *Bates*; had you been a *Soldier*, says he, I would have
doubled it. Ah! says the Sailor, we, *poor Negroes*, fight in our Way as hard as
you Gentlemen of the Army, *God help us*. At the word *Gentlemen*, Bates (for
'twas touching the very *String*) added another *Tester*:' And the Fellow stump-
ing on Quick, for fear of being over-heard, said to himself, – What the Duce
is this same Thing called *Rank*? Will it Feed or Cloath a Man? – No; will it
give you a Dinner when half-famish'd? – No; will it set a Broken Leg, or buy
me a new Wooden one of the *Doric Order*? – No; well, they shall have the
Rank if they will, with a *lean Carcass* to boot. Give me the Allowance for an
*English Appetite*, and your Servant for the *Rank*.[28]

Juxtaposed with a life of rank and privilege that is sarcastically denoted by
the luxury of an architecturally designed wooden leg of the '*Doric Order*', is
the meagre existence of a sailor, member of the 'oceanic proletariat'.[29] Short
of food and clothing, his labour appears to him a form of enslavement. The
awareness of inequality is palpable here, and remains unresolved, as the story
of Tristram Bates himself demonstrates. These scenarios testify to more than
a recognisable cause: the demand for the righting of a 'miscarriage' in which
veterans found themselves poorly rewarded for their service. Rather, they
articulate unease about the nature of that service itself. What happens to an
ethical dedication to the will of the nation – to notions of duty, self-sacrifice,
and just action – when that will is itself ultimately shaped by economic concerns, 'Money always in *View*'? To find out, I want to explore the spectacle
of the military veteran in more detail, focusing in particular on one much-
disseminated literary version – the popular figure of Sterne's uncle Toby – to
understand the wider cultural work at stake here.

### Uncle Toby's Wars: Historical Anamnesis

In one of the numerous satirical pamphlets generated by the publication of
the first volumes of *Tristram Shandy*, the anonymous writer claimed that
Sterne's work offered 'a compleat system of modern politics' in which references to the wars of the Spanish Succession might be read allegorically into
the present. Uncle Toby's concern with the siege of Namur thus transposes
into the doomed siege of Minorca, and his wound is said to represent 'the distress of the nation' at its loss.[30] However far-fetched this claim seemed to
some – and to others an elaborate puff engineered by Sterne himself[31]– the
figuring of Uncle Toby and his war games undoubtedly had contemporary
resonance, as did the stories of numerous old campaigners who populate the
literature of the time. Moreover Sterne's historical reference was precise. In

1936 Theodore Baird claimed uniquely that *Tristram Shandy* could be regarded as 'an exactly executed historical novel'. Using Sterne's historical source – Tindal's *The History of England, by Mr Rapin de Thoyras. Continued from the Revolution to the Accession of King George II* – Baird pointed out Sterne's borrowing and paraphrase, not to bring attention to that characteristic charge of plagiarism, but to suggest the novel's 'carefully planned and executed framework of calendar time in what is usually considered a chaos of whimsicalities'.[32] The historical events that form uncle Toby's recollections of Marlborough's campaigns, from Trim's joining of the army in 1689 to the listing of sieges and battles culminating in the Treaty of Utrecht in 1713, are delivered with an eye to sequential detail which is no less precise than Toby's enactment of the news from the Flanders mail upon his bowling green. And what we are presented with here is a particular construction of personal and public history that engages with the direction and inheritance of the 'militiating' mid-century.

The powerful historiographical task of making sense of the global enterprise of empire had been taken on by the public culture of the time. It was evident in the mushrooming of numerous histories, and in the circulation of miscellaneous fragments: from the great analyses of political history and memoirs bringing the 'progress' of the nation up into the present time (Hume,[33] Smollett,[34] Macaulay,[35] Walpole,[36] Wilkes[37]); to the histories of newly acquired territories and the ephemeral journals and accounts which accompanied their taking; to the historical narratives which plotted in more allusive ways parallel accounts of development, or the rise and fall of states, from Scott's *The History of Mecklenburgh*[38] to Gibbon (himself a militia man) and his magisterial account of Rome.[39] As J. G. A. Pocock discusses, the Seven Years' War brought about a major shift in historiography, addressing a shattering of borders in which an enlightened Europe post-Utrecht had 'found itself enlarged towards Russian Eurasia in one direction, towards the global ocean and the continents beyond it in another'. If Gibbon's *Decline and Fall* exhibited in 1776 the 'world history' also 'evident in the great global and American histories of Raynal and Robertson', the imperial conflict between 1757 and 1763 was instrumental in its emergence.[40] In the more uncertain climate of the 1760s, when the 'global' implications of events were still reverberating, the reader of such histories – accessed often in piecemeal weeklies and the compilations of material from the gazettes – may have been grateful for these bracing if provisional exercises in geopolitical orientation. Yet he or she would have experienced nonetheless a much more local and interstitial relation to 'universal' events than that promised by the interpellation: 'citizen of the world'.

Part of the work of public culture was to make that relation to the 'universal' one of identification. It is a work undertaken in institutionalising form, for example, in Joshua Reynolds' *Discourses on Art* from 1769, which valorise a tasteful and abstracted apprehension of 'general nature' in history painting rather than local particularity, as John Barrell ventriloquates: 'when we recognize – as, if we are men of taste, we will recognize – the representation of the central form of man (the argument works only for men) we recognize the ground of likeness between ourselves and all mankind, the universal character of human nature, and the ground of social affiliation.'[41] Francis Hayman's earlier paintings offered imaginative recreations of pivotal events from the war, in which the spectator was sutured into a realm of feeling that confirmed conquest as an extension of fellowship of precisely this kind. Recent events, still unfolding in the present, were thus constituted as 'historical', and rendered into matter for consumption; consumption thereby was itself transformed, into an encounter with a public spirit greater than nationalist opinion or private appetite. At the same time the rhetoric of humanitarianism bridged aporiae in the understanding of what such taking of territory entailed: its extent and management; its political and human consequences.

But the kind of history testified to by the bodies of those who had engineered it was of a different order. If the mutilated and sensitive body of the military veteran offered an indexical relationship to historical truth – such that, as in the case of uncle Toby, it was possible to point to a map of Marlborough's military campaign to show the 'location' of his wound – it was a troubled experiential account of history that emerged, despite an accompanying language of feeling that proffered its tale of bodily sacrifice as necessary to the securing of a wider 'universal happiness'. In part, the wounded body displayed on the streets suggested that historical experience to be unnameable; and yet it spoke volumes about the human cost of inheriting the past, and indeed about what such universal fellow-feeling might entail in the present. Suffering, wrote Soame Jenyns, 'should be considered but as the necessary Taxes, which every member of this great Republick of the Universe is obliged to pay towards the support of the Community'.[42] The figure of the veteran was often troped as a sympathetic advocate of just such a 'tax', and conversely, as its victim and sometimes complainant.

David McNeil divides eighteenth-century literary portraits of the veteran into two distinct kinds: 'the loquacious soul who, like uncle Toby, is always anxious to verbalise his experience; and the rather silent or pithy stoic whose experience has a significance that lies beyond language.'[43] On the one hand, then, McNeil suggests, we have a figure that generates discourse, such as Sir Charles Hanbury Williams's 'The Old General', who

If you name one of Marlbro's ten campaigns,
He tells you its whole history for your pains:

And Blenheim's field becomes, by his reciting,
As long in telling as it was in fighting.[44]

On the other, we are presented with a figure who has repressed the trauma of his experience into silence, a violence given eloquent testimony, however, by the often graphic nature of his wounds, as Oliver Goldsmith's poem attests:

The hardy veteran after struck the sight
Scarr'd, mangl'd, maim'd in every part,
Lopp'd of his limbs in many a gallant fight,
In nought entire – except his heart.[45]

If *Tristram Shandy* addresses what is, in McNeil's terms, 'a cultural sense of war memory',[46] then the figure of the veteran embodies that memory in a complex form. The discourse produced by attempting to name the trauma can be read as a talking cure, since 'the history of a soldier's wound beguiles the pain of it' (*TS* 1.25.88); in such a way memory enables the possession of a personal and temporal relation to events, allowing the historical subject to move on. In cultural terms an age might come to terms with itself and find direction through this process of anamnesis; thus, as McNeil records, Daniel Defoe's Colonel Jack, by listening to the tales of 'old Soldiers and Tars', claims 'I was a kind of an Historian, and tho' I had read no books'.[47] Yet, as the figure of uncle Toby testifies, loquacious as he is, 'his life was put in jeopardy by words': in seeking to tell his story intelligibly, to 'philosophize' upon his wound, he succeeds in miring himself even further in the ambiguities of military discourse:

No doubt my uncle *Toby* had great command of himself,—and could guard appearances, I believe, as well as most men;—yet any one may imagine, that when he could not retreat out of the ravelin without getting into the half-moon, or get out of the covered way without falling down the counterscarp, nor cross the dyke without danger of slipping into the ditch, but that he must have fretted and fumed inwardly . . . what sharp paroxisms and exacerbations of his wound my uncle *Toby* must have undergone upon that score only. (*TS* 2.1.95)

The problem for Toby is that far from therapeutically liberating him from his fixation with what Freud would have termed the 'traumatic accident' of his wound, language condemns him to repeat it, continually repositioning him in the situation he is unable to name, in all its immediacy. As he obsessively refines his understanding of the specialised military terminology of fortifications and projectiles, his inability to name the accident that castrated him becomes an exquisite source of pleasure and frustration, 'baking [his] blood with hectic watchings' (*TS* 2.3.104), and 'angering his wound' even more. It is only when he seeks a practical resolution to his problem by circumventing language altogether in the manner of Swift's Laputans, finding refuge in things rather than words,[48] that the war games he enacts with such accuracy bring about the 'cure'. In this sense Toby is both a hobbyhorsical producer of discourse and one whose experience will not only remain outside of language, but also, if the veteran is to be understood as a custodian of a form of historical memory, outside of the retelling of history itself. In *Tristram Shandy* McNeil's two types of veteran are in fact the same figure, 'speaking' the wounds sustained 'for the good of the nation', as Toby puts it, in a number of ways. Thus it becomes possible to read and weigh the significance of historical trauma of the wound, the event that cannot be named or owned: through the language of the body itself, by which the *miles gloriosus* becomes the man of feeling.

## 'In nought entire – except his heart'

The castrating 'blow' that Toby sustained at Namur causes an 'unparalleled modesty' that 'arose to such a height in him, as almost to equal, if such a thing could be, even the modesty of a woman' (*TS* 1.21.75). If historical experience has feminised Toby and rendered him impotent, for reasons yet to become clear, it at once positions him as a sentimental touchstone: an innocent whose frank tears and blushes suggest 'something in his looks, and voice, and manner', which 'let you at once into his soul' (*TS* 6.10.512). Toby's affective, bodily language appears to be a sensitive litmus test of the ravages of the 'scurvy, disasterous world' (*TS* 1.5.8), its modest blushes a passive register of external forms of violence: historical, sexual, social. The language of sentimental feeling, of the 'heart', which constellates around the figure of the veteran, proves both an antidote to that violence, and yet is also, in some sense, its measure.

Even as the language of sentiment is put to work, there is a density of symbolic administration present in its articulation of feeling. Corporal Trim's description of his master is a productive way in:

> I like to hear *Trim*'s stories about the captain, said *Susannah*.—He is a kindly-hearted gentleman, said *Obadiah*, as ever lived.—Aye,—and as brave a one too, said the corporal, as ever stept before a platoon.—There never was a better officer in the king's army,—or a better man in God's world; for he would march up to the mouth of a cannon, though he saw the lighted match at the very touch-hole,——and yet, for all that, he has a heart as soft as a child for other people.—He would not hurt a chicken. . .——I would serve him to the day of my death out of love. He is a friend and brother to me,—and could I be sure my poor brother *Tom* was dead,—continued the corporal, taking out

his handkerchief,—was I worth ten thousand pounds, I would leave every shilling of it to the captain.——*Trim* could not refrain from tears at this testamentary proof he gave of his affection to his master. (*TS* 5.10.437–8)

Trim's account bears all the hallmarks of the sentimental portrait that Sterne was to develop, replete with a litany of wounded victims from poor Maria to the old campaigner, in *A Sentimental Journey*. Relations between master and servant are re-presented in a quasifamilial light as they are between Yorick and La Fleur in that later novel: Toby is friend and brother, child, and, elsewhere, protector. A nominal equality is emphasised by Trim's willingness to serve Toby 'out of love' and leave his wealth, if he had it, to his master – a mystification and reversal of the economic relations of dependency that actually underpin the situation. To be a servant is to enter, as Eve Kosofsky Sedgwick describes, 'a pseudo-egalitarian space of familial pathos' where, as Yorick demands in *A Sentimental Journey*, 'are we not all relations?'.[49] And Trim clearly derives a lachrymose pleasure from dramatising the evidence of such relational 'sympathy' for his master.

The administrative dimension of this scenario lies in this production of equivalences. Trim's portrait of his master contains strategies that are at the heart of the sentimental project to reconcile a model of natural benevolence with the material interests of a particular class, interests naturalised within the obfuscations of familial ideology. Robert Markley has shown how these contradictions were perceived by writers such as Henry Mackenzie as a 'war of duties' between economic interests and Christian ethics,[50] a conflict arising from the socioeconomic maintenance of empire: 'the virtues of justice, of prudence, of economy, are put in competition with the exertions of generosity, of benevolence, and of compassion',[51] Mackenzie wrote of the sentimental novel. And, as Markley suggests, it is the materialist values that were to take precedence 'over sentimental virtues that in themselves are admirable but that, as [Mackenzie] demonstrates in *The Man of Feeling*, are naive and impractical in a post-lapsarian world'.[52] Thus, in *Tristram Shandy*, Toby's blend of virtue and nature is venerated while the novel at once points out his childlike innocence and powerlessness in an unjust world, in a manner reminiscent of Mackenzie: 'Thou blackened'st no man's character,—— devoured'st no man's bread: gently, with faithful *Trim* behind thee, didst thou amble round the little circle of thy pleasures' (*TS* 3.34.265).

If we return to Trim's portrait, however, it is clear that a concept of 'duty' figures large in his assessment of Toby's qualities: a duty to king and country that is equated with his worth 'in God's world'. 'Duty' is a social and ethical code of conduct that positions the soldier as an exemplary figure at the midcentury, a mediator of the relations between individual and public interest, representing the negotiation of boundaries between the self and God's universe. 'A wise man should surely be capable of doing what a good soldier holds himself at all times in readiness to do', wrote Adam Smith in his *The Theory of Moral Sentiments*:

> Good soldiers, who both love and trust their general, frequently march with more gaiety and alacrity to the forlorn station, than they would to one where there is neither difficulty or danger. In marching to the latter, they could feel no other sentiment than that of the dulness of ordinary duty: in marching to the former, they feel that they are making the noblest exertion which it is possible for a man to make . . . They cheerfully sacrifice their own little systems to the prosperity of a greater system. They take an affectionate leave of their comrades, to whom they wish all happiness and success; and march out, not only with submissive obedience, but often with shouts of the most joyful exultation, to that fatal, but splendid and honourable station to which they are appointed.[53]

Such an unquestioning form of duty, Smith argues, is analogous to that owed by society to 'the great Conductor of the Universe'. God, suggested Soame Jenyns, resembled 'the commander of a numerous army', who exercised his power for the good of the whole even though some would be exposed 'to danger, and some to destruction'.[54] Toby's seemingly reckless readiness to march up to a lighted cannon, if it is required of him, is thus a model of Christian conduct: symptomatic of his love for fellow man and selflessness in the name of the public good, and his disciplined acceptance of providential decree. In that a notion of public good both legitimates and is itself underpinned by an economic logic, which has actually initiated the warfare Toby is engaged in, a potential reconciliation of Mackenzie's ethical and material 'war of duties' is suggested,[55] one which Smith was later to explore in his *Wealth of Nations*. If the concept of duty effects a reconciliation of values, however, it is marked with their strife, and Toby exhibits its cost in bodily terms. Both *l'homme machine* and human sensorium,[56] a passive instrument of larger – economic, political – forces, Toby resembles a sentimental chameleon, advertising his powerlessness through an affective semiology in which his feelings are the measure of all things.

In this sense Toby does not quite fit the model of the sentimental hero who, as G. A. Starr describes, 'is subjected to ordeals and stresses of various kinds, but not to the pressure of having his character made dependent on training, habit, and . . . other contingencies of experience'.[57] Toby's character is precisely defined by those factors. If he is a natural innocent, he is not one in a position to choose to derive a sentimental pleasure from the repeated jarrings of a harsh world that serves up occasions for sympathy in manageable vignettes. Duty has uncompromisingly positioned him in that world. Toby is an innocent in spite of, and in response to, a world that has damaged him; its violence is such that he has turned away from it to a private realm where he can play out its effects. And unlike other sentimental figures, such as Mackenzie's Harley, the point is not that his innocence and natural affection will always position him outside the operations of the competitive world of Mandevillian self-interest, in the sense Janet Todd has suggested: 'the sentimentalist does not enter the economic order he condemns.'[58] Rather, Toby represents both a product of, and an ameliorative response to, such an order. He is part of it. We might ask why he and other military veterans, whose business is war, are constructed in this way at the mid-century; and why, indeed, the historical violence done to these sentimental touchstones appears almost totemic, 'scarr'd, mangl'd, maim'd', 'in nought entire', as Goldsmith described one such figure.[59] The irony in Toby's case is that the language of his body offers both a critique and a justification for this violence.

### The Legacy of Utrecht

> Never mind, brother *Toby*, he would say,—by God's blessing we shall have another war break out again some of these days; and when it does,—the belligerent powers, if they would hang themselves, cannot keep us out of play. (*TS* 6.31.552)

Toby's desire for the continuance of Marlborough's wars introduced, for critics such as Helene Moglen, a 'menacing aspect' to his childish pleasure in his military hobbyhorse.[60] A mid-eighteenth-century readership, however, would have had little difficulty in locating Toby's sorrow at the ending of war as a characteristic Whig position, given contemporary life by the debates surrounding the Seven Years' War. '*Calais* itself left not a deeper scar in *Mary*'s heart, than *Utrecht* upon my uncle *Toby*'s' (*TS* 6.31.552), Tristram notes in a volume that emerged at the end of 1761; for the more radical commentators in the *North Briton* early in 1762, the prospect of peace threatened to open the wound once again:

> I must own, that at present I am struck with the close similitude between the four last years of queen *Anne*'s reign, and the present times. The nation was then in a war with *France*, which had been carried on with amazing success, and, indeed, very little remained to be effected to reduce that exorbitant power, which had threatened the liberties of mankind within the most moderate bounds. All these just and glorious hopes were blasted by the infamous *Peace of Utrecht*, which compleated the disgrace of the sovereign, and the dishonour of *England*; for it was attended with ignominy to ourselves, and with the most shameful breach of faith to our allies. We have lately been engaged

in a war with the same power. It has been carried on with, at least, equal glory; but for all our blood and treasure we have only the wretched present of the *preliminary Articles of peace signed at Fountainbleau.*[61]

The Treaty of Utrecht in 1713 had secured and codified the imperial power of England as the culmination of the War of the Spanish Succession with France.[62] As the Whigs were to point out, the benefits of the Treaty were indefinite, and as Toby realises on his bowling green, the agreement was soon to be abused: 'a flame would inevitably break out betwixt *Spain* and the Empire' (*TS* 3.25.250). Yet in creating the largest free trade zone in the world the Treaty had inaugurated a certain logic of maintenance and mercantile expansion, a pressure to imperial aggrandisement, as Walpole was to discover to his cost, and which the mid-century was to inherit. As this commercial logic developed into foreign policy offensives such as the Seven Years' War, it brought English Hanoverian society into contradiction and conflict at home. In the reassembling of Parliament in 1758 before the year of victories, William Pitt had praised the First Duke of Marlborough in a manner that allows us to assess the historical significance of Toby's 'perverse wish' in that same society fifty years on: 'if he had been suffered to end the war which he so gloriously carried on, we should not have had the wars we have had since.'[63] If Toby's wish for the war to be prolonged had been granted, we may be led to conclude from Pitt that a more lasting peace, and a more certain hold on imperial power, would have been the outcome.

As if to play down the incongruity of a man with a 'heart as soft as a child' arguing for the 'prodigious consequences' of war, its 'treasure and blood-shed', Toby offers an 'apologetical oration' to his brother. His justification of war reveals more of how we are to 'read' the language of his heart. Do not think of your brother, he asks, 'that in wishing for war, he should be bad enough to wish more of his fellow creatures slain,—more slaves made, and more families driven from their peaceful habitations, merely for his own pleasure'(*TS* 6.32.555). Toby's heart 'pants' for war, but it also 'aches' for its distresses:

'Tis one thing, brother *Shandy*, for a soldier to hazard his own life—to leap first down into the trench, where he is sure to be cut in pieces:——'Tis one thing, from public spirit and a thirst of glory, to enter the breach the first man,—to stand in the foremost rank, and march bravely on with drums and trumpets, and colours flying about his ears:——'Tis one thing, I say, brother *Shandy*, to do this—and 'tis another thing to reflect on the miseries of war;— to view the desolations of whole countries, and consider the intolerable fatigues and hardships which the soldier himself, the instrument who works them, is forced (for six-pence a day, if he can get it) to undergo. (*TS* 6.32.556-7)

Both long-suffering 'instrument' of larger forces and glorious hero, the soldier acts, not in the name of pleasures associated with private interest, but self-lessly, as we have seen, in the name of liberty and wider public good. 'So soft a creature, born to love, to mercy, and kindness, as man is', engages in war by necessity: for what is war, Toby asks, 'but the getting together of quiet and harmless people, with their swords in their hands, to keep the ambitious and the turbulent within bounds?' (*TS* 6.32.557). This statement echoes the concern expressed in the *North Briton* above to contain the 'exorbitant' expansionism of the French, again on the agenda in the 1750s and 1760s. What is masked, however, behind these concepts of liberty and national honour, love and benevolence, is that drive for imperial competition and contest which positions Toby and his fellow veterans rather more ambiguously as 'instruments' of more abstract forces. Toby may feel that he is answering 'the great ends of our creation' in pursuing his vocation, but the truth uneasily expressed in his apology is that he is an agent for imperial violence, economic gain. Toby is subject to what Goldsmith's Citizen of the World called the 'strange absurdity' of an imperialist logic by which England had exchanged 'her best and bravest subjects for raw silk, hemp and tobacco . . . her hardy veterans and honest tradesmen . . . for a box of snuff or a silk petticoat'.[64] If God's benevolence is understood in utilitarian terms as producing what Adam Smith termed 'the greatest possible quantity of happiness',[65] then this is the expression of an underlying economic truth for Toby in addition to the ethical standard he champions, an economic truth that he is unable to countenance but which defines and subjects him all the same.

### The Benevolent Patriot

*Tristram Shandy* was regarded by the critic Richard Griffith as a work that aimed 'to inculcate that great Magna Charta of mankind, humanity and benevolence';[66] in the 'Advertisement' to Sterne's complete works in 1780 it was claimed that the more widely they were read, the more benevolence would be disseminated throughout society.[67] We have already seen how 'the good soldier' is a representative figure in Adam Smith's chapter on 'Universal Benevolence' in *The Theory of Moral Sentiments*, someone who 'cannot be too prodigal of his blood' if it is shed for the wider advantage of the nation.[68] The figure of the benevolent veteran who cannot kill a fly but would sacrifice his life if called upon to do so similarly carries the moral weight in Sterne's narrative. Yet though the political and economic resonances of Toby's desire for continuance of war have been suggested, more evidence is needed to locate the trauma of his wound in relation to debates about the economic direction of the mid-century. In his chapter on 'Benevolence' in *The Light of Nature Pursued*, written in the late 1760s, Abraham Tucker describes a benevolent act as one which 'must carry nothing of the self in view' – a definition that evidently applies to Toby's selfless commitment to the general good. The social application of such disinterested benevolence for Tucker enables us to 'read' Toby further:

> If the desire of promoting the general good were to prevail among all individuals so strongly as to overcome their averseness to labour and trouble, I am persuaded it would bring back the golden age or paradisiacal state again without any change in the elements.[69]

Interestingly, benevolence is here not equated with naive, pre-lapsarian virtue, largely ineffectual in the hard world of commercial values, as it is in the sentimental novel. Rather, it services and naturalises those values. Benevolence is a form of action which, in its selfless willingness to accept 'labour and trouble' in the name of a greater public good, satisfies the economic requirements of an age that was in the process of developing an abstract notion of labour. The golden age Tucker anticipates is a commercial one, in which individuals relinquish their labour power to greater social interests. Toby's concern at the instrumental role of soldiers as *les hommes machines* should be understood in this light. It is not only that the economic and moral imperatives for foreign wars turn out to be one and the same, but that the anxiety expressed at his powerlessness as a military instrument is analogous to that felt by an age whose interests are increasingly under the control of an economic 'hidden hand'. The violence done to Toby is connected with this realisation, for reasons that will become clear in a moment.

We would thus be right to expect Toby's bodily display of 'benevolence' to express the contradictions of an ideology that both services and protests against this economic imperative. Toby's affective semiosis is actually motivated by a vigorous moral polemic, however 'natural' and instinctive a language of virtue it presents itself to be. His 'benignity' of heart, we are told, 'interpreted every motion of the body in the kindest sense the motion would admit of' (*TS* 3.5.192). This benevolence of heart does not simply display the essential goodness of mankind Toby evidently represents, but argues for it according to a Shaftesburian affective hermeneutics that seeks to discover the best in human actions – in Toby's case, somewhat against the grain of reality. Toby's innocent, often misplaced reading of the motives of others thus works as a moral conscience that the narrative can draw upon at will. On the one hand, as we have seen, its naive faith is offered as a counterpoint to the corruption of the real world. Such humanity, as Smith puts it, 'is unfit for the world, because the world is unworthy of it'.[70] On the other, a strong case is made for the utility of the disinterested social values that accrete around him: duty, honour, liberty, equality, love, innocence, goodness, effeminacy, friendship, courage, feeling. It is these values that are the source of Toby's public spirit, which 'can only come from a social feeling or sense of partnership with human kind', as Shaftesbury wrote in his *Characteristicks*.[71] Toby is a Shaftesburian benevolist almost by virtue of his military hobbyhorse, since for Shaftesbury it is in war, occupation of 'the most generous Spirits', that the 'Knot of *Fellowship* is closest drawn': ''Tis in War that mutual Succour is most given, mutual Danger run, and *common Affection* most exerted and employ'd. For *Heroism* and *Philanthropy* are almost one and the same.'[72]

It is this connection between heroism and philanthropy that suggests the ideological potency of the wounded veteran. On one level such figures generate, as in the accounts of Corporal Trim, what might be seen as a reverse class discourse, in which inequalities are occluded by fellow feeling. Servants fantasise about leaving money to their masters, masters deny themselves in sympathy for the travails of their subordinates. Thus in the memoirs of Tristram Bates, one old campaigner relates the story of Lord Cadogan, 'who, when he saw me wounded and no Linnen at Hand, stript his shirt from his own Back (I shall never forget it) and gave it me to bind up my Wounds'– Bates wept! and wished he might ever have the same Opportunity of being *stript to the Skin*, too, for the sake of a *brave Soldier*'.[73] On another level, they provide a glimpse of a functioning collectivity, which acts unquestioningly according to sovereign interests: a vision perhaps of an ideal 'combination' of workers. Yet there is a danger here, as another instance from Tristram Bates suggests:

> But I shall ever Honour a Brother Corporal, who, in the Agonies Of a Death-Wound, said to his Friend, these *Breeches* are not the King's, – take them, – my own Money paid for them; my Tobacco Box (only Common Horn, but 'tis a Token) is in my Left Coat-pocket; and then finish'd, by saying, *Thank Heav'n*, there's Sixpence a Day for some Friend, – a Provision for some Body else.[74]

What appears from one perspective a death-bed scene that holds 'nothing of the self in view', in Tucker's words, is from another a reappropriation of the self and its collective economy from the sovereign space of the King. Yet the figure of the veteran provides a means of managing the threat of such a combination, since, despite the association with commonality, the loquacious soldier is, often as not, an isolato: 'I . . . am Sorry I have no Companions – scarce a Comrade to talk with'.[75] And such individuation had a political force.

'It will always be found, that a virtuous man is the best patriot, and the best subject the king has', Sterne declared in marking the occasion of a political anniversary (*Sermons*, 32.310). What lends the reactivation of

Shaftesburian values at the mid-century its particular inflection is the nature of patriot ideology during the period of the Seven Years' War. Shaftesbury had distinguished his model of a society based upon common affection and fellowship from that disruption caused by '*Love of Party*, and Subdivision by *Cabal*':[76] a distinction central to the political debates of the 1750s and early 1760s before the ascendence of a strong notion of 'party' via the Rockingham Whigs. The qualities associated with Toby, such as duty and love for country and community, equality, friendship, liberty, were all associated with the politics of the patriot, which were expected to be by definition disdainful of party spirit and resistant to 'combinations' of whatever kind. Such was the discursive power of the term 'patriot' to legitimate specific social interests, however, that it was a considerable ideological prize, claimed and fought over by various groupings. In Sterne's early writings in the *York Gazetteer*, on behalf of his uncle and Walpole's Ministry, he distinguishes between a Modern Patriot, evidently a term of abuse, and 'the Spirit of a Patriot of the Old Stamp'. The 'specious' Tory patriotism of the former, its defence of 'Country Interest (by which every honest Man in Britain knows they only mean their own Interest)', carried the country to 'the Brink of Ruin . . . by the Inglorious Peace made with France'.[77] In Toby we discover the public-spiritedness of 'the Old Stamp' brought to bear on the militiating mid-century as if to outdo Utrecht.

The figure who more than any other promised to vindicate the patriotism of the 'Old Stamp' was the 'Voice of Liberty', William Pitt, to whom *Tristram Shandy* is twice dedicated. Patriot ideology articulated in expansionist form sought to legitimise foreign commercial and imperial offensives through the very affective nationalism expressed by Sterne's military veteran, and was seen to be embodied at the mid-century by the Patriot Minister himself. As Jonathan Lamb has argued, Pitt's 'tactical eloquence' worked a powerful double movement, simultaneously drawing on an 'exilic dream language' (replete with visions of bucolic retirement) that removed him from the seeming corruption of political place (despite his later acceptance of a peerage), at the same time as reserving for himself a powerfully performative claim to authority, no less than the imperial measure of his voice.[78] Such a rhetoric could hold a notion of disinterested benevolence in play with the most strategic and adroit of manoeuvrings, whereby eloquence of public feeling might come to do the work of administration.

In Oliver Goldsmith's celebration of the successes of 1759, the prevalence of patriot discourse is evident: 'my king, my country, and I, are friends together, and by a mutual intercourse of kindness and duty, give and receive social happiness.'[79] Through the language of civic 'friendship', we witness the accommodation of those values of 'kindness and duty' by the political establishment in the 1750s and 1760s as servicing the imperial and commercial course of the nation. Toby Shandy is constructed, in this light, as a benevolent patriot, a version of the sentimental hero used to make a specific intervention in the political realignments of the mid-century, carrying with him values associated with a Whiggish militancy dating from the moment of Utrecht. Such a vision of the benevolent man is distinct from the narcissistic sensibility of the man of feeling that was to shape sentimental narratives later in the decade, though the tactics of such a sensibility are potentially at work in the self-authoring of patriot discourse as Lamb describes it, in which there may be 'no clear, mutually exclusive difference between the sincere and the insincere assertion of principles', in the words of J. C. D. Clark.[80] If the figure of uncle Toby is tossed in the shifts of such a discourse, both its victim and apologist, the violence which has 'unmanned' him, however, has yet to be explained.

## The New Effeminacy

In 1757 Samuel Johnson wrote that 'there was never from the earliest ages, a time in which trade so much engaged the attention of mankind, or commercial gain was sought with so general emulation.'[81] If there was general acceptance that the nation was set upon a commercial course, even amongst those who did not share the Whiggish enthusiasm for expansion, the period of the Seven Years' War was marked by an intense concern as to how that course was to be regulated. Who would gain in political terms from the consolidation of such economic power? What would the cost of such progress be to the traditional fabric of English life?

Public anxiety at such questions reached its height in 1757, exacerbated by rising prices and taxation brought about by a war that was yet to yield any dividends. The tract that encapsulated this public unease and added to the ferment was John Brown's popular *An Estimate of the Manners and Principles of the Times*, which we earlier saw ventriloquated in the diaries of Thomas Turner. Brown, who significantly had published essays on Shaftesbury's *Characteristicks* in 1751, was not alone in offering an indictment of the commercial degenerations of the age, its decline into 'luxury'; what made his contribution distinctive, as John Sekora has shown, was its topical allusions to the moment and its all-embracing reference.[82] Where other tracts looked to classical precedent, particularly the decline of Rome, to measure the pernicious effects of 'luxury' on a flourishing state, Brown examined the manners of his age. At every level of the body politic – within its institutions, its philosophical thought, its forms of artistic expression – he discovered evidence of the canker of what he saw as new commercial interests. 'Such a Nation', Brown wrote, 'can only resemble a large Body, actuated (yet hardly actuated) by an incapable, a vain, a dastardly, and effeminate Soul.'[83]

The *Estimate* measured the cultural cost of this commercial impetus in the realm of community and moral value, reading the changes brought about by material progress, in characteristic eighteenth-century manner, as a threat to the traditional balance of power between the moneyed city and the landed interest of the provinces. The 'flux of commerce' is held responsible for unparalleled migrations, shifts in the social landscape, later to be mourned by Oliver Goldsmith in his 'The Deserted Village':

> The Metropolis seems to augment in its Dimensions: but it appears, by the best Calculations, that its Numbers are diminished: And as to the Villages thro' *England*, there is a great Reason to believe, they are in general at a Stand, and many of them thinner of Inhabitants than in the beginning of this Century. (p. 188)

Moreover, in Brown's opinion, intrusive commercialisation had shackled the nation in 'Chains of Self-Interest' (p. 111), whereby 'love of our Country is no longer felt; and . . . except in a few Minds of uncommon Greatness, the Principle of Public Spirit EXISTS NOT' (p. 64).

Thus the nation was seen to languish in a 'vain, luxurious, and selfish EFFEMINACY' (p. 29), an enervated stupor of good living and fashionable pursuits made possible by the fruits of empire. 'Instead of Legislation, History, Policy and Philosophy . . . the securing of a Borough, Novels, Party Pamphlets, Irreligion; instead of Manners, Entertainment, Dress and Gaming'(p. 74). Patriot principles here follow a more conservative agenda, placed, as we might expect of a Shaftesburian commentator, in opposition to the distortions brought about by Mandevillian self-interest; Brown nevertheless allows for the possibility of some future reconciliation:

> Virtue may rise on the Ruins of Corruption; and a despairing Nation yet be saved, by the Wisdom, the Integrity, and unshaken Courage, of SOME GREAT MINISTER. (p. 221)

This reference to Pitt evidently did not require pointing out, yet what is interesting about Brown's critique is that the terms of his argument in any case succumb to the very drive of the commercial logic against which he rails. He has already set the stage for Pitt's integration of patriot and commercial principles. On the one hand, Brown has harsh words for the acquisitive decadence encouraged by economic success, which he equates with an 'effeminacy' that has apparently produced a worrying national impotence – suggested by the diminishing populace and 'lack of internal Strength'. On the other hand, one can sense a certain fear of unproductive stasis in his berating of 'an illegitimate Waste of Time, Honour, Wealth and Labour' (p. 120), which could be read as a demand for a more virile form of capitalist enterprise. Almost despite himself, Brown seems to argue that the problem has not been commercial progress as such, but the loss of a motivating work ethic and a 'national Spirit of Defence'.

The victories of 1759 under the direction of Pitt seemed to affirm Brown's 'spirit of Defence' once again. War, it appeared, could provide an impetus and competitive drive in a society dissipated by years of luxury. As Goldsmith cautioned:

> A COUNTRY at war resembles a flambeaux, the brighter it burns, the sooner it is often wasted. The exercise of war for a short time may be useful to society, which grows putrid by a long stagnation. Vices spring up in a long continued peace from too great an admiration for commerce, and too great a contempt for arms; war corrects these abuses, if of but a short continuance. But when prolonged beyond that useful period, it is apt to involve society in every distress. The property of a country by its continuance, is transferred from the industrious to the enterprizing. From men of abilities, to men of no other qualification but bravery; every man who is enriched by the trade of war, is only rewarded from the spoils of some unhappy member of society, who could no longer live by the trade of peace.[84]

War, then, purges a society of commercial stagnation – but it is continued at the price of a certain cultural enervation and a transfer of power and property from those who labour to the merely ambitious, 'the industrious to the enterprizing', old money to the new. Such was Goldsmith's rejoinder to those who argued for an outdoing of Utrecht.

How, then, is the 'unmanning' of uncle Toby to be understood in relation to both Brown's notion of 'effeminacy' and Goldsmith's virile concept of war? It is clear that the values he is made to represent – community of feeling, public benevolence, duty and love for country – are seen to be seriously under threat; while the qualities associated with his wound, such as feminine modesty, effeminacy and sympathy represent a form of cultural debilitation, symptoms of the national disease. Yet he is also an agent of forces able to 'correct these abuses'. The text that will allow us finally to locate the historical violence exacted upon Toby was first published in the same year as the *Estimate*: Edmund Burke's *A Philosophical Enquiry into the Origin of our Ideas of the Sublime and the Beautiful*. For it is in Burke's aesthetic categories that the disquiet at the heart of Mackenzie's 'war of duties' is articulated; and in the concept of the sublime in particular, as Tom Furniss has productively argued, that bourgeois thought 'responded to the potential costs of its own success', the contradictions of its hegemonic enterprise.[85]

### Sublime Labour

In his apology for war Toby recalls his boyhood: the tales of heroes and champions he had purchased with his pocket money, and in particular the impression made upon him by the story of the siege of Troy. 'Had I not three strokes of a ferula given me, two on my right hand and one on my left, for calling *Helena* a bitch for it? Did any one of you shed more tears for *Hector*? And when king *Priam* came to the camp to beg his body, and returned weeping back to *Troy* without it,—you know, brother, I could not eat my dinner' (*TS* 6.32.556). Toby's response to the pathos of the story of Troy is not unusual as a topos in eighteenth-century literature; in Pope's translation of the *Iliad*, for example, a characteristic lachrymose 'infectious Softness' affects the assembled soldiers: 'They bore as Heroes, but they felt as Man.'[86] However (as Pope well knew) the story of Troy also had considerable political significance, particularly within the foundation myth that had long linked the establishing of the nation with the travels of Aeneas. Claimed by both the Jacobites and the Hanoverians, it had been reinflected in Williamite terms by the Patriot Whigs in the 1730s, in ways that resonate with Sterne's construction of Uncle Toby, as the ballad might suggest:

> If Namur be compared to Troy;
> Then Britain's boys excelled the Greeks;
> Their siege did ten long years employ;
> We've done our business in ten weeks.[87]

In his mid-century *Enquiry*, however, Burke uses the legend of Troy to distinguish the 'amiable social virtues' of the weaker Trojans from the virile 'politic and military virtues' of the Greeks as alternative forms of cultural identity. 'With regard to the Trojans, the passion [Homer] chooses to raise is pity; pity is a passion founded upon love; and these lesser, and if I may say, domestic virtues, are certainly the more amiable.'[88] This distinction between 'amiable' and 'awful' virtues is observed in Hume's *Treatise*, but bears more relation to Adam Smith's developed use of Hume's terms in his *The Theory of Moral Sentiments*, where a balance between an ethic of love and a stoic ethic of self-command is advocated: 'the man who, to all the soft, the amiable, and the gentle virtues, joins all the great, the awful, and the respectable, must surely be the natural and proper object of our highest love and admiration'.[89] At stake here were not the opposing claims to rightful sovereignty that animated the earlier years of the century, but tendencies within the state form itself.

Toby is identified with the 'domestic virtues' of sympathy and love for fellow man, the sign of what Smith terms 'indulgent humanity'; yet in his castigation of the cause of the fall of Troy, Helen's 'fatal beauty' as Burke describes it, he aligns himself not with the effeminacy and weakness of the Trojan elders, but with the cool and stoical masculinity of the Greek military machine.[90] The account of the fall of Troy is testimony, for both Burke and Sterne's uncle Toby, that 'both death and defeat – the loss of collective liberty – accompany the amiable virtues', as Frances Ferguson puts it.[91] Troy becomes another cultural topos, like the decline of Rome, exhibiting the inevitable luxurious degeneration of a state that no longer evinces signs of 'internal Strength', in John Brown's words.

For Burke the question of the sublime arises in answer to the threat that nothing further might happen,[92] in a world bent on material progress but afflicted with luxurious indolence. If the three fundamental principles in the 'great chain of society' are those of 'sympathy', 'imitation' and 'ambition', then the two first – generally associated with the province of the 'beautiful' – are not sufficient to spur that social progress. The beautiful results from a sensation produced by an object in the observing subject; associated with affection, tenderness, 'the passion of love' and 'positive pleasure' it is inevitably linked with women in the *Enquiry*. Such a state of dangerous passivity and enjoyment is analogous to the realm of 'luxury', the stupefying fruit and Edenic temptation of commercial success. And the plenitude associated with the beautiful, the realm also linked with the sexual reproduction of society, becomes analogous to the spread of material prosperity. This, Burke is quick to remind us in puritan vein, is not a 'real pleasure':

> As we were not made to acquiesce in life and health, the simple enjoyment of them is not attended with any real pleasure, lest satisfied with that, we should give ourselves over to indolence and inaction.[93]

It is the indolence associated with luxury that Brown castigates in his *Estimate*, which, for Burke, is not a 'real pleasure': the necessary antidote to such lethargy is the 'swelling and triumph' of ambition – the sublime. If Helen's beauty induces the weakness of a Priam or the vanity of a Paris in cultural terms, then the sublime is represented by the strength and heroism of an Alexander, that 'power which arises from institution in kings and commanders'.[94] Such a power is beyond the dictates of the individual will, for 'whenever strength is only useful, and employed for our benefit or pleasure, then it is never sublime; for nothing can act agreeably to us, that does not act in conformity to our will; but to act agreeably to our will, it must be subject to us.'[95] The sublime can thus be linked, as it is in John Baillie's earlier *An Essay on the Sublime*, with universal benevolence,[96] since it can avowedly free a nation of the tangled self-interest that weakens what Brown termed 'the national Spirit of Union'.[97] It is a benevolence associated with the power of strong leadership. It thus involves the figuring of the state over and above the 'reciprocal commerce' of civil society. As both instrument of a publicly determined will – military man-machine – and a voice for the social utility of those amiable virtues, Toby seems curiously placed astride these Burkean categories, just as the patriot ideology, within which we have located him, attempts to straddle them.

Masked within such a virile notion of benevolence is, then, an economic imperative. Where the 'languid and inactive state' characteristic of the beautiful is seen in physiological terms as 'a relaxed state of the body', the sublime is a bracing of the body's Brownian 'internal Strength' by means of a concept of labour:

> The best remedy for all these evils is exercise or *labour*; and labour is a surmounting of *difficulties*, an exertion of the contracting power of the muscles; and as such resembles pain, which consists in tension or contraction, in every thing but degree.[98]

Emerging through Burke's formulation of his aesthetic categories is a version of that notion also contained in Tucker's notion of benevolence: the work ethic. The sublime is associated with a state of labour that resembles pain, one that produces a feeling of 'delight' rather than the pleasurable satedness of the beautiful. Commercial activity is not in and of itself sublime, and indeed can give rise, through the spread of material prosperity, to the enervation of luxury, but the spirit of competition – let loose, according to Goldsmith, in times of war – injects a vigorous sublimity into this enterprise. Thus, as Samuel Johnson saw it, the soldier's appetite for war might be explained: 'those who desire it most, are neither prompted by malevolence nor patriotism; they neither pant for laurels, nor delight in blood; but long to be delivered from the tyranny of idleness, and restored to the dignity of active beings'.[99]

Tom Furniss reads Burke's construction of the sublime as 'an aesthetic means through which bourgeois thought establishes itself, in face of the charges of luxury brought against it by traditional writers, as the locus of individual effort and virtue.'[100] The sublime becomes concomitant with an energy of individuation and innovation that is seen to propel social progress; moreover, it is an energy claimed by that middle order 'between the very rich and the very rabble', 'the true preserver of freedom, [who] may be called the People', as Goldsmith put it in *The Vicar of Wakefield*.[101] This middle order ascribes the contagion of luxury to aristocratic privilege or the laziness of the mob, seizing for itself a model of economic individualism and freedom as if to inoculate itself against the dangers of its own project. In so doing, Furniss contends, it contains the radical premise of the sublime, in a meritocratic model of ambition and progress seemingly available to all, but one on which, I would suggest, the soldier's body offers a spectacular commentary.

Of interest to the examination of Toby's affective semiotics is Burke's use of a *physiological* model upon which to ground his aesthetics of the sublime and the beautiful. As Furniss explores, Thomas Weiskel resists the physiological underpinning of Burke's notion of the sublime – such a model of 'homeopathic therapy, a kind of physiological catharsis . . . will hardly do' – preferring instead, in the interests of his own Romantic formulation, to site the purgative function of the sublime in the imagination.[102] Furniss argues productively that an assessment of this physiological model allows us to pursue the analogy worked in Burke's oeuvre between the figure of the body and that of the body politic, and thus the specific political purchase of Burke's early work on aesthetics. Further, I would suggest, it aligns Burke's model with the mid-century development of a physiological account of sentimentalism, which informs Sterne's narratives and the kind of reading practice they self-avowedly promote. 'True Shandeism' aims at just such physiological therapy in the wider social body. Yet the nature of its therapeutic diagnosis needs more explanation before the cultural weight of the military veteran can be fully located.

## Bodies Politic

The pressure to forge a connection between the individual body – its force, its duration, the horizon of its desires – and the body politic is especially intense at a time of war. The Seven Years' War was no exception, and a familiar mechanistic anatomy for the body of the state was available for just such incorporation, one that inserted individuals into the sovereign balance of assembled limbs and organs, the hierarchy of parts. In Sterne's sermon 'Follow Peace', such a commonplace analogy between natural and political bodies is furnished from biblical sources,[103] reconciling Christian ethics with the inequalities of the social order in a way that sentimentalism was to confirm:

> As a farther motive and encouragement to this peaceable commerce with each other,—God has placed us all in one another's power by turns,—in a condition of mutual need and dependence . . .The prince depends upon the labour and industry of the peasant;—and the wealth and honour of the greatest persons are fed from the same source.
>
> This the Apostle hath elegantly set forth to us by the familiar resemblance of the natural body;—wherein there are many members, and all have not the same office; but the different faculties and operations of each, are for the use and benefit of the whole.—The eye sees not for itself, but for the other members; and is set up as a light to direct them;—the feet serve to support and carry about the other parts; and the hands act and labour for them all. It is the

same in states and kingdoms, wherein there are many members, yet each in their several functions and employments; which, if peaceably discharged, are for the harmony of the whole state.—Some are eyes and guides to the blind;—others, feet to the lame and impotent;—some to supply the place of the head, to assist with council and direction;—others the hand, to be useful by their labour and industry. (*Sermons*, 41.388–9)

Sterne's rather laboured analogy reconciles the 'war of duties' between material and ethical concerns by describing all forms of social relations as a 'peaceable commerce'. The body is broken into its constituent parts, each of which functions to the harmony of the whole. Under a potential new peace, each individual offers up his labour selflessly to the good of the whole, and, significantly, the distinction between mental and manual labour, which in many ways had given rise to the public unease over the question of luxury, is fundamental to the functioning of the body politic.

The homeostasis of such a vision was deeply reassuring. What is interesting, however, is the extent to which it was under pressure in the political culture of the time. Imperial expansion severely tested its reach, such that, as Adam Ferguson reflected, the 'parts' could be seen to 'lose their relative importance to the whole', teaching 'the majority to consider themselves as the subjects of a sovereignty, not as the members of the political body'. Moreover, in the absence of a Sternean mutual dependence, force would need to be invoked 'to suspend the dissolution of a body, whose parts were assembled, and must be cemented, by measures forcible, decisive, and secret'.[104] No harmony there, and within the boundaries of the national body itself (where force had also long been applied in enforced clearances and deportation, as well as in the intensifying governmentality of enclosures) the distinction Ferguson was making in state thinking between belonging to the political body and the more abstract powers of sovereignty, also had its purchase. It was, then, an analogy that appeared in considerable disarray. The balance of members seemed to some severely out of kilter, as the flows of population (to the metropolis, and to the colonies) appeared to destabilise the metaphorical equilibrium of the whole, with the 'head' enlarging unsustainably, the body likely to go off . . . in a 'state-apoplexy' (*TS* 1.18.53), or the limbs drained of strength altogether.

Daniel Defoe had imagined the union in the terms of an indivisible body in 1706, one in which 'the very SOUL OF THE NATION, all its Constitution, Customs, Trade and Manners, must be blended together, digested and concocted, for the mutual, united, undistinguish't, good, growth and health of one whole united Body', but the repetition in his statement suggested more than a rhetorical strain.[105] It is an irony, as Katie Trumpener has powerfully detailed, that 'the conquest and administration of the domestic colonies [of

Wales, Ireland, and Scotland] served as a trial run for the colonisation of the overseas empire and caused the disproportionate representation of Scots and Irish in the British army that conquered the empire, as among the colonists who settled it'.[106] Consciousness of this 'disproportion' in the culture of 1760s could work for and against the imperial project itself, not least in the Scotophobia that laced the Wilkite brew of English nationalism at the time; and it revealed complexities and disjunctures at work in the crossings between nation and empire which the old mechanistic anatomy of the body politic could barely contain.

If the unchecked imperial constitution of the body politic appeared one dimension of the crisis, another was the impact of luxury, the fruit of imperial competition, which Smollett registers through the eyes of Matthew Bramble in *Humphry Clinker*. The perceived consequences of luxury threaten a fundamental vision of social order:

> there is no distinction or subordination left – The different departments of life are jumbled together – The hod-carrier, the low mechanic, the tapster, the publican, the shop-keeper, the pettifogger, the citizen, and the courtier, *all tread upon the kibes of one another*: actuated by the demons of profligacy and licentiousness, they are seen every where rambling, riding, rolling, rushing, justling, mixing, bouncing, cracking and crashing in one vile ferment of stupidity and corruption.[107]

In jeremiads and tracts even before the onset of war the analogy of the state and physical body generated a widely disseminated rhetoric of disease and corruption. Noting that the 'body as trope takes on an overwhelming importance' in the 1750s, Peter de Bolla shows that its literalisation often worked to prevent the identification of the physical and privatised body with the state.[108] Thus Patrick Murray, Lord Elibank (whose 'humanity and universal intelligence' is admired by Matthew Bramble), refuses such a metaphorical extension of the body in order to prevent the identification of public interest with individual, private interests that were seen to breed like a contagion. A contagion indeed which, as in the movement of paper money, would circulate throughout the nation 'like . . . blood in the human body', as Smollett described.[109] If the nation resembles 'a large Body', the comparison is not one John Brown similarly cares to pursue in his *Estimate*. His tract ends with a rejection of what he calls 'a trite and hacknied Comparison between the Life of Man and that of States': a refusal of metaphoric association in favour of a literal understanding of the natural decline of the body:

> The human Frame itself, after a certain Period, would grow into Rigidity; the Fluids would decrease, the Solids accumulate, the Arteries ossify, the Blood

stagnate, and the Wheels of Life stand still. BUT in Societies, of whatever kind, there seems no such necessary essential tendency to Dissolution.[110]

Despite the general pessimism of the *Estimate*, Brown's literalisation of the body prevents a cyclical history being projected onto the nation. The model of material progress remains unaffected by the inevitability of bodily decline that many saw as the lesson of the fate of Rome, the 'natural consequences' of the state of luxury, as the *London Magazine* described in 1758.[111] In disengaging that homologous relation between the private body and the state, Brown restricts the sense of contagion to the distortions and contingencies of private interest, that 'Enemy within' 'which must at all times break out into Factions' like some eruption of disease. Luxury is a danger that those possessing true public spirit – those benevolent figures 'with nothing of the self in view' as Tucker described[112] – can contain and eliminate. The purgative of war and the sublime benevolence of the 'Patriot Minister' William Pitt seemed to offer some hope: ''Tis something to have checked the Disease at its Crisis; the perfect Cure will require the Attention and Labour of an Age', Brown wrote in his *Explanatory Defence of the Estimate* in 1758.[113] Sterne's account of the medicinal benefits of laughter (driving 'the *gall* and other *bitter juices* from the gall bladder, liver and sweet-bread of his majesty's subjects, with all the inimicitious passions which belong to them, down into their duodenums' (*TS* 4.22.360)), is dedicated, significantly in this context, to Pitt.

The sublime, from a conservative and patriot perspective, was a means of actively identifying with the authority vested in the state while acknowledging and harnessing new social energies. If it potentially restrained the deracinating inroads of commerce, it also addressed a potential popular power of which it was an ambiguous sign. Both Furniss and De Bolla argue, differently, for the emergence of a new kind of modern subjectivity in the 1760s, burgeoning under the aegis of the sublime: a self-generating bourgeois agency, in the former, liberated to some degree from the customary practices of a traditional, paternalistic society; a discursive excess in the latter, loosed in the inflationary environment of public credit during the period of the Seven Years' War. It is my contention that the war for empire produces specific historical co-ordinates for these transformations, loosening and examining social ties in order to reimagine the relation between the subject and the state and codify it more extensively.

In part, the turn to the body I have been sketching dredges up residual conceptions of the physicality of the body politic consonant with a common reversion to seventeenth-century models of the polity I deal with in Chapter 3. But it is also important to think about the potential vitalism of such a turn, as a logic orientated towards the future. In Rousseau's account of the analogy of the body politic, for example, as Pheng Cheah has explored, there is an 'awkward' blending of the mechanistic model with a more 'organismic' sense of the living body of the people:

> The life of both bodies is the self common to the whole, the reciprocal sensibility and internal correspondence of all the parts. Where this communication ceases, where the formal unity disappears, and the contiguous parts belong to one another only by juxtaposition, the man is dead, or the State is dissolved.[114]

This is a *political* dissolution John Brown would not pursue the metaphor to imagine: an equation between the people and the state in which the latter is 'a corporate body whose *life* is in the union of its members'.[115] While Rousseau's discussion of political economy worries about luxurious excess, and emphasises the sublime virtue of the 'general will', a 'body of the State' in which individuality is subsumed in a patriotic love for the 'greater whole',[116] such a general will – 'Sovereignty' – is nonetheless collective and vital. In its generality 'it must come from all and apply to all', and thus testifies to the 'equality of rights and the idea of justice which . . . originate in the preference each man gives to himself, and accordingly in the very nature of man'.[117] In such potential organicism, then, is an emerging figure for political participation (and human nature) which overturns the hierarchical 'equilibrium' of the mechanical model of the body politic; the resonance of self-creating energies which might no longer find themselves corralled within the state boundaries of the body and its limbs.[118] Here is one horizon of the sublime that began to make itself felt in the tumults and combinations of the 1760s, though it would take much longer to find its political voice; one that soldiers were called on to contain in direct, as well as metaphorical, ways.

## The Spectacle of the Military Sublime

The sacrifice of the soldier is famously held to secure one powerful manifestation of the 'imagined community' of the nation.[119] Yet the nature of that service – a willing relinquishment of self-interest, a selfless labouring, for 'universal' public happiness – carried an exemplary weight in the climate of the Seven Years' War which took its significance far beyond the heroisms of conflict. If it was representative of what all good men would be prepared to do, to paraphrase Smith, such a sacrifice was also an extreme metaphorical marker of the self-denial incumbent on every member of the body politic. For Rousseau, risking and losing life in the defence of the State was no 'renunciation', but a form of contractual exchange: 'what more are they doing than giving back what they have received from it?'[120] If the sacrifice of British soldiers was not to be understood in such contractual terms, there was nevertheless a sense that notions of 'duty' and 'public good' did involve transactions of a complex kind, and that the literal cost of these was written on the bodies of those displaying their wounds in the public gaze.

What was the true 'Recompense of Virtue'? The spectacle of the wounded and the maimed suggested that offering up one's labour to the public good produced a return in no uncertain terms. It was a living critique for which answers had to be found, around which interpretations began to accrete. The body of the veteran, 'nought entire – except his heart'[121] – pulsating testimony to benevolence – became a site for the unveiling of the violence not just at the centre of the military 'sublime', but that associated with what was later to be termed 'alienated labour'. It was no surprise, perhaps, that soldiers called on to put down industrial riots often expressed sympathy for the wage conditions of the rioters they were meant to repress.[122] The inequality of their 'exchange' was evident and a source of disquiet, as we can see from Hogarth's engravings, for these were men whose sacrifices were inadequately rewarded in a manner characteristic of much sentimental fiction: by charity. At the same time, as visited on the spectacular body of the veteran rather than in the unrest of the late 1760s, such violence was safely kept at a remove. Pain and terror, as Burke's account of the sublime describes, were not allowed to 'press too nearly', but instead mediated and aestheticised.[123]

The body of the veteran is one vehicle for this aesthetic translation of labour and pain – a particular motivation of the metaphorisation of the body – within the literature of the mid-century. As we have seen, through the representation of a body that 'speaks' the narrative of its wound the historical inheritance and direction of the age is assessed. Yet by figuring this body as maimed, repressed, castrated (and by having it offer an apology for the very violence that has so 'unmanned' it) mid-century bourgeois culture exacts 'at one remove', in totemic fashion, the price of its enterprise. On the body of the veteran, viewed openly on the London streets, this society comes close to the literal truth of the economic logic that underwrote imperial war – that exchange, as Goldsmith described it, of the 'best and bravest subjects, for raw silk, hemp and tobacco . . . hardy veterans and honest tradesmen . . . for a box of snuff or a silk petticoat'.[124] On this physical body the sublime fiction is almost literalised, the pain associated with labouring for the nation graphically displayed: 'scarr'd, mangl'd, maim'd in every part'. In turn such a spectacle is repaid with charity: money in return for a pleasurable feeling of 'delightful horror'.

Competing claims were made for the significance of this maiming. In Smollett's *Humphry Clinker* the mutilation of captured soldiers by the Indians during the Seven Years' War is described in terms of ritual: one, ensign Murphy, is emasculated 'by women and children' and gradually eaten at the stake, heroically singing his way to a stoic death; the other, Lismahago, manages to hold on to his manhood, yet is 'wounded, maimed, mutilated, taken and enslaved, without ever having attained a higher rank than that of lieutenant'.[125] In owning his 'honest scar received in the service of my country', Lismahago refuses to acknowledge the injustice of the exchange of his labour for public good. Above the 'paltry considerations' of private interest, his is a familiar dedication to public service that hints at the disinterestedness of sublime benevolence: 'I am a gentleman; and entered the service as other gentlemen do, with such hopes and sentiments as honourable ambition inspires' (p. 225). The detailing of Lismahago's wounds testifies, like uncle Toby's affective semiotics, to the ambivalence of a society bent on commercial progress, and seeking a way to come to terms with its cost. Yet in Smollett's narrative the violence associated with the ritual maiming is in some sense 'explained' by the Indians' 'tenacious' resistance to invasive cultures – 'they were too virtuous and sensible to encourage the introduction of any fashion which might help to render them corrupt and effeminate' (p. 230) – the drive of the luxurious Europeans for the spoils of imperial gain is thus to be checked by the thrift and virility of those they seek to subject. Smollett's is a thoroughgoing attack on the commercial interests that have initiated such foreign offensives: he will have no truck with such effeminacy. Lismahago, we note, though scarred and maimed, is still able to fulfil the role of a traditional patriarch, his son becoming head of the Indian tribe. His wounds 'had not produced emasculation', the narrative states categorically (p. 228).

In Sterne's more ambiguously positioned text, as we see with uncle Toby, the nature of the emasculating wound is that it cannot, in a literal sense, be named. As Widow Wadman discovers to her frustration, its truth will always be at a remove. Toby's identity is constituted through a set of contradictions. His effeminacy resembles on the one hand a kind of impotence, a weakness and naivety that renders him vulnerable, like the court of Troy, to more worldly forms of power: this impotence is both the consequence and symptom of the economic interests he is made to serve. Yet that effeminacy is then recast, on the other hand, as a moral strength: these 'amiable virtues' are seen to be a source of social cohesion and fellow-feeling in a world where a notion of community is under threat due to the invasion of those very interests. Such a model, with its stress on innate virtue, is available as an alternative to the more hierarchical social order privileged by Smollett who has no such optimistic belief in human nature.

From a symptom, then, of luxurious material interests, Toby's effeminacy becomes a form of critique, in the name of the values such interests are seen to undermine. Yet it is possible to read that same effeminacy not only in terms of the Burkean category of the beautiful – sympathy, passivity, inaction, love – but also in terms of the sublime. For the ideological concept of benevolence draws its power from articulating a specific relation between both categories. It should be noted that sublime experience is seen to involve both a loss of individual will and a moment of passivity or feminised debility that has to be transcended through a galvanising of energy and effort. Toby's 'feminine modesty' becomes a sign of acquiescence to an overarching form of power. If, like Furniss, we understand this formulation of the sublime to be an aesthetic correlative of the work ethic, then Toby's willingness to be an unquestioning instrument of greater forces, to relinquish ownership of his labour-power, marks him as a victim of, and apologist for, an abstract economic logic. Toby becomes the ideal Shaftesburian figure who, straddling the Burkean categories, assures us of the continuity of 'domestic virtues' and fellow feeling while at once being prepared to act as an agent for the necessary, if threatening, inroads of the sublime. By replaying his war games on the bowling green, Toby can reposition himself as producer, originator, of the sublime fiction of war that has subjected him, just as the rhetoric of the sublime grants power to those who experience it. As Longinus attests: 'the true sublime lifts up our souls; we are filled with a proud exultation and a sense of vaunting joy, just as though we had ourselves produced what we had heard.'[126] Toby thus effects a reconciliation of Mackenzie's 'war of duties' in bodily terms: the ethical values suggested by his 'effeminacy' begin to justify the material interests driving this formulation of the sublime. War can thus be understood as the getting together of 'quiet and harmless people' to contain those with a thirst for expansion: in reality an aggressive argument for limiting French commercial interests abroad and consolidating the imperial gains of the nation 'beyond whatever history can show'.[127]

This, then, is the extraordinary cultural labour of 'consent'. Yet beneath the fictions which position the military veteran as a hero, spun to celebrate the 'glorious' purpose and sacrifice of war, there is, as at the end of *Tristram Shandy*, a fear of impotence, loss of autonomy. Is the exchange of the sublime fiction of public-spirited labour, and the literal fact of the 'intolerable fatigues and hardships which the soldier himself, the instrument . . . is forced (for sixpence a day, if he can get it) to undergo' (*TS* 6.32.556–7), a credible one? Is this metaphorical reworking of the literal pain and privation associated with labour sustainable? Glimpsed here is a certain resistance to a utilitarian argument at the heart of such metaphorical equivalences that the narrative of *Tristram Shandy* is attempting to formulate and examine through the figure of uncle Toby, the benevolent patriot. It is an argument that Jeremy Bentham later presents, using the figure of the military veteran, in his *A Table of the Springs of Action*, arguing for the equality of such an exchange:

For argument's sake, suppose even mutilation employed, – mutilation even in parts or organs more than one. Not altogether unsusceptible of reparation would even this punishment be; for suffering in this shape, reparation, and to a very wide extent, is almost everywhere in use: witness this, in the pensions granted in the sea or military service; and it is a matter generally understood, that by the individuals by whom on this account reparation in this shape and degree is asked, whether for the same reparation they would have originally have been content, or would now, if it were to do over again, be content to be subjected to the same suffering, the answer would be in the affirmative.[128]

No doubt for Uncle Toby the answer would be in the affirmative, content to repeat the event, even mutilation, of his injury as if to own it; happy, too, to believe in the fiction of an equality of exchange as the benevolent figure he is made out to be. Yet it is not simply the public concern during the 1750s and 1760s at the inadequacy of military pensions, Bentham's 'reparations', which indicates the gulf between such fictions and the literal pain and effort of labouring for the public good.

The popularity of sentimentalism during this period is in part an index of the need for such fictions of exchange to gain an explanatory power. The benevolent man, turned in Sterne's narrative into a contradictory sign of the cost of social labour, begins a process of metamorphosis that will result in the codification of the man of feeling. As the military veteran, a site of anxiety that at once acknowledges the possibility of castration (Toby's 'feminine modesty') while denying it (finding it, literally, unnamable) uncle Toby serves as a mid-century cultural totem. By requiring us, in the literal reading of Toby's 'swelling heart', to recognise the specific violence that has inscribed him into history, Sterne's narrative forces the reader to confront the historical contradictions of the mid-century, even as Toby offers his affective apologia. Yet, with the emergence of the man of feeling into a full-blown sentimentalism, the unstable, potentially explosive fiction of labour and its maiming is superseded and distanced by that of the charitable circulation of money. The 'amiable virtues' of the man of feeling, his delicate sensibility acutely tuned to the suffering of others, are required to erase evident socioeconomic inequalities in a charitable calculus that stands in for reciprocity.

In later chapters this affective calculus will be examined in more detail, not least for its management of the violences inscribed here on the bodies of military men. In *Tristram Shandy* the historical contradictions of this refiguration of the man of feeling are made manifest, exposed as part of the 'false imagining' of common life that Adam Smith dramatised in the *Wealth of Nations*: a deceptive simplicity – abstraction – forged from the labour of 'many thousands'.[129] Emerging, then, from the disavowal that marks the body of the military veteran – out of the unnamable gap between castration and its denial, instrumental violence and its affective justification – is a more uncompromising construction of historical relations in all their material contradiction: an imaginary, and yet literal, configuration of the nature and cost of social labour in the crucible of empire. Even as the British expansionist project was articulated in terms of the universalising of 'benevolence', it encountered, in the words of Marx's *Grundrisse*, 'barriers in its own nature',[130] imaged in the bodily limits and alternative affiliations of the military machine.

## Notes

1 Anon., *A Description Of Vauxhall-Gardens Being A Proper Companion and Guide for All Who Visit That Place* (London: S. Hooper, 1762), pp. 26, 25.

2 In this it exemplifies the so-called 'bracketing' of war that characterised the *jus publicum europaeum*, a 'rationalization and humanization' of conflict between just enemies, which Carl Schmitt invokes in deeply ideological form in his *The Nomos of the Earth in the International Law of the Jus Publicum Europaeum* trans. G. L. Ulmen (New York: Telos, 2003). Schmitt saw 'the classical transparency' of enlightened warfare and European order codified in Emerich de Vattel's 1758 work *Le droit de gens; ou Principes de la loi naturelle, appliqués à la conduite et aux affaires des nations et des souverains*, which was translated into English in 1760. Schmitt, p. 165. The 'bracketing' of just warfare is the satirical target of Voltaire's *Candide*.

3 As Brian Allen discusses, 'Nothing comparable to Hayman's scheme had been undertaken in England since Laguerre had covered the hall and staircases at Marlborough House with episodes from the Wars of the Spanish Succession, half a century earlier.' This earlier memorialisation of the moment of Utrecht was never shown publicly. Hayman's were 'the first genuinely popular history paintings and the public was eager to welcome pictures glorifying their contemporary history in the same way that theatre audiences welcomed a similarly jingoistic repertoire'. See Brian Allen, *Francis Hayman* (New Haven and London: Yale University Press, 1987), pp. 69, 70.

4 Benjamin West, *The Death of Wolfe* (1771).

5 *A Description Of Vauxhall-Gardens*, p. 54.

6 For one celebratory example of Wolfe's sacrifice, see Sir James Pringle, *The Life of General James Wolfe, the Conqueror of Canada: Or the Elogium of that Renowned Hero, Attempted According to the Rules of Eloquence. With a Monumental Inscription, Latin and English, to Perpetuate His Memory* (London: for J. Kearsly, 1760). Pringle's account makes dramatic use of the spectacle: 'HERE, what a Scene, mingled with Glory and Pity, Joy and Sorrow, Triumph and Mourning, presents itself to View!', p. 2.

7 Pierre Grosley, *Londres*, 3 vols (Neuchatel: Aux dépends de la Société Typographique, 1770), I, 242. My translation. Other spectators were less convinced. Hayman appears in Charles Churchill's poem *Gotham*: '. . . a likeness, as, thro' HAYMAN's works,/Dull Mannerist, in Christians, Jews and Turks,/Cloys with a sameness in each female face'. *Gotham. A Poem* (London: printed for the Author, 1764), p. 18.

8 Grosley, *Londres*, I, 242–3. My translation.

9 Ibid. p. 115 My translation.

10 Horace Walpole to Lady Ailsbury, 27 Sept 1761, in *The Yale Edition of Horace Walpole's Correspondence*, ed. W. S. Lewis (London and New Haven: Yale and Oxford University Presses, 1974), 38: II, p. 128.

11 [Josiah Tucker], *The Case of Going to War, For the Sake of Procuring, Enlarging, or Securing of Trade, Considered in a New Light, Being a Fragment of a Greater Work* (London: R. and J. Dodsley, 1763), p. 48. Tucker saw newswriters as one of a number of culpable social groups advocating war, adding that it was 'an indisputable Fact, that this Country is as much News-mad, and Newsridden at present, as ever it was Popery-mad, and Priest-ridden in the Days of our Fore-fathers' (p. 49).

12 Anon, *The Vocal Miscellany: A Collection of above Four Hundred celebrated Songs; Many of which were Never before Printed with The Names of the Tunes prefixed to each Song, Volume Second and Last* (London: A. Bettesworth and C. Hitch etc., 1738), p. 215.

13 The Militia Act of 1757 was deeply unpopular. It required a census to be taken of all men between 18 and 50 and a proportion, decided by ballot, to enlist for three years. Anyone chosen could avoid serving in the militia by finding a substitute or paying £10. As Ian Gilmore points out, it thus affected whole communities, and the poor in particular. 'Riots against the militia mingled with food riots, enclosure riots, and attacks on mills and millers. More than fifty towns in thirty-one different counties were affected, and some of the riots lasted for weeks.' Protests were most intense in Yorkshire, Sterne's county. Ian Gilmore, *Riot, Risings and Revolution: Governance and Violence in Eighteenth-Century England* (London: Pimlico, 1993), p. 297.

14 Samuel Johnson, *The Idler* 8 (3 June, 1758), p. 26.

15 Richard Gardiner, *An Account of the Expedition to the West Indies, Against Martinico, Guadelupe, and other the Leeward Islands; Subject to the French King, 1759*, 2nd edn (London: Zech Stuart, 1760), pp. 73–4. It is worth noting that 133,708 sailors died of scurvy and other diseases during the Seven Years' War, compared to 1,512 who died in action. See Linebaugh, *The London Hanged*, p. 130. Gardiner's complaint was thus no exaggeration.

16 Gardiner, *Expedition to West Indies*, pp. v, 74, v.

17 Ibid. p. 75.

18 William Hogarth, *The Times*, Plate II (1762).

19 John Collier, 'The Pluralist and Old Soldier', in his *Tim Bobbin's Toy-Shop open'd Or, His Whimsical Amusements* (Manchester, 1763); anthologised in Lonsdale, p. 511. The soldier concludes 'Send me, kind heav'n, the well-tanned captain's face,/Who gives me twelvepence and a curse, with grace;/But let me not, in house or lane or street,/These treble-pensioned parsons ever meet'. The association of begging soldiers and vagrancy is considered further in Chapter 3.

20 McNeil, *The Grotesque Depiction*, pp. 158–9.

21 Tobias Smollett, *Humphry Clinker*, ed. Angus Ross (Harmondsworth: Penguin Books, 1967), p. 225.

22 Tobias Smollett, *The Critical Review; or Annals of Literature* 2 (September 1756), 138.

23 The full title page reads as follows: '*THE LIFE AND MEMOIRS OF MR EPHRAIM TRISTRAM BATES, COMMONLY CALLED CORPORAL BATES, A broken-hearted SOLDIER; WHO, From a private Centinel in the Guards, was, from his Merits, advanced, regularly, to be Corporal, Serjeant, and Pay-master Serjeant; and had he lived a few Days longer, might have died a Commission-Officer, to the great Loss of his lamentable Lady, whose Marriage he had intended to declare as soon as his Commission was signed; and who, to make up for the Loss of so dear an Husband, and her Pension, which then no Duke on Earth could have hindered, in order to put Bread into the Mouths of seven small Children, the youngest now at her Breast, the sweet Creatures being two Twins, publishes these Memoirs from the original Papers, sealed up with the Seal of dear Mr BATES, and found, exactly as he mentioned in his last Will and Testament, in a Oven, never used, where, in his Life-time, he secreted many State-Papers, etc, etc, etc*' (London: Malachi * * * *, for Edith Bates, Relict of the aforesaid Mr Bates, and sold by W. Owen, 1756).

24 *The Life and Memoirs of Mr Ephraim Tristram Bates*, pp. 232, 8, 238.

25 Hester Thrale certainly thought Sterne had taken 'his first idea' from the novel, as Helen Sard Hughes reported in her 'A Precursor of Tristram Shandy', *JEGP* 17(1918), 227–51. On this point see Keymer, pp. 50–2.

26 Tobias Smollett, *Continuation of the Complete History of England to 1765*, 5 vols (London: Richard Baldwin, 1763–68), V, 19.

27 *The Life and Memoirs of Mr Ephraim Tristram Bates*, pp. 205–6.

28 Ibid. pp. 210–11.

29 See Linebaugh, *The London Hanged*, pp. 123–38 for a discussion of the 'oceanic proletariat' in the period.

30 *Explanatory Remarks Upon the Life and Opinions of Tristram Shandy*, pp. 44–5.

31 As Smollett says in the *Critical Review* 9 (April 1760), p. 319: 'To own the truth, we harbour some suspicions that the author himself is here giving breath to the trumpet of fame'.

32 Theodore Baird, 'The Time Scheme in *Tristram Shandy* and a Source', *PMLA* 51 (1936), 819, 804.

33 David Hume's influential *The History of England* was published between 1754 and 1762 in eight volumes. The Scottish Enlightenment in particular was central to the development of historiography at this time, not only because Scottish thought and enterprise was imbricated in imperial expansion, but also because, as Pocock argues, it saw Unionism and Anglicisation as integral to the

establishing of civil society, and thus 'the history of England, and of English emergence from the wars of religion, came to appear the history that Scotsman needed to know'. A historical narrative of the development of civil society became essential to the self-understanding of imperial culture at this time. See J. G. A Pocock, *Barbarism and Religion Volume One: The Enlightenments of Edward Gibbon 1737–1764* (Cambridge: Cambridge University Press, 1999), pp. 302–3. See also the chapter on 'Enlightenment and Empire' in Murray G. H. Pittock, *Inventing and Resisting Britain: Cultural Identities in Britain and Ireland 1685–1789* (London: Macmillan, 1997), pp. 128–52.

34 Tobias Smollett published *A Complete History of England deduced from the Descent of Julius Caesar to the Treaty of Aix- la-Chapelle* in 1757; *The History of England from the Restoration of 1688 to the death of George II* in 1757; and his five volume *Continuation of the Complete History of England to 1765* between 1763 and 1768.

35 Catharine Macaulay's *History of England from the Accession of James I to the Elevation of the House of Hanover* was published in eight volumes between 1763 and 1783; her *History of England from the Revolution to the Present Time, in a Series of Letters to a Friend* in 1778.

36 Horace Walpole's *Memoirs of the Reign of King George II* and *Memoirs of the Reign of King George III* were published posthumously in the nineteenth century.

37 John Wilkes, *The History of England from the Revolution to the Accession of the Brunswick Line* (London: S. Almon, 1768).

38 Sarah Scott, *The History of Mecklenburgh, From the First Settlement of the Vandals in that Country to the Present Time* (London: J. Newbury, 1762). Scott's history marked the ascendancy of the new king and his marriage to Sophia Charlotte of Mecklenburgh by celebrating the German empire and domestic bliss: 'How fortunate may that Princess be deemed, whose husband's heart is a far more valuable present than the throne'. (p. 360).

39 Edward Gibbon's *The Decline and Fall of the Roman Empire* was published in six volumes between 1776 and 1788. The project famously originated during a stay in Rome in 1764.

40 Pocock, *Barbarism and Religion*, I, 113.

41 John Barrell, 'Sir Joshua Reynolds and the Englishness of English Art', in Homi K. Bhabha, (ed.), *Nation and Narration* (London: Routledge, 1990), pp. 161–2. Barrell suggests that Reynolds changes his position, in what might be seen in this context as a response to shifting relations of state imagining, whereby the celebration of local, national forms came to serve as a route rather than impediment to the 'fully civic' (p. 166).

42 Soame Jenyns, *A Free Inquiry into the Nature and Origin of Evil*, 4th edn (Dublin: G. and A. Ewing, 1758), p. 55.

43 McNeil, *The Groteque Depiction*, p. 145.

44 Sir Charles Hanbury Williams, 'Isabella: Or, The Morning', *Gentleman's Magazine and Historical Chronicle* 35 (Jan. 1765), 38, ll. 48–51.

45 Oliver Goldsmith, 'Threnodia Augustalis', in Arthur Friedman (ed.), *The Collected Works of Oliver Goldsmith* (Oxford: Clarendon Press, 1966), IV, 338, ll.207–10.

46 McNeil, *The Grotesque Depiction*, p. 158.

47 Daniel Defoe, *The History and Remarkable Life of the Truly Honourable Col. Jacque, Commonly Call'd Col. Jack*, 2nd edn (London: J. Brotherton et al, 1723), p. 11; McNeil, p. 147.

48 'Since words are only names for things, it would be more convenient for all men to carry about them such things as were necessary to express the particular business they are to discourse on.' Jonathan Swift, *Gulliver's Travels* (Harmondsworth: Penguin Books, 2003), p. 230.

49 Sedgwick, p. 79. Laurence Sterne, *A Sentimental Journey through France and Italy*, collected with *Continuation of the Bramine's Journal: The Text and Notes*, The Florida Edition of the Works of Laurence Sterne, vol. 6, ed. Melvyn New and W. G. Day (Gainesville, FL: University Press of Florida, 2002), p. 90. Henceforth the *Journey* cited in my text as SJ and page number.

50 See Robert Markley, 'Sentimentality as Performance: Shaftesbury, Sterne, and the Theatrics of Bourgeois Virtue', in Felicity Nussbaum and Laura Brown (eds), *The New Eighteenth Century* (New York and London, 1987), p. 222. Henry Mackenzie coins the term 'war of duties' in *The Lounger* 20 (18 June 1785), p. 78.

51 Mackenzie, *The Lounger*, p. 79.

52 Markley, 'Sentimentality as Performance', p. 222.

53 Smith, *The Theory of Moral Sentiments*, p. 236.

54 Jenyns, p. 90.

55 Mackenzie, *The Lounger*, p. 78.

56 Julien Offray de La Mettrie's popular semi-clandestine work *L'Homme Machine* (1747), which linked sexuality and sensibility in a materialist theory of the body, was a text familiar to Sterne, who had attended soirées at the Paris home of the materialist and atheist Baron d'Holbach. His argument that states of the soul and the body are part of the same substance is parodied in *Tristram Shandy*.

57 G. A. Starr, 'Sentimental De-Education', in Douglas Lane Patey and Timothy Keegan (eds), *Augustan Studies: Essays in Honour of Irvin Ehrenpreis* (Newark, DE: University of Delaware Press; London: Associated University Presses, 1985), p. 254.

58 Todd, p. 97.

59 Goldsmith, 'Threnodia Augustalis', p. 338.

60 Helene Moglen, *The Philosophical Irony of Laurence Sterne* (Gainesville, FL: The University Presses of Florida, 1975), p. 85.

61 *North Briton*, 39 (26 February 1763), p. 257.

62 Specifically, the treaty secured English objectives: preserving the protestant succession, limiting French power through territorial concessions in Europe and acquiring territories and bases in North America (Newfoundland, Hudson's Bay, Nova Scotia) and in the Mediterranean (Minorca, Gibraltar), thus protecting shipping and strengthening naval power. Crucially, it resulted in the winning of the contract to supply slaves to central and South America: the *asiento*. Utrecht is constructed in some accounts as a caesura marking a new 'modern' geopolitical order in which British maritime (and commercial) power would prove determining; for others, while representing no 'break' with the past, Utrecht was a potent sign of British 'blue water' strategy: it 'exemplified not simply Britain's rise as a great power, but also its willingness and ability to regulate European affairs on a new principle of active balancing'. Such brokerage, in which war might be curtailed once weaker partners had recovered rather than when the common enemy had been destroyed, was not always appreciated domestically. Utrecht was often regarded (as uncle Toby's response suggests) as a Tory peace, bought prematurely. See Benno Teschke, *The Myth of 1648: Class, Geopolitics and the Making of Modern International Relations* (London: Verso, 2003), p. 258.

63 Quoted in Middleton, *Bells of Victory*, p. 97.

64 Goldsmith, Letter XVII, *Citizen of the World*, p. 75.

65 Smith, *The Theory of Moral Sentiments*, p. 236.

66 Biographer Triglyph [Richard Griffith], *The Triumvirate: or, the Authentic Memoirs of A(ndrews) B(eville) and C(arewe)* 2 vols (London: W. Johnston, 1764), I, xiv.

67 'The oftener they are read, the stronger will a sense of universal benevolence be impressed upon the mind.' See the 'Advertisement' to the 1780 ten volume edition of *The Works of Laurence Sterne*, anthologised in Alan B. Howes (ed.), *Sterne: The Critical Heritage* (London and Boston: Routledge and Kegan Paul, 1974), p. 247.

68 Smith, *The Theory of Moral Sentiments*, p. 191.

69 Abraham Tucker, *The Light of Nature Pursued*, 4 vols (1768–77; Bristol: Thoemmes Press, 2003), I, 255.

70 Smith, *The Theory of Moral Sentiments*, p. 191.

71 Anthony Ashley Cooper, Lord Shaftesbury, 'Sensus Communis: An Essay on the Freedom of Wit and Humour in a Letter to a Friend' (1709), in Philip Ayres (ed.), *Characteristicks of Men, Manners, Opinions, Times*, 2 vols (Oxford: Clarendon Press, 1999), I, 61.

72 Ibid., p. 63.

73 *The Life and Memoirs of Mr Ephraim Tristram Bates*, p. 205.

74 Ibid. p. 214.

75 Ibid. p. 206.

76 Shaftesbury, 'Sensus Communis', p. 63.

77 'An Address to the Protestant Freeholders of the County of York', *Daily Gazetteer* (23 October 1741), in Kenneth Monkman, 'More of Sterne's Politicks 1741–1742', *The Shandean* 1 (1989), 67.

78 Jonathan Lamb, 'Sterne and Irregular Oratory', in John Richetti (ed.), *The Cambridge Companion to the Eighteenth-Century Novel* (Cambridge: Cambridge University Press, 1996), pp. 155, 156, 166. Lamb sees a direct parallel between Pitt's patriot rhetoric and the discursive tactics of Sterne's narrative, in which the 'world being represented is subordinated in every sense to the demands of persuasively representing it' (p. 158).

79 Oliver Goldsmith, 'On Public Rejoicings for Victory', in Arthur Friedman (ed.), *The Collected Works of Oliver Goldsmith* (Oxford: Clarendon Press, 1966), III, 19. In Chapter 4 Goldsmith's response is examined as part of a wider debate about the nature of political friendship.

80 J. C. D. Clark, *The Dynamics of Change: the Crisis of the 1750s and English Party Systems* (Cambridge: Cambridge University Press, 1982), p. 151. Quoted in Lamb, 'Sterne and Irregular Oratory', p. 165.

81 Samuel Johnson, reported in Sekora, p. 306, n.38.. No specific reference.

82 Sekora, *Luxury*, p. 93.

83 Brown, *Estimate*, p. 191. All following references cited parenthetically by page number.

84 Goldsmith, 'On Public Rejoicings for Victory', p. 21.

85 Tom Furniss, *Edmund Burke's Aesthetic Ideology: Language, Gender and Political Economy in Revolution* (Cambridge: Cambridge University Press, 1993), p. 44.

86 Alexander Pope, *The Iliad of Homer*, in Maynard Mack (ed.), *The Twickenham Edition of The Poems of Alexander Pope* (London and New Haven: Methuen and Yale University Press, 1967), VIII, 563, ll.644, 646.

87 Matthew Prior, 'An English Ballad on the Taking of Namur by the King of Great Britain', quoted by Murray G. H. Pittock in his 'The Aeneid in the Age of Burlington: A Jacobite Text?' in Toby Barnard and Jane Clark (eds), *Lord Burlington: Architecture, Art and Life* (London and Rio Grande, OH: The Hambleden Press, 1995), p. 242.

88 Edmund Burke, *A Philosophical Enquiry into the Origin of our Ideas of the Sublime and the Beautiful*, ed. Adam Phillips (Oxford: Oxford University Press, 1990), pp. 143–4.

89 Smith, *The Theory of Moral Sentiments*, p. 152. For Hume's formulation of the amiable and awful virtues, see 'Of goodness and benevolence', in *Treatise*, pp. 602–6.

90 Smith, *The Theory of Moral Sentiments*, p. 23.

91 Frances Ferguson, 'The Sublime of Edmund Burke, or the Bathos of Experience', *Glyph* 8 (1981), p. 76. See the discussion of Helen of Troy and Burke's sense of the political dangers of the beautiful in Furniss, pp. 38–9.

92 For a discussion of Burke's anxiety at the 'vegetable stupor' of happiness in relation to Jean-François Lyotard's formulation of the sublime, see Meaghan Morris, 'Postmodernity and Lyotard's Sublime', in her *The Pirate's Fiancée* (London: Verso Books, 1988), p. 233.

93 Burke, *Enquiry*, p. 38.

94 Ibid. p. 62.

95 Ibid. p. 61.

96 John Baillie, *An Essay on the Sublime* (London: R. Dodsley, 1747). For a discussion of Baillie's *Essay*, see Samuel H. Monk, *The Sublime: A Study of Critical Theories in Eighteenth-Century England* (Ann Arbor: University of Michigan Press, 1960), pp. 63–83.

97 Brown, *Estimate*, p. 72.

98 Burke, *Enquiry*, p. 122.

99 Samuel Johnson, *The Idler* 21 (2 September, 1758), p. 67.

100 Furniss, *Edmund Burke's Aesthetic Ideology*, p. 34.

101 Goldsmith, *The Vicar of Wakefield*, p. 102.

102 Thomas Weiskel, *The Romantic Sublime: Studies in the Structure and Psychology of Transcendence* (Baltimore and London: Johns Hopkins University Press, 1976), p. 88.

103 The notes to the Florida edition point out the commonplace of this reference to St Paul's analogy (in Rom. 12:4 and 1 Cor. 12:12) of the natural body to the Church – and thus the body politic – in sermons from the late seventeenth century on. See *The Sermons of Laurence Sterne: The Notes*, ed. Melvyn New (Gainesville, FL: Florida University Press, 1996), pp. 415–16, n.388.26–389.1.

104 Adam Ferguson, *An Essay on the History of Civil Society* (Edinburgh: A. Kincaid and J. Bell; London: A. Millar and T. Caddel, 1767), p. 417.

105 Daniel Defoe, *An Essay at Removing National Prejudices Against a Union with Scotland, Part III* (1706: no place nor publisher), p. 7. Cited in *Katie Trumpener, Bardic Nationalism: The Romantic Novel and the British Empire* (Princeton: Princeton University Press, 1997), p. 128.

106 Trumpener, p. 249.

107 Smollett, *Humphry Clinker*, p. 119.

108 Peter de Bolla, *The Discourse of the Sublime: Readings in History, Aesthetics and the Subject* (Oxford: Blackwell, 1989), p. 12.

109 Smollett, *Humphry Clinker*, p. 317. Smollett's narrator notes how private 'schemes of interest and ambition' are rife, 'agents, commissaries, and contractors' have 'fattened, in two successive wars, on the blood of the nation' (p. 154).

110 Brown, *Estimate*, p. 214.

111 *London Magazine* 27 (May 1758), 223.

112 Abraham Tucker, *The Light of Nature Pursued*, p. 88.

113 John Brown, *An Explanatory Defence of the Estimate* (London: L. Davis and C. Reymers, 1758), p. 84.

114 Jean-Jacques Rousseau, 'A Discourse on Political Economy' (1755–6), in *The Social Contract and Discourses*, ed. P. D. Jimack, trans. G. D. H. Cole (London: J. M. Dent, 1993), p. 132. On the 'organismic' and mechanical dimensions of Rousseau's account of the body politic see Pheng Cheah, *Spectral Nationality: Passages of Freedom from Kant to Postcolonial Literatures of Liberation* (New York: Columbia University Press, 2003), pp. 29–31.

115 Jean-Jacques Rousseau, 'The Social Contract', in *The Social Contract and Discourses*, ed. P. D. Jimack, trans. G. D. H. Cole (London: J. M. Dent, 1993), p. 204, (my italics).

116 Rousseau, 'A Discourse on Political Economy', p. 148.

117 Rousseau, 'The Social Contract', p. 205.

118 My thinking here about the anticipations of the 1760s is shaped by Cheah, whose account of the emergence of organismic metaphor for the political body and its relation to the self-grounding nature of freedom is an important one.

119 As Ernest Renan described in 'What is a Nation?', 'a nation is . . . a large-scale solidarity, constituted by the feelings of the sacrifices that one has made in the past and of those that one is prepared to make in the future'. Ernest Renan, 'What is a Nation?', trans. Martin Thom, in Bhabha, p. 19. If the memorialisation of military sacrifice is one constitutive means of imagining the community of the nation, such sacrifice is no less ' "essential" and real' in historical terms, as Murray G. H. Pittock emphasises in his engagement with Renan and Anderson in *Celtic Identity and the British Image* (Manchester: Manchester University Press, 1999), pp. 129–30. Thanks to Ian Higgins for bringing this work to my attention.

120 Rousseau, 'The Social Contract', pp. 207–8.

121 Goldsmith, 'Threnodia Augustalis', p. 338.

122 This was also true of officers like James Wolfe, who recognised protesting weavers as 'poor devils' 'half-starved' through inadequate pay, as Gilmore records, p. 142.

123 Thus, as Tom Furniss argues in his excellent account, the metaphorical removal of labour and pain in Burke's model has a social correlative: '[The sublime] can be read as the resort of the 'civilized' classes whose lives no longer present sufficient mental and physical exertion or variety to prevent their degeneration into 'luxury'. The labour and pain which formed the daily experience of the majority provides the material ease which at once allows and makes it necessary that the new ruling classes transform labour and pain into aesthetic experience.' Furniss, p. 38.

124 Goldsmith, Letter XVII, *The Citizen of the World*, p. 75.

125 Smollett, *Humphry Clinker*, p. 224. The following references are cited parenthetically by page number.

126 Longinus, 'On the Sublime', in *Classical Literary Criticism*, trans. T. G. Dorsch (Harmondsworth: Penguin Books, 1965), p. 107.

127 Goldsmith, 'On Public Rejoicings for Victory', p. 17.

128 Jeremy Bentham, 'A Table of the Springs of Action', in J. Bowring (ed.), *The Works of Jeremy Bentham*, 11 vols (Edinburgh: W. Tait, 1843), II, 156.

129 Adam Smith, *An Inquiry into the Nature and the Causes of the Wealth of Nations*, ed. R. H. Campbell, A. S. Skinner and W. B. Todd, 2 vols (Oxford: Clarendon Press, 1976), I, 23.

130 'Capital drives beyond national barriers and prejudices as much as beyond nature worship, as well as all traditional, confined, complacent, encrusted satisfactions of present needs, and reproductions of old ways of life. It is destructive to all of this, and constantly revolutionises it . . . But from the fact that capital posits every such limit as a barrier and hence gets ideally beyond it, it does not by any means follow that it has really overcome it, and, since every such barrier contradicts its character, its production moves in contradictions which are constantly overcome but just as constantly posited . . . The universality towards which it irresistibly strives encounters barriers in its own nature, which will, at a certain stage of its development, allow it to be recognized as being itself the greatest barrier to this tendency, and hence will drive towards its own suspension'. Karl Marx, *Grundrisse*, trans. Martin Nicolaus (Harmondsworth: Penguin Books, 1973), p. 410.

# PRICKSONGS IN GOTHAM: OR, THE
# SEXUAL OECONOMY OF STATE IMAGINING

In the early volumes of *Tristram Shandy* the narrator refers to the 'world' he is representing as 'a small circle described upon the circle of the great world, of four *English* miles diameter' (*TS* 1.7.10). If this gesture registers the impossibility of comprehending the extent of that wider world in a single totalising vision, its use of the local is nonetheless a response to such a historical condition; a means, as I discussed earlier, of figuring a form of counter-modernity. Yet there is more to discover in Sterne's act of enclosure. It emerges in a gendered tale about the balance of power in that provincial community, which circulates around the birth of Tristram himself. Ranged on one side are the forces of the 'female part of the parish' and their elderly midwife, whose reputation forms the circumference of the circle, and, on the other, beleaguered exponents of patriarchal principle, intent on ensuring the male offspring's 'scientific' entry into the world. It is a short step from the contested boundaries of household and community to the imagining of the state in the mid-eighteenth century. Indeed there is a concerted turn towards the re-energising of older homologies of family and state, which is marked in the fictional, political and legal narratives of the period. In what follows, I explore the sexual politics of such imagining, in order to chart the complexity of the making and unmaking of the state at this time, and its particular fascination with the body political birth of 'a BEING guarded and circumscribed with rights' (*TS* 1.2.3).

## Tales from Gotham

Sterne's circumscription of his Shandean world had Cervantic parallels, as he was well aware. No sooner is the circle described than the quixotic figure of

Yorick is brought on to the scene, his horse a 'full brother to Rosinante' (*TS* 1.10.18). This is a space licensed for hobbyhorsical pleasures, in the manner of Bakhtin's carnivalesque, but as in the fact of carnival, the tilting at windmills can have its repercussions in violence and death. On the one hand there is a freedom and tolerance here for imaginative idiosyncrasies, as the narrator explains: 'so long as a man rides his HOBBY-HORSE peaceably and quietly along the King's highway, and neither compels you or me to get up behind him,——pray, Sir, what have either you or I to do with it?' (*TS* 1.7.12). On the other, hobbyhorses are also forms of social strategy, 'scampering it away like so many little party-colour'd devils astride a mortgage' (*TS* 1.8.13), which are exposed at one's peril, as Yorick discovers.[1] This is not simply a sentimental retreat into a universe of innocents and eccentrics, but a heterotopic engagement with the 'great world', in which the enclosure of household and community provides a means of thinking about wider forms of authority and the nature of social ties. It is also a space where it is possible to imagine alternative worlds. Sterne is borrowing in part from a tradition of political fantasy that includes utopian thought; the precedent is already there in Cervantes:[2]

> Was I left, like *Sancho Pança*, to chuse my kingdom, it should not be maritime —or a kingdom of blacks to make a penny of—no, it should be a kingdom of hearty laughing subjects: And as the bilious and more saturnine passions, by creating disorders in the blood and humours, have as bad an influence, I see, upon the body politick as body natural—and as nothing but a habit of virtue can fully govern those passions, and subject them to reason—I should add to my prayer—that God would give my subjects grace to be as WISE as they were MERRY; and then should I be the happiest monarch, and they the happiest people under heaven—(*TS* 4.32.402)

Quite what 'happiness' means here is a subject for later debate. The narrator's self-enthroning as king of an ideal state is a tactic shared by other satirists in the early 1760s. Charles Churchill, like Sterne a friend to John Wilkes and an Anglican minister, gives such laughter a keener critical edge in his verse satire *Gotham*. Gotham was a Nottinghamshire village associated for centuries with foolishness, its inhabitants reputedly having escaped punishment for insulting King John by faking imbecility. It is briefly mentioned in *Tristram Shandy* when the nonsense of Widow Wadman's strategy to seduce Uncle Toby deserves 'registering in letters of gold (I mean in the archives of Gotham)'(*TS* 8.23.704). Sterne's delineation of a 'crazy' (Shandean) community is paralleled in Churchill's use of Gotham as the scene for his satirical imagining of the state, but the poet is much more explicit about the imperial framing of that gesture. While

Sterne's narrator imagines his ideal happy kingdom as distinct from commercial interests and the rewards of the slave trade, *Gotham* offers a paradoxical reverse colonisation which reflects on the nature of imperial legitimation itself:

> EUROPE discover'd INDIA first; I found
> My right to GOTHAM on the self-same ground;
> I first discover'd it, nor shall that plea
> To her be granted, and denied to Me.[3]

Gotham is a virtual England[4] – an island however 'Not yet by modern MANDEVILLES disgrac'd./ Nor yet by *Map-jobbers* wretchedly misplac'd'. (p. 1).

The latent ludicrousness of Churchill's claim to 'discovery' works a clever double bind. First, it displaces and undermines the fantasy of conquest as the possession of 'virgin' territory, since England, like India, is already peopled, cultivated. There is something perversely Shandean about imperial enterprise, the delimiting and ownership of a space carved from an already existing world; and the satire reveals the brute interests that make such claims possible: 'Let SPAIN and FRANCE,/ In Slav'ry bred, as purchasers advance,/ Let them, whilst Conscience is at distance hurl'd,/With some gay bauble buy a golden world' (p. 3), declares the poet. In its acting out of an imperial claim, the poem voices an anti-imperial rhetoric marked by a blend of nationalist and anti-commercial sentiment. But the double bind then delivers its political twist. The luxurious design that characterises the imperial projects of other nations – the interest of 'modern MANDEVILLES' – *has* also subjugated England; to this extent the poet's 'discovery' of Gotham is indeed a *re*discovery of an originary freedom before the Fall of imperial accumulation. The claim to Gotham is thus a serious one, expressed in terms of *right*. The poem maps a shift from the enslavement and naked interest of absolutist forms of power to the stake of the sovereign individual who claims liberty as his birthright:

> An ENGLISHMAN, in charter'd FREEDOM born,
> Shall spurn the slavish merchandize, shall scorn
> To take from others, thro' base private views,
> What he himself would rather die, than lose. (p. 3)

It is possible to see in such a declaration the constitutional arguments against slavery – 'charter'd FREEDOM' – that would begin to consolidate in the work of lawyers like Granville Sharp a few years later.[5] But there is nothing inherently radical about this patriot celebration of the 'true-born Englishman', emerging umbilically from the twist of the imperial double-bind. It appealed to republican and blind nationalist sentiments alike, both of which in the early 1760s discovered their avatar.

Other tracts were less subtle in their ushering of the true-born Englishman onto the scene in the unmistakable guise of John Wilkes. Wilkes, Member of Parliament for Aylesbury, had harboured hopes of higher office, which had been dashed with the resignation of William Pitt in 1761, after the government refused to declare war on Spain. His publication of the *North Briton* between June 1762 and April 1763, vociferously countering the moves of Lord Bute's administration to bring the war to an early close, would have him arrested for seditious libel and committed to the Tower. Wilkes was synonymous with the popular cry for Liberty throughout the decade, though the militancy of the time was not reducible to Wilkite concerns alone, and the mob that demonstrated on his behalf was said to be 'of a far higher rank than common'. At his trial, as George Rudé's account details, Wilkes claimed on behalf of 'all peers and gentlemen' and 'what touches me more sensibly, all the middling and inferior set of people', that his case would determine 'whether English Liberty shall be a reality or a shadow'.[6]

In *An Essay on Woman. A Poem*, a spurious 'version' of the infamous poem that resulted in his expelling from Parliament, Wilkes is portrayed as 'among the foremost of your heroes militant', pitched against the forces of Gothamite corruption:

> In days of yore, when Gotham's pow'rful state
> Was rul'd by one supreme to senate join'd,
> There liv'd a gallant, bold intrepid wight,
> Whom goddess Liberty adopted her's,
> Tho' a pow'rful Faction labour'd to undo him;
> Because fair Freedom's voluntary champion,
> Unbrib'd, unpension'd, he stept forth, the cause
> Of ev'ry true born subject to maintain.[7]

There are faint echoes of Shakespeare's *Hamlet* here, the words 'unbrib'd, unpension'd' picking up on the cadences of Hamlet's father's ghost: 'unhousel'd, disappointed, unanel'd.' These are echoes worth registering.[8] The paternal dynamic controlling the true-born subject and his inheritance from the past was a complex one. The allusion might suggest it, since Freedom's champion stands simultaneously in the memorialising place of the paternal ghost and the avenging son. Such an articulation of duty in a corrupted present to the memory of forefathers had political resonance at this time, when the cabinet of George III and Bute in particular were vilified in radical circles for a perceived renewal of seventeenth-century Stuart absolutism. As Kathleen Wilson has shown, Wilkite radicalism was energised by a legacy drawn from the civil war and 1688: 'an effort which gave historical (and a more narrowly inclusive English) specificity to resistance arguments, identified past and present threats to the constitution and subjects' liberties, and so constructed a "tradition" of popular resistance to executive tyranny that legitimized extra-parliamentary action in the present'. Wilkes was thus very precisely located as the bearer of that 'tradition', the contemporary hope of the seventeenth-century Whig martyrs whose voices were still to be heard: 'Let not your great forefathers' ghost complain/ That all their blood was shed in vain', as one paper put it.[9] Yet in striking a blow for the political right of the sovereign true-born subject, Wilkite thought was caught in a contradiction. It had, on the one hand, to conduct a form of parricide, setting itself like the heroes of popular ballads against the entrenched forces of the state and its vested interests; yet, on the other, in its invention of a 'tradition' to codify that sovereignty it would succeed in internalising that very paternal authority in the process. This chapter takes a Shandean route into Wilkite territory to explore the cultural impact of such a contradiction, and the sexual rhetoric that animated it.

## 'True' Birth and Bastardy

What did it mean to be a 'true-born' subject? It was a symbolic construction of considerable ideological force, and densely worked: undoubtedly xenophobic and nationalist at root, specifically masculine, redolent of patriot principle and the defence of a constitutional inheritance of 'liberty', self-possessed and associated with a virile agency. If the figure of the true-born subject had great affective weight, condensing as it did a mass of desires, fears and identifications, it was also flexible, shifting in meaning depending on the 'enemy' it faced and who was claiming it. Those ranged against it might be imperial competitors, external French or Spanish aggressors, by definition enslaved and enslaving, effeminate and luxurious; or internal enemies, as is always the case in Wilkite literature, the Scots, 'like nature's bastards', their freedom one of strategy and barbarism.[10] At times, from the position of the state, the true-born subject was counterposed to domestic threats, a panoply of social illegitimates offending what William Blackstone termed 'the good order and oeconomy of the kingdom': the idle poor, gypsies, criminals and the vagrants who, as the statute put it, 'no man wot from whence they come, ne whither they go'. Thus the figure of the benevolent soldier met in Chapter 2 could occupy the position of the true-born subject, but he also had his illegitimate counterpart: 'idle *soldiers* and *mariners wandering* about the realm, or persons pretending so to be'.[11]

The true-born subject was thus often defined by its 'constitutive outside', a social zone of illegitimacy and counterfeiture.[12] As one MP put it in 1769, reflecting on petitioners to Parliament, there was 'a distinction between the genuine son of Liberty, and the base-born son of Licentiousness'.[13] But at the mid-century, I want to suggest, the figure of the true-born itself undergoes a form of remaking which the language of bastardy – if anything more intense in this period for distinct social and economic reasons – comes paradoxically to represent. Richard Savage's earlier poem of 1728, *The Bastard*, captures qualities that accrue to the repertoire of the true-born in the 1760s:

> BORN to himself, by no Possession led,
> In Freedom foster'd, and by Fortune fed;
> Nor Guides nor Rules his sov'reign Choice controul,
> His Body independent, as his Soul.
> Loos'd to the World's wide Range – enjoyn'd no Aim;
> Prescrib'd no Duty, and assign'd no Name;
> Nature's unbounded Son, he stands alone,
> His Heart unbyass'd, and his Mind his own.[14]

Savage's vision of autonomy, a deracinated freedom that involves being born *to* oneself, suggests an individualism that is representative of the experience of modernity, though it was a narrative that undoubtedly related to his own very public self-fashioning. Its rejection of paternal diktat – 'no tenth Transmitter of a foolish face'[15] – in the interests of independence and 'sov'reign choice' suggests a proto-Enlightenment stance that will find one *political* correlative in the reformulated resistance discourse of popular Wilkite radicalism. Thus while Wilkes's chosen constituencies are tagged by the word 'truth' – whether the sailors, 'true glory and stability of our country',[16] or London merchants, who 'understand more of the true interest of their country, than all the ministers of state ever discovered'[17] – their truth lies in an independence from the paternalist certainties of a political culture that Wilkes subjects to a sustained attack. One way he achieves this in the pages of the *North Briton* is to render the keywords of political administration suspect. 'Candour', 'oeconomy', 'universal satisfaction and harmony', a 'spirit of concord', are revealed as ideological, illegitimate; the king's speech, detailed in the notorious number 45, infiltrated by political spin. No wonder that lives are put 'in jeopardy by words', as *Tristram Shandy* put it (*TS* 2.2.101). At its most extreme, the radicalism released in the 1760s was expressed in terms of parricide and king-killing, but Wilkes's puncturing of the patrician elite – who would read *Essay on Woman* aloud in the Lords – was of a different order. His 'unbounded' nature, to recall the

Savage poem, seemingly exemplified in his libertinism and the mob action that followed him ('to laugh and riot and scatter firebrands with him was liberty'[18]), rendered him an outlaw to some, but he rode the same juridical energies that Blackstone was elsewhere working to control. As one anonymous Wilkite tract put it, cautiously: 'by liberty we understand the right a man has either to employ or dispose of his time, person or property in what manner he shall please, independent of the smile or frown of any individual of higher rank, etc., so that he shall not offend against the laws of his country, from whose protection he derives the indisputable charter of doing as beforementioned'.[19] Time, person, property. Wilkes was no revolutionary, and, it might be argued, effectively anchored popular desires and energies in the institutionalising of forms of sovereignty that well suited the new modelling of the imperial state.

The 'true-born' subject was thus not to be separated from the deracination expressed through a discourse of bastardy, but was rather constituted through it. Such a formation of identity was not simply a characteristic of the radical political culture of the time, which sought to harness the energies released by imperial accumulation in the new social subjects it brought into being, even as it envisioned a remodelled social order. It is also echoed in a general fantasy that repeatedly occurs in novels from the middling years of the century, which derive their pleasure and sense of risk from the loss and recovery of 'true' identity. The expulsion of a foundling or orphan from a known domestic world out on to the road is a common plot, which concerns how the stable location of individuals and communities is to be established within the deracinating experience of modernity. The deterritorialising effects of such movement introduce a contingency into the social environment that is often accompanied by violence: the threat of anonymity, rape and expropriation, misrecognition. Yet such a terrain is ultimately productive of that characteristic vision of 'domestic order' defined by the jurist William Blackstone: 'whereby the individuals of the state, like members of a well-governed family, are bound to conform their general behaviour to the rules of propriety, good neighbourhood, and good manners; and to be decent, industrious, and inoffensive in their respective stations'.[20] In these narratives a state of bastardy – 'loosed to the world's wide range' without 'aim', 'duty' and a 'name' as the Savage poem puts it – seems a necessary precondition to the establishing of the bounds of conformity; a condition to live through only to be bound in more tightly. The foundling Tom Jones eventually discovers an amiable state of legitimacy at the heart of the family. Roderick Random works his way towards his true paternal inheritance unexpectedly revealed in Argentina. Orphan Evelina wins patriarchal recognition and love.

These narratives are in distinctive ways about a form of class transition, the genealogical equivalent of Richardson's *Pamela*. Yet whereas hers is a story of upward mobility, 'Virtue Rewarded', theirs concern an originary status that is lost and regained. There is something perverse about these tales of 'accidental' misfortune, in which the genteel identity of the protagonist is reiterated in a manner that resembles a performative, continuously posited as an essential attribute that is in fact never lost at all. Illegitimacy is a zone of risk, full of the energies and anxieties of a life 'fostered' in modernity. As such, it provides a necessary rite of passage. Like the merchant's son in the *Spectator* who is abducted by gypsies, only to return to his father in later life well versed in the ways of the world, these bourgeois individuals are momentarily captured by such a bastard condition.[21] After venturing into such a wild zone, Tom's happiness, Roderick's work ethic, and Evelina's Christian virtue, make it possible for them to re-enter the moral city and transform the standard of gentility in the process. The distinction between a familial realm of property and order and a darker vagabond economy of money and interest is thus reinforced. Yet only just. As the case of Fielding's susceptible paternal figure, Mr Allworthy, suggests, the moral city has already fallen to the seductions and strategies of the vagabond, whose operations are not restricted to the highway. In the words of John Gay's *The Beggar's Opera*, there existed 'such a similitude of manners in high and low life, that it is difficult to know whether (in the fashionable vices) the fine gentlemen imitate the gentlemen of the road, or the gentlemen of the road the fine gentlemen'.[22]

If the eighteenth-century novel was concerned with the thematic plotting of illegitimacy, it was in part because it addressed the desires and moral values of the middle-class household, caught between the perceived excesses of the luxurious rich and the idle poor. Yet it was also a means of reflecting on that experience. Bastardy, I would suggest, is a symbolic form that operates in the mid-eighteenth century in the manner of the later narrative plot of the *Bildungsroman*. The disengagement of the central character from the social whole because he or she does not 'belong' sets in train a certain reflexivity, a mode of cognition by which the patterns and habits of social life might be observed, and the price of incorporation into that world assessed. Unlike their nineteenth-century counterparts, these protagonists are not generally in possession of this knowledge as an internal process of reflection and growth, except as a limited pedagogy. Historical cognition is rather a potential of the narratives themselves, as they rehearse for the reader the options and values that make sense of the characters' dislocation. The effects of such plotting generally prove to be normative, unwinding intricate familial entanglements (including the prospect of incest) into a reassuring confirmation (and re-formation) of the traditional order and the sanctity of marriage. But there is an exception.

## Bastardy: A Shandean Key

He calls from P_ M_. 'Take heed, my good friends,
'Tis a lie, a loud lie, to serve sinister ends,
Young Shandy may swear that he's born, but I tell ye,
The bantling is yet without breath in the belly!'
Derry down, etc.[23]

Sterne's *Tristram Shandy* organises the plotting of bastardy according to radically different principles. The plot is not predicated on the eventual recognition of the 'true' social identity of the illegitimate *inconnu/e*, the fact that she
or he belongs in the bosom of the family, but quite the reverse. Bastardy – the
lie with 'sinister' ends, in the words of the ballad – is uncovered in the heart
of familial relations which are increasingly unravelled, despite all attempts to
contain and 'fix' such a source of 'error'. Here the focus is on the pervasive-
ness of *misrecognition*: that what appears to be habitual and stable about
social life is no more than a fiction, but that, in Humean vein, fiction is all
there is to make sense of. The inauthenticity of a life in which persons are
'pretending so to be' becomes in a curious sense representative. Bastardy thus
can be read as a metaphor for a more general social alienation, a mark of an
inadvertent 'living to the self' in Sterne's words[24] that is both a form of
freedom and disorientation from the historical continuum, the passage of
generations. On the one hand this produces a new articulation of mid-century
masculine identity, to which I will return. On the other, it inaugurates in the
novel a thoroughgoing attempt to make sense of that disorientation, and the
anxiety that accompanies it: a mode of historical reflection about the nature
of authority itself.

  Tristram's definite assertion of the date and the circumstances of his conception – the primal scene – is of course a parody of the biographical 'Lives
of the Famous' genre that Samuel Johnson had made his own. 'Such were
the Life and Death of *Richard Savage*', Johnson intones, 'a Man equally distinguished by his Virtues and his Vices, and at once remarkable for his
Weaknesses and Abilities'.[25] The equilibrium of these statements is nowhere
to be found in Sterne's narrative, which in its search for stable origins sets
out 'ab ovo':

> I was begot in the night, betwixt the first *Sunday* and the first *Monday* in the
> month of *March*, in the year of our Lord one thousand seven hundred and
> eighteen. I am positive I was.—But how I came to be so very particular in my
> account of a thing that happened before I was born, is owing to another small
> anecdote known only in our own family. (*TS* 1.4.6)

By spelling out the details of his conception, and later his birth, 'as near nine kalendar months as any husband could in reason have expected' (*TS* 1.5.8), Tristram asserts a legitimacy that the Shandy family continues to protest. Yet at Tristram's genesis there lies a family fiction waiting to be told on which he, like his readers, must rely. As the first volume unfolds, the 'tokens of eccentricity' that mark the 'original character' of the Shandean males are linked to the fall of 'great aunt DINAH', who 'was married and got with child by the coachman' (*TS* 1.21.73). While the disgrace of Dinah's 'backslidings' to the family honour is evidently that of marrying beneath her, we are led to suspect that the account of events is chronologically somewhat different, and that bastardy is to blame.

Painted on the Shandy coach is a coat of arms, to which is added, on the occasion of Walter Shandy's marriage, the arms of his wife. The painter makes an error – 'the sinister turn which everything related to our family was apt to take':

> Instead of the *bend dexter*, which since *Harry* the Eighth's reign was honestly our due——a *bend sinister*, by some of these fatalities, had been drawn quite across the field of the *Shandy*-arms. 'Tis scarce credible that the mind of so wise a man as my father was, could be so much incommoded with so small a matter. The word coach—let it be whose it would—or coach-man, or coach-horse, or coach-hire, could never be named in the family, but he constantly complained of carrying this vile mark of Illegitimacy upon the door of his own. (*TS* 4.25.373)

Walter Shandy is unable to 'brush out' the sign of bastardy that marks his house by a reassertion of his paternal potency. The 'confounding' of the familial line is centrally about what Michael McKeon terms the 'categorial instability' of social class; the discovery, as Jonathan Swift puts it in *Gulliver's Travels*, of the consistent 'Interruption of Lineages by Pages, Lackies, Valets, Coachmen, Gamesters, Captains, and Pick-pockets'.[26] If Yorick's name has remained the same for 'nine hundred years', the narrator reflects (parodying the *Spectator* perhaps[27]), that is

> more than I would venture to say of one half of the best surnames in the kingdom; which, in a course of years, have generally undergone as many chops and changes as their owners . . . a villainous affair it is, and will one day so blend and confound us all together, that no one shall be able to stand up and swear, 'That his own great grand father was the man who did either this or that'. (*TS* 1.11.25)

Counterposed with a fantasy of paternal lineage are the genealogical irruptions of a vagabond class, without property or scruple. The novelistic plotting of bastardy is generally an antidote to these 'chops and changes' in social life, which rides on their energies but ultimately returns to a restatement of the irreduceability of genteel identity. Not, however, in Sterne's narrative.

What is distinctive in *Tristram Shandy* is the extent to which such instability is understood as a crisis of paternal power. The procreative abilities of the Shandy men have declined since the family's heyday in the Tudor Golden Age: even 'the greatest family in England' would find it difficult to withstand 'an uninterrupted succession of six or seven short noses' (*TS* 3.33.261). The mark of bastardy is thus compounded by increasing patrilineal impotence. This degeneration is marked by a shift in 'the monarchical system of domestic government' – a shift in the gendered nature of sovereignty – in which patriarchal authority is called to account. The woman not only begins to assume a degree of control in the 'mixed government' of the household, but alters the marriage contract in material terms: those of property. Thus, as Tristram relates, his great-grandmother demands 'jointure' for her part of the estate from her husband, 'because . . . you have little or no nose, Sir' (*TS* 3.31.257), a compensatory sum that is paid to her throughout subsequent generations despite male protestations that the inherited Shandean nose is growing in size.

Through the figure of Walter Shandy, Sterne's novel evinces a patriarchal anxiety that centres on the woman as the weak link in the patrilineal chain. She is the 'leaky vessel' who is not only unable to remember the name of the male child but also unlikely to ensure the safe passage and indeed identity of the masculine homunculus:

> what if any accident had befallen him in his way alone?——or that, thro' terror of it, natural to so young a traveller, my little gentleman had got to his journey's end miserably spent;——his muscular strength and virility worn down to a thread;—his own animal spirits ruffled beyond description,—and that in this sad disorder'd state of nerves, he had laid down a prey to sudden starts, or a series of melancholy dreams and fancies for nine long, long months together. (*TS* 1.2.3)

This melancholic grand tour within the body of the mother is fraught with castration anxiety; an anxiety, it turns out, which is well-founded but whose cause lies elsewhere. The damage is brought about by paternal attempts to control the birth scientifically, and by the consequences of Toby's war games. It is a form of patriarchalism that is seen to be at fault, but which nonetheless generates an intensely misogynistic vision of women, not limited in the narrative to Walter Shandy's seemingly outmoded traditionalism. Women are seen as both powerless – insofar as they are the property of their husbands ('*feme-covert*' in Blackstone's terms[28]) – and yet violently potent, in that paternity stands and falls by their actions. Mrs Shandy is thus bracketed out:

silent, stranded in mid-action by her filial narrator, a cipher of her husband. Her presence is measured by little more than a trace of obduracy in the text, and that natural desirous curiosity that eighteenth-century culture regarded as woman's post-lapsarian inheritance. Monodimensional, she can be no more than herself:

> What could my father do? . . . talked it over with her in all moods;—placed his arguments in all lights;—argued the matter like a christian,—like a heathen,—like a husband,—like a father,—like a patriot,—like a man:—My mother answered every thing only like a woman; which was a little hard on her;—for as she could not assume and fight it out behind such a variety of characters,—'twas no fair match;—'twas seven to one. (*TS* 1.18.55)

'Most Women', as the famous phrase went, 'have no Characters at all'.[29] Yet beneath that monovalence, a sign of the denial of their status as social individuals, is an alarming and contradictory prospect. Women are capable on the one level of extreme force, the 'violent compression and crush' of childbirth. On another, their desires suggest an all-consuming nymphomania, sketched in the comic concupiscence of Sterne's Widow Wadman. As the anonymous pamphlet, *Characterism, or the Modern Age display'd: being an Attempt to expose the Pretended Virtues of both Sexes* suggested luridly in 1750, women look 'as innocent as Angels, whilst the Devil himself has an Asylum under their Petticoats'.[30] As numerous popular manuals underlined, men approached sex with a certain risk, as the narrator of *Tristram Shandy* informs us with feigned distaste, and a number of puns on 'an old hat cocked':

> By all that is hirsute and gashly! I cry, taking off my furr'd cap and twisting it round my finger . . .
> ——No; I shall never have a finger in the pye (so here I
> break my metaphor)——
>      Crust and crumb
>      Inside and out
>      Top and bottom—I detest it, I hate it, I repudiate it——I'm sick at the sight
> of it——
>      'Tis all pepper,
>      garlick
>      staragen
>      salt, and
>      devil's dung——by the great arch-cook of cooks,
>      who does nothing, I think, from morning to night, but sit down by the fire-side and invent inflammatory dishes for us, I would not touch it for the world——(*TS* 8.11.670)

As Rousseau wrote in *Émile*, the 'boundless' desires of women, unconstrained by the natural curbing of modesty, were held to be a considerable threat: 'men, tyrannised ever by the women, would at last become their victims, and would be dragged to their death without the least chance of escape.'[31] The misogyny of *Tristram Shandy* thus draws its energies from much more broadly disseminated myths of women's sexual 'character', from accounts as diverse as the popular medical manual *Aristotle's Masterpiece* to Rousseau's meditation on masculine sovereignty, both of which find their way into the novel. Myths which are undoubtedly caught up in the exigencies of the moment. Widow Wadman's aggression, for example, was paralleled in mid-century wartime concerns about women's single state. As Elizabeth and Richard Griffith discussed in their letter memoirs of the period, with a neat martial metaphor: 'if this warm Weather, and the War, continue, Women will be obliged soon like the *Amazons* of old, to march off *in Troops* to the continent, and pick up Lovers for themselves'.[32]

Yet in the figure of Walter Shandy the novel's misogyny pulls a particular patriarchal model of history in its wake that has a broader purchase on the state imagining of the mid-century. While it is tempting to read Walter's as a regressive kind of nostalgia – on Sterne's part a parodic reponse to that Tory vision of a familial golden age lamented, for example, in Swift's *Gulliver's Travels* – his patriarchalism is far from backward-looking. Indeed it is carefully articulated around the prospect of the birth of 'a BEING guarded and circumscribed with rights' (*TS* 1.2.3). To discover what this might mean in the 1760s as *Tristram Shandy* emerged, is to tease out the political philosophy of the Shandy *père*.

### Filmerism at the Mid-Century

At issue in the aftermath of the Seven Years' War was the question of sovereignty. This was prompted, in part, by the accession of a new monarch in 1761, raising expectations of a centralisation of power around the throne, and fears for some about the consequences of a reborn 'patriot king'.[33] But it was also a necessary consequence of empire, in which the governance of newly-won territories and populations demanded a reformulation, and a strengthening, of the nature of the state. Increased taxation and rapid enclosure were not the only signs of this process. The nature of governmentality – the domestic management of population – intensified, not only to handle the large numbers of people forced from the land, but also in response to a felt crisis brought about by losses sustained in gaining such an immense extent of empire 'as must be measured by the Heavens, and probably never will be perambulated'. Would anyone be left at home to trade with the colonies, wondered 'Cato' in 1765.[34]

Depopulation was an issue that connected both to the move from the country to the city, mourned in Goldsmith's 'The Deserted Village', and to the future of the empire itself. What would happen to the seat of imperial power if Americans became more numerous? With a familialism long available to political imagining, connections between the state and household were repeatedly made, famously codified in Blackstone's *Commentaries*, but widespread and rearticulated in diverse forms to emphasise the natural law underpinning the empire. In Soame Jenyns's discussion of theodicy, for example, such familialism suggests a universal and aesthetic order:

> Thus the Universe resembles a large and well-regulated Family, in which all the officers and servants, and even the domestic animals, are subservient to each other in a proper subordination: each enjoys the privileges and perquisites peculiar to his place, and at the same time contributes by that just subordination to the magnificence and happiness of the whole.[35]

If the equation between state and household celebrated paternal order, it also linked procreation within the confines of marriage with national (and imperial) fecundity. Moreover the presence of illegitimacy could be seen not simply as a violation of Christian marriage, but also in xenophobic terms as an incursion of the state. In a tract on *The Present State of Matrimony* in 1739, 'Philogamus' had noted that the crime of an unfaithful wife was so great because she 'imposes a spurious Breed on her Husband's Family; makes a Foreigner Heir to his Estate'.[36] The economic fears behind such cuckoldry were nothing new. Such a formulation of domestic security through the equation of state and household was, however, at its most intense in times of war. The paternal crisis sketched in *Tristram Shandy* thus reflected political anxieties of the time.

Walter Shandy, constructed from the stuff of a previous generation, marks a seventeenth-century reversion that was very much part of the philosophy of mid-century culture, which had returned in complex ways to older models of property and oeconomy circulating around the settlement of 1688 to think its way into the future. Condensed in the portrayal of the Shandean patriarch – in his invoking and yet deliberate anachronism – are a mish-mash of views on contract theory, absolutism, and the worrying inroads of feminisation; the contradictions, perhaps, entailed by a liberal stance that recalled and resisted the arbitrary exercise of sovereign 'paternal' power while fantasising its own virile private dominion. Like many of his contemporaries Sterne turned to Locke's *Two Treatises of Government* to stage his parodic account of sovereignty, the work of political philosophy that had presaged the transformations of 1688, and which was repeatedly associated in radical circles with an anti-autocratic concept of natural law almost a hundred years later.

In Walter Shandy we are presented with a curious hybrid of Filmerian patriarchalism, against which Locke had polemicised, and a Lockean distaste for 'error'. Sir Robert Filmer had derived his concept of the origin of political right from the absolute power of fatherhood, exemplified in the granting of kingly right to Adam: *'the natural and private dominion of Adam* is the fountain of all government and propriety'.[37] Walter Shandy's pretensions to an Adamic model of language in the naming of his son can thus be understood as part of a wider formulation of the nature of social government: the transmission of a paternalist traditional order, for which he serves as a spokesman in Sterne's narrative.

The authority of the father for Filmer was not based on Locke's contractual concept of 'trust' – by which power is invested in those who govern by the governed – but upon the father's arbitrary will over both his offspring and spouse. The maternal body was regarded as no more than a vehicle for his procreative agency. Such a formulation of patriarchal right thus granted the father dominion in private and public realms, equating domestic and political authority, as Carole Pateman has argued:

> The original political right that God gives to Adam is the right, so to speak, to fill the empty vessel. Adam, and all men, must do this if they are to become fathers, that is to say, if they are to exercise the *masculine* procreative or generative power . . . Masculine procreative power creates new life; men are the 'principle agents in generation'. Men appropriate to themselves women's natural creativity, their capacity to give birth – but they also do more than that. Men's generative power extends to another realm; they transmute what they have appropriated into another form of generation, the ability to create new political life, or to give birth to political right.[38]

The origin of Filmerian paternal power lay, in the first instance, as Pateman points out, in conjugal right over the body of the woman. The one-Sunday-a-month sexual act, or 'family concernment', which Walter grudgingly performs is a continual re-enactment of that authority; though, as *Tristram Shandy's* opening drama suggests, it is an event not without its misfortune. Walter's Filmerian patriarchal duty is interrupted by that Lockean error, the false association of ideas exhibited by his spouse, which sets the small homunculus on his wayward course (and which, the satirical pamphlet *The Clockmakers' Outcry* suggested, played havoc with patterns of courtship in fashionable society where it became impossible for a gentleman to wind his watch in public without a woman suspecting his sexual design).[39] The authority of the Shandean patriarch is further circumscribed by legal means: the marriage document that makes provision for his wife's lying-in. Science, in the form of the new technology of obstetrics, and the art of the 'man-midwife', further promises to secure an absolute control over the process of reproduction, bringing with it the prospect of an 'ancient' form of love: that 'without mother' (*TS* 8.33.720).

Accepting Filmer's doctrine, 'that the plans and institutions of the greatest monarchies . . . were, originally, all stolen from that admirable pattern and prototype of this household and paternal power' (*TS* 1.18.55), Walter Shandy thus sets out his claim to dominion over his son and heir according to Filmerian principles. The *Tristra-paedia* that he constructs as a 'system of education' for his filial 'last stake' offers a patriarchal account of the origin of civil society as the 'getting together of one man and one woman'. Before political right can be established, the sex-right is secured, but it is one that denies any jurisdiction to the woman as partner in the marriage contract. 'the natural relation between a father and his child', Walter argues, is acquired through the various means of marriage, adoption, legitimation and procreation, but crucial to such paternal right is the exclusion of the mother. As Kysarcius argues at the Visitation dinner in volume four of the novel, '*the mother is not of kin to her child*' (*TS* 4.29.390), and Walter takes up this principle in a replaying of the debate in Locke's *Two Treatises*, Yorick providing the Lockean refutation:

> I own, added my father, that the offspring . . . is not so under the power and jurisdiction of the *mother*.—But the reason, replied *Yorick*, equally holds good for her.——She is under authority herself, said my father:—and besides . . . *she is not the principal agent*, Yorick.—In what? quoth my uncle *Toby*, stopping his pipe.—Though by all means, added my father (not attending to my uncle *Toby*) '*The son ought to pay her respect*,' as you may read, *Yorick*, at large in the first book of the Institutes of *Justinian*, at the eleventh title and the tenth section.—I can read it as well, replied *Yorick*, in the Catechism. (*TS* 5.31.468)

To underline Walter Shandy's commitment to the Filmerian model, Sterne's narrative rehearses one of its touchstones, the paternal origin of political obligation as founded on a particular interpretation of the Fifth Commandment: *Honour thy father and thy mother* . . . This is what Yorick means by reference to 'the Catechism'; moreover, as Gordon J. Schochet has shown, it was the commandment used from the time of the Stuarts to justify an absolutist form of monarchical government according to providential law.[40] Walter, like Filmer, interprets the catechism as an expression of a paternal right that subsumes the mother, who is deemed irrelevant in both political and procreative terms. Yet as Corporal Trim is made to recite the catechism aloud, it becomes clear that he is only able to remember it by rote: as a text it seemingly has no meaning for him. Walter Shandy offers to 'lay out all my aunt *Dinah*'s legacy, in charitable uses . . . if the corporal has any one determinate idea annexed to any one word he has repeated' (*TS* 5.32.470). The corporal's understanding of the Fifth Commandment thus, paradoxically, produces an acknowledgement of familial bastardy by the Shandean patriarch, a 'laying out' of Dinah's inheritance. For Trim, it transpires, naturally carries out his filial duty without the inculcation of scriptural values, without being subjected to patriarchal will. Paternal authority and its dictates thus appear largely irrelevant to the maintenance of traditional social ties, for reasons we will explore in a moment.

Sterne thus establishes Walter Shandy as a Filmerian patriarchalist in more than name, weaving into his narrative reference points that, at the beginning of the eighteenth century, had codified a set of Tory principles on the nature of government, collapsing the distinctions between domestic and political rule by literalising what had been posited as an analogous relation between the family and the state. Laurence Sterne would not have needed to be well-versed in the intricacies of these debates. As James Daly has argued, 'Filmer was the perfect straw man' for those of Whiggish allegiance opposed to the defence of the Stuart cause: 'one is tempted to say that, had he not existed, the Whigs would have had to invent him'. For the literate public at large, he was a figure associated with patriarchalism in any form, and 'wherever Locke went henceforth, Filmer was sure to go'.[41] Quite what this 'straw man' delivered in comic form at the mid-century is now the question, and castration is its symptom.

### Historical Castrations

In his response to Filmer's *Patriarcha*, John Locke had characterised his adversary's model of *patria potestas* in a manner that is suggestive of a repeated event in *Tristram Shandy*: castration. Filmer's concept of absolute sovereignty, he states, is that

> whereby a Father or a Prince hath an Absolute, Arbitrary, Unlimited, and Unlimitable Power, over the Lives, Liberties, and Estates of his Children and Subjects; so that he may take or alienate their Estates, sell, castrate, or use their Persons as he pleases.[42]

Sterne's novel pushes this account to its literal limits. Walter Shandy's control over the body of his expectant wife is informed by Sterne's reading in the new technology of obstetrics: in particular, the theories of John Burton, York surgeon and man-midwife, upon whom the 'squat, uncourtly figure' (*TS* 2.9.121) of Dr Slop is based. Burton was notorious as a Tory partisan – hence Sterne's (locally controversial) depiction of his 'Papist' (and, in the cockpit of York politics, intimated Jacobite) allegiances. Walter's attempt to determine the birth through the offices of this man-midwife draws on Burton's argument that only the male 'scientific operators' could guarantee the preservation of heirs to the families of the gentry, thus avoiding the 'blunders of the sisterhood'. Yet, as Arthur Cash describes, common opinion feared both the lecherous design of these gynaecological 'experts' – a point acknowledged by uncle Toby with his observation that 'Mayhap his sister might not care to let such a Dr Slop come so near her \*\*\*\*'(*TS* 2.6.116) – and their grisly scientific methods. The instruments that Dr Slop carries in his green baize bag struck terror into the hearts of expectant mothers, for whom the man-midwife appeared more like an adversary. As one woman wrote of the obstetrical enthusiasms of the followers of William Smellie, Burton's rival in the development of the forceps delivery, lampooned in *Tristram Shandy* as 'Adrianus Smelvgot':

> That multitude of disciples of Dr Smellie, trained up at the feet of his artificial doll, see the pack open in full cry: to arms! to arms! is the word; and what are those arms by which they maintain themselves, but those instruments, those weapons of death! . . . crochets, knives, scissors, spoons, pinchers, fillets, speculum matrices, all of which, and especially their forceps whether Flemish, Dutch, Irish, French or English, bare or covered, long or short, straight or crooked, windowed or not windowed, are totally useless or rather worse than good for nothing, being never but dangerous and often destructive.[43]

It is thus manly instruments of war, both obstetrical and playful – as in the affair of the sash window when the weights have been removed for the use of Toby in his military games – that bring about the double 'castration' of the Shandy heir. At the source of such violence is not, as the projections of patriarchal culture might have us believe, the uncertain physical origin, and sexual presence, of the mother, but rather the arbitrary will of the father. Castration is not simply a consequence of his attempt to control the course of nature by inflexible, rational means, though this is part of the novel's polemic against the unbending *recta via* of any form of dogma. It is a result of the father's arrogation of his son's person within particular historical constraints: a refusal to allow his heir the freedom to establish his own relation to familial tradition. As Locke had argued contractually in the *Two Treatises*:

> 'Tis true, that whatever Engagements or Promises any one has made for himself, he is under the Obligation of them, but *cannot* by any *Compact* whatsoever, bind his *Children* or Posterity. For this Son, when a Man, being altogether as free as the Father, any *act of the Father can no more give away the liberty of the Son*, than it can of any body else.[44]

Walter Shandy is thus responsible for the castration of his son to the extent that he tries to ensure his possession, in the manner of the Declaration of Right, of his 'heirs and posterities forever'. His use of Filmer's genetic theory of the nature of political right – the absolute identification of patriarchal household and paternal authority – is instrumental in this attempt. In this sense *Tristram Shandy* bears comparison with Rousseau's *Emile*, which offers the reverse scenario of an ideal paternal pedagogy that releases the son to the duties of citizenship and self-love: 'when the child is no longer feeble, when he is grown-up in mind as well as in body, does not he become the sole judge of what is necessary for his preservation? Is he not therefore his own master, independent of all men, even of his father himself? For is it not still more certain that the son loves himself, than that the father loves the son?'[45] Against the civic republicanism of the Rousseau, Sterne's is a vision of attempted paternal despotism – a despotism Tom Paine would later attack in *The Rights Of Man*[46] – revealed in its comic performance as continually doomed to fail. The authority of the father proves, as Locke put it appositely, 'a very shattered and short Power'.[47] Yet for all its comic diminution here, there is no doubt that fears of a powerful authoritarianism found their way into the cultural forms of mid-century Britain. The rise of gothic fiction at this time, with Walpole's *Castle of Otranto* in 1764, bears out such a Filmerian nightmare.[48] The Shandean child thus has an uncertain tutelage. Brought into the world by men, with a Tory partisan as a man-midwife, he is a citizen of the world whose inadvertent circumcision makes of him a Jewish cosmopolitan; finally abandoned by the failure of his father's 'government . . . of childhood', the *Tristra-paedia*, to his mother and his own self-making. How then are we to think of this resurgence of mid-century Filmerism and its attempt to bind that new-born being 'circumscribed by rights'?

## A Return to Gotham

> The minister cannot forbear, even in the *King's Speech*, insulting us with a dull repetition of the word *oeconomy*. I did not expect so soon to have seen that word again, after it had been so lately exploded, and more than once, by a most numerous audience, *hissed* off the stage of our *English* theatres. It is held in derision by the *voice of the people*, and every tongue loudly proclaims the universal contempt in which these empty professions are held by *this* nation. Let the public be informed of a single instance of *oeconomy*, except indeed in the household.[49]

The word 'oeconomy' carried archaic associations with the proper management of the domestic household, now projected onto the order of the state. As such it hooked neatly into the concerns of an expanding middle-class stratum of society, the small property owners, for whom, as Lawrence Stone describes, 'male property and status rights' and premarital female chastity remained functional as modes of exchange. In this fraction 'rigid ideas of patriarchy, extreme loyalty to the authoritarian state, and extreme sexual inhibitions tended to be the norm, among both husbands and wives.'[50] Sterne's fictional patriarch Walter Shandy was one of this number, the diarist Thomas Turner another. In his journals from the 1760s the discussion of his search for a second wife – a 'well-made woman' – is revealing. Among the qualities possessed by the fragrant Molly Hicks, his intended, are 'prudence' and the 'strictest honour'; qualities that guaranteed the sound maintenance of his affairs such that 'I can be assured in their management will be sustained no loss'.[51] Turner's account is testimony to the value placed upon domestic order. Marriage denoted the proper maintenance of accumulation, the balancing of expenditure exhaustively listed in his diary; profligacy in both sexual and economic terms, its haemorrhaging.

Yet like many independently-minded tradesmen, Turner was attracted by Wilkite calls for liberty. For John Wilkes the homology between household 'oeconomy' and the maintenance of the state was to be refused. It was one thing to acknowledge the mastery of domestic paternal order, which suggested a masculine virility, and another to accept patriarchalism at the level of the state, where it could in his view only represent an absolutist centralisation of power in the crown and Bute's ministry. In the *North Briton* he argued that the word masked the profligacy and corruption of those in power: 'We have heard of nothing but *oeconomy*, and we have seen nothing but profusion and extravagance.'[52] In the name of 'oeconomy' people would be made to pay for the cost of the war while an elite made lucrative benefits from it. As he put it in the incendiary number 45, the very autonomy of the household itself was under threat from an oeconomy that imposed the slavery of taxation and general warrants: 'private houses are now made liable to be entered and searched at pleasure'.[53] This was the moment when, in the words of the 'voice of the people', William Pitt's famous formulation, the Englishman's home might be defended as his castle.

Gothamite authority was thus pernicious in Wilkite eyes not simply because it inaugurated a renewal of Stuart patriarchalism, but because its oeconomy suggested confusion and excess rather than the self-mastery of balanced economic exchange. In Churchill's *The Times, A Poem*, published in 1764, this mismanagement is manifest:

> E're a great Nation, not less just than free,
> Was made a beggar by Oeconomy;
> E're rugged Honesty was out of vogue,
> E're Fashion stamp'd her sanction on the rogue,

Time was, that Men had Conscience, that they made
Scruples to Owe, what never could be paid.

. . .

Our Times, more polish'd, wear a diff'rent face;
Debts are an Honour; Payment a disgrace.
Men of weak Minds, high-plac'd on Folly's list,
May gravely tell us Trade cannot subsist,
Nor all those Thousands who're in Trade employ'd,
If faith 'twixt Man and Man is once destroy'd.
Why—be it so—We in that point accord,
But what is Trade, and Tradesmen to a Lord.[54]

Oeconomy has not only beggared the nation, but has also destroyed the social bond that allows trade to function, shattering the reciprocal exchange of debt and return – credit – properly monitored by 'conscience'. Moral 'scruples' are absent, in their place the luxurious effects of what was often termed 'the female oeconomy'[55] ('fashion', 'polish') and patrician class disdain. The peace brokered by Bute's ministry, attacked in number 45, was seen by many to betray a wartime exchange that was by no means abstract in nature. Lives had been sacrificed, and to what ends? As one satirical print, 'The Evacuations. Or an Emetic for Old England's Glorys' put it:

Here's a PEACE of the Puffmaster's wisdom – a Bubble
An empty exchange, for Men, Money and Trouble
Aloft the Dutch Boor and the French Ape are grinning
They laugh at our Losses and what they are winning.[56]

Churchill's poem *The Times*, like other Wilkite satirical texts, reads the failure of Gothamite authority and its political form – the relation ''twixt Man and Man' – in sodomitical terms. '*Woman* is out of date, a thing thrown by/ As having lost its Use', Churchill writes, 'kept for nothing but the breed; For pleasure we must have a GANYMEDE'. Homosocial friend-ship, the classical envisioning of political alliance, is rendered material, part of a realm of strategy in which misogyny is also a sign of a deeper design: 'beastly joy'.[57]

The figure of the sodomite was in Jonathan Dollimore's words 'the point of entry into civilisation . . . for the unnatural, the aberrant, the wilderness of disorder which beleaguered all civilisation; a disorder in part, but rarely only ever, sexual'.[58] Cameron McFarlane has usefully discussed the complex figuration of sodomy in the seventeeth and first half of the eighteenth centuries, and its linking with a range of diverse disorders that were seen 'to penetrate the social body of England': from the invasive nature of foreign luxury and its effeminate consequences to sometimes scatological (anal) visions of an unproductive (non-procreative) economy and consequent depopulation.[59] The cultural lexicon of sodomy he describes is particularly evident during the Seven Years' War and its aftermath, an indication perhaps not only of the fears of national degeneration (depopulation, defeats in battle, luxurious decline) but also of the excessive financial wealth that began to pour in to 'Nabob-land' following Clive's victories.[60] In 1757, when the outcome of the war was seriously in doubt, a tract entitled *THE TEN PLAGUES OF ENGLAND, Of Worse Consequences than those of EGYPT*, picks up on the themes of Brown's *Estimate*, listing the 'unnatural Appetites' of Noblemen and their 'He-minions' under the heading 'Effeminacy' alongside nine other 'CRIMES or FOIBLES . . . far more injurious to a NATION than bodily PLAGUES'. The first of these is England's failure to be a 'World in itself': the love for 'Exotics' encouraged by foreign trade. By the tenth heading, the 'Well-wisher to GREAT-BRITAIN' has placed sodomy in the full range of forms of excess amongst the rich and the poor, from the luxury and waste of great families to lower class envy and conspicuous consumption, from the rise of religious enthusiasm ('Field Preachers and Methodists) to gamblers whose 'Hearts are insensible of Martial Glory'.[61]

The language of sodomy circulating in discussions of oeconomy was at once a sign of the mass of material desires released in commercial society and their regulation. There was a direct relation between the Wilkite attack on Stuart oeconomy and the sexualised rhetoric of its satire. In late 1763 the House of Commons ordered Wilkes's offending *North Briton 45* to be burnt by the Common Hangman at the Royal Exchange, even as his *An Essay on Woman* was being denounced in the Lords.[62] *An Essay on Woman* scandalously rewrites Warburton's edition of Pope's '*general Map of MAN*', which had been addressed to Bolinbroke, the author of the *Patriot King*, and thus was of particular resonance in the early 1760s. Wilkes's text invokes a libertine priapism that recalls Rochester's seventeenth-century satire, substituting the philosophical pleasures of masculine friendship, and the universal authority it connotes, with a rampant phallic adventurism that sees (unlike Rochester) 'His Pego measur'd to the Female Case,/ Betwixt a Woman's Thighs his proper Place'. The anticipation of the 'latent' territories of women's bodies picks up on the language of imperial exploration:

> But of their Cunts, their Bearings and the Ties,
> The nice Connections, strong Dependencies,

The Latitude and Longitude of each,
Hast thou gone thro', or can thy Pego reach?
Was that great Ocean, that unbounded Sea,
Where Pricks like Whales may sport, fathom'd by Thee? [63]

The Essay was deemed blasphemous because it transfers a vision of providential order – 'Whatever IS, is RIGHT' [64] – to the condoning of such adventurism. The divinely-ordained progress of imperial expansion finds its porno expression. Those in positions of power have blocked the 'proper' course of such penetrative 'sport', not least, one surmises, through the brokering of the peace. The title page of the Essay suggests a wider patrician degeneracy in the colonies. Its engraved phallus carries a Latin inscription: 'From the original frequently in the crutch of the Most Reverend George Stone, Primate of Ireland, more frequently in the anus of the intrepid hero, George Sackville'. It was this, and the advertisement that continued the sodomitical theme, in particular, which caused a furore in the Lords.

What was at stake in such sexual political imagining? Clearly Wilkite texts share a great deal with the popular political caricature and ballads of the time, mining a pornographic seam within a long established satirical tradition. Figures of authority are positioned in a grotesque and perverse realm of disorder, counterposed with a 'natural' economy which is generative in sexual, economic and political terms: procreative, marked by proper exchange and the flow of masculine energies. However, the language of sodomy works this positioning in paradoxical ways, as can be seen in one satirical defence of Wilkes's *Essay*, also called *An Essay on Woman*, in 1763. Addressing the 'Fair Sex', the writer constructs Wilkes in a penetrative metaphor as 'among the foremost of your heroes militant, ever alert to push intrepidly forwards, and make himself absolute master of the covered way'.[65] In the poem women furiously defend their hero against the sexual degeneracy of the present, 'some knaves we know/ Who worship A, and startle at a C'. The Gothamite 'senators' who condemn him are decried: 'Old bearded babes, male prudes in solemn robes; Blush, blush for shame, leave procreants alone'. Yet in a sodomitical transference the 'bearded babes' become more than the object of verbal denunciation. They suddenly experience sexual transformation, after 'An instantaneous twinge in ev'ry groin,/ Like an electric stroke in breast or arm':

While th' oafs stand anxious by the sudden cramp,
Off fall their Vis, to all gape Cons in lieu—
What shuffling, waddling, shambling in their gait,
For Bungs, for Plugs, for Spunges, all cry out,
To fill the new made void; their steps to ballast:

And be more steady in their *walk*, than *principles*.
Tho' odd the change, 'twas strict poetic justice—.[66]

The penetrative force of this satire brings about its own 'justice' with a 'wave of a wand', recalling Rochester's libertine priapism: 'where'er it pierc'd, a cunt it found or made'. If patriarchal authority is the butt of attack, catastrophically feminised, the attack is nonetheless articulated within what McFarlane has usefully called a 'rhetorical hermaphroditism',[67] in which the heterosexual terms of the sexual act remain in place, and the 'proper' political relation ''twixt Man and Man' is rendered on one level at least free of libidinal confusion, even as the satire mimics the very 'sodomitical practice' it deplores. Wielding the phallus confirms masculine power. As McFarlane argues, 'because sodomy is conceived of as a deviant or confused form of the "natural" power hierarchy of "heterosexual" relationships, it can be a particularly useful figure, enabling the critique of a specific manifestation of power while leaving the power hierarchy itself intact'.[68] Corrupted forms of power thus give way to the sovereign authority of the masculine true-born subject, who may style himself 'absolute master of the covered way' in the home, but nonetheless resist the exercise of arbitrary will beyond it.

Continuously at stake in these texts is the birth of political right. Where the Filmerian household saw paternal power alone as producing and binding that right, the Wilkite son is 'born to himself' in the words of Savage's poem. Where the patriarchal political household feared and curtailed the role of women, mere empty vessels in the transmission of authority, Wilkite misogyny recognises women's desires, if only as a reflection of its own masculine potency. And if the mid-century reversion to a notion of Stuart oeconomy saw accumulation in terms of the household and the central regulation of taxation, the Wilkite economy took another route. Its political demands for liberty and independence found one correlative in libertine imagining, celebrating the tumescent pleasures to be had from the mastery – ownership – of desire. In the words of Wilkes's *Essay*: 'Spend when we must, but keep it while we can'. What such an economy of desire might mean is the subject that now concerns us.

## Other genealogies

The most hated sort of trade, and with the greatest reason, is usury, which makes a gain out of money itself, and not from the purposes it was meant to serve. For money was intended to be used in exchange, but not to increase at interest. And the term interest, which means the birth of money from money [*tokos*: born, engendered], is applied to the breeding of money because the offspring [*ta tiktomena*] resembles the parent. That is why of all modes of getting wealth this is the most unnatural.[69]

It was the credit economy that underpinned the British successes in the Seven Years' War, providing in the words of Immanuel Kant, 'a war chest exceeding the treasure of all nations taken together'.[70] Yet the words above from Aristotle's *Politics* capture something of the unease that accompanied its 'breeding' in the mid-eighteenth century, an 'unnatural' replication that threatened to undo the reciprocity of exchange. It was a fear also expressed in terms of the general sodomitical repertoire. Insatiable and compulsive, the generation of money from interest did not pass through the circuits that would socialise it. Moreover it suggested a degenerate weakness through which the son (to recall the Savage poem[71]) might endlessly transmit the father's face, and more shockingly, begin to engender it.[72]

The paternalist certainties of political culture were under pressure not only because of a resistance to the violence it took to keep them in place, but because of the need to respond to the new genealogies of this 'cosmopolitan–imperial regime',[73] the flows of variable capital. Those associated with John Wilkes were differently implicated in this process. The merchants of the slave-trading cities of London, Bristol and Liverpool had been party to the progress of the war, advising Pitt in the light of their interests in the East and West Indies, America and Africa, and resisted any restrictions on trade. Following Pitt's demise, many supported Wilkes's opposition to the peace, to the oligarchs, and to taxation. Numerous independent freemen looked to him to represent their grievances, petitioning in the name of the bill of rights printed in full in the newspapers. The skilled workers who rioted vociferously in the 1760s for better wages, lower food prices, and against foreign competition were also linked to his banner, though the 'sovereign choice' he advocated would not have been extended by Wilkes himself to many of them. If trade could be seen as a virtuous system, coextensive with a manly patriotism, the credit system and conspicuous consumption it released was seen by many as a moral abomination, an 'illegitimate Waste of Time, Honour, Wealth, and Labour'[74] in the words of John Brown's *Estimate*. Yet in the ideological conflict of the 1760s it was a view articulated from a number of positions. It was used to signal a dangerous irruption of acquisitive desire among the lower orders of society, threatening the 'inequality of goods' that in Adam Smith's view laws and governments needed to preserve, if they were to avoid the 'open violence' of equality that would express itself on the streets.[75] It was also used by both conservatives and radicals to attack the 'combinations of the rich', whose exhibition of luxurious wealth was often spectacular. 'But what is Trade, and Tradesmen to a Lord?'[76] If Wilkite thought found itself in the latter camp, it nonetheless had certain sympathies with the former's lawful defence of property, carefully distinguishing the rights of the 'people' from the presence of the motley crew, the 'mob'.

The discursive tropes circulating around the question of luxury and the credit system were potent indicators of the contradictions in mid-century imperial society. Some saw them as an 'imaginary evil'. As a Scot, Robert Wallace, argued with Brown in mind, 'it is ridiculous to be perpetually extolling trade and manufactures, while we are constantly railing at what it evidently connected with them, or necessary to procure them'.[77] Wallace understood luxurious accumulation and consumption, like Marx, as a moment of production. In the figure of his natural philosopher, Walter Shandy, Sterne argues it both ways: the Shandy patriarch lamenting (with an undoubted allusion to Brown) 'that the very foundations of our excellent constitution in church and state, were so sapped as *estimators* had reported' (*TS* 2.19.171; my italics) and nonetheless that 'it is the consumption of our products, as well as the manufactures of them, which gives bread to the hungry, circulates trade,—brings in money, and supports the value of our lands' (*TS* 2.14.137). For Brown, however, there was a distinction to be made. If the dominant 'spirit of commerce' had at least produced, he argued, invoking Mandeville, a form of 'regulated selfishness' that kept the bounds of property in place, the money economy seemed to refuse such regulation: 'The Passion for Money, being founded, not in Sense, but Imagination, admits of no satiety: like those which are called the natural Passions.'[78]

What might it mean to think of the War, underpinned by its 'main Engine', money, in such passional terms, as founded on the imagination? The question is not so far-fetched. In one of the many tracts giving advice on how to cope with the rapidly fluctuating financial markets of the period, Thomas Mortimer, pseudonymously known as 'Philanthropos', traced his own mythic genealogy of the present in characteristically florid terms: a story of the coming together of the 'fair Christian maid, of unsullied reputation, chaste as a vestal' known as 'Public Credit' with an amorous Jewish lover who aimed 'to bring her to the highest pinnacle of worldly power'. The narrator-child of this union is an 'Israel jobber', one with a philanthropic mission to navigate the dangers of the credit system for the benefit of all. Worldliness plus ethics: the ideological *sine qua non* of British imperial expansion. Beyond the popular and harmless purchase of lottery tickets, some amateur entrepreneurs turned 'coffee-house politicians' were, Mortimer reported, staking life and property on the merest of rumours and newspaper intelligence, prey to the insecurity that was the lifeblood of the trade of stockjobbing. The purpose of *Every Man His Own Broker* was to show how a man might learn to 'transact his own business' in such a speculative climate, in which even the outcome of military campaigns was said to be manipulated by generals with an eye to the fortunes of stocks and shares.[79]

Mortimer added his own pennyworth to the familiar discourse about the corruption of the system by the credit economy. Just as the liberty of the press had resulted in the decline of public taste, such that the most scurrilous and popular of works now issued from the pens of divines ('Vid T___m S___y, in 4 vols. said to be wrote by one who wears this sacred habit'), so the liberty of the financial markets and their transparency to foreign speculators had produced the 'diabolical art of STOCKJOBBING'.[80] Stockjobbers were deemed particularly iniquitous because they traded in stock without possessing it, controlling its value by 'raising rumours and spreading fictitious stories', as *The Imperial Magazine* put it in 1760.[81] Narrowly avoiding the digressive (and thus inflationary) tendency that he ascribes to the 'reigning Shandean taste', Mortimer offered his reader a way through the financial minefield to the 'profitable security' of India bonds.[82]

If Mortimer's tract is concerned with the consequences of financial freedom, it does not see it in terms of luxurious excess. His purpose is not to question the commercial credit system but to find a more rational means of navigating it. Four years after Brown's *Estimate* the situation had changed. The third edition of *Every Man His Own Broker* in 1761 anticipated security under a new king whose 'truly British brow' would shortly be crowned by the 'goddess of victory'.[83] Mortimer is convinced of the necessity of the credit economy – and the public debt – to the well-being of the nation:

> Surely the breast of every Englishman must glow with rapture and admiration, when he considers, that while the unhappy subjects of the other powers engaged in the present war are quite exhausted, and thousands of them totally ruined, by the demands made on them by their arbitrary monarchs, he is voluntarily contributing to wards defraying the public expenses of his country, in a manner that is so far from being a burden to him, that on the contrary, he is serving himself at the same time, by lending his money on parliamentary security.[84]

The operation of the public debt entailed a certain minimising of risk, since, as Marx was later to point out, 'as with the stroke of an enchanter's wand . . . [it] endows unproductive money with the power of creation and thus turns it into capital, without forcing itself to expose itself to the troubles and risks inseparable from its employment in industry or even in usury.' In investing his money in public bonds Mortimer's Englishman was in fact giving nothing away, since such securities continued to behave like hard cash in his pocket.[85] Despite Mortimer's concern about openness to foreign investors – a quarter of the national debt being underwritten by the Dutch at this time – his statement in fact marks a turning point in the financial power of the British imperial state, which was no longer dependent in those terms. The global successes of the Seven Years' War, in particular the booty from Bengal, meant that London, not Amsterdam, became in the 1760s the finance capital of the world.

Stockjobbers were of concern for Mortimer not because they represented the corruption of the system as such, but because as Walter Shandy might have said, they maximised the presence of 'error' within it. War brought uncertainty, and that palpable sense of risk was translated into financial trade. Any spark of rumour could serve a speculative purpose. 'Secret Intelligences, Important Events, Bloody Engagements, Flat-Bottomed Boats, Spanish Fleets joining with French, Difference with Foreign Powers, Death of a certain great Personage, a Principal in the present War, Breaking out of the Plague, Alterations in the Ministry, and that infinity of et ceteras' were the miscellaneous materials of the stockjobbing art, through which the 'bulls and bears', and their profits, would stand or fall.[86] If the credit system relied on trust and the checks and balances of public opinion, stockjobbing disturbingly showed the susceptibility of opinion to speculative inflation, to the inroads of *fiction*, a fact which exercised many commentators of the period. In Adam Smith's view, the potential of banking to enter into imaginative 'projections' 'endangered the security of the whole society'.[87] For Charles Davenant, 'of all beings that have existence only in the minds of men, nothing is more fantastical and nice than Credit; it is never to be forced; it hangs upon *opinion*; it depends upon our passions of hope and fear'.[88] Rather than securing trust, opinion threatened to render it radically unstable. As the *Imperial Magazine* put it, 'there is nothing so fallible as public opinion; which is often the instrument of power, and always the slave of fashion'.[89] Mortimer evidently saw increased knowledge on the part of investors as one way of limiting risk; the system could be judiciously used, and it was *productive*, as the prosecuting of the most successful imperial war of the century suggested. But there was nonetheless something dangerously aleatory about such excessive speculation, which appeared to undo the circuit of exchange that was second nature to eighteenth-century mercantile capitalism (and the many possessive individuals constituted by it). In exposing the very bonds of commercial society to unacceptable levels of risk, stockjobbing was, potentially, a sign of a wider crisis of belief: the opening of that society to the imaginary, 'the enchanter's wand' of capital. What did it mean if financial *realpolitik* extended not just to the sponsoring, but even to the *outcome*, of wartime events?[90] What if all social transactions in the mid-century polity were subject to similar manipulations of power and interest, and founded in 'fictitious stories'?

This was the suspicion of the Wilkite moment, discovering in the perspicuous terms of statecraft – 'candour', 'universal satisfaction and harmony' –

dark forms of brokerage. If the language of Stuart absolutism rendered this material revelation familiar to English ears, it also drew on a philosophical critique of hypocrisy that had its roots in classical culture, encapsulated in Horace's phrase *decimur specie recti* : 'we are deceived by the appearance of right'.[91] In *Tristram Shandy* it is articulated through the figure of Yorick, Sterne's alter ego, who true to his Shakespearean allusiveness knows the state to be corrupt. The counterfeit 'gravity' of those in authority encourages the investment of belief: 'more honest, well-meaning people were bubbled out of their goods and money by it in one twelve-month, than by pocket-picking and shop-lifting in seven . . . the very essence of gravity was design, and consequently deceit;—'twas a taught trick to gain credit of the world for more sense and knowledge than a man was worth' (*TS* 1.11.28). Yorick's fatal misunderstanding is in not realising that he too is implicated in the exchange of a credit economy, even as he satirically exposes the strategies of those who operate it to their own ends. The jester must repay the jestée. Caught up in a war of interests, Yorick is made to feel 'the full extent of [his] obligations' (*TS* 1.12.30) and suffers the mortal consequences. This sense of unease is inherited by the eponymous narrator:

> the planet is well enough, provided a man could be born in it to a great title or to a great estate; or could any how contrive to be called up to publick charges, and employments of dignity or power;—but that is not my case;—and therefore every man will speak of the fair as his own market has gone in it;—for which cause I affirm it over again to be one of the vilest worlds that ever was made. (*TS* 1.5.8)

It is interesting to reflect on the nature of 'opinion' emerging in this statement. 'If speculative man was not to be the slave of his passions', argues J. G. A. Pocock, 'he had to moderate these by converting them into opinion, experience and interest, and into a system of social ties which these things reinforced; and the reification followed by exchange of the objects on which his passions focussed was an excellent means of socialising them'.[92] These are the ties ''twixt Man and Man' all agreed were essential to commercial and social health.

Yet opinion is fully revealed in the 1760s as a zone of jeopardy: subject to linguistic ambiguities, the play of desires, and the strategies of the powerful. The 'social ties' invoked by Sterne's novel are shown to rest precariously on habit and desire, borrowing less from a Lockean formulation of the social compact (with its rational concern for the expunging of error) than a Humean acknowledgement of the sensual foundation of reason in the imagination. Opinions thus 'disturb', for while they can be reified and possessed 'as a man in the state of nature picks up an apple.—It becomes his own' (*TS* 3.34.262–3),[93] they are also unreliable, and subject to the most passionate forms of *libido sciendi*. Rather than acting as an honest public broker for private interests, opinion is itself radically privatised and reified; subject to idiosyncratic desires and hobbyhorsical appropriations. Sterne's satirical exposure of the ways in which people are captured by the logics and appetites of opinion is a comic index of the instrumental rationality at work in mid-century culture. It is consequently haunted by a symbolic violence, the potential for repression, sometimes fatal in its effects: 'so long as a man rides his HOBBY-HORSE peaceably and quietly along the King's highway, and neither *compels* you or me to get up behind him . . .' (*TS* 1.7.12; my itals). If 'force' is 'always on the side of the governed', in Hume's words, such rationality is born out of the fear of what this might mean.

Opinion, understood as the right of 'every man to speak of the fair as his own market has gone in it', takes on new significance in such a climate. The Shandean narrator's determination to speak 'my case' and refusal of class deference hints at the contractualism that renews itself in the 1760s: a radical Lockeanism that reiterated the power of the governed to confer political 'trust'. Opinion can legitimate the governors, but it can also be taken away. Such a declaration of dissent presages the pressing of broader political claims: the imagining of a new transparent realm in which the workings of authority might be held to account, and the 'reciprocal commerce' of society mediated and reformed by new forms of association, the choices of sovereign individuals. Opinion in this sense expressed the critical hope of Wilkite politicking, connecting to issues of press freedom and the right to report parliamentary debates, to the challenging of legal warrants, to the strengthening and extension of political representation rather than its purchasing. Yet the reality of these demands, and the forms of radical organising that grew from them, were not fully apparent until beyond the close of the decade. This critical hope seemed to many in the early 1760s a marvellous fiction. The problem, Sterne's novel suggests in an appropriately Mandevillian metaphor for private interests, is that motives cannot be read as if observing through the transparent window of a 'dioptrical bee-hive' (*TS* 1.23.82). 'If we would come to the specifick characters of [men's minds], we must go some other way to work' (*TS* 1.23.83). 'Shandean taste', in Mortimer's phrase, is thus a sign of the material effects of reification, in which the 'opinion, experience and interest' exchanged in the maintenance of public virtue collapse back into the opacity and unease of fetishism, a mystery of social relations. Socialisation *itself* becomes an object of fascinated scrutiny, whereby 'we must go some other way to work'.

## Pricksongs in Gotham

For some the Wilkite critique, for all its political pertinence, was under-mined by the licentiousness that accompanied it. If patriarchal authority could be shown to be a cover for financial 'profligacy', so its radical oppo-sition was animated by libertarian energies, and sexual excess. As Kathleen Wilson notes, 'the men who split off from the SSBR (Society of Supporters of the Bill of Rights) to form the Constitutional Society in 1771 cited the banishment of "regularity, decency and order" from the Wilkite camp as a main cause; and some middle-class supporters of radical politics incre-asingly had recourse to an ideal of conjugal domesticity that proscribed such discrepancies between public and private virtue'.[94] The status of this ideal equation is the subject of Chapter 4. Yet it might be argued that the obscenity of Wilkite satire was a precise, if perverse, symptom of the deeply interested nature of the imperial present, testimony to the fact that power and commercial desire were inextricably combined and defining. The love of liberty was synonymous with the entrepreneurial energies of the time. Alongside the political fictions of the mid-century, whether that celebrating the perfect balance and order of the family, or the vision of a virtuous man exercising his sovereign choice, is a phallic adventurism which suggested that there was no alternative but to ride the desires of the moment, no 'outside' high ground from which to view the material exigencies of com-mercial life.

One of *Tristram Shandy*'s tales-within-tales, published in volume four in 1760, anticipates this imagining in an absurdist allegory of the war that takes priapism as its method. 'Slawkenbergius's Tale' is ostensibly taken from the life's work of a German pedant – a digest on noses, translated from the Latin. It describes the 'riot and disorder' caused by a marvellously endowed Spanish stranger, as he passes through the 'imperial city' of Strasburg (sic) on his Cervantic quest to find his lost love. The speculative rumour mill that follows generates a frenzy of epistemophilia that takes hold of every citizen, from the ecclesiastics and natural philosophers, to the doctors and logicians of the universities ('Nosarians' and 'Antinosarians') and the inn keeper's wife: it 'turned the whole stream of all discourse and wonder towards it . . . every eye in *Strasburg* languished to see it——every finger—every thumb in *Strasburg* burned to touch it' (*TS* 4.*Tale*.303–4). In anticipation of the stranger's return, the population turns out in its thou-sands. 'What a carnival did his nose make of it' (*TS* 4.*Tale*.303): the novel's humour is in part the acknowledgement of the sensual, passional founda-tion of experience and knowledge, which forms of unmediated authority ignore at their peril.

Yet the story does not end there. Such is the pitch of agitation that the French forces are able to walk in and take a city 'garrisoned with five thousand of the best troops in all the world' (*TS* 4.*Tale*.318). History records this episode, the narrator explains, as crucial to the system of 'Universal Monarchy' developed by the French – the history of Empire – but it is only Slawkenbergius who knows the truth:

> What a fatal thing is the popular pride of a free city! cries one historian—The *Strasburgers* deemed it a diminution of their freedom to receive an imperial garrison—and so fell prey to a *French* one.
>
> The fate, says another, of the *Strasburgers*, may be a warning to all free people to save their money—They anticipated their revenues—brought themselves under taxes, exhausted their strength, and in the end became so weak a people, they had not the strength to keep their gates shut, and so the *French* pushed them open.
>
> Alas, alas! cries *Slawkenbergius*, 'twas not the French— 'twas CURIOSITY pushed them open—The *French* indeed, who are ever upon the catch, when they saw the *Strasburgers*, men, women, and children, all marched out to follow the stranger's nose—each man followed his own, and marched in.
>
> Trade and manufactures have decayed and gradually grown down ever since—but not from any cause which commercial heads have assigned; for it is owing to this only, that Noses have ever so run in their heads, that the *Strasburgers* could not follow their business.
>
> Alas! alas! cries *Slawkenbergius*, making an exclamation—it is not the first—and I fear will not be the last fortress that has been either won——or lost by NOSES. (*TS* 4.*Tale*.323–4)

The familiar euphemistic 'science' of fortification is put into play here and the joke adds up to no more than a bawdy reference to sex, one that Thomas Jefferson would later reflect on in a letter to Maria Cosway.[95] However, the story rehearses fragments of political opinion that would have been recognisable to Sterne's readers at the height of the Seven Years' War, at the moment when Spain had just entered the conflict alongside France. The sovereign state of Strasburg falls, but not because it refused to accept a foreign imperial garrison (Britain, by comparison, had allowed large numbers of Prussian troops to be billeted across the South of England and was caught up in a recurrent debate about the necessity for a standing army). Nor even because its strength had been spent in taxes and debt (the great anxiety of the late 1750s). But rather because of *curiosity*, a state of temptation and 'unbounded' desire, as a tract put it in 1736, in which the desire 'to know most Things' was directly connected to imperial accumulation, the desire for 'universal Conquest'.[96] The Strasburgers are taken in by a fascination for the exotic.[97] Their enervated condition is thus a parodic version of the crisis described by John Brown, in which the British imperial city appeared weakened by speculation, and libidinously ensnared by its ruling passions.

The fantasy at stake in Wilkite satire, linking *An Essay on Woman* to the phallicism of Sterne's novel, is control over such an economy of desire. The sexual politics of this misogynistic imagining always posits feminine territory as the very sign of consumption: whether as the curious woman reader or concupiscent widow of the Shandean world, or as in the Gothamite universe, the neglected and available universe of the 'Female Case'. Met with such insatiable desire, the masculine subject answers a God-given calling. The phallic 'enchanter's wand' conjures up visions of impossible plenitude, acted out in onanistic encounters,[98] or in pornographic money-shots which suggest new trajectories of expenditure: 'spend when we must, but keep it while we can', 'oft when we spend we propagate unknown', 'and now a Hymen burst, and now a World'. There is a presumed procreative reciprocity, here, but the emphasis is on masculine force and pleasure, and the boundaries of such an economy are unclear, the consequences unintended. This is the very theatre of imperial commerce, a Smithian pornography, if such a thing can be imagined. For Sterne there is always a stopping short, a note of failure, ultimately handing over the negotiation of such materiality to conscience and medicinal laughter. In Wilkite satire the language of sodomy provides one means of projecting unrecuperable forms of material excess onto others, while retaining its own libidinous forms of exchange. Yet at the libertarian heart of this celebration of the virility of the true-born subject is another unrecuperable vision, unacknowledged and yet defining; a measure of the 'force of the governed' in Hume's words, who, even for Wilkes, remained firmly outside the circuits of legitimate exchange. When the Wilkite 'volcano'[99] erupted in the 1760s, it offered a constitutive drama for the bourgeois imperial subject and thus for the mid-century state. Its (pro)creative energies nonetheless intimated on the streets the presence of other tactics of 'bastardly digression' (*TS* 8.1.655), the desires of others '*to tell their stories their own way*' (*TS* 9.25.785).

### Notes

1 The views about the inequalities of social rank expressed in the first volumes of the novel were widespread, and sometimes phrased in similar terms. As one commentator put it in the *Norfolk Gazette* in 1764, 'There is a hobby horse in the world called Nobility by Right of birth; but this nobility, that consists in sound, is an empty and chimerical grandeur.' Quoted in Wilson, *Sense of the People*, p. 231.

2 Though contemporary tracts were not averse to Cervantic parallels of the most topical kind: in one the 'people of England' are compared with 'Sancha Pancha', who loves his master (Pitt) but wishes 'his conduct were a little more reconcileable to their plain capacities'. See *A Letter to the Right Honorable The Earl of B\*\*\* on A Late Important Resignation, and its Probable Consequences* (London: J. Coote, 1761), p. 56.

3 Churchill, *Gotham*, p. 6.

4 And in characteristically Wilkite and nationalist terms, specifically England, rather than a Britain that had incorporated Scotland.

5 Granville Sharp had first taken on English slaveholders in the courts in 1765. In his famous test case defence of James Somerset in 1772, a slave whose master wanted to compel him to return to Boston, Sharp had argued that slavery was contrary to the constitutional liberty of England. Lord Mansfield, himself a slaveholder, had judged that he could not be deported because 'So high an act of dominion must derive its authority, if any such it has, from the law of the Kingdom where executed.' It was a conclusion that, as Robin Blackburn states, 'gravely weakened the position of all slaveholders in England: the Scottish courts went somewhat further in 1778 ruling that no slaveholder rights could be upheld in that country'. See Robin Blackburn, *The Overthrow of Colonial Slavery 1776–1848* (London: Verso, 1988), p. 100. I discuss aspects of Sharp's anti-slavery arguments and his relation to Phillis Wheatley in Chapter 4.

6 George Rudé, *Wilkes and Liberty. A Social Study of 1763 to 1774* (Oxford: Clarendon Press, 1962), pp. 26–7.

7 *An Essay on Woman. A Poem*, By J. W. Senator (London: Printed for the Editor, 1763), p. 21. This is one of several texts using the name of John Wilkes's notorious *Essay on Woman* ascribed to the author in circulation in the 1760s, in this case attacking those who had decried the *Essay* in the Lords.

8 *Hamlet*, I.v.77. The comic allusiveness to *Hamlet* in the early pages of *Tristram Shandy*, to a 'scurvy, disastrous world' somehow out of joint, is a topical staging of mild dissent at the height of the war that assumes serious political import in the following decade. Yorick is, explicitly, a critical figure, as well as a literary joke. The reference to 'unpension'd' is certainly directed at Pitt, who had controversially accepted a pension as Lord Chatham (which Sterne defends in the dedication to Volume IX of *Tristram Shandy*). The phrase 'Alas Poor Yorick!' may also have been prompted by the anonymous war-time 'life' of the soldier Ephraim Tristram Bates, as I discussed in Chapter 2.

9 Wilson, *The Sense of the People*, pp. 213, 214.

10 See Charles Churchill, *The Prophecy Of Famine. A Scots Pastoral* (London: for the Author, 1763), which reads the Peace of Paris in terms of a Scottish plot. The line about 'nature's bastards, reaping for our share/What was rejected by the lawful heir', is on p. 21 of the fourth edition.

11 Blackstone, *Commentaries*, IV, 165, 170, 165. Thus in Edward Long's anonymous narrative *The Anti-Gallican; Or, the History and Adventures of Harry Cobham Esquire* (London: T. Lownds, 1757) the begging 'Sailor' turns out to be a highwayman.

12 I have in mind Judith Butler's formulation of the 'constitutive outside', in which social subjectivity is seen to constitute itself through exclusionary tactics whereby 'unlivable' and 'uninhabitable' zones of social life are densely populated by those 'who do not enjoy the status of subject', and yet serve to reinforce 'the defining limits of the subject's domain'. Social subjectivity is thus marked by a founding repudiation, a 'constitutive outside', through which it will 'circumscribe its own claim to autonomy and to life' in the very invocation of those who are deemed to possess neither. See Judith Butler, *Bodies That Matter: On the Discursive Limits of 'Sex'* (New York and London: Routledge, 1993), p. 3. This exclusionary self-constitution, shaped by the administrations of mid-century sentimentalism and its negotation of slavery in particular, is the matter of Chapter 4.

13 Rudé, *Wilkes and Liberty*, p. 136.

14 Richard Savage, *The Bastard: A Poem* (Dublin: S. Harding, 1728), p. 1, ll.11–18.

15 Ibid. p. 1, l.6.

16 Rudé, *Wilkes and Liberty*, p. 30.

17 John Wilkes, *North Briton* 19 (9 October 1762), in *The North Briton Revised and Corrected by the Author* (Dublin: John Mitchell, 1764), I, 105.

18 'Though he became martyr of the best cause, there was nothing in his principles or morals that led him to care under what government he lived'. The words are Horace Walpole's. See Adrian Hamiliton, *The Infamous Essay on Woman or John Wilkes Seated Between Vice and Virtue* (London: André Deutsch, 1972), p. 10.

19 Anon., *England's Constitutional Test for the Year 1763* (London: J. Morgan, 1763), p. 23.

20 Blackstone, *Commentaries*, IV, 162.

21 See *Spectator* 130 (Monday July 30, 1711), in Donald F. Bond (ed.), *The Spectator* (Oxford: Clarendon Press, 1965), II, pp. 17–18.

22 Quoted in Gilmore, *Riot, Risings and Revolution*, p. 79.

23 Anon., '*The* BIRTH of SHANDY; *A new* BALLAD', *The Imperial Magazine, or, Complete Monthly Intelligencer*, October 1760, 551.

24 'No one therefore who lives in society, can be said to live to himself,—he lives to his GOD,—to his king, and his country.——He lives to his family, to his friends, to all under his trust, and in a word, he lives to the whole race of mankind' (*Sermons*, 7.68).

25 Samuel Johnson, *An Account of the Life of Mr. Richard Savage, Son of the Earl Rivers* (London: J. Roberts, 1744), p. 179.

26 Swift, *Gulliver's Travels*, p. 185; on the fiction of noble birth see Michael McKeon, *The Origins of the English Novel 1600–1740* (Baltimore and London: Johns Hopkins University Press, 1987), pp. 343–4.

27 See the first issue of *The Spectator* (Thursday, 1 March 1711), where the paternal inheritance of a 'Hereditary Estate' has been passed down 'from Father to Son whole and entire, without the Loss or Acquisition of a single Field or Meadow, during the space of six hundred Years'. I, 1–2.

28 Blackstone, *Commentaries*, I, 15, 430.

29 'NOTHING so true as what you once let fall,/ "Most Women have no Characters at all" '. Alexander Pope, 'Epistle to a Lady', in F. W. Bateson (ed.), *The Twickenham Edition of the Poems of Alexander Pope*, 2nd edn (London and New York: Methuen and Yale University Press 1961), IIIiii, 46, ll.1–2. These lines were used for the definition of 'character' in Johnson's *Dictionary*.

30 Anon., *Characterism, or the Modern Age display'd: being an Attempt to expose the Pretended Virtues of both Sexes; with a Poetical Essay on each Character* (London: printed for the Author, 1750), p. 13. For a discussion of this anonymous work in relation to Henry Fielding's 'An Essay on the Knowledge and Characters of Men', see Felicity A. Nussbaum, *The Autobiographical Subject: Gender and Ideology in Eighteenth-Century England* (Baltimore and London: Johns Hopkins UP, 1989), pp. 150–2.

31 Jean-Jacques Rousseau, *Émile*, trans. Barbara Foxley (London: J. M. Dent, 1993), p. 386.

32 [Richard and Elizabeth Griffith], *A Series of Genuine Letters Between Henry and Frances*, 6 vols (London: J. Bew, 1786), III, 16. My thanks to Jumana Al Dahnak, 'Women's Conceptualisation of Selfhood in Relation to Marriage: A Study of Selected Fiction by Women Writers of the 1770s' (Unpublished PhD Thesis, University of Leeds, 2002), for bringing this to my notice.

33 Henry St. John Bolinbroke's *The Idea of a Patriot King* had been published in 1749 and written ten years earlier. Its particular brand of Tory patriarchalism, and vision of a virtuous monarch rising above factional politics to unify the family of the nation, was said to have been influential in shaping the new king's political creed.

34 'Cato', *Thoughts on . . .*, p. 47.

35 Jenyns, *Free Inquiry*, p. 30.

36 'Philogamus', *The Present State of Matrimony: or, the Real Causes of Conjugal Infidelity and Unhappy Marriages* (1739), in Vivien Jones (ed.), *Women in the Eighteenth Century: Constructions of Femininity* (London and New York: Routledge, 1990), p. 78.

37 Sir Robert Filmer, *Patriarcha and Other Political Works* (ed.), Peter Laslett (Oxford: Blackwell, 1979), p. 71.

38 Carole Pateman, *The Sexual Contract* (Cambridge: Polity Press, 1988), pp. 87–8.

39 'That I should live to see the unhappy day, when sober and well-regulated clocks are treated as the alarms of lust'. Anon., *The Clockmakers' Outcry Against the*

*Author of the Life and Opinions of* Tristram Shandy. *Dedicated to the Most Humble of Christian Prelates* (London: J. Burd, 1760), p. 43.

40 Gordon J. Schochet, *Patriarchalism in Political Thought. The Authoritarian Family and Political Speculation and Attitudes, Especially in Seventeenth-Century England* (Oxford: Blackwell, 1975), p. 79.

41 James Daly, *Sir Robert Filmer and English Political Thought* (Toronto and Buffalo: University of Toronto Press, 1979), pp. 160, 165.

42 John Locke, *Two Treatises of Government*, ed. Peter Laslett, 2nd edn (Cambridge: Cambridge University Press, 1967), p. 148.

43 Quoted in Arthur H. Cash, 'The Birth of Tristram Shandy', in Paul-Gabriel Boucé (ed.), *Sexuality in Eighteenth-Century Britain* (Manchester: Manchester University Press, 1982), p. 208.

44 Locke, *Two Treatises*, p. 346.

45 Rousseau, *Émile*, p. 507. Rousseau had attacked the 'detestable system' of Filmerian patriarchalism, and with it the equation of state and family, in his *Discours sur l'inégalité* in 1755.

46 Paine contrasts the despotic 'family tyranny and injustice' of the aristocracy and 'hereditary powers' of the monarchy with a notion of distributive justice. 'Every age and generation must be free to act for itself, *in all cases*, as the ages and generations which preceded it'. Thomas Paine, *The Rights of Man* (Harmondsworth: Penguin, 1985), pp. 83, 122, 41.

47 Locke, *Two Treatises*, p. 323.

48 If gothic fiction deals with absolutist forms of paternal power, it might be said to emerge with specific social content in the 1760s for all its projection into the catholic and medieval past. Markman Ellis suggests Walpole's *Castle of Otranto* picks up on the perceived despotism of the government during the Wilkes affair, Walpole having been caught up in scandal because of his support for Wilkes in Parliament. He notes also that no contemporary readers appear to have understood the novel as a 'serious satire . . . attacking the administration's unwarranted and despotic attempts to silence its enemies'. See Markman Ellis, *The History of Gothic Fiction* (Edinburgh: Edinburgh University Press, 2000), pp. 39–42.

49 Wilkes, *North Briton* 45 (23 April 1763), II, 265.

50 Stone, *The Family, Sex and Marriage*, p. 402.

51 Turner, *Diary*, 14 April 1765, p. 319.

52 Wilkes, *North Briton* 42 (19 March 1763), II, 243.

53 Wilkes, *North Briton* 45 (23 April 1763), II, 266.

54 Charles Churchill, *The Times, A Poem* (London: for the Author, 1764), pp. 6–7.

55 See for example 'The World as it Goes', in *The Imperial Magazine, Or Complete Monthly Intelligencer* (December, 1760), 699: 'The whole business of female oeconomy, at present, is to ask, What is the fashion now? And then directly to repair to new regulate the dress of the succeeding day. This sets the whole kingdom in an uproar.'

56 See Hamilton, p. 77. Hamilton notes that of 500 satirical prints in The British Museum that deal with Bute, 400 are violently opposed, and around 6 supporting.

57 Churchill, *The Times*, pp. 19, 20.

58 Jonathan Dollimore, *Sexual Dissidence: Augustine to Wilde, Freud to Foucault* (Oxford: Clarendon Press, 1991), p. 239.

59 Cameron McFarlane, *The Sodomite in Fiction and Satire 1660–1750* (New York: Columbia University Press, 1997), p. 33.

60 The term 'Nabob-land' is Horace Walpole's. Clive's excessive wealth – about £30 million in today's terms – was seen as responsible for his moral degeneration. In later life rumours would ruin his reputation, accusing him of consorting with prostitutes, producing numerous children out of wedlock, and participating in homosexual orgies: all part of the 'sodomitical' repertoire.

61 Anon., THE TEN PLAGUES OF GREAT BRITAIN of Worse Consequences than those of EGYPT, DESCRIBED Under the following HEADS: I. Disregard to our own Productions II. Luxury and Waste in Great Families III. Effeminacy IV. Gaming V. Love of Novelty VI. Hypocrisy VII. Drunkenness VIII. Avarice and Usury IX. Pride X. Idleness. The Whole intended to show, That Whatever CRIMES or FOIBLES infect the Minds of a PEOPLE, are far more injurious to a NATION than bodily PLAGUES. By a Well-wisher to GREAT-BRITAIN (London: R. Withy, 1757).

62 See Rudé, p. 33. *The Essay on Woman* was attributed to Wilkes, though the bulk had, it appeared, been written by fellow member of the Hell-Fire Club, Thomas Potter, between the mid-1740s and 1750s, and finished by 1759, and the notes and additions to it added by Wilkes. The title page in particular was the object of Sandwich's attack in the Lords, linking the sexuality of George Sackville to his reputed cowardice during the war. See Kathleen Wilson's discussion of Wilkite libertarianism in her *The Island Race: Englishness, Empire and Gender in the Eighteenth Century* (London and New York: Routledge, 2003), pp. 38–9; and Anna Clark, 'The Chevalier d' Eon and Wilkes: Masculinity and Politics in the Eighteenth Century', *Eighteenth-Century Studies* 32 (1998), 19–48.

63 *An Essay on Woman*, by Pego Borewell, Esq. (London: printed for the Author, 1763), pp. 20, 16–17.

64 Pope, *Essay on Man*, p. 51, l.294.

65 *An Essay on Woman, A Poem*, by J. W. Senator, dedication.

66 Ibid. pp. 23, 25, 26.

67 McFarlane, p. 44.

68 Ibid. p. 52.

69 Aristotle, *Politics*, quoted in Éric Alliez, *Capital Times: Tales from the Critique of Time* (Minneapolis: University of Minnesota Press, 1996), p. 9.

70 Immanuel Kant, 'To Perpetual Peace. A Philosophical Sketch', in *Perpetual Peace and Other Essays*, trans. Ted Humphrey (Indianapolis and Cambridge: Hackett

Publishing Company, 1983), p. 109. As John Brown put it in his *Estimate*, 'MONEY, it is true, hath of late, more than ever, been among *us* regarded as the main *Engine of War.*' Brown, *Estimate*, p. 92.

71 Savage, *The Bastard*, p. 1., l.6.

72 As Alliez suggests, 'Thus *tokos*, interest, whose root *tek-* evokes the son being called by the name of the father, cuts itself off from the order of *phusis* and of natural reproduction to become the symbol of a monstrous filiation. If money does not engender interest but is engendered by it in some fashion, doesn't that invert the Just Relation of Generations? Isn't the child giving birth to the procreator?' Alliez, p. 9.

73 Arrighi, *The Long Twentieth Century*, p. 219.

74 Brown, p. 120.

75 Smith, *Lectures on Jurisprudence*, p. 83.

76 Churchill, *The Times*, p. 7.

77 [R. Wallace] *Characteristics of the Present Political State of Great Britain*, 2nd edn (London, 1758), pp. vi, 50. Wallace makes a case for the commercial benefits derived by Scotland in particular, noting that the English at the metropolitan centre show 'less curiosity than the Scots', in a nod to the instrumental role Scots played in the extension of imperial trade (p. 137). For a brief account of Wallace's place in the Scottish radical liberal tradition see Caroline Robbins, *The Eighteenth-Century Commonwealthman: Studies in the Transmission, Development and Circumstance of English Liberal Thought from the Restoration of Charles II until the War with the Thirteen Colonies* (Cambridge, MA: Harvard University Press, 1959), pp. 202–11.

78 Brown, *Estimate*, p. 155.

79 Philanthropos [Thomas Mortimer], *Every Man His Own Broker, Or A Guide to Exchange Alley* (London: S. Hooper, 1761), pp. xviii, 54. Henceforth first edition noted under pseudonym.

80 Ibid. p. 26.

81 *The Imperial Magazine, or, Complete Monthly Intelligencer*, August 1760, 407.

82 Philanthropos, pp. 27, 147. As the *DNB* reports, Mortimer had himself 'lost a genteel fortune' through speculation in 1756. He made quite a profit from his tracts on risk management however, not only from the much reprinted *Every Man*, but also from the engagingly entitled book *Die and Be Damned: Or, A Policy of Insurance for Every Family in Great Britain Against Methodism.*

83 Thomas Mortimer, *Every Man His Own Broker*, 3rd edn (London: S. Hooper, 1761), p. 174.

84 Philanthropos, p. 3.

85 Karl Marx, *Capital Volume One*, trans. Ben Fowkes (Harmondsworth: Penguin Books, 1976), p. 919.

86 Philanthropos, *Every Man His Own Brother*, pp. 32–3.

87  Smith, *Wealth of Nations*, I, 324. For a discussion of Smith's view of the paper money crisis in Scotland and his criticism of stockjobbers see John Dwyer, 'The Civic World of Adam Smith', in Peter Jones and Andrew S. Skinner (eds), *Adam Smith Reviewed* (Edinburgh: Edinburgh University Press, 1992), pp. 190–213.

88  Charles Davenant, *The Political and Commercial Works of that Celebrated Writer Charles D'Avenant LLD, Relating to the Trade and Revenue of England, the Plantation Trade, the East-India Trade, and African Trade, collected and revised by Sir Charles Whitworth*, 5 vols (London: printed for R. Horsfield et al. 1771), I, 151. Quoted in Brewer, *The Sinews of Power*, p. 187.

89  *The Imperial Magazine, Or, Complete Monthly Intelligencer* (February, 1760), 83.

90  In his speculation that generals were almost prepared to throw the outcome of particular battles to adjust share values, Mortimer adds to the current debates about the moral fibre of the nation's military leaders, which had emerged vociferously around the execution of Admiral Byng in 1756. But it was of course true that the outcome of events was ultimately determined by economic criteria; Pitt's endgame played off territorial gains from the French and Spanish in the Caribbean, Central America, Africa and the Mediterranean against the conquest of Canada and North American markets. See Richard Pares, *War and Trade in the West Indies 1739–1763* (London: Frank Cass & Co, 1963). Moreover, intended invasions were often publicised by Britain's opponents precisely to cause financial panics, and thus undermine the state, rather than for any designs on territory. See Brewer, *Sinews of Power*, p. 227.

91  For a pertinent discussion of the critique of hypocrisy in Rousseau's thought and Horace's dictum, which has strong parallels with and indeed influence on the debates in England, see James Swenson, *On Jean-Jacques Rousseau* (Stanford, CA: Stanford University Press, 2000), p. 67ff.

92  J. G. A. Pocock, *Virtue, Commerce and History* (Cambridge: CUP, 1985), p. 115.

93  Sterne is directly referring to a passage in Locke's *Two Treatises of Government* here.

94  Wilson, p. 221. The SSBR had been set up to defray Wilkes's costs and expenses, but became the model for later political organising. See Rudé, p. 194.

95  'I could think of nothing at Strasbourg but the promontory of noses . . . Had I written to you from thence it would have been a continuation of Sterne upon noses, & I knew that nature had not formed me for a Continuator of Sterne'. Thomas Jefferson to Maria Cosway, 24 April 1788, in *Writings*, ed. Merrill Peterson (New York: The Library of America, 1984), p. 921.

96  *A Letter on the Nature and State of Curiosity*, p. 63.

97  Another trait associated with the dangers of luxury and the parlous state of the nation in the late 1750s, as suggested by *The Ten Plagues of England*, p. 3: 'nothing is of the least Esteem in *England*, without it is either French, Spanish, Italian, or any other Country'.

98 As in the Shandean narrator's mutual rapture with his ideal reader, whose brains
   are 'injected and tunn'd into, according to the true intent and meaning of my wish,
   until every vessel of them, both great and small, be so replenished, saturated and
   fill'd up therewith, that no more, would it save a man's life, could possibly be got
   either in or out' (*TS* 3.20.228–9).

99 Wilkes described himself as an 'extinct volcano' in later political life. See Rudé,
   p. 191.

# CHAPTER
## 4

# FRIENDSHIP, SLAVERY AND THE POLITICS
# OF PITY, INCLUDING A VISIT FROM
# PHILLIS WHEATLEY

SOCIETY *subsist* among Men by a mutual Communication of their Thoughts to each other. Words, Looks, Gesture, and different Tones of Voice, *is* the Means of that Communication. I *speaks*, and in an Instant my Ideas and Sentiments *is* communicated to the Person *which hear I*; my Soul in a Manner *pass* into his. This Communication of my Thoughts *are* again the Occasion of others in *he, who* he *communicate* to *I* in his Turn. Hence *arise* one of the most lively of our Pleasures; by *this* Means too *us enlarges* our Knowledge, and this reciprocal Commerce *are* the principal Source of our intellectual Wealth.[1]

The 'Private Young Gentlemen and Ladies' whose task it was to correct this 'promiscuous exercise' from James Buchanan's *The British Grammar* of 1762 were engaged in more than a simple test of linguistic competence. As the passage, entitled 'On Conversation', itself suggests, in removing the last grammatical distortions from this model of polite discourse, Buchanan's students would earn their right to be members of a privileged community. As soon as the way to a certain transparency of sense could be cleared, so the social channels of communication would be opened to them. The errors concern what Locke had generally termed the 'particles' of language, essential, he believed, to the coherence of a discourse in addition to 'the clearness and beauty of a good style'. These 'particles', Locke had explained, 'are all marks of some Action or Intimation of the Mind';[2] by correcting these wayward pronouns and verb endings, students could demonstrate both their comprehension of the logical connections between ideas, and their own involvement in the dynamic of reciprocity that was the very object of the exercise. The action of correction, the curbing of linguistic 'promiscuity', was not simply a passport into the world of civic politesse, but a form of *consent* to a model of public sociability that defined the private interactions between its members. It was a lesson to be absorbed and enacted catechistically by the young readers of Buchanan's *Grammar*: their identity and birthright as eighteenth-century subjects was inseparable from their constitution as members of the linguistic community.

This chapter begins with an exercise from a grammar book because it reveals one pedagogical instance of the investment in sociable commerce that took place in the mid-eighteenth century, a cultural labour that informed and shaped the realm of popular politics in the period. Dedicated to the wife of the new king, Queen Charlotte, the grammar captures the triumphalist tone of the moment, celebrating 'the Language of the bravest, wisest, most powerful, and respectable Body of People upon the Face of the Globe! Highly distinguished with the additional Glory, of being the Vernacular Tongue of the most Virtuous, most Potent, and best beloved MONARCH upon Earth!'[3] The teaching of the English language – the connections between grammar and the imposition of law – had long been part of an imperial project, as John Barrell has shown, and was instrumental in consolidating the union with Scotland after 1707.[4] In the 1760s the teaching of the 'manly Diction of BRITONS'[5] took on a new impetus, with the accession of the first king for generations who was a native speaker of English, and the vision of a global theatre that needed to be newly defended, in Buchanan's view, against French and provincial barbarisms alike. As the Grammar informed '*Teachers of Youth in* Great Britain *and* Ireland', and in a later Boston edition, '*Teachers of Youth in* America', the English language had to be regarded 'with an Esteem equal to and becoming the Glory of our Arms', 'no less designed for Conquest than our Swords!'[6] The pedagogical intent of the Grammar was not only to clarify the proper working of the spoken and written language, but also to inculcate the sociable values of such a 'Conquest'.

The formative link between society and language in the first sentence of the exercise is characteristically Lockean in its assertion of what appears to be a natural law. In his *Essays on the Law of Nature*, Locke's second law urges each individual 'to enter into society by a certain propensity of nature, and to be prepared for the maintenance of that society by the gift of speech and through the intercourse of language'.[7] Social intercourse is thus inextricably linked with the preservation of human community. A 'common Tye' guarantees the subsistence of society; it is agreed by mutual 'compact', terms invested for Locke with the values and practices of the post-revolutionary polity, but rather differently inflected at the mid-century by Buchanan. Glimpsed in his exercise is the utopian prospect of a community able to converse freely and equally within an ordered and perspicuous discourse: a realisation, it might seem, of Locke's project to discover the 'right use of words'. 'Propriety of speech', Locke had argued, 'is that which gives our Thoughts entrance into other Men's Minds with the greatest ease and advantage'.[8] At first glance, this statement would seem to differ little from the sentiments of *The British Grammar*: 'In an Instant', expounds the no longer promiscuous exercise, 'my Ideas and Sentiments [are] communicated to the Person [who hears me]; my Soul in a Manner [passes] into his.'

Yet Buchanan's written exercise actually describes a model of speech that identifies the interior, affective state of the speaker with 'his' bodily language of gesture and physiognomy, as well as translating his thoughts effortlessly into words. As Thomas Sheridan put it with similar assurance in his *A Course of Lectures on Elocution*, published in the same year as Buchanan's *Grammar*, decorous speaking in public entailed the harmonious expression of 'two languages':

> The one is, the language of ideas; by which the thoughts which pass in a man's mind, are manifested to others; and this language is composed chiefly of words properly ranged, and divided into sentences. The other, is the language of the emotions; by which the effects that those thoughts have upon the mind of the speaker, in exciting the passions, affections, and all manner of feelings, are not only made known, but communicated to others; and this language is composed of tones, looks, and gesture.[9]

In Buchanan's exercise the distinction between these two forms of language is eclipsed in a model of 'conversation' that expresses the certain commensurability of external appearance and inner substance. Unlike Locke, for whom the dark corporeal recesses of the self were a space of passionate seduction and linguistic error that needed to be controlled, in Buchanan the affective dimension of the self is rendered legible, and thus seemingly transparent. It is a model that opens private subjectivity – 'the passions of the mind'[10] – out onto the world only to display its inalienably public nature, in which individual, bodily expression and public rhetoric might be regarded as one and the same.

The members of numerous eighteenth-century associations aspired to just such an ideal form of 'conversation' in the constitution of their communities. Participation in middle-class and artisanal debating societies, friendly associations and political clubs was usually governed by rules defining propriety of speech and behaviour that shaped the public culture of the period. As Kathleen Wilson has explored:

> clubs and societies provided largely homosocial enclaves of conviviality, sociability and social discipline that . . . endowed their members with greater social

and political authority than they could get on their own. Animated by the code of civic patriotism and respectability, voluntary associations were seen by their advocates to benefit the public as well as the private, promoting through social reconstruction both individual character and the public good and forming a dense network for social and political action.[11]

The 'reciprocal Commerce' that took place in such associations was diverse, as Wilson shows. It included mutual financial welfare in addition to political sponsorship, the organising of patriotic spectacles as well as radical petitions demanding the accountability of political elites, demands which were galvanised, as we have seen, in the Wilkite controversies of the 1760s. Crucially, these clubs extended participation in the public culture of the metropolis and provinces to sectors of the population beyond the genteel elite. Some clubs were open to all comers for a small weekly fee; others, like the freemasons, had more byzantine levels of access and secrecy. Discursive freedom was generally defined by the exclusion of those who did not conform to its normative requirements (women, drunken rabble-rousers, 'effeminate' men) and also in many cases by the regulation of the dissemination of opinion itself, the management of its proper circulation.[12] Yet as Donna T. Andrew has explored, by 1780 such friendly societies were numerous and generally mixed in their audiences, and there were four debating societies in London reserved for women alone. This extension was for some a source of unease, though as 'Junius Junior' wrote in the *Public Advertiser* and the *Morning Chronicle*, 'when gentlemen meet together for the purpose of communicating their sentiments to each other . . . although the company may be very numerous, 'tis nevertheless, in a more enlarged sense, conversation'.[13] The stakes were high nonetheless. As William Jones reminded in 1783, 'remember, that a free State is only a more numerous and more powerful club, and that he only is a free man, who is a member of such a state'.[14] Not only did such communication appear to render transparent what it was to be enfranchised by the proper membership of the state, but it also encouraged participants to have a stake in a state imagining that rose above the tawdriness of interest, potentially transforming the nature of authority in the process.

The grammar exercise 'On Conversation' thus contains the kernel of a political hope, concerning the wider significance of communication between conversing souls. The back pages of *The British Grammar* include other exercises that underline this point. Another, demonstrating the use of ellipsis, brings the notion of such mutual exchange into a political sphere by reframing it in terms of *friendship*:

> Friendship is the Union of two Souls by means of Virtue; the common Object and Cement of their mutual Affection: Without Virtue, or the Supposition of

it, Friendship is only a mercenary League, an Alliance of Interest, which must dissolve of course, when that Interest decays, or subsists no longer.[15]

These were lessons evidently drawn from a civic humanist tradition that saw such self-control and clarity of exchange as synonymous with virtue, a virtue filtered in this case through the sympathetic sociability of Scottish moral philosophy. It is this distinction between different forms of friendship – one an ideal union of souls among virtuous equals, another that appears to collapse back into utility and interest – which I want to test as particularly generative in terms of the domestic cultural work of empire at the mid-century. What was the nature of such 'reciprocal commerce', and who was admitted to, and excluded from, such a vision of transparent exchange? In what ways was it put to use in the imperial context, to communicate with others who might also be brought within the community of the nation? Moreover what happened to such perceived reciprocity when excluded others took on the terms of that participation: when a slave and a woman, the poet Phillis Wheatley, elegantly mastered the language of civic virtue for herself?

### The Work of Friendship

The grammar's vision of friendship as the mutual communication of souls had numerous sources in classical antiquity, notably in Ciceronian discussions of the perfection of ideal homosocial friendship, and in Aristotelian philosophy, where the 'work' of friendship produces 'everything that comes to pass in the polis'.[16] This classical inheritance was mediated by the Renaissance humanism exemplified by Montaigne, and as such continued to circulate in eighteenth-century France and Britain as a means of imagining the ties that bound men, and specifically men, to the happiness of the state. While various forms of political and familial friendship could be seen to exist based on what Aristotle saw as 'utility', the state of virtuous character that made possible a disinterested reciprocity between men was by definition not available to all. As Montaigne's famous essay 'De l'amitié' suggests, 'what we normally call friends and friendships are no more than acquaintances and familiar relationships bound by some chance or some suitability, by means of which our souls support each other. In the friendship which I am talking about, souls are mingled and confounded in so universal a blending that they efface the seam that joins them together so that it cannot be found'.[17] Such a vision of friendship promised an ideal suturing of the friend to the active and virtuous production of the polity; the state was thereby imagined as a transparent expression of this 'universal . . . blending' and above the mercenary interests of exchange.

In his account of the rise of the 'egalitarian family' amongst the aristocracy in the eighteenth century, Randolph Trumbach suggests that friendship was instrumental in the modification of patterns of authority, 'the strongest of all ties' in the maintenance of the power of the elite. It was, perhaps accordingly, the 'most protean word in the vocabulary',[18] despite the scarcity attributed to its ideal form. Tracts from the period place friendship within a range of affective relationships in a taxonomic echo of Montaigne and Aristotle's ethics. William Fleetwood's sermons in 1705 are characteristic:

> There is a love peculiar to every Relation, that a Man can stand in by Nature, or can contract by Choice, and it is truly distinct from every other Affection. Thus there is a love of honour and esteem, due to Vertue, Excellence and Perfection, and this is commonly the love we pay to Princes, great and brave People of all sorts, and commonly our Superiours. There is also a Love of *Friendship*, due to Merit and good Qualities, either real or imagined, generally paid our Equals. There is also a love of Natural Relations, different from the rest, and which grows up with us insensibly from our Infancy. And the mutual love of Marriage is distinct from all the rest.[19]

The different forms of love that constitute the social bond would at the mid-century be variously rearticulated, in debates about romantic marriage, discussions of the virtuous nature of patriotism, and not least through a powerful notion of sympathy that carried with it a hierarchical sense of the reciprocities of social positioning: emulative love for one's betters, benevolence and pity towards one's subordinates. Yet the middle ground of friendship, that 'paid our Equals', also crucially expands its meaning at this time, and gains a renewed significance. It is worked over repeatedly in the sentimental fictions of the period, as will be seen shortly. And it is a common currency in mid-century public culture. Oliver Goldsmith's response to the imperial victories of 1759 provides one example:

> How blest am I, said I to myself, who make one in this glorious political society, which thus preserves liberty to mankind and to itself; who rejoice only in their conquest over slavery, and bring mankind from bondage into freedom. Thus solitary as I am, am I not greater than an host of slaves? I, who in my little sphere contribute to the happiness of mankind; am I not greater than the greatest monarch, whose only boast is unbounded power?
>
> LET him dictate to his slaves, and ride upon the neck of submission. My king, my country, and I, are friends together, and by a mutual intercourse of kindness and duty, give and receive social happiness.[20]

Brushing fireworks from his wig amidst the rejoicing crowds, Goldsmith is transported by the turning point of the war somewhat against his sceptical nature.[21] But his statement reveals the 'work' of friendship in all its complexity, revisiting classical precedent in the context of the mid-century moment. The global expansion of the liberty of British political society is celebrated in biblical tones, the bringing of 'mankind from bondage into freedom'. It is a characteristic paradox of course that the spread of British imperial power is equated with the 'preservation of liberty to mankind'; like the untutored Indians, in Pope's poetry, who welcome their subjection to the British state rather than fall prey to the violences of the Spanish colonial system. If the battle is framed in universalising terms, against the 'unbounded' forces of absolutist subjection, it is fought by a community of friends whose strength lies in singularity and reciprocity. Goldsmith 'make[s] one', 'solitary . . . yet greater than a host of slaves'; this sense of countable number gestures towards a question of democracy which, as Jacques Derrida has discussed, is present in Aristotle's discussion of friendship: 'It is possible to love more than one person, Aristotle seems to concede; to love in number, but not too much so – not too many. It is not the number that is forbidden, nor the more than one, but the numerous, if not the crowd . . . There is no belonging or friendly community that is *present*, and first present *to itself*, *in act*, without election and without selection'.[22]

Goldsmith's response to the public rejoicing expresses the affective nationalism of wartime through a vision of friendship which has a number of effects. His essay transforms the crowd into a differentiable body of 'fellow countrymen', thus defusing the excessive multiplicity of the crowd into an identifiable yet generalised (and non-calculable) national community in which his own 'satisfaction' is increased, 'as if by reflection from theirs'. This is an image that diverts reciprocity into narcissistic self-affirmation. The language of the friend, one might argue, actively works against the numerous presence of 'combinations' of the multitude that puts such equality under pressure, while drawing on the egalitarian affinities of a civic republicanism for its own purposes. Goldsmith's singular election as a friend to king and country uses the language of the patriot to suggest an unmediated and transparent relation with the monarch, one free from personal or party interest and evoking the constitution itself, a relationship described by the new king as 'the most beautiful combination that ever was framed'.[23] The bondage vanquished by British liberty thus has a number of political meanings: simultaneously invoking imperial enemies abroad, and the 'slavery' of factional interest at home, as the Tory journal *Con-test* put it in 1756.[24] Goldsmith thus writes in the name of the 'middle order of mankind', in the words of his novel *The Vicar of Wakefield*, his invocation of friendship constituting 'the true preserver of freedom . . . called the People', whose task it is 'to preserve the prerogative and the privileges of the one principal governor with the most sacred circumspection'.[25]

The protean vocabulary of friendship enables a continual process of political re-translation, state imagining. But it is also unstable, liable, as the grammar exercise describes, to collapse into interest and expediency where virtue is absent; to enter into a jeopardy of words where different kinds of friendship become fatally confused. Goldsmith's breaking open of reciprocity into a 'mutual intercourse of kindness and duty' reveals the 'seam' (in Montaigne's words) where friendship can fold into calculation and misunderstanding. Derrida summarises the Aristotelian distinction between two forms of political friendship in an account that illuminates the problem:

> When it is grounded on consent, consensus, convention . . . this friendship is at once political and legal . . . It is, then, a matter of a homology of reciprocity, as in the case of a contract, an agreement between two subscribing parties. When, on the other hand, the parties leave the matter to each other's discretion, in a sort of trust without contract, credit becoming an act of faith, then friendship 'wants to be' moral, ethical . . . and of the order of comradeship.[26]

What is at stake here in the terms of Goldsmith's formulation? Firstly a friendship of legal consent to the power of a monarch over a people – nominally a relationship of equality in which the place of each is the provision of duty. It was possible to envisage such a 'love' as an equality of proportion, in Aristotelian terms, in which each gives and receives the love due to him according to his status. And secondly, an ethical friendship based, in this instance, on 'kindness', 'trust without contract'. This reciprocal exchange – of duty and kindness – is what produces 'social happiness'; a conflation of the two forms of friendship is seen to bind the polity together in common nationalist cause. It is this exchange that accounts for sentimentalism's ideological power during this period, in which, for example, dedication to one's country in times of war and 'distracted'[27] peace can be seen to be a matter of duty *and* selfless choice. It is a rapprochement evident, as we have seen with the case of Sterne's uncle Toby, in the compound figure of the 'benevolent man' and 'good soldier' in ethical discourse at the mid-century.

Yet instability nonetheless enters the equation. As Derrida's account beautifully describes, different kinds of friendships can be mistaken, suffer a 'recoil'. Ethical friendship can be confused with legal, expectations of reciprocity clash, friendship based on pleasure is 'smuggled into . . . virtue's mask'. This is the dilemma for public culture in mid-eighteenth-century Britain. 'Everything can function as long as love is there', Derrida argues, but 'when love ceases, the two lovers strive to calculate their respective share, and they wage war'.[28] What happens when love for the state is not present? Friendship becomes, as the exercise put it, a 'mercenary League', dissolving into expediency and interest. 'Reciprocity' becomes a question of calculus, of what constitutes a fair exchange. What did it mean to invoke such a community when a man could be said to 'consent' just by walking down the king's highway[29] (a place from where he might well be pressed into military service)? What did such reciprocity mean, as Goldsmith himself acknowledged, when veterans returned from the war without a pension, for the 'strange absurdity' of an economic logic that valued fur or silk over a man's life?[30] Or when bread was short and taxes high? Or when the labour of many produced luxurious accumulation for others? Or when the most perfect friend of the state measured his honour in the gold coin of a peerage?[31] The rise of utilitarian thought in the 1760s marks this moment of 'recoil', as does the development of what might be seen as a sentimental cultural formation, which emerges to register and crucially, to *manage and administer* its effects.

The invocation of a model of sentimental community might serve, in ideological terms, as an apology for the sacrificial cost of imperial expansion at home, but it also registered the conflicts the model was intended to explain. Unmoored from the fiction of legal exchange, ethical friendship generated that familiar defensive topos of the sentimental family, speaking to one another from the heart, at the mercy of an unfeeling and violently self-interested economic world. While at the same time legal friendship took on a utilitarian character, operating a calculus of just recompense – money for suffering – or found radical articulation in a discourse of rights. Such instability was thus productive, new political subjects emerging from what was a far-reaching re-evaluation of authority, though in the hegemonic interests of a strengthening of authority nonetheless. Yet quite what it was that produced this 'recoil' with some violence at the mid-century, is something to examine: it came, ironically, from within the very logic of friendship itself.

### Ideal Friendship and its Limits

The perfection of friendship was such a potent fiction because it suggested both a transparency of communication – that seamless merging of souls celebrated by Montaigne – and a realm distinct from calculation, interest and even law. As such it provided a place from which to critique the excesses of commercial empire and to build a vision of a virtuous state. Jean-Jacques Rousseau's thought connected both, as James Swenson has discussed, contrasting a virtuous ideal of 'an ease of reciprocal penetration', in which the feelings of the heart could not be separated from their expression in the 'exterior countenance' of the body, with 'the opacity of our social relations' which could only appear 'factitious and unnatural'.[32] While Wilkite radicalism's dream of transparency was cheerfully animated by the material opacities – the desires and interests – of commercial society, Rousseau's state imagining took another, utopian form, in the light of such virtue, removing from that society altogether. In the fictional world of *Julie, ou la Nouvelle Heloise* removal takes the form of provincial retreat; in *The Social Contract*, it distinguishes the interested realm of the will of all, from the ideal abstraction of the general will: 'to follow this will it is necessary to know it, and above all to distinguish it from the particular will, beginning with one's self: this distinction is always very difficult to make, and only the most sublime virtue can afford sufficient illumination for it'.[33] It was an abstraction that might take the most radical of forms – the imagining of fraternal liberty as an equality for all – which would take a revolutionary direction in France several decades later. Not so in Britain, though the consequences of imagining friendship as an equality began to be registered at the mid-century nonetheless.

It is perhaps not surprising that exemplary Ciceronian friendship found various forms of cultural expression in Britain in the late 1760s, its language of pastoral and patrician retreat countering the popular clamour that seemed to some to threaten wider imperial disorder.[34] Yet if unsullied friendship could bring such a fallen world to its senses, as some believed, it nonetheless had to undergo some modification if it was to be extended within a society that ultimately throbbed, as Wilkes and more sanguine commentators knew, to a commercial beat. The sociable exchange of clubs and societies provided one patriotic means of extending public-minded virtue throughout the capillaries of the national body. Here nonetheless came the inevitable confrontation, as I suggested earlier, with the question of *number*, and thus with governmentality, complicated in the aftermath of the Seven Years' War, by issues of geographical extension, imperial projection.

> In proportion as territory is extended, its parts lose their relative importance to the whole. Its inhabitants cease to perceive their connection with the state, and are seldom united in the execution of any national, or even of any factious, designs. Distance from the seats of administration, and indifference to the persons who contend for preferment, teach the majority to consider themselves as the subjects of a sovereignty, not as the members of a political body. It is even remarkable, that enlargement of territory, by rendering the individual of less consequence to the public, and less able to intrude with his counsel, actually tends to reduce national affairs within a narrower compass, as well as to diminish the numbers who are consulted in legislation, or in other matters of government.[35]

What could unite such a society, asked Adam Ferguson, 'where the friendship of particular men was out of the question'?[36] It was a question for public culture at large. While Ferguson clearly addresses the question of the representativity of the state, describing the deracinating abstraction accompanying a notion of sovereignty, his answer, particularly for 'distant provinces', was unequivocal: force. Others tried out utopian solutions. In the steps of Thomas More, Robert Wallace argued for the global extension of a model of ideal communication, and the equal distribution of its wealth and knowledge:

> uniting all mankind under governments which shall preserve the same language, maintain an universal correspondence among the most distant inhabitants of the globe, and raise the whole human race to the highest perfection. Let us not immediately take it for granted that such a government is utterly impracticable. Let us suspend our judgment till once we have considered whether we can conceive a consistent idea of it.[37]

But Wallace's vision of perpetual peace, as William Godwin was later to point out, was also haunted by the question of number, which he resolved 'rather surprisingly', in the words of Caroline Robbins, by suggesting the 'Providence or nature would set due bounds to the establishment of any government unsuited to a limited earth'.[38] Others saw the benevolent restrictions of providence beginning at home. For Oliver Goldsmith, it was rather an issue of hegemony, about who could be said to share the reciprocities of the social bond, be brought to love and identify with the state, and thus the kinds of interest that might define that love. Force was not the answer, but then neither was equality:

> It were to be wished then that power, instead of contriving new laws to punish vice, instead of drawing hard the cords of society till a convulsion come to burst them, instead of cutting away wretches as useless, before we have tried their utility, instead of converting correction into vengeance, it were to be wished that we tried the restrictive arts of government, and made the law the protector, but not the tyrant of the people. We should then find that creatures, whose souls are held as dross, only wanted the hand of a refiner; we should then find that wretches, now stuck up for long tortures, lest luxury should feel a momentary pang, might, if properly treated, serve to sinew the state in times of danger; that, as their faces are like ours, their hearts are so too.[39]

Goldsmith's advocacy of 'the restrictive arts of government' marks the point where friendship, that 'paid our Equals' as the sermon put it, discovers its utilitarian limits. How were the effects of such an ideal reciprocity to be extended even beyond the 'middle order of mankind'[40] to those 'whose souls are held as dross', except by finding a means of their 'refining'? A means moreover, in which the interiority – 'hearts' – of the unskilled and vulgar might be brought to the light of public day, transformed in the process to become more 'like us'.

Sentimentalism, a cultural work linking a realm of affective feeling to institutionalised measures then changing the face of social life, provided the means. It managed the point of friendship's recoil in active and directly translatable ways, paralleling moments of textual pathos with forms of social regulation and welfare. One practical example is the intense focus on *debt* in sentimental texts, both as a material crisis that has to be eradicated, and as an affective metaphorics retained as ideological testimony to a reciprocal social relation, a bond across the classes. These narratives repeatedly come across families and individuals who have experienced a catastrophic loss of status, sometimes deliberately seeking them out to release them from debtors' prison, or providing the destitute the means of an income so that they can live out the middle-class values of virtue and independence to which they have already been assigned. The effect is to shore up the boundaries of that 'middle order of mankind' by returning them to the fold, at the same time as articulating a particular social truth: that gentility is not enough to 'make you a worthy member of the community', in the words of Henry Brooke's *The Fool of Quality*: 'It is industry alone, employed on articles that are useful and beneficial to society, that constitute the true riches of mankind'.[41] If sentimental fictions chart and even protest against friendship's inevitable descent into interest, they also manage to make a virtue of it by passing it through the carefully calibrated realm of social labour. Some, like the unfortunate Mr Clement of Brooke's novel, become teachers of an embryonic man of feeling; others are returned to live on the land, in familial cottages built for 'improvement', self-sustaining and grateful.

Yet there are also those who fall outside such refinement, their 'souls held as dross': the *non-friends*. If we remember the linguistic exercise from Buchanan's *Grammar*, it is clear that the 'Private Young Gentlemen and Ladies' are deemed to have the capacity to bring together propriety of diction (the sign of the mind able to think in abstract terms) *with* the realm of feeling. As Murray Cohen's rich survey of eighteenth-century attitudes to language suggests, theirs would have been just one of numerous language communities addressed within the rapidly proliferating field of manuals, dictionaries and grammars at the mid-century.[42] It was a field that discriminated between the needs and levels of different social fractions, such that 'practical' grammars were directed for 'the use of Youth designed for mechanick and mercantile Arts',[43] and others (like Buchanan's) included more theoretical knowledge that was for the purview of the educator alone. The rational facility of Buchanan's ideal community was key to the sociable commerce of the whole, however: some were brought to awareness of their 'consent', while the unskilled would simply learn the dictates of custom. Others inhabited the 'constitutive outside' of such a commerce, consigned to the realm of inarticulate feeling, or even (like slaves, in some accounts) did not have souls with which to converse. The 'laborious multitude', for example, were seen to be caught in a sensual world of brute experience, their language tied to the things upon which they laboured. As James Harris put it, the 'vulgar' were so 'merged *in Sense* from their earliest infancy' that they 'imagine nothing to be *real*, but what may be *tasted*, or touched'.[44] Sheridan's 'two languages' of ordered thought and wayward emotion thus had a clear social analogue.

In so far as sentimentalism routed its sociable commerce through the body, it promised (where friendship could not) to maintain a vision of transparent exchange between these 'two languages'. The language of the heart might communicate where rational discourse failed, and it is the production of this language that is central to the cultural work – Goldsmith's 'refining' – which I have described. As the enigmatic benevolent man of *The Fool of Quality*, Mr Fenton, explains:

> I am persuaded that there is not a single sentiment, whether tending to good or evil in the human soul, that has not its distinct and respective interpreter in the glance of the eye, and in the muscling of the countenance. When nature is permitted to express herself with freedom by this language of the face, she is understood by all people; and those who never were taught a letter, can instantly read her signatures and impressions; whether they be of wrath, hatred, envy, pride, jealousy, contempt, pain, fear, horror, and dismay; or of attention, respect, wonder, surprise, pleasure, transport, complacence, affection, desire, peace, lowliness, and love.[45]

The 'language of the face' is thus a *lingua franca*, a communicative bond between all ranks of society including the illiterate. And it is here that sentimentalism powerfully goes to work in its production of an extensive lexicon of emotion that erupts as a wordless gestics in the body itself, a gestics that nonetheless had to be tamed if such imagined reciprocity was not to dissolve into conflict and impotence.

### The 'Restrictive Arts' of Sentiment

In its purest form friendship appeared testimony to the benevolent eradication of the self in its relations with an other. Montaigne had regarded the perfect union of friends as rare and indivisible, a love which had driven out 'all terms of division and difference, such as good turn, duty, gratitude, request, thanks and the like': 'they can neither lend nor give anything to each other'.[46] This logic, of a gift economy in which the other is by definition not brought into debt, continues as a *promesse de bonheur* in the contortions of the sentimental writings of the mid-eighteenth century, which are fascinated by numerous *secret* acts of kindness, the presence of true 'friends' in disguise. Yet what Robert Markley has termed a 'theatrics of bourgeois virtue' is already acting out friendship's recoil in these texts.[47] As Sarah Scott expresses it in *The History of Sir George Ellison*:

> The mutual intercourse of civilities should be public, they harmonize the mind; such debts we incur with pleasure, because we can easily repay them: as tokens of reciprocal regard, they cultivate friendship; but we should receive much greater pleasure from conferring benefits, if we could do it secretly.[48]

Reciprocity is here inevitably a matter of debt and exchange, which leads in some texts to the difficulty of assessing the motives and actions of others. The theme of disguise runs through many sentimental tales, emphasising the opacity of social relations rather than their transparency. While misprision is part of the moral game for the reader, like the Vicar of Wakefield who dismayingly mistakes the identity of his benefactor, uncertainty nonetheless survives the resolutions of plot. The public 'intercourse of civilities' is revealed as a mask for strategy, as the Man of Feeling discovers when the gentleman he has been conversing with turns out to be a excise-man imitating the ways of upper class. Harley's conclusion is that 'the fault may more properly be imputed to that rank where the futility is real, than where it is feigned'.[49] A dimension of such recoil, then, is the articulation of inequality, but one that is not accompanied by the demand for justice, as I will explore in a moment.

Mutual exchange is also destabilised by the presence of *pleasure*: the gratification to be experienced in benevolent acts that reaches its apogee in the ironies of Sterne's *A Sentimental Journey*. Giving would produce a more exquisite pleasure, Scott observes, 'if we could do it secretly'. The misanthropist of Mackenzie's *The Man of Feeling* offers his negative opinion of such a desire: 'There are some, indeed, who tell us of the satisfaction which flows from a secret consciousness of good actions: this secret satisfaction is truly excellent – when we have some friend to whom we may discover its excellence.'[50] The presence of the friend is here a sign not of selflessness, but of vanity; a suspicion voiced by many critics of sentimentalism in the period, who distrusted declarations of the pleasures of benevolent feeling.

'*Rare* indeed are *reliable* friends, writes Derrida, 'those, then, who are able to renounce all public profit, all political or institutional consequence, to the possession or circulation of this secret.' The difficulty, however, as he discusses in the context of Kant's treatise 'On the Most Intimate Union of Love with Respect in Friendship', is the establishing of the limits of that secret, since 'no-one knows in all certainty where discretion begins and ends'. Moreover, 'the secret is that which one *thinks must* remain secret because an *engagement* has been entered upon and a *promise* made in certain non-natural conditions'.[51] Such a secret takes a specifically gendered form at this moment in history, not least because in its recoil it relies fundamentally on the limited agency of women; women, who, like many of the aspiring benefactresses in sentimental fiction, want to seize the opportunity of benevolent action, seeing in it the chance to extend beyond their domestic sphere. Women who are not, in a classical political sense, 'friends', whose thereby impossible 'promise' has been made in 'certain non-natural conditions'. For, as many tracts of the period declared, women were deemed naturally 'less rational' in their benevolence, 'existing . . . more in themselves, and in the objects of their sensibility, and perhaps being less fitted than men by nature for the civil institutions in which they have less share, they must be less susceptible of that enthusiasm, which makes a man prefer the state to his family, and the collective body of his citizens to himself'.[52]

The productive nature of women's friendship as a *state imagining* is a secret disclosed in Sarah Scott's work, where it enters into discourse staged as a chance discovery, witnessed by male tourists in the seclusion of provincial retreat. In this ideal community run by women the pleasure of benevolence is socialised so that it is not simply the self-affirmed property of the benefactor as spectator, producing its own version of reciprocity in the process. *Millenium Hall* stages a dialogue between Mrs Mancel and the sceptical Mr Lamont, who sees the regulation of this women's community as a possible form of slavery:

> 'You seem, madam, answered Lamont, to choose to make us all slaves to each other?' 'No, sir, replied Mrs Mancel, I would only make you friends. Those who are really such are continually endeavouring to serve and oblige each other; this reciprocal communication of benefits should be universal, and then we might with reason be fond of this world.' 'But, said Lamont, this reciprocal communication is impossible; what service can a poor man do me? I may relieve him, but how can he return the obligation?' 'It is he, answered Mrs Mancel, who first conferring it, in giving you an opportunity of relieving him. The pleasure he has afforded you, is as far superior to the gratification you have procured him; as it is more blessed to give than to receive . . . much

obliged are you to that poverty, which enables you to obtain so great a gratification. But do not think the poor can make no adequate return. The greatest pleasure this world can give us is that of being beloved, but how should we
obtain love without deserving it? Did you ever see any one that was not fond
of a dog that fondled him? Is it then possible to be insensible to the affection
of a rational being?'[53]

Scott's message joins Christian scripture with a utopian strain in radical
liberal thought that dares to imagine a future where 'there may probably be
no inequality'.[54] For the present, however, it is a question of the learning of
good behaviour and rational reciprocity: 'what I understand by society is a
state of mutual confidence, reciprocal services, and correspondent affections;
where numbers are thus united, there will be a free communication of sentiments, and we shall then find speech . . . a valuable gift indeed'.[55] The lesson
of Millenium Hall is actualised in her later *George Ellison* as a practice which
the labouring inhabitants are only too happy to voice: 'in accepting their
bounty, we seem to confer an obligation, and do in reality confer a benefit,
by being the cause of so much refined pleasure to them' (I. 277). If this seems
to promise a curious if limited reversal of social status, it also correspondingly
modifies the role of authority within a pleasurable oeconomy. As Ellison
declares:

> Now, I am so great an epicure, that I love to raise my pleasures as high
> as I can carry them, and while I amuse myself with improvements, would enjoy
> the additional satisfaction of intentionally benefiting others; and the best
> means I know to procure this, is, to make the pursuit of my own gratification
> so far subservient to the good of the labourer, as to hasten, or retard the first,
> as shall prove most conducive to the latter. (I. 136–7)

'Self-love and social are the same', the text declares (I. 138). The point of Scott's
secret is that it has to circulate, as secrets do. The realm of sentimental fiction
thus seems to offer a supplement to a vision of society characterised by the virtuous 'friendship of particular men', one in which the very implosion of such
affinities into the material world of competing interests might be redeemed.
Not only, in Sarah Scott's model at least, are those in authority brought to
'retard' their own pleasures in the name of 'the good of the labourer', but the
disadvantaged are shown to participate willingly in the very form of their subjection. This was a version of the exchange described by Goldsmith, the giving
and receiving of social happiness, which reveals how despite the modification
of authority the vision of an ideal patrician order remained intact. Scott's
utopian thinking maintains the estate values of 'ancient patriarchs' even as
they are mediated by necessary forms of feminisation. The 'secret' of Scott's

narratives – the friendship of women – has to be framed by those who look on, by the benevolent transformation of men.

### The Work of Community: Women and the State

The merging of souls that Montaigne had seen as a rare and ideal form of friendship was by definition a form of homosocial relation among equals. Yet sentimental affinities were of a different order, and required the capacity to open the self to relations with unknown and subordinate others. 'The formation of a collectivity', writes Luc Boltanski of such sentimental bonding, takes place 'through an emotional contagion which transmits the *sociable* from interiority to interiority'. Moreover:

> when the spectator opens his heart to accept the trace left by suffering in the unfortunate's heart, it is at the same time a moment of the greatest *emotion* and the moment of truth. The quality of the emotion, which does not deceive, is the test of the reality which makes it possible to allay an always possible doubt about the authenticity of the suffering endured by the unfortunate.[56]

As we have seen such doubt extended not just to the sufferer, who may well be counterfeit, but as Boltanski points out, also to the spectator who theatricalises the sensitive pleasures of charitable feeling. Hannah More's poem 'Sensibility' thus extols the truth of Mackenzie's man of feeling even as she warns of the dangers of counterfeiture (exemplified by 'polish'd Sterne'):

> There are, who for a dying fawn display,
> The tend'rest anguish in the sweetest lay;
> Who for a wounded animal deplore,
> As if friend, parent, country were no more;
> Who boast quick rapture trembling in their eye,
> If from the spider's snare they save a fly;
>
> . . .
>
> Yet, scorning life's dull duties to attend,
> Will persecute a wife, or wrong a friend . . . [57]

This was the risk of what many saw as the peculiarly *feminine* state that the man of feeling had to embody. It was not just that many of the unfortunates paraded before the sentimental observer were distressed women, thus eliciting various degrees of voyeuristic excitement as well as identification (as the case of Sterne's 'poor Maria' will show in Chapter 5). Nor only that the opening up to an other could involve a loss of self-mastery that was integral to notions of manliness at the time. It was also that the sociable 'contagion' represented by sentimental feeling was connected to the contradictory presence of women in the realm of public culture: marked on the one hand by their domestic virtue, and yet by a 'self-love' to which they were said to be particularly prone.

One interesting example of this emerges in William Russell's *Essay on the Character, Manners and Genius of Women in Different Ages*, 'enlarged' and translated from a French source, and published in 1773.[58] At one point the writer stages a dialogue with Montaigne on the nature of friendship, and the possible inclusion of women into its ideal union. 'You undoubtedly agree', the writer says to Montaigne, 'that friendship is the sentiment of two souls, which seek and which have need of the support of each other'. Why is it then, he asks, that men, as 'the sex whose head and hands are most occupied; which is most free; which has the greatest ability of expanding its ideas, and of employing its sentiments . . . which in all conditions has a consciousness of its powers, and which glories in them' (II. 25), should have need of it, when women do not:

> Woman, in short, to whom externals are nothing, and her feelings are everything; woman, in whom every thing produces a sentiment, to whom indifference is violence, and who knows almost only to love and to hate, must feel more exquisitely the liberty and pleasure of a secret commerce, and the tender confidence which friendship gives and receives. (II. 26)

Women (like the labouring multitude) were seen as caught within a realm of sense, and thus friendship is here imagined as a kind of measured release from the turbulence of their passions, from a love that possesses no reserve, and which can as quickly turn into its opposite, hate. Montaigne's ventriloquated reply warns that women, particularly those in cities, are too 'intoxicated' by flattery and self-love to show the necessary restraint for the 'happy equality friendship imposes' (II. 27). The friendship 'he' defines reiterates a manly self-command that shares a current of stoicism also to be found in the moral thought of Adam Smith:

> Friendship . . . is a sentiment which requires energy of soul, and a solidity of mind as well as of character; it is a sacred and almost holy union, which by a devotion peculiar to itself, consecrates a heart entirely to a heart; it is a passion which transforms two wills into one, and gives to two beings the same life and the same soul. Friendship is bold and severe: for, properly to fulfil its duties, it must be able to speak and to hear the harsh and ungrateful language of truth.

> It must possess a courage, which is neither alarmed at sacrifices nor at dangers, and it demands, above all other things, that unity of character which, from the variety and the eternal fluctuation of their passions, we seldom find in women, and which only can enable us to feel, to think, and to act as a friend, at all times, and upon all occasions. (II. 28)

Manly friendship can bear the exacting challenges of abstraction, and it has, these tracts are bound to tell us, a power and constancy lacking in women's affection. Like Smith, for whom a 'feeble spark' of benevolence alone was not enough to cause someone to 'sacrifice their own interests to the interests of others', it offered a 'stronger love' than 'the love of our neighbour'.[59] It was the very medium for the transmission of disinterested, 'sacred', virtue, a rational binding of souls. In Kant's view, such 'love in friendship cannot be an *affect*; for emotion is blind in its choice, and after a while it goes up in smoke'.[60] What distinguishes such friendship from mere affection is that it is shaped by an overarching idea of the state, which makes it more than a form of sentimental philanthropy. Yet in order for such friendship to exist beyond the exclusivity of its limits, it has to pass through a realm of sensibility normally associated with the feminine. Thus Russell has to come back to the character of women, and argue once again with Montaigne:

> But women have a sensibility which is never absent, which never forgets or omits any thing. Nothing escapes them: they divine the hidden friendship; they encourage the bashful or timid friendship, and they offer their sweetest consolations to friendship in distress. Furnished with finer instruments, they treat more delicately a wounded heart, they compose it, and prevent it from feeling its agonies: they know, above all things, to give an importance to circumstances which have none in themselves. We ought therefore perhaps to desire the friendship of a man upon great occasions; but, for general happiness, we must prefer the friendship of a woman. (II. 30)

Manly friendship needs the supplement of sensibility for the everyday production of 'general happiness', in order to *take place* in the interested realm of the social. In Kant's essay, Derrida notes, this results in a 'pragmatic' form of friendship, which 'out of love, burdens itself with the ends of other men, this time of an indeterminate number':

> In history, in space, and in time: yes, friendship does happen. Hence sensibility is part of the game. And this cannot happen except against a backdrop of what unites mankind, this effective and sensible sharing out [*partage*] whose *aesthetic* dimension is thus required. What happens must be able to happen.

And the condition of possibility must be universal. All this supposes, then, a general or generic possibility, the possibility of what Kant calls here the *friend of man*.[61]

The imagining of just such a 'humanitarian solidarity' begins to take place in the Britain of the 1760s, in part as a consequence of empire; an answer to the philosophical and political need to formulate what it was that bound man to man. As Russell stated mournfully towards the end of his *Essay*, 'we seem to be attached to all the world, and we are attached to nobody' (II. 118). Such an attachment had to be more than sentimental. It was rather a rational and virtuous extension, within the realm of sensibility, of the 'Love of Friendship . . . generally paid our Equals'.[62] This was the state imagining at the heart of what has been termed the feminisation of culture, and it is exemplified in Scott's texts. Femininity traces the limits of what a society will recognise of itself, as Jacqueline Rose has written;[63] embodied by men like George Ellison, or indeed Sterne's uncle Toby, it is manifested as the height of fellow-feeling. In women's form such affection is contrastingly transformed either into modest communities, like that of Millenium Hall, or into visions of excess: the 'arbitrary power' of Ellison's wife (I. 92), who feels more for her lap-dog than her slaves, or the woman in More's poem who weeps over *Werther* 'while her children starve'.[64] As Ellison argues in terms which echo Russell's concluding of the dialogue with Montaigne, 'I shall not be ashamed of endeavouring to imitate the ladies who gave rise to this conversation . . . benevolence appears with particular lustre in a female form, the domestic cares to which the well educated have been trained, qualifies them better for discerning and executing the offices of humanity' (I. 111–12). Sensibility thus had a necessary rapprochement with stoic virtue in the 1760s, and if the 'lustre' of the modest woman facilitated it by anchoring humanity in the local and everyday, her passion-bound sister exposed its limits.[65] Sensibility could provide the conditions for universalised feeling, but in its passional expansiveness it also had to be reined in. It was sentimentalism, I want to suggest, which carried out this task at the mid-century.

What is it, then, that characterised this gendered friendship for mankind? It was animated, suggests Derrida, by an Idea of equality:

It is not only an intellectual representation, a representation of *equality* among men, but *consideration* for this representation of equality, a '*just consideration*' for such a representation. Equality *is necessary*. There is no equality, but there must be. For it is *obligation* that the soundness or justice of this *consideration* adds to the representation: 'the Idea that in putting others under obligation by his beneficence he is himself under obligation'. Consequently, equality is not only a representation, an intellectual concept, a calculable measure, a statistical objectivity; it bears within itself a feeling of obligation, hence the sensibility of duty, debt, gratitude. This is inscribed in sensibility, but only in sensibility's relation to the purely rational Idea of equality.[66]

This is the reciprocity of obligation – the giving and receiving of social happiness – repeated almost catechistically within Scott's narratives, a pedagogy in which one must 'learn, that to oblige is as much an exertion of your power, as to mortify, and far more rational, as well as amiable' (I. 72), discovering as a consequence that one's subordinates are only too happy to reciprocate. Yet if there is a 'just consideration' for the 'representation of equality' that shapes *The History of George Ellison* – the 'sudden sense of right' associated with sensibility in Hannah More's poem which becomes a 'prompt sense of equity'[67] – one which sets out to acknowledge 'the distinguishing marks of humanity' (I. 27) among all whatever their 'rank or station' (II. 112), there is also a specific cultural work taking place here that manages the risk of such a friendship with mankind. Sentimental writing turns the *necessity* of an equality into a *not yet*. Its gestures towards a posited equality in fact defuse attendant claims for justice. For imagining society in terms of a 'great SENSORIUM of the universe' (*SJ* 155) had its repercussions.

## Universal Friendship and the Question of Slavery

I suggested earlier that the 'recoil' of friendship arrived with some violence in the 1760s because of a logic internal to political friendship itself. The logic I have been tracing has to do with *number*: the need to extend forms of fellowship beyond a patrician elite into the wider sociable commerce of mid-century public culture, which at this point promised to circulate around the globe. Yet there was something potentially incendiary about the universalising of that friendship 'paid to Equals',[68] glimpsed in the language of rights that begins to articulate itself at this time in tracts and 'tumults': the view that liberty and equality were to be thought as inextricably, and unconditionally, bound up with each other. In friendship's recoil arrives the incontrovertible question of justice. There was no greater challenge to the ideal community of friends than the presence of slavery, opposition to which begins to be articulated with increasing vociferousness in the 1760s.

Quite what it was that intensified public debate on the question of slavery in the late 1760s is a complex question. The effects of imperial conflict and expansion are certainly factors. As Robin Blackburn has discussed, opposition to slavery often came from those who saw slave labour as undercutting their own interests in this most commercial of wars; or through an attack on the vested interests of the powerful West Indian lobby. Others saw the generalisable condition of slavery as providing a rhetoric for their own demands, as we will see shortly, demands that for those like the American colonists arose out of the claims for a just recompense for their wartime sacrifices. If the aftermath of the Seven Years' War was for many a period of turmoil alongside the usual maelstrom of trade – high prices, increased taxation, shifting relations with the colonies, and large movements of people spilling from the countryside and arriving home from battle – the resulting reframing of authority contained within it a moment of deterritorialisation in which new claims might be heard. Such opposition achieved a defining moment with the court case of James Somerset in the early 1770s, a slave who took the much vaunted 'liberty' of England's air at its word.[69]

At the same time there was undoubtedly a utopian strain in the universalising impetus of this new imperial 'civilization' (a word first coined in this decade). As James Otis wrote from colonial Boston in 1764, with an agenda of his own:

> I should say that the world was at the eve of the highest scene of earthly power and grandeur that has been ever yet displayed to the view of mankind. The cards are shuffling fast throughout all Europe. Who will win the prize is with God . . . The next universal monarchy will be favourable to the human race, for it must be founded on the principles of equity, moderation, and justice.

Slavery appeared in this light a violation of natural law, one that debased the 'inestimable value of liberty' and made 'every dealer in it a tyrant, from the director of an African company to the petty chapman in needles and pins on the unhappy coast'.[70] Similar arguments were framed in Christian terms. Slavery was impious, wrote the anonymous author of *Two Dialogues on the Man-Trade* in 1760, because all men were the offspring of God, in possession of 'rational immortal souls', and connected by a common 'bond of humanity' 'spread over the face of the whole earth'. Such a traffic offended the divine foundation of human society in its reduction of men to beasts and commodities, 'things inanimate'.[71]

The universalising imperatives within the experience of imperial expansion – the imagining of the self within the community of 'mankind' – thus registered the presence of non-friends whose subjection was defining of the 'inestimable' freedoms of others. This was a zone of recoil, since it was in the encounter with such exclusion that seeming universals had to be weighed and accounted for. Slaves' existence, Orlando Patterson has argued, resembled a form of social death.[72] What would it mean to imagine their birthing as subjects 'circumscribed by rights', in Sterne's words; their 'resurrection' as an 'apparent elevation of a piece of human property into the place of reason', as

Joan Dayan has explored?[73] In James Otis's discussion of the rights of the British colonies, for example, the notion of what it is to be a free-born subject is extended to all men, 'white or black'. But the effect of this is to put the notion of a society based on the compact of natural law – a notion re-emerging at the mid-century, as we have seen – under severe pressure. The result was an indeterminacy that Otis details in his rhetorical questioning. 'What man is or ever was born free, if every man is not? . . . If every man has such right [to make an original compact], may there not be as many original compacts as there are men and women born or to be born? Are not women born as free as men? Would it not be infamous to assert that the ladies are all slaves by nature? If every man or woman born or to be born has, and will have, a right to be consulted, and must accede to the original compact before they can with any justice be said to be bound by it, will not the compact be ever forming and never finished, ever making and never done?'[74]

The antidote to such vertiginous thinking came for some, like the notorious Governor of Jamaica, Edward Long, in racist accounts of slavery that sought naturalising biological and religious explanations for such subordination: these were people without souls, incapable of rationality, no better than beasts, living out the biblical 'curse' of Ham. While the sentimental fiction of the period radically refutes in the name of a common humanity the inequality of a natural law read in the colour of a woman's skin or the features of a man's face, it also deals in its own racist forms of naturalising constraint. The elevation of the slave to the status of an equal subject can only be 'conditional', as Dayan shows.[75] Thus Sarah Scott's George Ellison justifies his recognition of slaves as 'fellow creatures' to his wife, 'when you and I are laid in the grave, our lowest black slave will be as great as we are; in the next world perhaps much greater; the present difference is merely adventitious, not natural' (I. 27). 'I am exerting a power meerly [sic] political', he explains, 'I have neither divine, nor natural right, to enslave this man' (I. 35).

Yet the text contains its own stereotypes of the childlike 'faithful and affectionate' slaves, who speak in pidgin ventriloquated by the text: 'Oh! master, no go, no go; if go steward whip, beat, kill poor slave; no go, no go; you go we die' (I. 82). Recognition of the plight of slaves brings with it new enlightened versions of paternalist subjection, always expressed in familial terms. While the 'shocking subordination' of slaves is seen to be an abhorred necessity in Jamaica, Ellison is able to hold up the liberty of Britain as a counterpoint, 'a country, that with all its faults is conspicuously generous, frank and merciful, because it is free; no subordination exists there, but what is for the benefit of the lower as well as the higher ranks; all live in a state of reciprocal services' (I. 37–8). This was a view of freedom that was to be legally tested on behalf of individual slaves, to the chagrin of plantation owners like Long; but it is a claim for liberty as justice that Scott's texts elide even as they hint at a future in which 'there may probably be no inequality'.[76]

## Sterne's Politics of Pity

But why *thy* brethren? Why to *thee* confin'd?
Why not allied to *me*? – to all mankind?[77]

The anti-slavery positions adopted in sentimental fiction of the period are thus woven into what Luc Boltanski has termed a 'politics of pity',[78] rather than a discourse of rights, in which individualised vignettes of distress connote generalisable states of wretchedness, the 'millions born to suffering' acknowledged in *A Sentimental Journey*. They do not articulate a 'metaphysics of justice', in Boltanski's words. If Sterne's work became for many representative of sentimental feeling on a universal scale, it was because such a politics is generated in the pages of his sermons and novels in ways that are definitive for the 1760s. His writing charts the links between the local tingling of the nerve endings and sympathetic tears, and the wider, global spectacle of tragedy by which the observer's 'mind is taken captive at once', 'without any observable act of the will', as his sermon 'Philanthropy Recommended' described (*Sermons*, 3.23). On the one hand Sterne offered vignettes, representations, through which readers could enjoy the same spectatorial identifications, the pleasures of instantaneous communion with the suffering in the name of a shared humanity. On the other, his work provided forms of philosophical reflection anatomising such a process that meant that some degree of cognitive control was retained. This was evidently more possible to maintain in his sermons, since a mode of exegetical reflection was there to be expected, than in fictional form, where the gap between feeling and thinking seemed to open up a moral ambiguity that was more difficult to justify. Yet in whatever genre, Sterne's writing was indicative of the discursive investment in a 'friendship with mankind', making the mute gestics of the affective body speak a 'universal' language.

In the last volume of *Tristram Shandy*, as a digression within one of the embedded sentimental tales, Sterne included a vignette that illustrates this process precisely. Corporal Trim describes the spectacle in a Portuguese shop, witnessed by his soldier brother Tom, of 'a poor negro girl, with a bunch of white feathers slightly tied to the end of a long cane, flapping away flies—not killing them.——'Tis a pretty picture! said my uncle Toby—she had suffered persecution, Trim, and had learnt mercy——'. This 'picture' is followed by discussion of the 'nature' of the slave girl, who is shown to be educable and inherently good, and to possess a story 'that would melt a heart of stone', which he promises to relate at a later point. The encounter gives rise to reflection:

> A Negro has a soul? an' please your honour, said the Corporal (doubtingly).
>
> I am not much versed, Corporal, quoth my uncle Toby, in things of that kind; but I suppose, God would not leave him without one, any more than thee or me——
>
> ——It would be putting one sadly over the head of another, quoth the Corporal.
>
> It would so; said my uncle Toby. Why then, an' please your honour, is a black wench to be used worse than a white one?
>
> I can give no reason, said my uncle Toby——
>
> ——Only, cried the corporal, shaking his head, because she has no one to stand up for her——
>
> ——'Tis that very thing, Trim, quoth my uncle Toby, – which recommends her to protection——and her brethren with her; 'tis the fortune of war which has put the whip into our hands *now*——where it may be hereafter, heaven knows!——but be it where it will, the brave, Trim! will not use it unkindly. (*TS* 9.6.747–8)

Sterne's '*now*' suggests the stakes might one day be reversed, and that it is only power, political dominion, that holds such barbarousness in place. The language of the passage resembles Sarah Scott's work in its concern for 'protection' of a mute and persecuted victim and her learned reciprocity. The two authors, who were related by marriage (Sterne's wife was her cousin), met in 1765. Like many writers of the period, she acknowledged a debt to this touchstone of benevolence by choosing an epigraph from his *A Sentimental Journey* for her later pamphlet reprise of *Ellison, The Man of Real Sensibility*, in 1774.

If there is nothing other than kindness that can be done to change the circumstances of the slave girl, who suffers persecution 'without reason', she is nevertheless brought within the circle of divinely orchestrated equality. Yet while the notion that a slave and a woman might possess a soul suggests an equity before God that writers like Phillis Wheatley would grasp in their own terms, it certainly did not entail parity in the ideal realm of conversing souls that we saw earlier. Christian deliverance suggested equality was a matter for the afterlife; the acknowledgement of a slave's soul was in the view of many testimony to his or her ability to learn to accept things as they were. As Richard Nisbet, a slave owner, put it in his *The Capacity of Negroes for Religious and Moral Improvement Considered* in 1789:

> The letters of Ignatius Sancho, the Latin compositions of Francis Williams, and the more natural ingenious productions of Phillis Wheatley, a slave whose

mind was cramped by her condition, and whose only tutor was the strength of her own faculties; each of these has already furnished a publick and ample testimony of, at least, as considerable a portion of mental ability as falls to the lot of mankind in general.

Yet it was quite possible to recognise the abilities of a Phillis Wheatley without conceding, in a 'fruitless discussion', as Nisbet put it, that the presence of a black Milton or Newton argued for equality on earth. Indeed in an address to his own slaves, Nisbet concluded that 'I no longer troubled to find out whether you could read or write, and to do all other such things, so well and so soon as white people; it was enough for me to know that God is too merciful, too just, and too kind to us all, to put it out of your power to become good, if you were properly taught.'[79]

Sterne had been writing the interpolated story of the slave girl in 1766 when he received the first of his letters from Ignatius Sancho, asking him as an 'epicurean in acts of charity. – You who are universally read, and as universally admired –' to address the question of West Indian slavery further in his work. 'Dear Sir, think in me you behold the uplifted hands of thousands of my brother Moors. – Grief (you pathetically observe) is eloquent; – figure to yourself their attitudes; – hear their supplicating addresses! – alas! – you cannot refuse. – Humanity must comply'.[80] Sterne replied that he aimed to 'weave' in the tale 'at the service of the afflicted', and, in an exchange that was later widely circulated and even versified, he claimed Sancho's 'brethren' as his own:

> There is a strange coincidence, Sancho, in the little events (as well as in the great ones) of this world; for I had been writing a tender tale of the sorrows of a friendless poor negro-girl, and my eyes had scarse done smarting with it, when your Letter of recommendation in behalf of so many of her brethren and sisters, came to me – but why *her brethren*? – or your's, Sancho! any more than mine? It is by the finest tints, and the most insensible gradations, that nature descends from the fairest face about St James's, to the sootiest complexion in Africa: at which tint of these, is it, that the ties of blood are to cease? and how many shades must we descend lower still in the scale, 'ere Mercy is to vanish with them? – but 'tis no uncommon thing, my good Sancho, for one half of the world to use the other half of it like brutes, & then endeavour to make 'em so. For my own part, I never look *Westward* (when I am in a pensive mood at least) but I think of the burdens which our Brothers & Sisters are *there* carrying – & could I ease their shoulders from one ounce of 'em, I declare I would set out this hour upon a pilgrimage to Mecca for their sakes –[81]

Sterne's response carries painterly references to a scale of tints and shades that suggest he is for all his humanitarian solidarity dealing in *representations*; like colonial paintings that register the infinitessimal calibrations of interracial breeding, for which the Spanish colonists had invented new and fantastical names. His is no taxonomy charting degrees of miscegenation, but the passage is nevertheless haunted by such 'gradations'. Blood ties are here evidence of 'consanguinity' even as they are precisely the sign of what Joan Dayan has termed 'a pseudorational system for the distribution of a mystical essence: blood = race',[82] and thereby of racial distinction and subjection. Sterne's invocation of his friendship for mankind is thus built upon an enabling (for him) disavowal, producing an imagined kinship without barriers. As he declares in *A Sentimental Journey*, 'are we not all relations?'(*SJ* 90): a rhetorical question, easier to pose against the grain of the servitude of the French *fille de chambre* than the more unrecuperable state of the 'friendless poor negro-girl'.

Ignatius Sancho had been prompted to write to Sterne because of a passage on slavery in his sermons, one that would be reworked in the *Journey* and widely exerpted and anthologised thereafter: 'Consider slavery——what it is,——how bitter a draught, and how many millions have been made to drink of it;—which if it can poison all earthly happiness when exercised barely upon our bodies, what must it be, when it comprehends both the slavery of body and mind?' (*Sermons*, 10.99–100). The examples of bondage Sterne had provided there were general, rooted in the misery of war, poverty and religious oppression (anti-Catholic sentiment conjuring up the torture of the Spanish Inquisition here as in the pages of *Tristram Shandy*), the universal panorama that Voltaire had also addressed in *Candide*. It was not a consideration specific to the plight of African slaves in his own time, as Sancho saw. Yet the universality of the lesson, describing the way 'all ranks and conditions of men' suffer and are thus 'put out of love with human life', is one reason why Sterne's passage was so potent. Many saw the rhetoric of slavery as a means of articulating their own sense of disenfranchisement, not least the women writers who, as Moira Ferguson has charted, took up the anti-slavery cause and thereby addressed their own sense of subjection.[83] Sterne's passage on slavery became a touchstone. Even in the early nineteenth century it continued to circulate. On board the Seven Years' War relic the *Namur*, during the Napoleonic wars, the young press-ganged sailor Clarkson Stanfield wrote to his father: 'Disguise thyself as thou wilt (says Sterne) still slavery, still thou art a bitter draught, and though Thousands in all ages have been made to drink of thee, thou art no less bitter on that account'.[84]

If, as uncle Toby stated, 'no reason' could be found for the state of slavery, the biblical story of *Job* from which Sterne's lesson originated offered one explanation. As the most upright of God's servants, Job is tested by an extreme suffering that is 'without cause', a 'captivity' which his friends attempt to explain through surmisings about the nature of divine justice, the imputation of crimes for which this must be some form of punishment. Theirs is the mistake. Only God knows why Job suffers. Job, in turn, keeps hold of his righteous 'integrity' and loudly declares his conscience is clear, even as he acknowledges the inscrutable nature of God's will.[85] In Immanuel Kant's view, the story of Job allegorised the nature of theodical reasoning – the relation of evil and pain in the world to God's wisdom – in its reiteration of the limits of human rationality: 'Job declares himself for the system of *unconditional divine decision*. "He has decided," Job says, "He does as he wills".'[86] Slavery in this light was not to be explained as some kind of retributive calculus on God's part (as some argued); nor, in Kant's view at least, was such worldly pain to be answered by reward in heaven (the reassuring message of a Christianity that preferred the temporality of deferral). The point was 'a religion of good life conduct', and 'sincerity in taking notice of the impotence of our reason';[87] or, as Sterne put it, if the 'dark sides' of human life were 'out of our power to redress', 'it is necessary every creature should understand his present state and condition, to put him in the mind of behaving suitably to it' (*Sermons*, 10.101).

The story of Job emphasised a stoicism that ran like a current through mid-eighteenth-century culture, moderated by Christian values. Not, Sterne countered in his sermons, a 'stoical stupidity', but an acceptance based in a 'just sense of God's providence' (*Sermons*, 15.145). Interpreted in this way, the existence of slavery was beyond rational comprehension, but might nonetheless be alleviated through the practice of benevolence. Sarah Scott's George Ellison thus improves the lot of his slaves, allowing them to marry, to be educated, to gain financial security. But he does not free them. Within a politics of pity, Boltanski suggests, 'the urgency of the action needing to be taken to bring an end to the suffering involved always prevails over considerations of justice. From such a perspective it is only in a world from which suffering has been banished that justice could enforce its rights'.[88] In the Christian universalism of the mid-eighteenth century, this was a matter for God, and while some like Granville Sharp underpinned their radical demand for justice with scriptural support, others felt more comfortable with a more conservative (and paternalist) reading of God's inscrutability. Seeing bondage as the lot of mankind undoubtedly strengthened the humanitarian framing of misery, so that all might feel implicated. As Sancho put it, 'Grief . . . is eloquent', and 'Humanity must comply': the purpose of sentimentalism was a discursive realignment of the mute gestics of the suffering such that moral action might be possible.[89] But it was one thing to acknowledge and weep at the commonality of human misery, to feel the guilt and pity prompted by the plaint of slaves ventriloquated in sentimental vignettes, and quite another to recognise the extent of public culpability in the particular violence of the slave system, and to remove the checks and balances that defined and denied the personhood of those who were captured within it.

The politics of pity dealt in spectatorial distance, internalised in the figure of conscience, Adam Smith's 'man within'. It thus offered an almost phantasmatic extension of the ideal friendship we have been exploring, a feeling projected beyond the boundaries of self and nation, underwritten by the Christian commandment of loving thy neighbour as thyself. This was the disinterested meaning of self-love. Yet its benefits of fellow-feeling generally flowed in one direction only, for all the concern for mutual reciprocity, as the incontrovertible and violent truth of slavery revealed. Friendship's 'recoil', marked by the demands for rights and freedom that found legal expression in the 1770s, eclipsed this comforting distance. In the language of Granville Sharp, we can see its calculus at work: '*With the same* MEASURE *that ye* METE (says he) *shall it be* MEASURED *unto you again* . . . What MEASURE of *Benevolence*, therefore, have these Men to expect, who endeavour to enrich THEMSELVES by *enslaving* and *oppressing* their BRETHREN'?' And again: SELF-LOVE . . . must be the RULE OR MEASURE . . . It must not be SOLE TENANT of the heart; but is always to leave *equal* room for a due balance of *that Love which we owe to our Neighbour*.'[90] Through this invocation of calculation, 'due balance', an unconditional demand began to assert itself in friendship's uncompromising extension, an ideal expressed in Étienne Balibar's Arendtian words as 'the right to rights'.[91] Thereafter not only would the truths of the barbarity of the slave system be articulated in court rooms and at Westminster, but the place of the suffering and mute victim, so crucial to sentimental narratives, would also be refused in the claim to subjecthood, to the shock of white observers like Hester Piozzi:

> Well! I am really haunted by *black shadows*. Men of colour in the rank of gentlemen; a black lady covered with finery, in the Pit at the Opera, and tawny children playing in the Squares . . . with their Nurses, afford ample proofs of Hannah More and Mr. Wilberforce's success in breaking down the *wall of separation*. Oh! how it falls on every side! and spreads its tumbling ruins on the world! leaving all ranks, all custom, all colours, all religions, *jumbled together*.[92]

If such a seeming ruination (in the emergent form of a black middle class) was only intimated in the 1760s, it was a prospect that sentimentalism attempted to contain. At the same time, and sometimes even in the same breath, it became possible to envisage a different permutation of fellow-feeling, one that acknowledged not simply the incorporation of all into the fundamental unity of mankind, but the presence of difference, even antagonism, in the encounter with the non-friend and thus the making of community. Here, as always, there was a scriptural precedent, linking the sermons of Laurence Sterne with the radical demands of lawyers like Granville Sharp.

The tale of the Good Samaritan graced the walls of many charitable institutions in the eighteenth century. The parable was a conventional sign of the virtue of practical charity, the alleviation of suffering as and where encountered. In Luc Boltanski's account, the story of the Samaritan is an example of localised compassion, lacking both the generalised condition and eloquence of a politics of pity. Yet Sterne's version turns it into precisely such a politics. The Samaritan's ability to relieve the plight of a stranger is testimony to 'a settled principle of humanity and goodness' (*Sermons*, 3.27) and thus to a 'universal benevolence' (*Sermons*, 3.22) 'planted in the heart of man' (*Sermons*, 3.28–9). To underline this, Sterne ventriloquates the thoughts of both the victim, a Jew, and his rescuer. Shunned by both a Priest and Levite, the Jew wonders '*what hopes*' he can have of a stranger: '*not only a stranger, – but a Samaritan released from all obligations to me, and by a national dislike inflamed by mutual ill offices, now made my enemy, and more like to rejoice at the evils which have fallen upon me, than to stretch forth a hand to save me from them*' (*Sermons*, 3.26). In turn, the Samaritan provides the answer:

> he is a Jew and I a Samaritan.—But are we not still both men? partakers of the same nature—and subject to the same evils?—let me change conditions with him for a moment and consider, had his lot befallen me as I journeyed in the way, what measure I should have expected at his hands.—Should I wish when he beheld me wounded and half-dead, that he should shut up his bowels of compassion from me, and double the weight of my miseries by passing by and leaving them unpitied?—But I am a stranger to the man—be it so,—but I am no stranger to his condition—misfortunes are of no particular tribe or nation, but belong to us all, and have a general claim upon us, without distinction of climate, country or religion. Besides, though I am a stranger—— 'tis no fault of his that I do not know him, and therefore unequitable he should suffer by it. (*Sermons*, 3.27–8)

It was certainly not unusual, as Melvyn New reminds us, for an eighteenth-century sermon writer to dramatise the thought processes of his characters.[93] But Sterne's 'copious' reflections, and the first-person form they take, reveal and animate the production of a politics of pity. Central here is the presence of the stranger and *enemy*, who can transcend his threatening alterity, outside the realm of 'obligation' and reciprocity, to reframe that equality on another level altogether.

The biblical lesson, that one must 'go and do likewise' could remain within the comforting defusal of sentimentalism, and the exhortations of the Sterne's charity sermon undoubtedly rest there. But the lesson also intimates a more radical message. In Granville Sharp's polemic it entails the ethical recognition not simply of the estrangement of another, but the alterity of the self. The lesson came from Leviticus: 'But *the stranger*, that dwelleth with you, shall be unto you *as one born among you*, and THOU SHALT LOVE HIM AS THYSELF, for *ye were strangers* in the land of Egypt'. And in the form of the Good Samaritan, a 'professed enemy', it had a political charge: 'the same benevolence which was due from the Jew to his brethren of the house of Israel is indispensably due, under the Gospel, to OUR BRETHREN OF THE UNIVERSE, howsoever opposite in religious or political opinion'.[94] Embedded in the story of Job's endurance was a similar lesson, the experience of what it means to be transformed into an 'alien' in the sight of family, friends and servants, 'abhorred' and 'forgotten' by all. God, Job declaims, 'counteth me unto him as one of his enemies'.[95]

It might be argued that an effect of the 'shadow' of slavery on the enlightened spread of universal benevolence was a chink in its security, an unsettling of the balance of power such that the subject of benevolence had to take the force of just such an alienation. This was in part an issue of imperial realpolitik, the verso of an imagined cosmopolitanism. Alongside the supremely confident triumphalism of imperial expansion were much more tentative narratives of dislocation and anxiety, about who it was that constituted the 'enemy' for whom. Voltaire's absurdist vision evokes this in *Candide*, in a global theatre where people change sides, mete out punishments and are enslaved by each other with equal alacrity. Yet the presence of the stranger as the self, signalled in the thematics of bastardy developed in Chapter 3, also concerned the constitution of political community, and the registering of a necessary deracination – the irruption of difference – in the remaking of sovereignty that would allow its extension. It found radical expression. The condition of friendship, that 'paid to Equals' in the words of Fleetwood's sermon, had to be reframed as a community forged in non-relation. Jacques Derrida reminds us of a quote from William Blake: 'Thy Friendship oft has made my heart to ake/ Do be my Enemy for Friendships sake'. It was, he suggests, 'a seismic revolution in the political concept of friendship'.[96]

### Phillis Wheatley comes to London

The reverberations of just such a revolution began to be felt with its release of the emergent voices of black writers and artists in the 1770s. Ignatius Sancho's claiming of Sterne as a friend was no insignificant gesture. It suggested not only his right to be part of public culture – the desire to 'mix . . . with all countries, colours, faiths'[97] – but also the garnering of cultural capital for quite radical ends: the constitution of social subjecthood. As Sukhdev Sandhu has argued, Sancho's work exhibits a 'studious creolisation of Sterne's aesthetic', the adoption of a formal play which in his hand deliberately ironises the racist commonplace that black people were unable to cope with linearity and thus with rational thought.[98] Sterne's attack on linearity in the pages of *Tristram Shandy* has a moral force; for Sandhu, it is the very meaning of Samaritanism; 'a doctrine which urges us to be concerned with the defective, the maimed, those who are unable to hasten along the straight paths of economic or social success'.[99] The appropriation of these tactics had far-reaching effects. Sancho's affiliation with Sterne, and his epistolary connections with numerous other friends in enlightened circles in London and the thirteen colonies, constitute an active claim for equal status in the sociable commerce of the period. Others appeared more seamless and thus dependent in their appropriation of the cadences of white culture, as if they had undergone an assimilation without remainder.

In 1773 the Boston poet Phillis Wheatley arrived in London with her master's son, ostensibly for her health. She was about nineteen, and had been bought by Susannah Wheatley in 1761, after her transportation from West Africa on the slave ship *Phillis*. The preface to her first collection of poems sketched her biography, underwritten by the testimony of various Boston luminaries including the Governor of the Massachusetts Bay Colony. She had reportedly been brought from Africa to America aged seven or eight, 'an uncultivated Barbarian',[100] but within sixteen months had mastered English enough to read the most difficult passages from the Bible 'to the great Astonishment of all who heard her'. She had been drawn to writing through 'Curiosity', first writing a letter to the Mohegan Indian minister Samuel Occom, and then to prominent Methodist figures like Selina Hastings, Countess of Huntingdon, who had connections to the Wheatleys and to whom she dedicated her poems.[101] Phillis Wheatley was at this point prolific, turning her hand to the elegy, to occasional poems, and to religious and polit-ical subjects which had begun to include advocacy of America's cause in the light of palpable examples of British repression. It was the Countess who would fund the publication of her poetry, selected for British eyes.[102] The col-lection was in preparation as she arrived, in a London that was more con-ducive to her recognition than the Boston she had temporarily left behind.

Ignatius Sancho read her poems five years after their publication, sent over with anti-slavery tracts by a friend in Philadelphia:

> Phyllis's poems do credit to nature – and put art – merely as art – to the blush.
> – it reflects nothing either to the glory or the generosity of her master – if she
> is still his slave – except he glories in the *low vanity* of having in his wanton
> power a mind animated by Heaven – a genius superior to himself. – The list
> of splendid – titled – learned names, in confirmation of her being the real
> authoress – alas! shows how very poor the acquisition of wealth and knowl-
> edge is – without generosity – feeling – and humanity. – These great good

folks – all know – and perhaps admired – nay, praised Genius in bondage – and then, like the Priests and the Levites in sacred writ, passed by – not one good Samaritan amongst them.[103]

Sancho was right that her figuring as 'Genius in bondage' served to reflect aspects of the white culture that framed her, though she had already been manumitted by the time of his writing. Many were astonished that her poetry could so perfectly provide in its balanced classical couplets and Miltonic repertoire, a seemingly untrammelled occasion for their own self-recognition. Some dismissed it as wholly imitative, without acknowledging the powerful part classical imitation had to play in the public culture of the period, and the extraordinary fact of its wielding by someone who had no right to its cultural capital at all. It was, in Thomas Jefferson's words, 'below the dignity of criticism'.[104] Yet there was something potentially incendiary about her talent that some were prepared to recognise. Phillis Wheatley was cited as an exemplary case study, a sign of what 'uncultivated nature' was capable of, with education; even a moral counterpoint to the savagery of those whose happiness was measured in wealth.[105] Within anti-slavery debates Wheatley became a touchstone of natural rights arguments. Thomas Clarkson included extracts of her poems in his *Essay on the Slavery and Commerce of the Human Species*, concluding that 'if the authoress *was designed for slavery* . . . the greater part of the inhabitants of Britain must lose their claim to freedom'.[106] In the very year of her visit, in the aftermath of the Somerset case, British reviews of her collection expressed dismay at her slave status. *The Gentleman's Magazine* saw the accompanying testimony of the great and good as 'disgraceful': 'Youth, innocence, and piety, united with genius, have not yet been able to restore her to the condition and character with which she was invested by the Great Author of her being. So powerful is custom in rendering the heart insensible to the rights of nature, and the claims of excellence!'[107]

Phillis Wheatley was freed shortly after her visit, 'at the desire of my friends in England', also managing to secure the proceeds from her intellectual property.[108] They would not sustain her, and like many who were freed but without a means of support, she would die destitute in Boston in 1784. Yet at this moment there was enormous hope in the discovery of such a transatlantic community of friends. Granville Sharp himself took her to see the crown jewels and lions in the Tower. She was fêted by prominent Methodists such as the Earl of Dartmouth, Secretary of State for North America, whose appointment and 'Friendship' for America she celebrated in verse. She was called upon by Benjamin Franklin, who noted Nathaniel Wheatley's unease at not being present in the room when she received him. It was a commonplace that the slaves of West Indian and American visitors were 'notoriously hard to control' in the free air of the metropolis;[109] in her case it was a sanctioned liberty.

Schooled in the Whitefieldian strain of Methodism and shaped by the values of the Great Awakening, she was able to write to her aristocratic patron Selina Hastings in the most deferential tones and yet as a fellow witness to the divine 'Friend of Mental Felicity', 'our great & common Benifactor'.[110] As Moira Ferguson has explored, Phillis Wheatley was hailed without reference to her slave status by the poet Mary Scott in *The Female Advocate* as one of the 'Female Authors of late [who] have appeared with honour', arguing implicitly, Ferguson suggests, that 'cultural equality . . . must be on a par with spiritual equality'.[111]

Many of Phillis Wheatley's poems address this question in their careful positioning of the poetic voice. She underwrites her right to have a voice at every opportunity. In 'A Hymn to Humanity', Christ, 'Divine *Humanity*', is commanded by God: 'Each human heart inspire:/ To act in bounties uncon-fin'd/ Enlarge the close contracted mind,/ And fill it with thy fire'. His descent to earth is paralleled by the arrival of the nine Muses: 'O'er me methought they deign'd to shine, /And deign'd to string my lyre'. It is the '*Friendship*' central to a Christian universalism, then, which legitimates the poetic act:

> Can *Afric's* muse forgetful prove?
> Or can such friendship fail to move
>     A tender human heart?
> Immortal *Friendship* laurel-crown'd
> The smiling Graces all surround
>     With ev'ry heav'nly *Art*.[112]

Yet if the act of writing is sanctioned by such piety, and the demand for tolerance and benevolent action is thereby woven in to her art, Phillis Wheatley's poetry has seemed to some a forgetting nonetheless. Hers has often appeared a willing assimilation into the sensibilities of white Christian culture, not least in the recasting of slavery in redemptive terms as a God-given mercy that had brought her from Africa. As John Shields, the editor of the modern *Collected Works*, put it: 'her works were (and continue to be) viewed as typical of eighteenth-century blacks who sold their blackness for a pottage of white acceptability'.[113] The general absence of reference to 'her own situation' was noted by *The Monthly Review* in 1773; to the more recent critical demand for some overt form of memorialisation of her pain and struggle in her poetry – that would see expressive protest as a horizon of her own historical self-consciousness – it has appeared a sign of denial, even bad faith.

The tactics of her work argue against simplistic conclusions, and the charge of selling out effects its own form of subalternisation. Her refusal to provide eloquent testimony of her own trauma and passage in poems such as 'On Being Brought from Africa to America', an experience often explicitly narrativised as a sentimental plaint by white anti-slavery poets of the time, can be seen to work in this particular moment against the victimhood reserved for such a spectacle. There is much evidence in her work of what Moira Ferguson terms 'subversive and camouflaged responses to representations of her life', articulated through a 'subtle mimicry' of white culture that 'expropriates their view of her by gazing back and commenting on what she sees';[114] a form of reflexivity that I want to consider again in a moment. There were also other, traceable, textual forms of dissent available to her. Sondra O'Neale, for example, has explored the use of biblical myth in her work within a tradition of African–American protest.[115] There were undoubtedly radical currents within the religious Great Awakening in the thirteen colonies who took Whitefield's doctrine of free grace literally, the view that a slave could be baptised into freedom. It is possible to see a demand for liberation slipping through the gaps between versions of single poems, even as Wheatley articulates a more mainstream Whitefieldian line.[116] And throughout, the imaginative flight of her verse suggests the search for a sublime transcendence, as John Shields has explored, one that yokes religious redemption with the 'mental optics' of a liberated, 'unbounded soul'.[117]

If the racialised tactics of Phillis Wheatley's writing afford ample evidence of the struggle with subjection, they also celebrate the Christian values espoused by the white New England community she lived among: worthy women and men addressed in the most elevated and generous of tones, slave-owners all. Yet it is clear that this too is a strategy, as she reveals in a widely circulated letter to Samuel Occom in 1774, just after her manumission. Here she makes her position plain in underlining Occom's argument for the natural rights of 'the Negroes':

> Those that invade them cannot be insensible that the divine Light is chasing away the thick Darkness which broods over the Land of Africa; and the Chaos which has reigned so long, is converting into beautiful Order, and reveals more and more clearly, the glorious Dispensation of civil and religious Liberty, which are so inseparably united, that there is little or no Enjoyment of one without the other: Otherwise, perhaps, the Israelites had been less solicitous for their Freedom from Egyptian Slavery; I do not say they would have been contented without it, by no Means, for in every human Breast, God has implanted a Principle, which we call Love of Freedom; it is impatient of Oppression, and pants for Deliverance; and by the Leave of our Modern Egyptians I will assert, that the same Principle lives in us.[118]

'Civil and religious Liberty' are one and the same: this is the enlightened lesson she takes to the 'Modern Egyptians' who have enslaved her. The unconditional link between friendship and equality has been broken by them: 'How well the

Cry for Liberty, and the reverse Disposition for the Exercise of oppressive Power over others agree, – I humbly think it does not require the Penetration of a Philosopher to determine'.[119] If this was a fundamental contradiction that colonial society revealed – 'how is it that we hear the loudest yelps for liberty among the drivers of negroes?', as Samuel Johnson had recognised[120]– her strategy might appear unusual. While 'deliverance' is a matter for God, she asks that he 'get him honor' on those whose 'Avarice' underlines the slave system, 'not for their Hurt, but to convince them of the strange Absurdity of their Conduct whose Words and Actions are so diametrically opposite'.[121] This is an odd statement, where 'Absurdity' is generated not through Shandean irony (as in the case of Ignatius Sancho), nor even answered immediately by retribution, but rather through an excessive embracing of those responsible for her subjection. It explains the positive drive and reflexive movement of many of her poems, which concern 'recollection' of the honour conferred by God: 'Forgive the muse, forgive th' advent'rous lays,/ That fain thy soul to heav'nly scenes would raise'.[122]

It becomes possible to read, in this light, the intense cultural *work* taking place in Phillis Wheatley's seamless appropriation of the cadences of white transatlantic culture. The realm of 'reciprocal Commerce' that we saw enacted in the grammar exercise at the beginning of this chapter is where she chooses to locate herself, in the seemingly effortless production of transparent exchange, the animation of a conversation in which she can ventriloquate the parts. In this way she participates equally in a discourse that, as the exercise reminded us, founds public sociability. Her poetry attempts to render the rhetorics of religious and civic discourse commensurable, to erase the disjunction between 'Words and Actions'. And the community of voices orchestrated in her writing – from the public encomium to freedom in the mouth of a dying general, to the intimacy of parents asking for their dead child – play off her own: a poetic voice that engages with its own fort/da game with authority, at times emphasising its marginality, elsewhere controlling the exchange, but always weighing the nature of reciprocal relations, and the calibrations of power that lie within them.

It is significant that the story of Wheatley's own capture is uniquely introduced in her poem to Lord Dartmouth, addressing America's sense of grievance, in 1768:

> Should you, my lord, while you peruse my song,
> Wonder from whence my love of *Freedom* sprung,
> Whence flow these wishes for the common good,
> By feeling hearts alone best understood,
> I, young in life, by seeming cruel fate
> Was snatch'd from *Afric's* fancy'd happy seat:

What pangs excruciating must molest,
What sorrows labour in my parent's breast?
Steel'd was that soul and by no misery mov'd
That from a father seiz'd his babe belov'd:
Such, such my case. And can I then but pray
Others may never feel tyrannic sway? [123]

This invocation of 'my case' draws on the spectacular nature of a politics of pity in its intense reimagining of the scene of capture. But it also contains evidence of removal – '*seeming* cruel fate', '*fancy'd* happy seat' – that render her position ambiguous: Africa is already the stuff of representation, while her violent abduction turns out, as she states elsewhere, to be a sign of 'Mercy'. This suggests an incommensurability in the positioning of a figure like Phillis Wheatley, caught and yet self-fashioning within the complex structuring of loss plotted out in numerous Atlantic crossings: neither American, nor African, yet both; abducted and enslaved yet claiming a right of public belonging, marking the presence of that incontrovertible demand for liberty in the universalising rhetoric of the colonial culture of the moment. Like the Samaritan of Sterne's sermon, she identifies reciprocally with the plight of others because she knows what it is like to feel 'tyrannic sway'; 'my case' becomes not only a mark of her otherness, but the very condition of her belonging, her right to speak for the 'common good'.

What does the 'case' of Phillis Wheatley reveal about the state imagining I have been charting? Her own engagement with the constitution of community, sanctioned by divine 'Friendship', suggests the potential for its radical remaking against the grain of oppressive authority. As Robert Kendrick has perceptively explored, Wheatley's use of the epic, in which she borrows and excerpts past fragments and forms (a Sternean tactic in itself, one might think), becomes representative of an American culture that is itself self-constituting at this time. Imagining that her poetry might rival '*Virgil's* page'[124] (itself a heavily worked allusion to state imagining in the eighteenth century), she produces a textual indeterminacy within an emergent national mythmaking that disrupts notions of belonging and exclusion. 'As a result', Kendrick argues, 'one cannot say that either African or European Americans "belong" in Christian culture. One can only practice "belonging" in Christianity, and racial marks cannot determine who practices this process'.[125] For a woman who saw civil and religious liberty as synonymous, such an equality had secular, political meaning, which gradually became embodied for her in an ideal form: the American republic. In her writing a transition is charted, from the rebus celebrating the British taking of Quebec to the emergence of a 'new-born *Rome*', a rival 'Realm of Freedom'.[126] The loss of the thirteen colonies was one consequence of friendship's recoil as a state imagining, shaping the aftermath of the Seven Years' War. In Wheatley's work it is accompanied by the renewal of imperial fantasy as a *pax Americana*. Even as her poems chart the flight of her liberated imagination, from an Edenic vision of Gambia to the harvest of 'Britain's favour'd isle',[127] the expansionist rhetoric of empire is also present:

> From star to star the mental optics rove,
> Measure the skies, and range the realms above.
> There in one view we grasp the mighty whole
> Or with new worlds amaze th' unbounded soul.[128]

In the New World of 1784 she celebrated the sunlight of a 'Heavenly *Freedom*' in her poem 'Liberty and Peace', writing at the same time an elegy to her own leavetaking, which mourns the loss of her 'poetic flame'.[129] Phillis Wheatley paid the absolute cost of imagining the unconditional relation between liberty and equality. It is doubtful that any of the 'Private Young Gentlemen and Ladies' who picked up Buchanan's *Grammar* in the Boston edition of that year would have grasped the meaning of 'reciprocal Commerce' with anything like the same awareness of its violence, and hope.

## Notes

1. James Buchanan, *The British Grammar: Or, an Essay in Four Parts towards Speaking and Writing the English Language Grammatically and Inditing Elegantly for the Use of the Schools of Great Britain and Ireland, and of Private Young Gentlemen and Ladies* (London: A. Millar, 1762), p. 202.

2. John Locke, *An Essay Concerning Human Understanding*, ed. Peter H. Nidditch (Oxford: Clarendon Press, 1975), p. 472.

3. Buchanan, 'Dedication'.

4. See particularly the chapter on 'The language properly so-called' in Barrell, *English Literature in History*, pp. 110–75.

5. Buchanan, *The British Grammar*, p. 73, and 'Dedication'.

6. Buchanan, 'Dedication', p. xxxiv. The shifting context for the 'manly Diction of BRITONS' in the Boston of 1784, however, suggests that the triumphalism of 1762 might later have been read and appropriated by the former colonies in unintended ways.

7. John Locke, *Essays on the Law of Nature*, ed. W. von Leyden (Oxford: Clarendon, 1970), p. 157.

8. Locke, *Essay Concerning Human Understanding*, p. 514.

9. Thomas Sheridan, *A Course of Lectures on Elocution* (London: np, 1762), pp. 132–3.

10  Buchanan, *The British Grammar*, p. 67.

11  Wilson, *The Sense of the People*, p. 61.

12  An example of this regulation was the expelling of Thomas Spence from the Newcastle Philosophical Society in 1775, which Wilson discusses. The rules for this Society were particularly stringent, and were offended when Spence published his radical tract *The Real Rights of Man*, which advocated the complete redistribution of property among the English population. Though his argument had been previously debated, Wilson records, it clearly did not tally with the views of the property owning tradesmen who were fellow members of the Society, and who baulked at its circulation 'in the manner of a halfpenny ballad and . . . hawked about the streets to the manifest dishonour of the society'. See Wilson, p. 68.

13  Quoted in Donna T. Andrew, 'Popular Culture and Public Debate: London, 1780', *The Historical Journal* 39:2 (1996), p. 417. As Andrew discusses, the four women's debating societies in London were La Belle Assemblée, The Female Parliament, the Carlisle House Debates for Ladies Only and the Female Congress. I am indebted to Angela Escott for this reference. As her own work on the drama of Hannah Cowley shows, women's debating was itself reflected on in theatrical satire. See Angela Escott, 'Generic Diversity in the Plays of Hannah Cowley' (unpublished PhD thesis, University of London, 2005).

14  Jones, William, p. 14.

15  Buchanan, *The British Grammar*, p. 215.

16  Jacques Derrida, *The Politics of Friendship*, trans. George Collins (London and New York: Verso Books, 1997), p. 199. Derrida is referring to Book III of Aristotle's *Politics*.

17  Michel de Montaigne, 'De l'amitié', usually translated as 'On Friendship' but by M. A. Screech as 'On affectionate relationships', in *The Complete Essays* (Harmondsworth: Penguin Books, 1991), pp. 211–12. Screech points out that the first syllable of *amitié* would have sounded like *âme* (soul) in Renaissance French.

18  Randolph Trumbach, *The Rise of the Egalitarian Family: Aristocratic Kinship and Domestic Relations in Eighteenth-Century England* (New York and London: Academic Press, 1978), pp. 14, 64.

19  W. Fleetwood, *The Relative Duties Of Parents and Children, Husbands and Wives, and Masters and Servants, Consider'd in Sixteen Sermons* (London: Charles Harper, 1705), pp. 297–8.

20  Goldsmith, 'On Public Rejoicings for Victory', p. 19.

21  Ibid. p. 17.

22  Derrida, *The Politics of Friendship*, p. 21.

23  This vision of unmediated access to the king was powerfully present at the accession of George III, as Laurence Sterne's letters report: 'The King seems resolved to bring all things back to their original principles, and to stop the torrent of

corruption and laziness . . . The present system being to remove that phalanx of great people, which stood betwixt the throne and the subjects, and suffer them to have immediate access without the intervention of a cabal.' Sterne to Stephen Croft, December 1760, *Letters*, p. 126. This hope soon diminished with the torrent of criticism of the king's involvement with Bute, and continued with Burke's attack in 1770 on the 'second cabinet' around the monarch: 'knots and cabals of men who have got together avowedly without any public principle . . . ought never to be suffered to domineer in the state; because they have no connection with the sentiments and opinions of the people.' See Burke, 'Thoughts on the Present Discontents', p. 269.

24 *The Con-test* 4 (14 December 1756), cited in J. A. Gunn (ed.), *Factions No More: Attitudes to Party in Government and Opposition in Eighteenth-Century England* (London: Cass., 1972), p. 171.

25 Goldsmith, *The Vicar of Wakefield*, p. 102.

26 Derrida, *The Politics of Friendship*, p. 204.

27 Horace Walpole responds to the unrest of the time in a letter to Horace Mann dated 26 June 1765: 'I never knew a more distracted [situation] in times of peace'. See Walpole, *Correspondence* 22:VI, 301.

28 Derrida, *The Politcs of Friendship*, pp. 205, 206.

29 See Barrell, *English Literature in History*, p. 115.

30 Goldsmith, *Citizen of the World*, p. 75.

31 I am thinking of William Pitt's elevation on his resignation to Earl of Chatham, which was particularly controversial because of his patriotic construction as the Great Commoner, which I discuss in Chapter 2.

32 Swenson, *On Jean-Jacques Rousseau*, p. 70.

33 Rousseau, 'The Social Contract', p. 135.

34 As David H. Solkin notes in an excellent essay, Cicero was deemed significant because of his defence of aristocratic virtue against a vociferous and increasingly powerful citizenry, his *De legibus* marking the moment when a free republic gave way to imperial tyranny. Solkin traces the parallels with the furore over Wilkes's success and executive removal as MP for Middlesex, and the repeated references to Cicero in the culture of the period, in particular the Wilkite context for Richard Wilson's Royal Academy exhibit of 1770, *Cicero and His Two Friends, Atticus and Quintus, at his Villa at Arpinium*. See David H. Solkin, 'The Battle of the Ciceros: Richard Wilson and the politics of landscape in the age of John Wilkes', in Simon Pugh (ed.), *Reading Landscape: Country – City – Capital* (Manchester: Manchester University Press, 1990), pp. 41–65.

35 Ferguson, *An Essay on the History of Civil Society*, p. 417.

36 Ibid. p. 211.

37 Robert Wallace, *Various Prospects of Mankind, Nature and Providence* (London: n. pub., 1761), p. 37. See Caroline Robbins, *The Eighteenth-Century Commonwealthman: Studies in the Transmission, Development and Circumstance of*

*English Liberal Thought from the Restoration of Charles II until the War with the Thirteen Colonies* (Cambridge, MA: Harvard University Press, 1959), p. 206.

38 Ibid. p. 209; brief reference to Godwin on p. 207. Godwin discusses Wallace's view of 'a community of goods to be maintained by the vigilance of the state' in 1793, in his *Enquiry Concerning Political Justice and Its Influence on Modern Morals and Happiness*, ed. Isaac Kramnick (Harmondsworth: Penguin Books, 1985), pp. 729, 767.

39 Goldsmith, *The Vicar of Wakefield*, p. 151.

40 Ibid. p. 102.

41 Henry Brooke, *The Fool of Quality* (London: George Routledge, 1906), p. 74. The interpolated story of Hammel Clement and his family, discovered starving in a field, is one pedagogic example of what I have been describing: the son of a rich retailer, he is educated to be a gentleman and man of letters, and is thus ill-equipped to survive after his father cuts him off without a penny.

42 See Murray Cohen, *Sensible Words: Linguistic Practice in England 1640–1785* (Baltimore: Johns Hopkins University Press, 1977).

43 James Gough, *A Practical Grammar of the English Tongue* (Dublin: Isaac Jackson, 1754), p. xii.

44 James Harris, *Hermes: Or, A Philosophical Inquiry Concerning Language and Universal Grammar* (London: H. Woodfall, printed for J. Nourse and P. Vaillant, 1751), pp. 350–51.

45 Brooke, *The Fool of Quality*, p. 129.

46 Montaigne, 'De l'amitié', p. 214.

47 Markley, 'Sentimentality as Performance', p. 223.

48 Sarah Scott, *The History of Sir George Ellison*, 2 vols (London: A. Millar, 1766), II, 22. All futher references cited by volume and page number in the text.

49 Henry Mackenzie, *The Man of Feeling*, ed. Brian Vickers (Oxford: Oxford University Press, 1967), p. 29.

50 Ibid. p. 42.

51 Derrida, *The Politics of Friendship*, pp. 258, 259.

52 William Russell, *Essay on the Character, Manners and Genius of Women in Different Ages. Enlarged from the French of M. Thomas*, 2 vols (Philadelphia: R. Aitken, 1774), II, 34. I am mindful here of Harriet Guest's discussion of Russell in *Small Change*, where his sense of women's incompatibility with patriotism is contrasted with its domestic, local refiguring in the 1770s and 1780s. See Guest, *Small Change*, pp. 181–2. I argue below that his debate about the nature of ideal friendship and its relation to the role of women gestures to such a refiguring despite its separation of women from the business of the state.

53 Scott, *Millenium Hall*, pp. 112–13.

54 Ibid. p. 245.

55 Ibid. p. 111.

56 Luc Boltanski, *Distant Suffering: Morality, Media and Politics* (Cambridge: Cambridge University Press, 1999), pp. 81–2.

57 Hannah More, 'Sensibility: A Poetical Epistle to the Hon. Mrs Boscawen', in *Sacred Dramas: Chiefly Intended For Young Persons: The Subjects Taken from the Bible. to which is added Sensibility. A Poem* (London: T. Cadell, 1782), pp. 284–5.

58 Russell, *Essay*. All further references will be cited by volume and page number in the text.

59 Smith, *The Theory of Moral Sentiments*, p. 137.

60 Immanuel Kant, *Conclusion of the Elements of Ethics* in *Doctrine of Virtue, Metaphysics of Morals*, trans. Mary Gregor (Cambridge: Cambridge University Press, 1991), p. 262. See Derrida, p. 253–63 for a discussion of Kant's short treatise on friendship.

61 Derrida, *The Politics of Friendship*, p. 260.

62 Fleetwood, *Realistic Duties*, p. 297.

63 Jacqueline Rose, 'Margaret Thatcher and Ruth Ellis' in her *Why War? – Psychoanalysis, Politics, and the Return to Melanie Klein* (Oxford: Blackwell, 1993), p. 51.

64 More, 'Sensibility', p. 282.

65 On the notion of the 'lustre' of the woman of sensibility see Harriet Guest, 'A Double Lustre: Femininity and Sociable Commerce, 1730–60', *Eighteenth-Century Studies* 23 (1989–90), 479–501.

66 Derrida, pp. 260–1.

67 More, 'Sensibility', p. 282.

68 Fleetwood, *Relatives Duties*, p. 297.

69 As discussed earlier, James Somerset was a slave of a Boston customs official who wanted to force him to return to the colonies. In a landmark case, prosecuted by Granville Sharp, Lord Mansfield chose not to support the rights of the slave-holder given the constitutional liberty enshrined in British law. See Chapter 3, n.4.

70 James Otis, *The Rights of the British Colonies Asserted and Proved* (Boston, MA; London: J. Almon, 1764), pp. 61, 44.

71 Anon., *Two Dialogues on the Man-Trade* (London: J. Waugh, 1760), pp. 12, 9, 19.

72 Patterson, Orlando, *Slavery and Social Death: A Comparative Study* (Cambridge, MA; London: Harvard University Press, 1982).

73 Joan Dayan, 'Legal Slaves and Civil Bodies', *Nepantla: Views from South* 2:1(2001), p. 14.

74 Otis, pp. 4–5. This reasoning was quoted approvingly by the American editor of Granville Sharp's later *Essay on Slavery*, a text that attacked Thomas Thompson's tract which had argued that 'the African Trade for Negro Slaves' was 'consistent with the Principles of Humanity'.

75 Dayan, 'Legal Slaves and Civil Bodies', p. 14.

76  Scott, *Millenium Hall*, p. 245.

77  From a versified version of Sterne's exchange with Ignatius Sancho, in Ewan Clark, *Miscellaneous Poems* (Whitehaven: J. Ware, 1779), p. 217. Many of the poems – 'The Monk, 'The Captive', 'Sensibility', The Dead Ass', 'Maria' – are poetic paraphrases of vignettes in *A Sentimental Journey*.

78  Boltanski, *Distant Suffering*, pp. 3–19.

79  Richard Nisbet, *The Capacity of Negroes for Religious and Moral Improvement Considered: With Cursory Hints, to Proprietors and to Government, for the Immediate Melioration of the Condition of Slaves in the Sugar Colonies: to which are subjoined Short and Practical Discourses to Negroes on the Plain and Obvious Principles of Religion and Morality* (1789) (Westport, CT: Negro Universities Press, 1970), pp. 31, 1, 199.

80  Ignatius Sancho to Mr Sterne, 21 July 1766, in *The Letters of Ignatius Sancho*, ed. Paul Edwards and Polly Rewt (Edinburgh: Edinburgh University Press, 1994), p. 86.

81  L. Sterne to Ignatius Sancho, 27 July 1766, in Edwards and Rewt, p. 274.

82  Dayan, 'Legal Slaves and Civil Bodies', p. 12.

83  See Moira Ferguson's excellent *Subject to Others: British Women Writers and Colonial Slavery, 1670–1834* (New York and London: Routledge, 1992) for the valencies of anti-slavery sentiment among women at this time.

84  Clarkson Stanfield was a famous theatre designer, named by his father James Stanfield after the abolitionist Thomas Clarkson, with whom he had corresponded. The letter, which quotes directly from *A Sentimental Journey*, dates from 22 October 1814, and is cited in Pieter van der Merwe, 'The Life and Theatrical Career of Clarkson Stanfield 1793–1867' (unpublished Ph.D. thesis, University of Bristol, 1979), p. 26. I am indebted to Pieter van der Merwe for making his research available to me. The general appropriation of the term slavery also had reactionary repercussions. In the 1770s the example of impressment as a form of slavery was used by the anti-abolitionist Samuel Estwick to argue against the view that Britain's constitution was incompatible with slavery, which was key to James Somerset's claim to liberty on British shores.

85  Job 2: 3, 42: 10, 27: 5.

86  Immanuel Kant, 'On the miscarriage of all philosophical trials in theodicy', in his *Religion and Rational Theology*, trans. and ed. Allen W. Wood and George di Giovanni (Cambridge: Cambridge University Press, 1996), p. 32.

87  Ibid. pp. 33, 34.

88  Boltanski, *Distant Suffering*, p. 5.

89  As Sancho wrote, 'Sterne's Sermons – . . . chiefly inculcate practical duties, and paint brotherly love and the true Christian charities in such beauteous glowing colours – that one cannot help wishing to feed the hungry – clothe the naked, &c. &c.' Sancho to Mr. M[eheux], 23 July 1777, in Edwards and Rewt, *The Letters of Ignatius Sancho*, pp. 93–4.

90 Granville Sharp, *The Law of Liberty, Or Royal Law, by which All Mankind Will Certainly Be Judged! Earnestly Recommended to the Serious Consideration of all Slaveholders and Slave-Dealers* (London: B. White, E. & C. Dilly, 1776), pp. 39, 10.

91 Balibar, 'Ambiguous Universality', p. 167.

92 Hester Piozzi, in Oswald G. Knapp (ed.), *The Intimate Letters of Hester Piozzi and Penelope Pennington 1788–1822* (London: John Lane, 1914), p. 243. Quoted in Edwards and Rewt, p. 15.

93 See in particular the connections drawn between the sermons of Thomas Herring, Archbishop of York and then Canterbury in the 1740s and 1750s and Sterne's writing in this regard, in New's useful volume of notes to the sermons, pp. 75–83.

94 Granville Sharp, *The Just Limitation of Slavery in the Laws of God, Compared With the Unbounded Claims of the African Traders and British American Slaveholders* (London: B. White, E. & C. Dilly, 1776), pp. 9, 40.

95 Job 19: 11–19.

96 Derrida, *The Politics of Friendship*, pp. 26, 27.

97 Ignatius Sancho to Mr. M[eheux], 23 July 1777, in Edwards and Rewt, *The Letters of Ignatius Sancho*, p. 96.

98 It was not only those who wrote tracts about race like Edward Long who promulgated these views. James Grainger's *The Sugar Cane* of 1764 is a 'West-India georgic' that integrates the racialised perception of linearity into a conventional form of estate poetry, adapted for the colonial planter: 'As art transforms the savage face of things,/And order captures the harmonious mind;/ Let not thy blacks irregularly hoe;/But, aided by the line, consult the site/ Of thy desmesnes, and beautify the whole.' See James Grainger, *The Sugar-Cane* (London: R. and J. Dodsley, 1764), ll.266–70. I return to this in my conclusion.

99 Sukhdev Sandhu, 'Ignatius Sancho: An African Man of Letters' in Reyahn King, Sukhdev Sandhu, James Walvin and Jane Girdham, *Ignatius Sancho: An African Man of Letters* (London: National Portrait Gallery, 1997), pp. 52–3.

100 See the Attestation to her authorship, in John C. Shields (ed.), *The Collected Works of Phillis Wheatley* (New York and Oxford: Oxford University Press), p. 7.

101 Details from the short biography sketched in a letter from her master John Wheatley, prefacing her volume, in Shields, p. 6.

102 In the English publication of her poetry many of the more overtly political poems were left out. Following its earlier celebration of British victories in the Seven Years' War, like the taking of Quebec, her writing became increasingly partisan with the growing opposition to British interests in the thirteen colonies. It included addresses to Generals Washington and the captured Lee, the death of General Wooster, the events surrounding the Boston Massacre, 'America', and the encomium to American freedom, 'Liberty and Peace', published in 1784. These were proposed for an American volume of poems and letters that were to be dedicated to Benjamin Franklin, but were never published.

103 Ignatius Sancho to Mr. [Jabez] Fisher, 27 January 1778, in Edwards and Rewt, *The Letters of Ignatius Sancho*, p. 122.

104 'Religion indeed has produced a Phyllis Whately [sic]; but it could not produce a poet. The compositions published under her name are below the dignity of criticism'. Jefferson, *Notes on the State of Virginia* (1787), in *Writings*, p. 267.

105 She was 'a young Affrican, of surprising genius', in the words of *The Royal American Magazine*, which reflected: '*By this single instance may be seen, the importance of education. – Uncultivated nature is much the same in every part of the globe.It is probable* Europe *and* Affrica *would be alike* savage *or* polite *in the same circumstances; though, it may be questioned, whether men who have no* artificial *wants, are capable of becoming so ferocious as those, who, by faring sumptuously every day, are reduced to a habit of thinking it necessary to* their *happiness, to plunder the whole human race'.* Quoted in Shields, p. 302.

106 Thomas Clarkson, *An Essay on the Slavery and Commerce of the Human Species Particularly the African, Translated from a Latin Dissertation which was Honoured with the First Prize in the University of Cambridge for the Year 1785* (London: J. Phillips, 1786), p. 175.

107 See 'Poetical Essays', where her poem 'Recollection' is fully reproduced, *The Gentleman's Magazine and Historical Chronicle*, 43 (1773), p. 456. *The Monthly Review* also expressed concern at finding 'this ingenious young woman is yet a slave', particularly given that 'the people of Boston boast themselves chiefly on their principles of liberty', though it dismissed her poetry as 'merely imitative'. See *The Monthly Review; Or, Literary Journal* 49 (June 1773 – January 1774), 458–9.

108 Phillis Wheatley to David Wooster, 18 October 1773, in Shields, *The Collected Works*, p. 170.

109 See Julie M. Flavell, 'The "School for Modesty and Humility": Colonial American Youth in London and Their Parents, 1755–1775', *The Historical Journal* 42:2 (1999), 393.

110 Phillis Wheatley to the Countess of Huntingdon, 17 July 1773, in Shields, *The Collected Works*, p. 168.

111 Ferguson, pp. 128, 129.

112 Wheatley, 'A Hymn to Humanity', in Shields, *The Collected Works*, pp. 96, 97.

113 'Preface', Shields, *The Collected Works*, p. xxviii.

114 Ferguson, *An Essay on the History of Civil Society*, p. 127.

115 See Sondra A. O'Neale, *Jupiter Hammon and the Biblical Beginnings of African-American Literature* (Metuchen, NJ and London: Scarecrow Press, 1993).

116 See her three versions of an elegy to George Whitefield, where the contradictions of his religious discourse are made manifest. Whitefield had argued that slave rebellions were a judgement from God, and that the situation could only be resolved if slave owners attended to the souls of both masters and slaves, recognising their relative duties to each other – slaves would then become better

servants, and masters, if they averted brutality, would avoid divine retribution. This ameliorist Christian message is strongly to be found in Wheatley's poems and letters. Whitefield became himself a slave owner, and, worried about being seen to incite insurrection, had explicitly forbidden slaves to disobey their masters. Yet the liberationist reading of free grace also registers. In Phillis Wheatley's American published poem she addresses the black slave population: 'Take him, ye Africans, he longs for you,/*Impartial Saviour* is his title due:/ Wash'd in the fountain of redeeming blood, / You shall be sons, and kings, and priests to God'. This offers up the Christian prospect of a life of freedom after death that works throughout her poetry, and remains within the orthodox and conservative account of Whitefield's message. But one variant poem (published in London) puts it differently: 'If you will walk in Grace's heavenly road,/ He'll make you free, and Kings, and Priests, to God.' Wheatley, 'On the Death of the Rev. George Whitefield', Shields, *The Collected Works*, p. 23, LL.34–7. Variants in Shields, *The Collected Works*, pp. 206–11. On this point see Shields, *The Collected Works*, p. 195; also the chapter 'Sable Patriots and Modern Egyptians' in Rafia Zafar, *We Wear the Mask: African Americans Write American Literature 1760–1870* (New York: Columbia University Press, 1997), 15–39. On the doctrine of free grace and the insurrectionary potential of the Great Awakening see Linebaugh and Rediker, *The Many-Headed Hydra*, pp. 190–3.

117 Wheatley, 'On Imagination', in Shields, *The Collected Works*, p. 66, ll.19, 22. See Shields, pp. 252–67 on her use of a sublime aesthetic.

118 Phillis Wheatley to Samsom Occom, 11 February 1774, in Shields, *The Collected Works*, pp. 176–7.

119 Ibid. p. 177.

120 Samuel Johnson, 'Taxation no Tyranny: An Answer to the Resolutions and Address of the American Congress' (1775), in *Political Writings*, p. 454.

121 Phillis Wheatley to Samsom Occom, 11 February 1774, in Shields, *The Collected Works*, p. 177.

122 Wheatley, 'To His Honour the Lieutenant-Governor, on the Death of his Lady', Shields, *The Collected Works*, p. 118, ll.43–4.

123 Wheatley, 'To the Right Honourable WILLIAM, Earl of DARTMOUTH, His Majesty's principal Secretary of State for North America, &c.', Shields, *The Collected Works*, p. 74, ll.20–31.

124 Wheatley, 'To Maecenas', Shields, *The Collected Works*, p. 10, l.23.

125 Robert Kendrick, 'Re-membering America: Phillis Wheatley's Intertextual Epic', *African American Review* 30:1 (1996), 77. Kendrick is particularly illuminating on the role of mourning in her writing, and its relation to the 'process of "becoming" American' in which 'one's "origin" no longer serves as a teleological mark'. (83)

126 Wheatley, 'An Answer to the Rebus', Shields, p. 124; 'Liberty and Peace', Shields, *The Collected Works*, pp. 154, 155, ll.22, 30.

127 Wheatley, 'Phillis's Reply to the Answer', Shields, *The Collected Works*, p. 144, l.31.
128 Wheatley, 'On Imagination', in Shields, *The Collected Works*, p. 66, ll.19–22.
129 Wheatley, 'Liberty and Peace', Shields, *The Collected Works*, p. 156, l.64; 'An Elegy on Leaving—', Shields, *The Collected Works*, p. 156, l.18.

# WOMEN'S TIME AND WORK-DISCIPLINE: OR, THE SECRET HISTORY OF 'POOR MARIA'

The only possible Means of preventing a Rival Nation from running away with your Trade, is to prevent your own People from being more idle and vicious than they are . . . So the only War, which can be attended with Success in this Respect, is a War against Vice and Idleness; a War, whose Forces must consist of – not Fleets and Armies – but such judicious Taxes and Wise Regulations, as will turn the Passion of private Self-Love into the Channel of Public Good.[1]

Imperial competition was the most aggressive of enterprises, even in times of peace. For Josiah Tucker, a pacifist during the Seven Years' War in the name of *le doux commerce*, the war at stake was an internal one, to be welcomed in its rigorous conquest of the domestic population. If the realm of sociable commerce made such an imperative palatable through the forms of affective 'reciprocity' I have been exploring, it nevertheless could seem a war in all but name. It had, to continue the metaphor, its casualties and deserters, as well as its enemies within. And central to its campaign was the regulation of time: in particular, *women's* time, which appeared at once to be a cause of, and antidote to, the widespread 'Vice and Idleness' Tucker deplored. This chapter considers the relation of 'women's time' to the state imagining of the 1760s and 1770s, by tracking the fortunes of one popular sentimental image, Sterne's 'Poor Maria', across the social landscape of the period.

'Poor Maria', I will suggest, was not only a highly bankable visual image, increasingly cut loose from its literary origins, but an index of a wider aesthetic labour whose changing lineaments can be read in the domestic culture of Britain in the latter decades of the century. She has a 'secret history'.[2] It is one which involves the abstractive translation of social misery, yet nonetheless articulates, in the same gesture, a wordless form of resistance. Not unlike a detective faced with a mystery of signs, I want to think about what it means to read her aleatory figure within the drawing rooms of bourgeois life, and in particular – since *time* is the mystery central to this chapter – to find her reproduced on the surface of a watch-case.

### Ur-Marias

Sterne's Maria was one of the most iconic and widely disseminated sentimental emblems of the second half of the eighteenth century. This pastoral image of a melancholic young woman, distracted by thwarted lost love, was 'a subject seemingly tailored to fit . . . the sensibility of the late eighteenth-century spectator', as Catherine Gordon relates, uncovering twenty versions of the subject exhibited and engraved between 1774 and 1819, and at least ten other paintings by the end of the century.[3] New technologies of reproduction and interior design meant that Maria turned up decorously in elegant drawing rooms across Europe, on walls and textiles, and on furniture from fire-screens to commodes, most often taken from Angelica Kauffman's popular representations of Sterne's literary figure (Figure 5.1).[4] In Germany, where the sensitivity to visions of romantic abandon was at its height, Maria became the occasion for quasi-touristic homage: her grave was constructed in a park, and elsewhere a young woman impersonated her wandering distress, accompanied by a pet lamb. The vogue for Sterne's *A Sentimental Journey*, which was the main source for the image in the last decades of the century, can only partially account for this fascination.[5] Both the novel, and the much-reprinted anthology of highlights from Sterne's work aimed at 'the Heart of Sensibility', *The Beauties of Sterne*, prompted a number of imitators who attempted to complete Maria's story in narrative, poetic and even operatic form.[6]

Maria is twice encountered in Sterne's work in the late 1760s. In *Tristram Shandy* the narrator comes across her in volume nine, while travelling across France with the tale of uncle Toby's amours forming in his mind. With 'the kindliest harmony vibrating within me', he declares, 'every thing I saw, or had to do with, touch'd upon some secret spring either of sentiment or rapture' (*TS* 9.24.781). Maria provides the occasion for both. Music from her pipe, querulously playing the 'evening service to the Virgin' morning and night, sets his 'feeling heart' vibrating, and her history takes 'full possession' of him. Maria's marriage has been prevented by the 'intrigues' of the parish curate, who has obstructed the reading of the banns; she consequently loses her senses, taking

Figure 5.1 Angelica Kauffman, *Maria* (1777), oil on metal. Courtesy of the
Burghley House Collection

refuge in the music that speaks eloquently of her plight while she remains mute.
The sketch of Maria is meant to emphasise her Ophelia-like distress:

> We had got up by this time almost to the bank where Maria was sitting: she
> was in a thin white jacket with her hair, all but two tresses, drawn up into a

> silk net, with a few olive-leaves twisted a little fantastically on one side——
> she was beautiful; and if ever I felt the full force of an honest heart-ache, it
> was the moment I saw her——(*TS* 9.24.783)

Overcome with enthusiasm, the narrator steps down to sit between Maria
and her goat:

> MARIA look'd wistfully for some time at me, and then at her goat——and
> then at me——and then at her goat again, and so on, alternately——
> ——Well, Maria, said I softly——What resemblance do you find?
> I do intreat the candid reader to believe me, that it was from the humblest
> conviction of what a *Beast* man is,——that I ask'd the question; and that I
> would not have let fallen an unseasonable pleasantry in the venerable presence
> of Misery, to be entitled to all the wit that ever Rabelais scatter'd——and yet
> I own my heart smote me. (*TS* 9.24.783–4)

The precise symbolism of the goat, a familiar sign of lechery in the period, is
one that I will return to. The joke marks a moment of textual embarrassment,
a clashing of registers, which the narrative is prepared to confess: a fascination with the relationship between powerlessness and seduction. What is, in
the formal contradictions of *Tristram Shandy*, an opportunity to savour and
reflect upon the moral ambiguities of spectatorship in the 'presence of
Misery', will return a year later bound seamlessly into the ironies of a more
extensive sentimental lexicon.

'Some time, but not *now*, I may hear thy sorrows from thy own lips' (*TS*
9.24.784), the Shandean narrator had advertised in 1767, as if to excuse
himself from the taint of exploitation. In *A Sentimental Journey* the reciprocal exchange between Maria and Yorick, the sentimental tourist and reader,
is obligingly fully developed, but each element is now given an iconic weight.
She is staged emblematically as a melancholic and thus contemplative figure,
'sitting with her elbow in her lap, and her head leaning on one side within
her hand': a pose echoed in the prints and paintings, recalling a tradition of
representation that has its roots in the work of old masters such as Dürer.[7]
And the pictorial detail Sterne provides is also faithfully reproduced:

> She was dress'd in white, and much as my friend described her, except that her
> hair hung loose, which before was twisted within a silk net.—She had, super-
> added likewise to her jacket, a pale green ribband which fell across her shoul-
> der to the waist; at the end of which hung her pipe.—Her goat had been as
> faithless as her lover; and she had got a little dog in lieu of him, which she had
> kept tied by a string to her girdle; as I look'd at her dog, she drew him towards
> her with the string.—'Thou shalt not leave me Sylvio,' said she. I look'd in

Maria's eyes, and saw she was thinking more of her father than of her lover or her little goat; for as she utter'd them the tears trickled down her cheeks. (*SJ* 150)

What is clear from Sterne's description is that it is already mediated by compositional principles drawn from a knowledge of art, and, I would suggest, shaped by the culture of popular prints. This Maria differs from the first because she already connotes a density of affective meanings translated into aesthetic form. Moreover she is encountered by Yorick (and the reader) as an already commodified sentimental touchstone, generating proven effects that Yorick as a spectator aims to reproduce: his pulse languidly beating, tears falling, emotions indescribably melting. Maria's purpose is, as the text attests, to confirm that the spectator has a 'soul'. As Sterne was well aware, prompted by the reviewers who argued that his real skill lay in the delineation of the pathetic, these effects were highly marketable. The Maria scenes of *A Sentimental Journey* are one more exercise in the creation of vignettes of singular suffering which the narrator is only too happy to explain. As he states in the famous episode where he imagines a Captive, incarcerated in the Bastille:[8]

> I was going to begin with millions of my fellow creatures born to no inheritance but slavery; but finding, however affecting the picture was, that I could not bring it near me, and that the multitude of sad groups in it did but distract me—
>
> —I took a single captive, and having first shut him up in his dungeon, I then look'd through the twilight of his grated door to take his picture. (*SJ* 97)

The point of such 'pictures' is the production of the right kind of proximity to the 'presence of Misery'.[9] In the case of Maria, the encounter is abstracted away from the generalised collective scene of harvest plenty, 'the hey-day of the vintage', in which 'music beats time to labour'. Maria has an aesthetic quality that removes her from the social landscape: she is 'of the first order of fine forms—affliction had touch'd her looks with something that was scarce earthly' (*SJ* 154). Yorick's approach is also framed in a number of ways. He is a Cervantic figure (Cervantes is invoked in each Sternean version of Maria): a 'Knight of the Woeful Countenance, in quest of melancholy adventures' (*SJ* 149). He is also overdetermined in scriptural terms: a compassionate Good Samaritan, pouring 'oil and wine' onto her wounds, and a paternal figure who takes such an innocent lamb to his bosom. If this framing locates Yorick's actions, it does not provide a moral distance from which to judge them. Aesthetic removal is accompanied by an eclipsing of spectatorial detachment. The overt symbolism of the lecherous goat, and the textual awkwardness that accompanied it, are removed. Instead, as if double entendre has become the very territory of feeling, the episode is reflexively buffered within the complex transformations of philanthropy: voyeurism *is* concern, vicarious identification *is* sympathetic communion, sexual desire *is* Christian, paternal love.[10] The line Yorick utters when she dries his handkerchief on her breast – 'And is your heart still so warm, Maria?' (*SJ* 153) – appears to be without tonal embarrassment. Not, however, for Mary Wollstonecraft, when trying to convey 'the temperature of her soul' thirty years later: 'I must love and admire with warmth, or I sink into sadness. Tokens of love I have received have rapt me in elysium – purifying the heart they enchanted. – My bosom still glows. – Do not saucily ask, repeating Sterne's question, "Maria, is it still so warm?"'[11] If Sterne's Maria had by this point become a cliché in the discourse of feeling, she also carried with her a trace of ironic disavowal that I want eventually to account for.

There is, I am suggesting, a *passage* between Sterne's two versions of Maria in the late 1760s in which a deliberate form of aesthetic work takes place. Such a shift was undoubtedly market-driven, since the taste for sentimental scenes of this kind, particularly among women readers, was intense, and Sterne, even in the final months of his life, had an eye to fame and income. Yet it also anticipated the concerns of newly founded academicians, who, in the form of Sir Joshua Reynolds, would argue that 'beauty and grandeur' was the proper subject for painting, and if the heart of the spectator was to be warmed, it would be achieved by rising above 'all singular forms, local customs, particularities and details of every kind'.[12] To discover what was at stake in such abstraction, and the more silent forms of instrumentality at work there, it is important to mine the figure of Maria in more detail, to unravel precisely those local particularities and details which were undergoing aesthetic transformation and occlusion at this time.

### Magdalen Marias: their 'Secret History'

Maria is of course one of many examples of 'virtue in distress' peopling mid-century narratives, a multitude of often interchangeable sentimental figures whose antecedents include Ophelia, Clarissa, traditional characters such as Patient Griselda and the tragic Lucrece. These *exempla* had a pedagogical purpose, often embedded in the novel as it mimicked the techniques of conduct manuals, guiding the reader along the moral *recta via* of domestic life. If there is something vertiginous about this path, it is because the women of these narratives often risk a catastrophic loss of status. In this sense, these are middle-class dramas about the very real fear of *economic* destitution, as much as the maintenance of female sexual probity, and the sense of risk is heightened by the sexualised theatrics of the loss, degradation and abduction of vulnerable women. At its most extreme, there was something scandalously close to the pornographic, and thus excitingly sensational, about the representation of these distressed women, far in excess of the logics of plot. This is the proto-melodrama of the mid-century, sharing with the later cultural form a focus on inarticulate and often hysterical women, their bodies 'seized by meaning' as Peter Brooks has discussed;[13] texts which correspondingly revel in vicarious spectatorial pleasures. 'Melodrama might best be seen', Tom Gunning suggests appositely, 'as a dialectical interaction between moral significance and an excess aimed precisely at non-cognitive affects, thrills, sensations, and strong affective attractions'.[14] The figure of 'virtue in distress' is one mid-century site for this 'interaction'; one which acknowledges a wider field of popular feeling and sensation – shocks, desires and fears – which melodrama will later turn into a pedagogy of mass emotion.

Markman Ellis has argued rightly that there is more specificity to Sterne's Maria than this, suggesting that she is constructed within a mid-century confluence of two discourses of the libertine woman, which he begins to trace. On the one hand, there is the tradition of the wandering whore, in which the ungovernability of women takes a picaresque and sexually threatening form, picked up perhaps in the brief sketch of Maria's travels in *A Sentimental Journey*. This was to some extent formalised in the eighteenth-century popular imagination by Hogarth in his series *The Harlot's Progress*. On the other hand, Maria seems to owe even more to the narrative of the sentimental magdalen, in which the pathetic victim might through benevolence be brought to reform: a more pietistic vision, in which, as he explains, Mary Magdalene is figured iconically as a weeping and penitent saint. It is not then that Maria is a prostitute, Ellis contends, but rather that there is something 'masterless' and curiously powerful about her, which the language of madness and sexual abandon attempts to locate and control.[15] It is my view that the sentimental magdalen is particularly relevant here, and I want to take this hunch about her masterlessness further.

The figure of the magdalen was enormously potent in ideological terms at the mid-century because a number of live and pressing issues coalesced around her; indeed, she is constituted by them. Central were questions of governmentality: the management of population as a means of 'strengthening' the state. In the years during and after the Seven Years' War this inevitably meant thinking urgently about the effects of empire, which, as we have seen, were often connected to fears of depopulation. Thus, as the philanthropist Jonas Hanway writes in *Virtue in Humble Life*, it is a '*trade of lawless love*' that 'is a further reason why our numbers in general *diminish*, or that they do not *increase* in a due proportion, to answer the drain of people for *Asia*,

*Africa* and *America*'.[16] The connection of sexual licentiousness – whether conjugal infidelity or prostitution – to sterility was a common one, and it had far-reaching political consequences. As Vivien Jones points out, 'the reform of prostitutes is offered as a means of bolstering national strength through an efficiently reproductive population, and subscription [to the Magdalen House charity] thus becomes a patriotic duty'.[17] The asylum sermons are uncompromising on the subject. 'Matrimony is the source of population', preaches William Hazeland. 'Fornication and adultery have been punished as crimes against the State, as well as against Religion'.[18]

The magdalen was thus a significant figure of institutionalised concern, the object of a mid-century notion of national security. She was a spectacular site from which it was possible to argue for the sanctity of marriage, the binding in of her deviance thus shoring up the link between family and state. As Hanway put it in terms that were widely shared, 'whatever pretensions *men* may make to a superior degree of knowledge in the government of a *state*, *women* have a larger share in the direction and management of *families*, which compose kingdoms'.[19] The discursive role of the Magdalen Asylum in the public culture of the period, beyond its immediate practical effects, was to emphasise the importance of inculcating this sense of domestic governance, and the sexual division of labour underpinning it. In achieving the benevolent restoration of these women to the proper oeconomy of their own lives, the machine of mid-century life would run more smoothly. It is philanthropy, declared Dr William Dodd, in a description that recalls the sentimental vignette, who 'shews you the chambers of deserted infants, of little out-casts, and unfriended orphans, kindly sheltered from the rude blasts of infamy, of ignorance, of ruin; and made instrumental to the commerce, the defence, and the domestic necessities of the nation'.[20] The asylums of the mid-century were in many ways fashioned as theatres of this kind, displaying on their walls works that confirmed the Christian benevolence of their benefactors.[21] Whatever the ideological spin, reformation often entailed the addressing of extremes of poverty, providing these asylum seekers with an alternative means of earning their subsistence to prostitution.[22] Those not redeemed by institutional, paternal care were correspondingly portrayed as permanently lost, to themselves, and to society. As Goldsmith described in 'The Deserted Village':

> Now lost to all; her friends, her virtue fled,
> Near her betrayer's door she lays her head,
> And pinch'd with cold, and shrinking from the shower,
> With heavy heart deplores that luckless hour,
> When idly first, ambitious of the town,
> She left her wheel and robes of country brown.[23]

Lurking behind the administrative fantasy of redemption lay a fear which was related to that of depopulation, though it appears paradoxically to be its reverse: that of overwhelming *number*. John Brown gives it characteristically florid form in his sermon *On the Female Character and Education* in 1765:

> From the vast Concourse of Men and Women, pouring daily into this vast metropolis from every Quarter of the Globe, and destitute of all legal Settlement, a Number of unhappy Children are annually born.[24]

Brown's account links the global reach of empire with a vision of the teeming numbers massing in the metropolis. It is clear that this sense of crisis – of the numbers of children born 'without community'[25] – was supported by the realities of urban life.[26] A means of control had to be found, not only to improve the condition of the poor, but also to defuse the threat from those outside the social bond who might form motley combinations of their own. Foundling children who turned to crime to survive were a 'class', as the Philanthropic Society later described, 'which belongs to no rank of the civil community':

> They are excommunicates in police, extra-social, extra-civil, extra-legal; they are links which have fallen off the chain of society, and which going to decay, inure and obstruct the movements of the whole machine.[27]

Social crises such as these have long been laid at the door of the supposed sexual incontinence of women, one of a number of ideological fantasies contributing to mid-century nationalistic sentiment.[28] There had undoubtedly been, as Lawrence Stone discusses, a 'dizzy rise' in illegitimate births among working women at this time, which he attributes to 'a rise in the proportion of the propertyless with no economic stake in the value of their virginity', and to the increasing 'proportion of men removed from the pressures of family, community and priest which previously would have contrived to force them into marriage'.[29] But behind the changing realities of the sexual economy lay a 'secret history' of broader economic transformations, harsher forms of coercion.[30] As Oliver Goldsmith's 'prospect' of 1764 saw it, the desuetude of 'Nature's ties' – Stone's family, community, and priest – had been met with the creation of 'fictitious bonds, the bonds of wealth and law'.[31] These 'bonds' were the very instruments of what Marx would later call 'primitive accumulation', the violent process by which the labouring population were denied their traditional forms of livelihood and subsistence in order to bring them into the wage economy, a violence which, as we will see, also takes a symbolic form.

The 'release' of agricultural workers from the land with the uneven decline of rural industry, and the extraction of land through enclosure, which accelerated radically in the 1760s, increased the numbers journeying to London and other manufacturing centres in search of work and a dream of wealth. Arthur Young described the exodus in his *The Farmer's Letters to the People of England* in 1771: 'Young men and women in the country fix their eye on London as the last stage of their hope; they enter into service in the country for little else but to raise money enough to go to London . . . And the number of young women that fly thither is almost incredible'.[32] Some saw the deeper pressures behind this movement. Oliver Goldsmith's 'The Deserted Village' mourns the process that has seen 'trade's unfeeling train/ Usurp the land and dispossess the swain'. A series of sentimental figures are paraded through his poem: 'Ah, turn thine eyes/ Where the poor houseless shivering female lies./ She once, perhaps, in village plenty blest,/ Has wept at tales of innocence distressed'. Gradually these figures become ciphers of a historical crisis: 'She, wretched matron, forced, in age for bread,/ To strip the brook with mantling cresses spread,/ To pick her wintry faggot from the thorn,/ To seek her nightly shed, and weep till morn;/She only left of all the harmless train,/ The sad historian of the pensive plain'.[33]

Maxine Berg has discussed the centrality of women and children to the pool of labour at this time. Their access to certain trades, and to better wages, was highly restricted, and put under pressure in the years following the peace when returning soldiers and sailors joined those 'pouring' into the cities.[34] They were a reserve army, expendable, their place in the division of labour easily obliterated. Pitiful wages could keep them off the parish, yet the more casual and mobile they were – a deracination in fact encouraged by the vagrancy laws which turned parishes against one another 'like states at war'[35] – the more likely they and their children would be constituted as 'without community' and thus outside the bounds of poor relief. There is an economic liminality here in which women trod the boundaries of what it was to be intelligible within the 'machine' of eighteenth-century life; boundaries increasingly distinguished by subordination to a realm of work which, if not new, was certainly more invasive than ever before. As one asylum sermon described, some women could not find recognition within its legitimating terms:

> I cannot but observe here, that so scanty are the means of subsistence allowed the female sex; so few the occupations which they can pursue, and those so much engrossed by our sex: so small are the profits arising from their labours, and so difficult often the power of obtaining employment, especially for those of doubtful character; and frequently, so utter their unskilfulness in any branches of their common industry, from a mistaken

neglect of their parents in their education . . . that, it is but too well known, many virtuous and decent young women, left desolate with poor unfriended children, have been compelled to the horrid necessity . . . of procuring bread by prostitution![36]

It is possible to read the cultural labour of sentimental fiction as reversing such a prospect, in part as producing, beyond its protest, a fantasy of economic intelligibility for the litany of unfortunates who wander across its pages. As we saw in the case of George Ellison, redemptive action repeatedly involved the defraying of debt, and the incorporation of outcasts into renewed forms of economic self-sustaining: idealised cottage economies for some, and a restitution of leisured middle-class status for others. And the figure of the magdalen is particularly significant in this, because her narrative of loss – the loss of virtue, status and reputation – carries with it the Christian possibility of recuperation into either deserving narrative . She is the potential point where the 'secret history' I have begun to sketch, replete with its violences and exclusions, surfaces, and is negated by familial (state) belonging.

Others remained locked outside. As the plantation owner Edward Long reflected characteristically, 'the true wealth and greatness of a nation are not upheld solely by the multitude of its people, but by their being civilised, industrious, and constantly well employed'.[37] The empire required not just the generation of population, but the reproduction of the proper kind of subject. Secret equations were at work. 'In China it is a maxim', wrote William Blackstone, 'that if there be a man who does not work, or a woman that is idle, in the empire, somebody must suffer cold or hunger'.[38] If mid-century governmentality tightened invisible lines of causality across the empire, they were connections that could be expressed in a number of ways. Long, for example, argues for his own slaving interests by partially defending the plight of the unemployed and idle at home. Noting the 'amazing increase' in beggars, which had 'overspread the streets in all our populous towns, cities, and even our villages, to the dishonour of this nation', he concludes:

we are overburthened with an enormous number of very poor, distressed white subjects; who, for want of some employment suited to their ability, are thus thrown, as a rent-charge, upon the industrious class of our people.

The word 'white' is the key term here. It turns the distinction between the idle and industrious classes temporarily on its head. The multitude 'turned adrift' are white, their idleness the consequence of competition with multifarious foreign others, in this case, 'the multiplication of Negroe domestics',[39] but a charge also laid at the door of the Irish and the Jews. The xenophobic fear here is revealed: not simply in the racist sense of being 'swamped' by people pouring in to the metropolis from all quarters of the globe 'destitute of all legal Settlement' as John Brown put it,[40] but actually of their gaining legitimacy within the body of the nation. These anxieties were then a consequence of imperial and commercial power. The furore around the naturalisation controversies of the 1750s – of the Jewish population in particular – is one instance of this concern, captured in the 1751 print *The Dreadful Consequences of a General Naturalization to the Natives of Great Britain and Ireland*, which shows master manufacturers and their labourers leaving on a ship as the immigrants crowd around the British cornucopia. Long's assault on Granville Sharp is another later instance, where it is the commercial future of the empire, and not just the strength of the domestic market, which is seen to be at stake: 'Nothing less is demanded by the Negroe advocates, than a total sacrifice of our *African trade* and *American possessions*, to their fantastic idea of *English liberty*'.[41] The consequence of such legal recognition, for Long, was a 'universal licentiousness', which he sees simultaneously as a sexual (in the sense of miscegenate) and economic catastrophe. It is perhaps not surprising that the magdalen became so ideologically potent in such a nationalistic climate, a moral and sexual figure through which it was possible to fantasise the rescue and protection of the domestic realm, the support and simultaneous refusal of the consequences of empire.

### Prodigality and Rural Life: Maria's Melancholy

Such a 'secret history' might appear a rather weighty burden to lay in the lap of Sterne's Maria. Indeed her location in a pastoral landscape might contrastingly suggest a rural retreat from the degeneracy of the metropolis, carrying connotations of Horatian retirement and bucolic innocence. If she is one of Goldsmith's 'sad historians', as I believe, then she is also a sign of an aesthetic labour that disavows the actuality of rural experience: the process definitively explored by John Barrell in his *Dark Side of the Landscape*. Alongside the eighteenth-century pastoralism that saw the countryside as a place of happy, comedic pleasures and lusty abandon is a civic humanist inheritance that saw it as the seat of moral values, and which often took the Virgilian georgic as its form. As Barrell shows, the relation between these traditions shifts as the century changes, and with it the image of the rural poor:

> The effect is always to claim that the rural poor are as contented, the rural
> society as harmonious, as it is possible to claim them to be, in the face of an
> increasing awareness that all was not well as it must have been in Arcadia. The

jolly imagery of Merry England, which replaced the frankly artificial imagery of classical Pastoral, was in turn replaced when it had to be by the image of a cheerful, sober, domestic peasantry, more industrious than before; this gave way in turn to a picturesque image of the poor, whereby their raggedness became of aesthetic interest, and they became the objects of our pity; and when that image would serve no longer, it was in turn replaced by a romantic image of harmony with nature whereby the labourers were merged as far as possible with their surroundings, too far away from us for the questions about how ragged or contented they were to arise.[42]

I want to place the melancholic construction of Maria, and the confusion around a proper proximity to her, in the context of these changes, and also within the pressures specific to the late 1760s. Not only were there fears of the haemorrhaging of population from the countryside into the cities and the distant reaches of the empire (fears also shared, interestingly, in the colonies themselves), but also of the threat of 'tumults', and the self-organising of the masses in to 'combinations' of the poor. For philosophers like Adam Smith, removal to the country and husbandry of the land enabled a classical vision of virtue largely occluded in the cities; and it was this aestheticised vision that would accompany his writings on political economy. In the interests of social cohesion it appeared necessary to show, in the words of Sarah Scott, that 'virtue is within the reach of every station'.[43] It was a view echoed by Jonas Hanway in his *Virtue in Humble Life*, which targets the experience of 'common people' in its construction of lives of idealised piety. 'Wandering through the humble haunts of peasants' convinces him that a certain form of reflection is embodied in the labour of such ordinary lives:

> We are not indeed to seek for reasoning *philosophers* in villages, but there *are* more, in that situation, who are *practically* such, than the *great* imagine . . . with the *humble* and *laborious*, the *body* and the *mind* are both kept in action.[44]

Sterne's depiction of Maria draws on the common moral construction of rural life. Like Hanway's farmer's daughter, the exemplary Mary, she connotes a 'state of innocency' rather than the 'ambiguous circumstances of a *Pamela*'.[45] Yet if Maria borrows from the conventions of pastoral that had long been popular in the eighteenth century, there are mid-century details which work against the topos of rustic retirement and harmony, and indeed the natural industriousness that is increasingly seen to underpin it. Maria is, in both versions, dislocated from her community, a fracturing which is registered as madness in *Tristram Shandy*, and as both an aleatory wandering and contemplative stasis in *A Sentimental Journey*. She will not be pulled back into the fold, and the paternal gesture, acted out by Yorick in the absence of a dead father, does not convince. Maria's melancholic reflection refuses the co-ordination of *active* mind and body celebrated by Hanway in his account of practical philosophy; nor does she exemplify the rural 'happy oeconomy' in which, as he put it, 'the heart of man keep[s] time with peace and concord'.[46] I want to argue in a moment, however, that in departing from such an exemplary vision she embodies a kind of thought nonetheless, and with it a different register of time.

The loss of Maria's senses is due, we recall, to the machinations of authority in the form of the Church. The curate's 'intrigues' suggest predatory forms of interference which later versions of Maria were only too happy to write up in gothic form. Sterne's representation of the goat as a sign of lechery within the vignette is not just a sign of the sensationalism attending the figure of the magdalen.[47] It also links forms of sexual exploitation with social power, a codification which was familiar in the political prints of the period. As David H. Solkin has explored, for example, the artist John Collet lampooned the patrician vision of rural retirement in the 1760s and 1770s by representing the seduction of labouring countrywomen by their social betters, local squires and clergymen. In *Landscape with a Farmgirl and a Squire*, which echoes in formal terms Hogarth's depiction of Moll Hackabout, the encounter is given meaning not simply by the ubiquitous goat, but also by a distant but dominant image of the gallows, to which the Squire gestures. As Solkin explains, 'the hanged man's presence tells us something of utmost importance: that the landed gentry controlled the law, and could exploit that control as a means of constraining the liberty of their poorer subjects'.[48] This was a lesson often repeated in the sentimental fiction of the time, where the rescue of women from the clutches of aristocratic libertines is accompanied by an acute sense of social class: as the Vicar of Wakefield puts it, 'he can triumph in security; for he is rich, and we are poor'.[49] *Tristram Shandy* is, as we have seen, a narrative which engages in its own comic attack on authority, the narrator distancing himself from those born to 'power and great estates', but he is nonethless ambiguously implicated in such exploitation. While the encounter with Maria is set at a safe distance in a newly vanquished France, and the offending curate is a Catholic and therefore less troubling as a hate figure (as is the priest in Goldsmith's *Vicar*), the potential lecher is nonetheless the narrator himself, which raises broader questions about the culpability of spectatorial power in the 'presence of Misery', animated and even indulged by the ironies of the text. Accusations of such sensual cynicism would haunt the reception of Sterne's work thereafter.

If the lineaments of broader social struggles and meanings are suggested in the first encounter with Maria, they undergo an aesthetic transformation by the time Yorick seeks out the same experience in *A Sentimental Journey*.

This shift takes place initially through the conventional use of the magdalen narrative. It was generally held that consent to marriage carried with it particular dangers, marking the moment at which unsuspecting women could fall into disrepute. As Hugh Kelly's novel of 1767, *Memoirs of a Magdalen: Or, the History of Louisa Mildmay*, related:

> Of all the stages of a woman's life, none is so dangerous as the period between her acknowledgement of a passion for a man, and the day set apart for her nuptials. Her mind, during that interval, is susceptible of impressions unusually tender; and the happy lover is admitted to a number of familiarities, which are in themselves the strongest temptations.[50]

The marriage act had exacerbated the problem, in Jonas Hanway's view, since it had formalised a legal delay between the reading of the banns and the closure of the marriage: 'the parties under the sanction of mutual promises, or frequently by mere delay, come together before the ceremony: the consequence of which is, that the *hind*, who is generally the most of a mere animal, or the least sensible of moral obligations, often fails of his promise'.[51] This is the drama that is described in the most sensational of terms in *Memoirs of the Magdalen*, where the rake both savours and castigates a 'woman thus lost to sentiment'.[52] It is also intimated in the predicament of Sterne's Maria.[53]

The aim of magdalen narrative is to chart the loss and redemption of a woman's virtue. One obvious literary model is Richardson's *Clarissa*, where the innocent yet fallen heroine finds transcendence in the afterlife. It is the novel which Hugh Kelly's penitent Louisa Mildmay reads with an 'instinctive kind of terror', finding her own situation literally enacted in its pages (in a characteristic move, her abductor, the second male villain of the piece, reads *Tristram Shandy* until he falls asleep). Luckily for her, she has 'chosen in her delirium' a haven to take refuge in – the Magdalen Asylum – rather than death.[54] While some 'authentic' magdalen accounts end in the institutional recognition of 'true reformation', their lives sometimes culminating in sickness or death nonetheless,[55] sentimental versions are often more expedient, bringing about suprising reversals of fortune, discoveries of hidden benefactors, or marriages in which the rake is reformed whether he wills it or not. Above all, they concern the rebuilding of the family, the parental acceptance of the ruined child. Ellen G. D'Oench has fascinatingly explored the incorporation of the biblical story of the prodigal son into these stories of distressed women, and its connection of sentiment and paternal care with social reform.[56] As she shows, Sterne's own sermon on the lesson of the prodigal son stresses both unselfish fatherly love and an acknowledgement of the 'fatal passion' for travelling 'wove into the frame of every son and daughter of Adam'. Sterne's object is the temptations of the grand tour, but there are undoubtedly parallels here with his staging of the encounter with Maria in *A Sentimental Journey*, not only in Yorick's confession of protective paternal love, but also in her errant behaviour, and possession of an 'ingenuous heart too open for the world', as the sermon puts it (*Sermons*, 20.192, 190).

If the magdalen narrative operates according to established patterns of plotting, not least through those of biblical parable, it also has to account for the sometimes rapidly changing psychological state of the heroine. The fallen woman suffers hysteria and fainting fits, delirium or madness, entering a melancholic phase that will end in the restoration of some form of equilibrium. The intended husband and seducer of Louisa Mildmay in *Memoirs of the Magdalen* has his own interpretation of this movement:

> Women, however, though their sensibility may be more piercingly exquisite than ours, are nevertheless much readier to conquer the remembrance of misfortune: they feel more deeply indeed at first; but from the osier-like pliability of their minds, the moment the first hurry of the tempest is sustained, they gradually rise to their former situation; the anguish inperceptibly [sic] softens from affliction into melancholy, from melancholy into languor, and from languor into tranquility, whereas, the masculine mind, like the oak in the fable, is shattered by the severity of a conflict, when it might have recovered the most violent shock by a happy facility in bending.[57]

This assessment is shown by the culprit's sister to be misguided, viewing women through the 'contracted eye of a narrow-minded libertinism'.[58] But it does identify one difficulty: how to interpret what we might see as a feminine anatomy of melancholy. On one level, running through this view of women's supposed adaptability to emotion, is a fear of autonomy and calculation that has its parallels in the tracts of the period,[59] as if the very stylisation of sentimental emotion brings with it the dangers of counterfeiture. It is women, here, who are associated with conquest; in this case the mastery of feeling. On another level, there is a kind of resistance to the reading of affect embodied in the magdalen figure, which renders her enigmatic. In *The Vicar of Wakefield*, the father thus misreads his fallen Olivia, as he tends to do the world: 'She appeared from that time more calm, and I imagined had gained a new degree of resolution: but appearances deceived me; for her tranquility was the languor of over-wrought resentment'.[60] It is this often final reflective state of tranquillity – as a calmness, waiting, suspension – that has to be made sense of, and which is captured in the paintings of Maria as a melancholic figure.

The passage from the madness and inarticulacy of Sterne's first Maria, to the second, who has a more complex story to tell, and a more evolved aes-

Figure 5.2. Joseph Wright of Derby, *Maria and her dog, Silvio* (1781), oil on canvas. Copyright Derby Museums and Art Gallery

thetic character, might be said to follow the psychological movement sketched in Kelly's novel. The melancholy sketched in *A Sentimental Journey*, and represented with gravitas in the paintings of Joseph Wright of Derby (Figure 5.2) and Angelica Kauffman, offers a form of abstraction that is also an aesthetic resolution. In both of Wright's versions, for example, Maria is represented in solitude, in a sylvan landscape, light seemingly fading. She gazes pensively across the frame, as if her mind is elsewhere. Her lap-dog seems focused on her mood. The relaxation of her body, emphasised by classical drapery, suggests that she is wrapped in thought. One of the most important functions of such singular melancholic abstraction is to allow the spectator to identify with her emotional state, providing a means of recognition, the pleasurable suturing of sympathy to distress. As an earlier poem by Thomas Warton had expressed it: 'Ye Youths of Albion's beauty-blooming isle,/ Whose brows have worn the wreaths of luckless love,/ Is there a pleasure like the pensive mood,/ Whose magic wont to sooth your soften'd souls?'[61] 'Melancholy', explains Goldsmith's narrator, 'which is excited by objects of pleasure, or inspired by sounds of harmony, sooths the heart instead of corroding it'.[62] What begins as a musical vibration in *Tristram Shandy* binds the narrator of the later narrative into a fascinated mimesis, governed by the 'great SENSORIUM of the world' (*SJ* 155). While in *The Vicar of Wakefield* (in what might appear an extraordinary act of affective violence), the parents of poor Olivia thrill to the exquisite pathos of the melancholy ditty that they oblige her to sing, in which, as the lyrics describe, only the 'art' of death can 'wash her guilt away'.[63]

Beyond the to-ings and fro-ings of sympathy, however, melancholic abstraction opens up a specific relation to time. It carries traditional associations: of death – the mortal limits of the *memento mori* – and of recollection, understood in the sense of a renewed link with an eternal order and the place of the penitent within it. Sterne's Maria recalls the 'sad Virgin' Melancholy of Milton's *Il Penseroso*, whose conjuring of orphic song 'made Hell grant what love did seek'.[64] Despite its 'prophetic strain', melancholy also names an increasingly secularised relation to experience, a form of temporal spatialisation. It suggests a private realm abstracted from the everyday, which has an unrecuperable dimension to it, as if its melancholic gesture might be a form of catachresis, misnaming. I want now to explore women's experience in terms of this unrecuperability, as a form of *duration* which is embodied in the sentimental image. In what ways might it be related to the secret history I have begun to sketch?

## Ways of Killing Time

In *Virtue in Humble Life*, Jonas Hanway stages a dialogue between Thomas Trueman, a farmer, and his daughter, Mary. The effect resembles the catechism: through questioning and demonstration, Mary learns to recognise the devotional nature of ordinary life, and the reader is provided with prayers tailored to the specific lesson of the moment. Central to Mary's learning is the proper husbandry of time. As Thomas reflects, at length:

> How quickly do the hours glide on from morn to noon, and from noon to night; when we first fall into the arms of sleep, which is the image of death!

Nothing is more true, than that *yesterday* is already *dead*; and *to-morrow* not yet *born*; what have we then except *to-day*? And shall one *poor day*, and this not *certain*, create such distress, as to make us think of murdering it? . . . Time is the representative of *immortality* with regard to our present state, and the guide to *eternity*! *O Time, how awful, how adorable thou art! How precious to mortal man!* What is life, *Mary*, but *time*? And what the various ways of spending it, but so many proofs of our inclination to *wisdom* or *folly* . . . In every condition, pray for the proper use of time; and the most whole-some maxim is, that *innocence* and *idleness* cannot exist in the same person.[65]

The connection between the experience of the mortal present and reflection on eternity is of course part of the labour of melancholy; a state, moreover, in which innocence and a form of idleness are precisely brought into relation. For Hanway, however, there is a direct parallel between a day profitably used and a life well-spent. Mary learns her lesson dutifully: 'If *time* be a treasure of such vast value, and the means by which we acquire immortal happiness, we should guard it as the apple of the eyes, and see that it suffers no injury.'[66] Time has to be actively surveilled and monitored, the present moment actively occupied. Misuse of time is portrayed in literal terms as an 'injury' or even 'murder', and maps directly onto distinctions of social rank. While time-discipline among the labouring poor is integral to 'immortal happiness' (as Methodism was also to teach), it is the rich in particular who kill time. The story of prodigality here takes a temporal turn. 'They think they have a vast superfluity, because they cannot tell what to do with it. But they often repent the loss of it, as many a prodigal hath done, who has squandered a large fortune, and been reduced to poverty and distress! Those who know the *value* of time, treat it as prudent people do their money'.[67]

Women were often regarded as particularly susceptible to the squander-ing of time's resources, probably because they were also ideologically central to its domestic oeconomies, the point at which the surplus value of time – leisure – might be imagined as reined under control. It is interesting that for all his discussion of the 'levelling' need to address ordinary people, Hanway is concerned that his wealthy woman reader should persevere with his text, imagining her yawning at the weight of piety (a reaction one might sympa-thise with). She has, after all, responsibilities. It is clear that his book is in part about the inculcation of proper values among the servant classes, revealed in his telling observation that 'it is easy to perceive how much the calm succes-sion of a lady's hours depends upon the good humour and respect shewn her by her servants'.[68] Middle-class women, unlike their labouring counterparts, had 'an extraordinary portion of time on their hands' as William Alexander put it in his *The History of Women*, which the domestic duties that fall to their share are not sufficient to fill up; such is human nature, especially where the spirits are active, and the imagination lively, that time of this kind is of all others the most disagreeable: in order, therefore, to fill up this blank, as well as the to vary the scene of human life, a variety of little employments, diversions, and amusements, have been contrived; many of them adapted to both sexes, and some of them to the fair sex only.[69]

There are then many gendered ways of filling the 'blank' of time, including the prodigal excess of the imagination, which from another perspective appears a form of murder. If there is something 'disagreeable' about time, it relates to its consumption rather than husbandry. Hannah More would later be more explicit about the domestic 'invaders', 'fine ladies, who, always afraid of being too early for their parties, are constantly on the watch, how to disburden themselves for the intermediate hour, of the heavy commodity *time*; a raw material, which, as they seldom work up at home, they are always willing to truck against the time of their more domestic acquaintance'.[70]

Hanway's pious compendium is one of numerous mid-century tracts devoted to the inculcation of time-discipline. Many similarly relate the 'natural' temporal organisation of the day – early rising, early to bed – to the maintenance of religious observance. And it is not just the 'fine ladies' who sleep in. These texts do not only address the leisured lifestyle of the rich, which, for all the moral associations with indolence, is nonetheless linked to the necessary production of surplus value within the economy, and therefore at its root to be tolerated. They are concerned with a more pressing problem: the disturbing effects of such a surplus on the wider population. As John Clayton's *Friendly Advice to the Poor* declaimed in 1755, 'Luxury, this shameful devourer of Time and Money, has found its Way into the Houses of our Poor'. Many members of the multitude appeared in any case resistant to the 'Rules of Regularity and good Order' he recommends, such as the 'Sluggard' who 'spends his time in Sauntring', or the 'swarms of Loyterers' only too happy to while their time away spectating in the streets.[71] Clayton's pamphlet echoes the language of the vagrancy laws, but it also reveals the presence of masterless numbers who are not fully interpellated by the administration of time. This task ultimately falls, in Clayton's view, to the domestic 'good Husbandry' of 'the Mistress of the House'.[72]

### Duration: Regulation and Resistance

Edward Thompson famously explored the long process of changes in the 'inward notation of time' in his influential essay, 'Time, Work-Discipline and Industrial Capitalism'.[73] It is Thompson who reminds us that the opening anecdote of *Tristram Shandy* is itself a skit on the topic of time-discipline. The Shandy patriarch, a 'slave' to 'extreme exactness', winds the house-clock on the first Sunday of the month, a time which he also gives over to 'family concernments' with his wife, 'to get them all out of the way at one time' (*TS* 1.4.6). His son is conceived on one of these occasions, when his wife, in a characteristic Shandean double entendre, asks '*have you not forgot to wind up the clock?*' (*TS* 1.1.2). The effect of this anecdote on the readership of the early 1760s was reputedly immediate. A pamphlet, entitled *The Clockmaker's Outcry against the Author of the Life and Opinions of Tristram Shandy* was published in 1760, ostensibly written by a clockmaker dismayed by a loss of trade, though some have suggested it was highly likely to have been penned by Sterne himself. 'The common expression of street-walkers', he reported, is 'Sir, will you have your clock wound-up?' 'The directions I had for making several clocks for the country are countermanded; because no modest lady now dares to mention a word about *winding-up a clock*, without exposing herself to the sly leers and jokes of the family'.[74]

Such debauchery, the clockmaker suggests, threatens 'to overturn church and state':

> for clocks and watches being brought into contempt and disuse, nobody will know how the time goes, nor which is the hour of prayer, the hour of levee, the hour of mounting guard, &c. &c.&c. consequently an universal confusion in church, senate, playhouse, &c. must ensue . . .
>
> Time's out of rule; no Clock is now *wound-up*: TRISTRAM the *lewd* has *knock'd* Clock-making up.[75]

The joke involves, then, the capturing of the very orientation of bourgeois life by alternative logics, the aleatory movements of sex and desire. Significantly, it is women who trouble such an ordering, in the figure of the wife (whose literal adherence to domestic habit exposes Walter's sexual inadequacy) and the prostitute, who ventriloquates the wife's words, turning such exposure to her own instrumental ends.[76] For Thompson this Shandean anecdote and the furore surrounding it is one indication of the internalisation of clock time, which by this point in the eighteenth century had reached the most intimate levels even as it calibrated the operations of church and state. His argument then eschews the 'gross impressionism' of these and other literary examples to pose the question central to his enquiry: namely, 'if the transition to mature industrial society entailed a severe restructuring of working habits – new disciplines, new incentives, and a new human nature upon which these incentives could bite effectively – how far is this related to changes in the inward notation of time?'[77] There is nothing accidental about the way disciplinary pressures registered in the cultural forms of the mid-eighteenth century, which laboured to redefine human nature in precisely these terms, while posing questions for us about the 'transition' Thompson describes. I want for the moment to press such impressionism further.

The drama of *Tristram Shandy* involves reflection on shifts in time-sense, which are often put into conflict. The regularity favoured by the paternal principle in the novel is troubled by a notion of *duration*, in which the bad associationism deplored by Locke has its sway, an inner time governed by a digressive logic of perceptions and impressions, which even the mechanistic philosophy favoured by Walter Shandy is unable to contain. At one point Walter undertakes to explain the nature of duration to his wise fool of a brother, attempting to show the mechanism by which the 'eternal scampering of the discourse from one thing to another . . . had lengthened out so short a period to so inconceivable an extent'. Toby replies that it relates 'entirely . . . to the succession of our ideas' (*TS* 3.18.222), but is unable to explain how he comes by this enlightening connection or what it means. Walter Shandy anticipates a future in which clock time will have been internalised so thoroughly that duration will no longer be distinct from it:

> in our computations of *time*, we are so used to minutes, hours, weeks and months,——and of clocks (I wish there was not a clock in the kingdom) to measure out the several portions to us, and to those who belong to us,—— that 'twill be well, if in time to come, the *succession of our ideas* be of any use or service to us at all. (*TS* 3.18.224)

Yet even as he tries to account for duration, the exchange between the Shandy brothers suggests the opposite of such a vision, in which Toby's inexplicable associationism, and Walter's own epistemophiliac pleasures, testify to the thwarting of the measure of clock time. There is a resistance here to its determinism, and one that I want to account for.

Tristram Shandy describes a world pressured by time. He needs to live '364 times faster than [he] should write' to keep up with the experiences that assail him (*TS* 4.13.342). This writerly crisis is due to his need to register the activity of duration: the daydreams and burgeoning associations which hollow out the private space of the everyday, and which give the novel its digressive form. Register, but not regulate. It was this space that the late eighteenth century aimed to 'restructure', in Thompson's words, as Thomas Wedgwood describes in a letter to William Godwin:

> Let us suppose ourselves in possession of some detailed statement of the first twenty years in the life of some extraordinary genius; what a chaos of per-

ceptions! . . . How many hours, days, months have been prodigally wasted in unproductive occupations! What a host of half formed impressions & abortive conceptions blended into a mass of confusion . . .

In the best regulated mind of the present day, had not there been, & is not there some hours everyday passed in reverie, thought ungoverned, undirected?[78]

It is precisely the 'prodigal' ungovernability of experience, and thus resistance to disciplinary pressure, which describe the space of the everyday in *Tristram Shandy*. Ranged against it are forces of regulation – taxonomic, mechanistic, rational – that struggle comically (and often irrationally) to hold it in check. It is no accident that the paternal figure of Walter Shandy, whom, as I have argued, is linked with notions of seventeenth-century political authority, believes despite himself in the order of clockwork. As Otto Mayr has shown, it was a widely used analogy for the absolutist order of the state and universe, which could be figured as a harmonious machine.[79] If Walter is 'enslaved' by his belief, and consequently always bedevilled by accident and association, Sterne's narratives make the most of this drama.

Yorick's encounter with Maria in *A Sentimental Journey* is thus marked not just by sentimental affirmation but by a brief moment of philosophical reflection: 'I am positive I have a soul; nor can all the books with which materialists have pester'd the world ever convince me of the contrary' (*SJ* 151). Sterne's engagement with the mechanistic philosophy favoured by Walter Shandy also takes place here, in a debate with the work of French materialists such as La Mettrie and the Baron d'Holbach, whose salon he had attended in Paris. And it is also re-enacted in an earlier moment of Shandean travel around France, where it is the scientific inheritance of the Royal Society that provides the connection. Sterne clearly has Robert Boyle's writing on the famous monumental clock of Strasbourg Cathedral in mind when he has his narrator visit Lyons, and the 'wonderful mechanism of the great clock of Lippius of Basil' (considered second in importance to that of Strasbourg) on his tourist itinerary. I'm going to quote in full:

Now of all things in the world, I understand the least of mechanism——I have neither genius, or taste, or fancy—and have a brain so entirely unapt for every thing of that kind, that I solemnly declare I was never yet able to comprehend the principles of motion of a squirrel cage, or a common knife-grinder's wheel —tho' I have many an hour of my life look'd up with great devotion at the one—and stood by with as much patience as any christian ever could do, at the other——

I'll go see the surprising movements of this great clock, said I, the very first thing I do: and then I will pay a visit to the great library of the Jesuits, and procure, if possible, a sight of the thirty volumes of the general history of China, wrote (not in the Tartarian, but) in the Chinese language, and in the Chinese character too.

　　Now I almost know as little of the Chinese language, as I do of the mechanism of Lippius's clock-work; so, why these should have jostled themselves into the first two articles of my list——I leave to the curious as a problem of Nature. (*TS* 7.30.626)

Sterne's source for this information was the travel writing of Jean-Aimar Piganiol de la Force, author of the *Nouveau Voyage de France* of 1755.[80] In Sterne's hands this material becomes an occasion to think about attempts to explain a universal order (either through the mechanism of the clock, or the formulation of Chinese, which many believed was the representation of a universal language) via the mysteries of associationism, to ask what might inexplicably connect clockwork with the Jesuits and the history of China, and why, when the traveller comes to marvel at these wonders, he actually prefers to visit the anonymous 'Tomb of the two lovers', his own sentimental 'Mecca'.

　　Like many of the events which unfold in *Tristram Shandy*, this episode condenses a number of levels of reference, from philosophical and religious debates to the most topical of contemporary issues. The tourist's progress is interrupted by a Commissary of the post office who demands the payment of a tax for his intended use of a post-chaise, even though he has suddenly decided to go by boat, because 'REVENUES are not to fall short through your *fickleness*'. 'If fickleness is taxable in France', the narrator declares, we have nothing to do but make the best peace with you we can——AND SO THE PEACE WAS MADE' (*TS* 7.35.637–8). This allusion to the Treaty of Paris of 1763, which had concluded the Seven Years' War, many felt, to the disadvantage of the British victors, gives an imperial spin to this touristic experience and the narrator's associations. The Jesuits were famously connected to expansionist religious and state missions across the globe. (Indeed as Hegel's *Philosophy of History* recounts, their colonisation of the Indians in the American continent took a disciplinary form, in which the organisation of time even extended to the ringing of a bell at midnight to 'remind them of their matrimonial duties' – not unlike the beginning of *Tristram Shandy*[81].) The secret and highly unified administration of the Chinese empire was a source of fascination to competing European imperial powers, and gifts of scientific objects such as clocks and planetaria were one means of convincing them, as Leibniz put it to a French minister, that 'divinity communicates itself most particularly to Christians', and to French Catholics in particular.[82] In the case of Sterne's tourist, such mechanistic communication is more uncertain: Lippius's great clock, he discovers, 'was all out of joints, and had not gone for some years', the great library containing the history of China is closed because '*all the* JESUITS *had got the cholic*', and the tomb of the two lovers turns out never to have existed (*TS* 7.39, 40.642–3).

Sterne's narratives, then, ultimately reject the clockwork analogy, and indeed the imperial determinism it connotes, by producing their own Shandean ('crazy') counterpoint. Like Walter Shandy, the narrator and reader are confronted by 'riddles and mysteries', a realm of inexplicable connections. One proper response in the face of such a condition of non-knowledge, for an Anglican vicar like Sterne, might have been the assertion of a contemplative faith in divine order, echoed in Walter's contemplation of the fishpond – a gesture arguably embodied in a more uncertain, secular form by the melancholic figure of Maria. Yet his novels rather imagine this space of mystery as shaped by the desires, attachments and corporeal idiosyncrasies of the everyday world that refuse to be disciplined in instrumental ways. The biggest mystery turns out to be the opacity of everyday life.

## The Double-Bind of the Everyday

Sterne's Maria conforms in many ways to the resistance I have been describing. She is linked with disordered sense of time in *Tristram Shandy*, playing the evening hymn to the virgin at all times of the day and night. *A Sentimental Journey* emphasises her abstraction from the community of rural workers, for whom 'music beats time to labour'. Her wanderings suggest an aleatory and masterless quality, the 'fatal passion' of prodigality, perhaps, or the distraction of those who saunter and daydream rather than enter the proper oeconomy of time. Yet to explain the precise nature of the time accumulated in her image, I want to introduce one vision of aesthetic abstraction in more detail, a contemporaneous reading of the experience of everyday life.

Adam Smith's *The Theory of Moral Sentiments* chooses to think the nature of the universal system through a metaphor of clockwork that paraphrases the mechanistic philosophy of Robert Boyle:

> The wheels of the watch are all admirably adjusted to the end for which it was made, the pointing of the hour. All their various motions conspire in the nicest manner to produce this effect. If they were endowed with a desire and an intention to produce it, they could not do it better. Yet we never ascribe any such desire or intention to them, but to the watch-maker, and we know that they are put in motion by a spring, which intends the effect it produces as little as they do. But though, in accounting for the operations of bodies, we never fail to distinguish in this manner the efficient from the final cause, in accounting for those of the mind we are very apt to confound those two different

things with one another. When by natural principles we are led to advance those ends, which a refined and enlightened reason would recommend to us, we are very apt to impute to that reason, as to their efficient cause, the sentiments and actions by which we advance those ends, and to imagine that to be the wisdom of man, which in reality is the wisdom of God.[83]

Smith holds onto the clockwork analogy which is one means of grasping the rationality of the universal system as he understands it, and indeed the machinic operation of language itself. The nature of social abstraction in fact demands this disinterested ticking out of equal units of time, the measured pointing of the hour. Yet, as he describes, it is the mind which puts this order under pressure, abrogating to itself the enlightened workings of reason and its sentimental praxis, rather than attributing such facility to the divine watchmaker himself. This identification of the mind's autonomy is shared by *Tristram Shandy*, which pushes it to its comic limits by exploiting an associationism that incorporates reason into its own wayward logic. In Smith's *Moral Sentiments*, by contrast, such autonomy is defused; the self becoming host to the surveillance of conscience, the 'man within' or 'impartial spectator', who teaches the 'real littleness of ourselves'.[84] Accompanying this disciplinary vision, significantly, is an *aesthetic* sense of the universal order. What may appear a mystery from one perspective, or falsely simplistic from another, is just a question of finding the right level of 'abstract and philosophical' contemplation:

> The perfection of police, the extension of trade and manufactures, are noble and magnificent objects. The contemplation of them pleases us, and we are interested in whatever can tend to advance them. They make part of the great system of government, and the wheels of the political machine seem to move with more harmony and ease by means of them. We take pleasure in beholding the perfection of so beautiful and grand a system, and we are uneasy till we remove any obstruction that can in the least disturb or encumber the regularity of its motions.[85]

The production of an aesthetic space, in Sterne's narratives, suggests a realm of freedom that thwarts the instrumental pressures of the mid-century world. In Smith, by contrast, the aesthetic binds judgement and sensibility into the maintenance of the system; a disinterested perspective by definition not within the purview of all. *The Wealth of Nations* turns such a perspective on what he terms the 'false imagining' of common life, the mystery of the everyday yielding a vision of the perfect harmony of the division of labour. Behind the simple tools and commodities that provide a man with his basic subsistence – warmth, food, shelter – are the hidden complex operations of 'knowledge and art', the 'assistance and co-operation of many thousands'.[86] The everyday is thus experienced through a form of false consciousness, haunted by the presence of secret histories that undergo aesthetic sublimation.

At the same time therefore as the everyday is imagined as distinct from the regulation of economic life, or even as a zone of freedom, it is already incorporated into the logics of capital. This is the double-bind exposed by *Tristram Shandy*, as we have seen, theatricalising its status as a commodity even as it protests its autonomy in the face of the market. The paradox is that the imagining of a space resistant to instrumental forms of rationality is precisely *required* in order for such discipline to 'bite effectively', in Thompson's words.[87] Such a zone undergoes an intense ideological construction at the mid-century, in some versions appearing to be outside social time altogether; a place that, depending on nature of the exercise, is peopled by the feckless and idle, by (proto-Romantic) eccentrics distracted by daydreams and excessive imagination, by those suffering a surfeit of leisure and luxury, by masterless outsiders, and especially, by women. This double-bind – in which particular constituencies are said to be both internal to, and excluded from, the time of social labour – is crucial to the ordering of eighteenth-century life. It takes the form of a type of symbolic violence, not least in the constitution of what I am going to term 'women's time'.

## The Conquest of Women's Time

Writing of the 'unthinkable history' of Spanish imperial reason, Alberto Moreiras argues that 'the history of every process of hegemony is always already the history of a forgetting: hegemony is always the forgetting of primitive accumulation, the original sin of political economy'. As he continues:

> And then what about the state, every state, insofar as every state is necessarily founded upon colonial territorialization, territorial reason, imperial reason; insofar as every state reproduces itself through internal colonialism?: an ongoing colonialism which we can perhaps identify as the politico-cultural translation of primitive accumulation in all its varieties.[88]

I have been reading poor Maria as a symptom of just such a 'politico-cultural translation'. If, as Marx stated, and Moreiras considers, 'primitive accumulation plays approximately the same role in political economy as original sin does in theology',[89] then I am suggesting that the figure of the fallen woman here articulates the translation of that originary violence, in a movement that is also 'the history of a forgetting'. But how, precisely?

In William Russell's *Essay of the Character, Manners and Genius of Women in Different Ages*, published in the early 1770s, a distinction is made between men and women's relation to time and history, and thus to the formation of the imperial state. Men can 'transform their existence entirely into the body of the state', he writes.[90] 'It is only by the power of arranging his ideas, that the philosopher is able to overleap so many barriers; to pass from a man, to a people; from a people, to human kind; from the time in which he lives, to ages as yet unborn; and from what he sees, to what he does not see'. *Pace* the embattled Walter Shandy, the rational organisation of ideas is what makes it possible for man to manage future time – the very action of politics – on a universal scale. By contrast,

> The tender sex do not love to send their souls so far a-wandering. They assemble their sentiments and their ideas about them and confine their affections to what interests them most. Those strides of benevolence to women are out of nature. A man, to them, is more than a nation, and the hour in which they live, [more] than a thousand ages after death. (pp. 35–6)

Women are tied to the everyday, Russell's account suggests, representing particularity, magnifying an hour into a 'thousand ages'. Yet their alternative husbandry of time is essential to the harmonious working of the system. 'Society [has become] a complicated machine, and demands more dexterity to regulate its movements' (p. 38), he explains: such dexterity is provided by women, whose 'finer instruments' (p. 30) sense the secret connections and minute circumstances that comprise the everyday world. The particularity of women supports the overarching Enlightenment values which only men have the vigour and disinterest to bear.

Such a vision of the moral and affective functions of the women's sphere of course becomes increasingly powerful within the ideology of middle-class domesticity which takes hold in the last decades of the eighteenth century and so centrally in the nineteenth. There is a substantial body of critical work that has discussed the historical constitution of separate spheres and its relation to industrial capitalism, a separation that many have sought to trouble in gendered terms while recognising the ideological potency of the divide. To the same end it is worth reflecting again on the distinction that Russell wants to make here, which while reinforcing the sexual division of labour hypostatised in the notion of separate spheres – public/private, political sphere/domestic realm, state/family – also unravels it. In Chapter 4 I discussed the way he stages a dialogue with Montaigne about the gendered nature of friendship. With their 'vigour of the soul', which 'strengthens and extends political capacity' (p. 15), men are able to project themselves beyond immediate limits; elevating 'themselves to that patriotism, or disinterested love of one's country, which embraces all its citizens, and to that philanthropy or universal love of mankind, which embraces all nations' (p. 33). The point about such philanthropy, as we saw, is that it is accompanied by an Idea: the rational spirit of freedom embodied in the state. In other words, men are perceived as integral to such a process of political abstraction. Women, by contrast, are said to exist 'more in themselves, and in the objects of their sensibility, and perhaps being less fitted than men by nature for the civil institutions in which they have less share, they must be less susceptible of that enthusiasm, which makes a man prefer the state to his family, and the collective body of his fellow citizens to himself' (pp. 34–5). Thus far we remain within the terms of the distinction. To women, however, falls a different form of *conquest*:

> Women correct that rudeness which pride and passion introduce into the company of men. Their delicate hand smooths the asperities of human life. Politeness is a part of their character; it is connected with their mind, with their manners, and even with their interest. To the most virtuous woman society is a field of conquest. (p. 38)

This notion of conquest can be connected to the 'internal colonialism' mentioned in the Moreiras quotation above. 'Humanity is the virtue of a woman', writes Adam Smith.[91] The 'feminised' values celebrated in mid-century society may appear to take a non-political, ethical form, yet they have for all their philanthropic sensibility, directly administrative effects. The ideal construction of women's lives, associated with moral instinct and the sensitive grasp of human affections, is central to the 'restrictive arts of government'. While such 'conquest' might appear to relegate women to the ameliorative domestic role commonly assigned to them, I want to suggest that it also posits a relation between women and a process of social abstraction that is temporal and historical in form. Russell's view of the density and significance of a middle-class woman's 'hour' is interesting in this regard. It appears to be outside the time of the nation and the monumental reach of historical time. Yet it suggests the continual activity of minute adjustments, 'the crowd of little notices and polite attentions, which are every moment necessary in the commerce of life' (p. 12), and the particularist recognition of the 'importance of circumstances which have none in themselves' (p. 30). Such temporal attention facilitates 'the regulation of the machine' (p. 38). It is also in itself a concrete, social form of time. This density is interpreted as a form of time-killing – the filling of a temporal space – *and at the same time* as a useful productivity that elasticates the duration of the hour. How can it be both?

Moishe Postone has discussed with clarity the distinctions between two related forms of time that are socially constituted in capitalism, and which have a direct bearing on my analysis. One is abstract time, determined by the measure of value, which is a mathematical constant. As Lukács argued, abstract time has a spatial character that establishes, in Postone's words, 'an abstract, homogeneous temporal frame that is unchanging and serves as the measure of motion . . . its equable constant "flow" is actually static'. Its constant form is that of present time. The second is historical time, the concrete 'movement *of time*' which registers a dynamic of ongoing social transformation and activity: from objective changes in the state and family, shifts in work, production and technologies, to newly constituted forms of subjectivity, values and needs. It can take the most intimate of forms. Historical time is related to abstract time in economic terms because it moves it along through the production of a density of use–value; thus, while the unit – the hour – is an unchanging measure, productivity can increase, and thus transform its value. What interests me about this interaction however is the way it is experienced (as an acceleration: the 'treadmill' effect of capitalism), and also how it is interpreted.[92]

For Postone, this 'historical flow exists behind, but does not appear within, the frame of abstract time'. This observation bears, I think, on the ideological double bind I have been exploring, since the 'flow' of changing needs and activities can appear to be distinct from the uncompromising imperatives of economic rationality. But it would be wrong, Postone argues, to interpret this historical flow as a 'non-capitalist moment', and thus as constituting a 'critique that points beyond that social formation'. As he explains:

> As opposed to Lukács – who equates capitalism with static bourgeois relations and posits the dynamic totality, the historical dialectic, as the standpoint of the critique of capitalism – the position developed here shows the very existence of an ongoing, 'automatic' historical flow is related intrinsically to the social domination of abstract time. *Both* forms of time are expressions of alienated relations. I have argued that the structure of social relations characteristic of capitalism takes the form of a quasi-natural opposition between an abstract universal dimension and one of 'thingly' nature. The temporal moment of that structure also has the form of an apparently nonsocial and nonhistorical opposition between an abstract formal dimension and one of concrete process. These oppositions, however, are not between capitalist and noncapitalist moments, but, like the related opposition between positive–rational and romantic forms of thought, they remain entirely within the framework of capitalist relations.[93]

The 'quasi-natural opposition' Postone identifies is central to the ordering of eighteenth-century life, in which particular subjects are to be located either side of the divide. It is women who are part of ' "thingly" nature', and also in a more subtle sense, moral middle-class guardians of 'concrete process', smoothing the path of change, ensuring the necessary interpellation of those in their charge into new forms of human nature. From one perspective they appear to inhabit a realm that escapes the instrumental ravages of economic life, from which it is possible to construct, sometimes in utopian form, a moment of anti-capitalist critique.[94] Yet this potential is defused by an ideological positioning of their time as leisured and idle, a domestic non-time or 'blank', which at the same time naturalises the occlusion of forms of labour that keep such 'false imagining' in place. As Harriet Guest explores perceptively in her book *Small Change*, the analogy of the household as a machine returns in the writing of Hannah More, echoing Adam Smith's account of the invisible hand (and for my purposes, the mechanistic analogy of his *Theory of Moral Sentiments*). The housewife is the 'moving spring' guaranteeing the 'order, regularity and beauty of the whole system'; moreover such ideal domestic oeconomists:

> execute their well-ordered plan as an indispensable duty, but not as a superlative merit. They have too much sense to omit it, but they have too much taste to talk of it. It is their business, not their boast. The effect is produced, but the hand which accomplishes it is not seen. The mechanism is set at work, but it is behind the scenes. The beauty is visible – but the labour is kept out of sight.[95]

In Smith's clockwork metaphor he had warned against attributing intention to the working of the mechanism rather than the divine clockmaker who fashioned it; in Hannah More's version an analogous argument is used to disavow the intentionality of women's labour, as Guest points out. 'Labour is kept out of sight'. The sleight of hand is clearly explained: it is a matter of polite taste. This is part of the aestheticised 'conquest' Russell describes, and no less part of the dominative history of abstraction than the industrial embracing of time-discipline.

'Women's time', as I have argued elsewhere, names an ideological ruse that positions women outside the time of social labour, naturalising their exclusion; while making their activity symbolically central to the maintenance of the social.[96] It thus has implications for the organisation of the social order as a whole. It becomes instrumental, for example, in the division of the deserving and undeserving poor, in which, as John Barrell has shown, those seeking charity must be marked by domestic labour despite their exclusion if they are to qualify.[97] In Hannah More's words, summing up the distinction forged in the later decades of the eighteenth century, 'it is neatness, housewifery, and a decent appearance, which draws [sic] the kindness of the rich and charitable, while they turn away in disgust from filth and laziness'.[98] Predicated as it is on the life of the middle-class domestic oeconomist and her polite disavowal of necessary labour, this vision of women's time elevated bourgeois women as domestic guardians of the moral city, such that they might find, in John Brown's words, 'subordination' to be 'a source of genuine and lasting Pleasure';[99] and, one might add, limited power. Others, and sometimes these women themselves, nevertheless saw and experienced the violence of its contradictions; indeed, as a form of slavery.

The process of 'a historical forgetting' Moreiras describes is by no means ever complete or homogeneous, and contested in complex ways. It poses a problem analagous to that raised by Thompson's essay: to what extent the process of time-discipline might be seen as inevitable and exhaustive, such that it became impossible to think and experience the nature of social life – for those in Britain and in its colonies – 'outside' its universalising terms. As Dipesh Chakrabarty has explored in his critique of Thompson's historicism, however, the opposition of inside and outside is itself caught within the ideological terms of development (and within the division Postone also refutes). Marx acknowledges, he suggests, that the 'contradictory development' of bourgeois society always contains a remainder, of 'partly still unconquered' remnants:

> signaling by his metaphor of conquest that a site of 'survival' of that which seemed pre- or noncapitalist could very well be the site of an ongoing battle. There remains, of course, a degree of ambiguity of meaning and an equivocation about time in this fragment of a sentence from Marx. Does 'partly *still* unconquered' refer to something that is 'not yet conquered' or something that is in principle 'unconquerable'?[100]

For Chakrabarty the history of capitalism is rather to be thought as a battle marked by disjuncture and difference: an array of 'intimate and plural relationships to capital' that reveal the 'deep uncertainty' at its heart; the recognition of other temporalities, different 'pasts', that both 'inhere in' and 'interrupt' its logics.[101] One might see the ideological labour of women's time, as I have termed it, as an attempt to organise such a heterogeneity into the binaries that take on a symbolic and foundational form. And as thus also revealing, in its cultural work, a specific performative aspect to the process of social abstraction that Chakrabarty generalises to the capitalist process as a whole: 'To organise life under the sign of capital is to act *as if* labor could indeed be abstracted from all the social tissues in which it is always embedded and which make any particular labor – even the labor of abstracting – concrete.'[102] In the decade when Smith's vision of the division of labour was already in manuscript, the *as if* was imagined with the material force of a premonition. If hegemony might be thought a *dominant imaginary*,[103] to borrow the terms in which Judith Butler has reflected on the nature of a reified symbolic order, then its 'conquest' took, in part, a cultural form in which the embeddedness of the 'social tissues' of mid-century life became the time and territory of women; the realm of the 'abstract human' the prerogative of certain men.

### Struggling for Time: A Woman's Labour

Traces of contestation of the ideological capture of women's time can be glimpsed throughout the eighteenth century, in popular forms such as balladry, in the works of 'plebeian poets', in the discursive traces left by wandering figures, refusing the proper time-discipline of the day, long before its radical political articulation in the last decades of the century. It is also marked in the writing of those who seem to have embraced and indeed benefited from the terms of its interpellation: middle-class women, who despite their celebration of the domestic realm were faced with the negativity of the home, as Harriet Guest has shown, brought to represent it as 'a space evacuated of almost any possible subjectivity', a place of distraction and sleep.[104] The battle is present too in debates about the imagination, the unrecuperable, prodigality of the mind: a proto-Romanticism that might be constituted, as Postone describes, 'entirely within the framework of capitalist relations',[105] but which is nevertheless increasingly posited as a space of freedom: a *'Time to Dream'* as the poet Mary Collier put it.

Collier's poem 'A Woman's Labour' can be read as dramatising a struggle with the imposition of women's time, revealing aspects of its secret history. First printed in 1739 to counter what Collier saw as a misleading account of women's work in Stephen Duck's *The Thresher's Labour*, it found a wider readership in 1762 with the general publication of *Poems on Several Occasions by Mary Collier, Author of the Washerwoman's Labour*.[106] Collier's poem is an important document, exposing as it does an acute consciousness of the role of women's labour as underpinning an economy based on the male breadwinner. Duck's poem renders women's work invisible – 'our hapless Sex in Silence lie/ Forgotten, and in dark Oblivion die' (p. 8, ll.39–40) – or in their seeming leisure and gossip a foil for the labour of men – 'on our abject State you throw your Scorn,/And Women wrong, your Verses to adorn' (p. 8, ll.41–2). Collier's response is to detail the continuous cycle of work in which poor women are trapped. It was, Edward Thompson suggests, the rural labourer's wife who experienced the 'most arduous and prolonged work of all',[107] and it is this collective figure – the working mother – who Collier ventriloquates in her poem, bringing her children from the hearth to the field and back again, making meals and clothes for her family,

waiting to be let in to the House to start charring, sleepy and 'Oppress'd with
Cold' (p. 12, l.153), washing, polishing, brewing and mending by candle-
light. In characteristic classical fashion Collier imagines women's present
state as a kind of Fall from grace – from a golden age when sexual difference
presented no antagonism but rather reciprocity, in which men had been
brought to recognise 'as from us their Being they derive,/They back again
should all due Homage give' (p. 7, ll.23–4). Her poem resembles a manifesto
because it acknowledges that women's reproductive role, their domestic
labour, continues to produce the 'Being' of men even as they work alongside
them in the fields:

> We must make haste, for when we home are come,
> We find again our Work but just begun;
> So many Things for our Attendance call,
> Had we ten Hands, we could employ them all.
> Our Children put to Bed, with greatest Care,
> We all Things for your coming home prepare:
> You sup, and go to Bed without Delay,
> And rest yourselves till the ensuing Day,
> While we, alas! but little Sleep can have,
> Because our froward Children cry and rave;
> Yet, without fail, soon as Day-light doth spring,
> We in the Field again our work begin. (pp. 10–11, ll.105–16)

Mary Collier's work is powerful in its refusal of an aesthetic pastoralism
that surfaces in Duck's georgic. As Donna Landry has discussed, as a
spinster Collier herself has a limited leisure for thought, speculating on her
bed 'Eas'd from the tiresome Labours of the Day' (p. 6, l.12). There is,
Landry suggests, a 'dream-work' acknowledged here.[108] It is leisure too that
Goldsmith associates with the lost pastoral community of rural life in 'The
Deserted Village', a claim radicalised, as John Barrell shows, in the political
debates of the 1790s.[109] In Jonas Hanway's *Virtue in Humble Life*, this
demand is circumvented by imagining the very labour of men and women
as a kind of practical thought. In Collier's poem the association of time and
reflection also takes a radical form, though of a different order, one that in
the 1760s would have run against the grain of many of the texts promul-
gating time-discipline.

   The sexual politics of time appears to produce the political consciousness
of Collier's text. The cyclical patterns of life – diurnal, seasonal – are cut into
by the necessities of labour of all kinds. Time is no longer passed, but as
Thompson describes, is rather increasingly subject to a disciplinary logic:
spent, measured, husbanded, costed, squandered, saved, expropriated. In

Collier's case it is experienced as a continual and inexorable pressure: ''tis often known,/ Not only Sweat but Blood runs trickling down/ Our Wrists and Fingers; still our Work demands/ The constant Action of our lab'ring Hands' (p. 13, ll.184–7). The cyclical times of day and night, of the harvest, are incorporated into the grind of work to produce an impossible rhythm in which there is never enough time. Collier's women labourers 'fear the Time runs on too Fast' (p. 13, l.167), piecing 'the *Summers* day with Candle-light' (p. 14, l.193) in a phrase that picks up simultaneously on the domestic metaphor for assembling, or adding on to, and the notion of piece-rated wages (p. 22). The effect of this in the poem is to disorder and render more urgent the sense of time: women often begin their work in the evening, getting up at midnight and working on several tasks simultaneously, while juggling domestic responsibilities to home and hearth. It is not true for the labouring mother, as the tracts argued, that early rising means the working day will fall into its rightful place, with time for sleep and religious observance. Such is the intensity of labour that, at times, there is no respite to be had: 'Our Toil and Labour's daily so extreme/ That we have hardly ever *Time to Dream*' (p. 11, l.134).

No time to dream: such is the disciplinary penetration of time into women's mental space, that, if we might read the phrase in its strongest sense, there is 'hardly' any utopian potential for imagining that things might be otherwise. That future moment anticipated by Walter Shandy, in which the time of the clock might achieve synchronicity with the inner time of duration and thus do away with it altogether, has seemingly already arrived. What we witness in this text, emerging in a world increasingly shaped by the not so hidden hand of capital, is the space of the everyday, but here revealed in all its regulation: the everyday defined, as Henri Lefebvre has argued, as a crushing of the cyclical patterns of reproduction by the instrumental repetitiveness of work. It is women, Lefebvre declares, 'who are sentenced to everyday life'.[110]

Edward Thompson suggests that the hours of work detailed in 'The Woman's Labour'

> were only endurable because one part of the work, with the children and in the home, disclosed itself as necessary and inevitable, rather than as an external imposition. This remains true to this day, and, despite school times and television times, the rhythms of women's work in the home are not wholly attuned to the measurement of the clock. The mother of young children has an imperfect sense of time and attends to other human tides. She has not yet altogether moved out of the conventions of 'pre-industrial' society.[111]

Yet though Thompson goes on to question the easy categorisation of historical change in terms like 'pre-industrial', the complexity of Collier's text also demands closer consideration of the way women's experience is understood in historical terms, then as now. For the sense of oppression, of 'external imposition', in her poem is palpable, and the 'slavery' she describes takes place as much in the home as elsewhere. While Thompson's account identifies the problem of the naturalised 'necessity' of domestic labour – and this is the disavowal engineered by 'women's time' I have been describing – part of the force of Collier's argument is to situate that necessity within the wider world of work increasingly marked by 'the measurement of the clock'. It is not just that women's labour is rendered visible, but that it is framed temporally in a number of ways. What emerges from her poem, then, rather than an 'imperfect sense of time'[112] in Thompson's terms (once again the time of 'reproduction' proving outside the reach of history – in this missing the very point of the poem itself), is an acute and practised awareness of it: as a series of differentials simultaneously and multiply lived in everyday life (at the workplace and home, and in the home *as* workplace); marked by the passage of the days and the seasons; according to the task, the employer, the technological means available; as representing various degrees of autonomy and imposition (that is, the extent to which it suggests agency and subjection, coercion and leisure, often simultaneously); as ideological, to the extent that the 'time' of reproduction and the home might appear to be no time at all – marked by other rhythms, 'other human tides'; and differently experienced by diverse men and women, according to their class, their wealth, their access to consumption and thought. There is nowhere for this heterogeneity to go, no political means of making her claim heard for *'Time to Dream'*. As Donna Landry shows, Collier's is ultimately a position of resignation, one that finally consents in the other poems in her collection to the piety later celebrated by Jonas Hanway, a belief in a better world to come.[113] Yet 'A Woman's Labour' does memorialise a point of struggle nonetheless, and indeed, in the terms not of singular suffering but of a collectivity – the daughters of Danaus – who turn the violence back on the culture from whence it came.

## Maria: An Afterlife

It is this long secret history of women's time that I am arguing accumulates in the figure of poor Maria. I do not imply by this an essentialist notion of a time specific to women: the fluidities valorised by modernist feminism, for example, or the 'cyclical' time of reproduction that has often been seen as outside the 'linear time' of history. Rather, I am using it to name the ideological ruse, whereby women are located outside the time and values of the social, while also being central – in sometimes ethical and aestheticised form – to its maintenance. It is a double-bind that is naturalised as the condition of women's lives. Maria might now appear as a site of struggle: a vision of imaginative autonomy and yet sentimental dependence; aleatory freedom and yet alienation.

Yet these are contradictions that sentimentalism largely defuses. In the prints and surfaces of late-eighteenth-century drawing rooms Maria was a sign of amnesiac consumption, a comfortable proximity to 'the presence of Misery'. As she made her way through a number of narrative guises in the decades after the emergence of Sterne's novels, her status as sympathetic touchstone, testimonial to the benevolent reader, was reinforced.[114] The author of *Maria; Or, The Generous Rustic* weeps tears of sympathy over impoverished rural 'sons and daughters of affliction', incorporating her lover in a captivity narrative in North Africa, and ending the story in madness and death.[115] Sterne's *Maria; A Pathetic Story. With an Account of her Death at the Castle of Valesine* borrowed heavily from Sterne, though produced sisters to maximise the number of melodramatic outcomes.[116] The anonymous *Letters of Maria; to which is Added, an Account of her Death* imagines her wanderings in terms of a pilgrimage, emphasising the virtue of rural retreat:

> Humanity is not confined to crouded cities, in these solitary cottages, far, far distant from the busy haunts of men, she lives in her greatest purity: The humble cottagers, untainted by vice, are intent only on the means of subsistence, and of paying their adoration to God.[117]

And the anonymous *Maria; Or the Vicarage* transforms her distraction in 1796 as the very image of time-discipline. Not only is her sensibility 'tempered with firmness' nor 'the dupe of licentious passion', but

> she had studied with success the arts of music and painting, which, while they harmonized her, mind, and formed the elegance of her taste, served to fill up those vacant hours which the solitude of retirement, and want of society, would otherwise have extended to a tedious length.[118]

However, the sentimental conquest of Maria is perhaps not quite as total as it might appear. The figure of the distressed woman continues to surface in the latter decades of the century in discussions of the social intelligibility of women, not always in ways which collude with the cultural work of the time. In the 1790s it becomes possible to articulate her plight, and the symbolic violence that defines her, in political terms. In Mary Wollstonecraft's *A Vindication of the Rights of Woman* she reflects on women thus 'broken off from society':

> many innocent girls become the dupes of a sincere, affectionate heart, and still more are, as it may emphatically be termed, *ruined* before they know the

difference between virtue and vice: – and thus prepared by their education for infamy, they become infamous. Asylums and Magdalens are not the proper remedies for these abuses. It is justice, not charity, that is wanting in the world![119]

Wollstonecraft can name the arbitrariness of the 'unnatural distinctions' that constrain both men and women, defining their social being. If a man can slip through 'loop-holes' and 'dare to think and act for himself', a woman is enslaved, her escape a 'herculean task' requiring 'almost superhuman powers'.[120] The interpellative capture is exposed.

In *Tristram Shandy* Sterne's narrator promises that the story of Maria's 'sorrows' will later be told from her own lips. What would it mean for her to relate her secret history? There remains something necessarily subaltern about it. Yet in Wollstonecraft's work there is nonetheless an attempt to tell a different version of her story from below. In the posthumous narrative, *The Wrongs of Woman: Or, Maria, A Fragment*, Wollstonecraft relates the predicament of the distressed woman in more than one voice. Her Maria has been institution-alised in an asylum, her madness fabricated, but also temporarily induced in the form of melancholia, by the patriarchal despotism that has confined her and snatched her child.[121] She is attended by Jemima, the daughter of servants, whose own tale is one of abuse and poverty, seduction and eventual prostitu-tion: 'I was, in fact, born a slave, and chained by infamy to slavery during the whole of my existence, without having companions to alleviate it by sympathy, or teach me how to rise above it by example.'[122] 'Infamy' for Wollstonecraft is not just a loss of reputation, but the material consequence of women's oppres-sion. She counters it by imagining a cross-class solidarity between women (though Jemima's diction and abilities are notably polite) as 'out-laws of the world', and by demanding her rights, albeit fruitlessly, before the law. Her notes suggest that the narrative would have ended melodramatically in degra-dation, an unfaithful lover and miscarriage, and finally in the prospect of suicide, averted by Jemima's discovery of the lost child.

It is clear that Wollstonecraft is demanding a specific form of social recog-nition: an equality of subjecthood that extends logically in her *Vindication* to women's ultimate representation by the state. The figuring of Maria as senti-mental *victim* has to be sloughed away. And with it the libertinism of the male spectator, whose desires and exquisite privations derive pleasure from her dis-empowerment. There's no doubt that Wollstonecraft has Sterne in mind when her Maria describes the sympathies of 'a man of feeling' with a subtle allu-sion to *A Sentimental Journey* (the italics are my own):[123]

A man of feeling thinks not of seducing, he is himself seduced by all the noblest emotions of his soul. He figures to himself all the sacrifices a woman of *sensi-*

bility must make, and every situation in which his imagination places her, touches his heart, and fires his passions. *Longing to take into his bosom the shorn lamb*, and bid the drooping buds of hope revive, benevolence changes into passion.[124]

It is here that Wollstonecraft's unease with Sterne's portrayal of Maria might be understood. His sensualism is akin to the lasciviousness she finds in Rousseau, a sensibility that turns desirously in on itself rather than attaining the clarity of a moral and rational perspective. As John Whale has explored, hers is a complicated negotiation of sensibility, one that sees in its 'anguish' 'the potential to highlight the social capacity for feeling' while recognising that 'if it is only a limited materialism it can provide no escape from the dangers of egoism'. 'True sensibility', he suggests, 'as well as being virtuous, must also be original: part of the creative and genial spirits of individuality. It must also be an act of choice, a product of intellectual free-thinking.'[125] It is this affective agency that Wollstonecraft wants to bring within the purview of women, one that would allow them to wander 'astray' like men beyond the limits of the everyday.

Mary Wollstonecraft possesses the contemplative space signalled by melancholy, countering its associations with idleness, reworking its relationship to time. The aesthetic removal of Sterne's Maria, the difficulty of reading her enigmatic figure, becomes late in the century a question of the sublime imagination, the Romantic 'intimation of immortality' that Whale describes.[126] Wollstonecraft claims Collier's '*Time to Dream*' against the deadening indolence and yet instrumentality of commercial life, seeing it however in terms of an *awakening* that has both a religious and political force. This is not an idle daydreaming that 'build[s] airy castles in a future world', but the imagining of futurity through the vigorous labour of a transformed present.[127] It is as if, fusing sensibility and abstraction, Wollstonecraft can position herself as the philosopher celebrated by William Russell, able to move from 'the time in which [she] lives, to ages as yet unborn; and from what [she] sees, to what [she] does not see':[128] 'Rousseau exerts himself to prove that all *was* right originally: a crowd of authors that all *is* now right: and I, that all will *be* right'.[129]

There is then a utopian dimension to Wollstonecraft's critique of the brutalities of women's time. The melancholy nonetheless persists. It is not possible to sustain the separation of 'contradictory things' – 'God and Mammon', wealth and virtue – as she advocates in her *Vindication of the Rights of Women*, as if from the pages of *The Pilgrim's Progress*: 'Do not imagine you can bound from one road to the other without losing the way.'[130] Her own work is caught up in the capture of these and related contradictions, marked by the presence of time-discipline in the very terms of its strenuous imagining of freedom. This is a drama central to Romantic aesthetics, but it has already found expression in the cultural work of the mid-eighteenth century: the lesson of the wayward ironies that attend the figure of poor Maria, carried in her wake. Ironies that articulate less the predilections of Laurence Sterne than lineaments of disjuncture in an ongoing secret history; tracking a story of a wider social 'capture' and forgetting that is exemplified in the reported reproduction of the image of poor Maria, among prints, commodes and fire-screens, on the case of a watch.

## Notes

1  Josiah Tucker, *Four Tracts*, pp. 44–5. On the war on sloth, with reference to Tucker, see Michael Perelman, *The Invention of Capitalism: Classical Political Economy and the Secret History of Primitive Accumulation* (Durham, NC and London: Duke University Press, 2000), pp. 16–24. Tucker was unfashionably pacifist during the Seven Years' War because he saw conflict as an anathema to trade. As he wrote in *The Case of Going to War* in 1763, he preferred to create customers and peaceable exchange rather than 'knock a Man on the Head', p. 57.

2  I am picking up on the Perelman, p. 1, here, and in particular his suggestive use of the Althusserian notion of the 'inner darkness of exclusion', the 'forbidden vision' within and defining of the intelligible and seen, taken from Althusser and Balibar, pp. 25–6, which relates the non-knowledge with which my book began.

3  Catherine M. Gordon, *British Paintings of Subjects from the English Novel 1740–1870* (New York and London: Garland, 1988), pp. 74–5. These were images informed by the vogue for sensibility which took *A Sentimental Journey* as their source. Gordon also notes that about fifteen versions of the subject were exhibited between 1830 and 1870, overwhelmingly taking *Tristram Shandy* as their point of reference. It is likely that critical responses to Sterne in the nineteenth century, she suggests, were often mediated by the material culture surrounding Maria and related sentimental scenes (pp. 87–9).

4  Angelica Kauffman's versions of Maria were most widely reproduced in copies and prints. These included her single figure study, and the two figure composition of Yorick and Maria, *Moulines – The Handkerchief*, engraved in 1782. What was significant about Kauffman was not simply her status as a history painter and co-founder of the Royal Academy, but her domination of the rapidly expanding market in the decoration of domestic interiors. Her work was widely disseminated through the mediation of copyists, furniture designers, engravers and print makers. Her paintings found their way into book illustrations and onto walls as 'furniture prints', not framed and mounted but framed by gilt covals on the walls. The development of new engraving techniques such as

stipple techniques meant that more copies could be reproduced, and the fine quality meant that wealthy women could incorporate them into interior design. They were also used as embroidery motifs, sometimes printed directly onto satin: Emma Hamilton's needlework version of the two figures of Sterne and Maria (held at the National Maritime Museum) reprised her own romantic coupledom with Nelson. It is known from a journal early in the nineteenth century that prints from Ryland's stipple after Kauffman's Maria were circulated over all Europe. See Wendy Wassyng Roworth (ed.), *Angelica Kauffman: A Continental Artist in Georgian England* (Brighton: Reaktion Books, in association with The Royal Pavilion Art Gallery and Museum, 1992); David Alexander, *Affecting Moments: Prints of English Literature Made in the Age of Romantic Sensibility 1775–1800* (York: University of York, 1993).

5  *A Sentimental Journey* ran to 120 editions by 1820. Gordon notes that over fifty paintings and prints from the novel were produced in the last twenty-five years of the eighteenth century. Gordon, p. 76.

6  Gordon also makes the point that the sentimental figures taken as the subject of paintings from Sterne's work tally exactly with the fragments anthologised in *The Beauties of Sterne* (1786).

7  See in particular the two versions of Maria by Joseph Wright of Derby, *Maria, from Sterne* (1777), and *Maria, from Sterne, a Companion to the Picture of Edwin* (1781). Durer's engraving *Melencholia I* (1514) informs the characteristic pose, which is repeated in a number of Wright's works, including the earlier companion piece to the second Maria, *Edwin, from Dr Beattie's Minstrel* (1777–8) and *The Widow of an Indian Chief watching the Arms of her deceased Husband* (1785). Wright had earlier penned a 'Study of a Melancholic Girl' while in Rome in 1775 which bears close relation to the later Maria. Both versions of Maria dress her in classical drapery rather than contemporary clothing, as Gordon notes, p. 76. See Judy Egerton, *Wright of Derby* (London: Tate Gallery, 1990).

8  *The Captive* was another popular image which found its way quickly onto the art scene.

9  Thus, as Robert Markley has discussed, Sterne is 'ideologically constrained by a culture which refuses to acknowledge the legitimacy of a vocabulary to describe large scale political oppression'. While sentiment recognises the affective rights of individuals whatever their social status, contributing to the critique of aristocratic authority, it does so by limiting them within the hierarachical gradations of reciprocity I discussed in Chapter 4. As Markley argues, to acknowledge the suffering of ' "millions" ' . . . would be to move from sentiment to social injustice, from pity to either outrage or fear, and from passive sympathy to the spectres of outright repression and revolutionary action'. Markley, pp. 226–7. It is the pressure of these 'millions', and their disavowal, which I read in the lineaments of 'poor Maria'.

10 The biblical reference underlines the slippage here. Beneath the parable from the second book of Samuel (chapters 11 and 12) quoted by Sterne – that Maria might 'lay unto him as a daughter' – is the lesson about David's coveting and possession of Bathsheba, another man's wife.

11 Mary Wollstonecraft, 'Letters Written in Sweden, Norway and Denmark', in Marilyn Butler and Janet Todd (eds), *The Works of Mary Wollstonecraft* (London: Pickering and Chatto, 1989), IV, p. 280. Wollstonecraft also quotes another phrase from the Maria episode when writing to Gilbert Imlay about leaving her daughter in July 1795: 'It may run very well in a tale, that "God will temper the winds to the shorn lamb!" but how can I expect she will be shielded, when my naked bosom has had to brave continually the pitiless storm?' (Letter LVIII, VI, 421).

12 Joshua Reynolds, 'Discourse III', in *Discourses on Art*, ed. Robert R. Wark (New Haven and London: Yale University Press, 1997), p. 44.

13 Peter Brooks, 'Melodrama Body Revolution', in Jacky Bratton, Jim Cook and Christine Gledhill (eds), *Melodrama: Stage Picture Screen* (London: British Film Institute, 1994), p. 18.

14 Tom Gunning, 'The Horror of Opacity: The Melodrama of Sensation in the Plays of Audré de Lorde', in Bratton et al., *Melodrama*, p. 51.

15 I am grateful to Markman Ellis for making his unpublished paper 'Being Sterne with Maria' available to me. For the moral construction of the magdalen see also the chapter on 'The Politics of Prostitution' in his *The Politics of Sensibility: Race, Gender and Commerce in the Sentimental Novel* (Cambridge: Cambridge University Press, 1996), pp. 160–89. On the 'wanton chase' of Hogarth's harlot, and the 'entire industry of desire' accompanying it, see James Grantham Turner, ' "A Wanton Kind of Chace": Display as Procurement in *A Harlot's Progress* and Its Reception', in *The Other Hogarth: Aesthetics of Difference*, edited by Bernadette Fort and Angela Rosenthal (Princeton and Oxford: Princeton University Press, 2001), pp. 38–61. Turner notes that Hogarth's etching, *The Battle of the Pictures*, which annouced the auction of the series in 1745, shows the third plate of the harlot being 'speared in mid-air by a Penitent Magdalene'. p. 55.

16 Jonas Hanway, *Virtue in Humble Life: containing Reflections on the Reciprocal Duties of the Wealthy and Indigent, the Master and the Servant: Thoughts on the Various Situations, Passions, Prejudices, and Virtues of Mankind, Drawn from Real Characters: Fables Applicable to the Subjects: Anecdotes of the Living and the Dead: the Result of Long Experience and Observation. In a Dialogue between a Father and his Daughter, in Rural Scenes. A Manual of Devotion, comprehending extracts from Eminent Poets*, 2 vols (London: J. Dodsley, 1774), I, xxiii.

17 Jones, Vivien, p. 59.

18 William Hazeland, *A Sermon Preached in the Chapel of the Asylum, Near Westminster-Bridge, on the Sunday before Christmas-Day, 1760* (London: J. Beecroft, 1761), pp. 5, 6.

19  Hanway, *Virtue in Humble Life*, p. xiv.

20  Dr Dodd, 'The Third Sermon, preached at the anniversary meeting of the Governors, March 18 1762', quoted in Jones, Vivien, p. 88.

21  For an example of this institutional display see David H. Solkin's discussion of the Foundling Hospital in *his Painting for Money: The Visual Arts and the Public Sphere in Eighteenth-Century England* (New Haven and London: Yale University Press, 1992), pp. 159–74.

22  As Vivien Jones notes, the Magdalen House Charity, established in 1758 by private subscription, 'offered shelter and an ascetic regime of work and worship for prostitutes who petitioned for entry, were judged genuinely penitent, and who were not "infected with the foul disease". Of the 1,036 prostitutes who passed through the Hospital in the first ten years, 509 were "reconciled to, & received by their Friends or placed in Services in reputable Families, and to Trades" '. Jones, p. 93.

23  Oliver Goldsmith, 'The Deserted Village', in Arthur Friedman (ed.), *The Collected Works of Oliver Goldsmith* (Oxford: Clarendon Press, 1966), IV, 299–300, ll. 331–6. For an excellent discussion of this passage in the context of the representation of extreme degradation and the redemptive figure of the magdalen, see Ellen D'Oench, 'Prodigal Sons and Fair Penitents: Transformations in Eighteenth-Century Popular Prints', *Art History* 13:3 (1990), 318–43. I am indebted to Markman Ellis for the reference.

24  John Brown, *On the Female Character and Education: A Sermon Preached on Thursday the 16th of May, 1765, at the Anniversary Meeting of the Guardians of the Asylum for Deserted Female Orphans* (London: L. Davis and C. Reymers, 1765), p. 20.

25  A phrase from a talk by David Washbrook describing the status of the mobile and anonymous, quoted by Maxine Berg in her 'Women's Work, Mechanization and the Early Phases of Industrialization in England', in R. E. Pahl (ed.), *On Work: Historical, Comparative and Theoretical Approaches* (Oxford: Basil Blackwell, 1988), p. 87.

26  The figures, which Jonas Hanway's tireless administrative activism did much to begin to uncover, are shocking. As M. Dorothy George describes, when the Foundling Hospital temporarily opened its door to all child arrivals between 1756 and 1760 to alleviate the failings in parish welfare, 14,934 children were admitted, of whom just 4,400 lived to find an apprenticeship. These were children 'brought in a dying state and even stripped of their clothes, so that they might be buried at the expense of the Hospital. Many were sent from the country, and many died on the way. Infants were entrusted to carriers, wagoners, and even to vagrants. Disreputable people trafficked in the conveying of children to London. Many parish officers both in London and in the country sent children to the Hospital, sometimes openly, sometimes secretly. Sometimes legitimate children born in workhouses were forcibly taken from their mothers'. See

M. Dorothy George, *London Life in the Eighteenth Century* (Harmondsworth: Penguin (Peregrine) Books, 1966), p. 57.

27  From the first report of the Philanthropic Society (1788), quoted in George, p. 221.

28  The ideological scapegoating of the 'single mother' by successive British governments in the 1980s and 1990s is one modern example of the same phenomenon.

29  Lawrence Stone, *The Family, Sex and Marriage in England 1500–1800* (Harmondsworth: Penguin Books, 1979), p. 403.

30  See Perelman p. 156 for an account of the ways in which classical political economy debated the promotion of a 'taste for labour' among working people, in the words of Sir James Steuart in 1767.

31  Oliver Goldsmith, 'The Traveller; Or a Prospect of Society', in Arthur Friedman (ed.), *The Collected Works of Oliver Goldsmith* (Oxford: Clarendon Press, 1966), IV, 264, ll. 349, 351.

32  Arthur Young, *The Farmer's Letter to the People of England* , 2nd edn (London: np, 1771), pp. 353–4.

33  Goldsmith, 'The Deserted Village', p. 289, ll.63–4; p. 299, l.326; p. 292, ll. 131–6. See also Goldsmith's 'The Revolution in Low Life', published in the *Lloyd's Evening Post* (14–16 June 1762) for his sense of the impact of enclosure and the parcelling out of the country 'among the rich alone'. 'Let others felicitate their country upon the encrease of foreign commerce and the extension of our foreign conquests; but for my part this new introduction of wealth gives me but very little satisfaction'. In Arthur Friedman (ed.), *The Collected Works of Oliver Goldsmith*, (Oxford: Clarendon Press, 1966), III, 197–8.

34  On the cheapness of women's labour and their time-discipline, see Berg, p. 73. Weaving was a good example of an organised trade which *The Book of Prices* for 1769 which set piece rates for weaving attempted to restrict women in peacetime from the better paid branches of the trade, which was overwelmingly reliant on their labour. See George, p. 183.

35  The Settlement Act of 1662 gave magistrates the power to return the immigrant poor to the parish of their birth. Edmund Burke argued in 1774 that the restrictions imposed by 'laws of settlement and removals are the essence of slavery'. Moreover 'instead of the kingdom being equally and properly burthened with their poor; instead of the parishes of it drawing in concert to one end, and forming so many parts of one whole: they are in a system of repulsion; every one driving away the poor, and being to every intent hostile against each other, like states at war'. 'Speech on the Poor Removals Bill', pp. 402–3.

36  Dr Dodd, quoted in Vivien Jones, p. 89.

37  [E. Long], *Candid Reflections upon the Judgement lately awarded by the Court of King's Bench in Westminster-Hall on what is commonly called the Negroe-Cause, by a Planter* (London: T. Lowndes, 1772), p. 67.

38  Blackstone, *Commentaries*, IV, 169.

39  Long, *Candid Reflections*, p. 52.

40  Brown, *On the Female Character and Education*, p. 20.

41  Long, *Candid Reflections*, p. 60.

42  John Barrell, *The Dark Side of the Landscape: The Rural Poor in English Painting 1730–1840* (Cambridge: Cambridge University Press, 1980), p. 16.

43  Scott, *The Life of Theodore Agrippa D'Aubigné*, p. xiv.

44  Hanway, *Virtue in Humble Life*, p. xxxviii.

45  Ibid. p. xxxvi.

46  Ibid. pp. 296, xxxiv.

47  This found specific articulation in the reception of certain widely disseminated sensual images, like Correggio's *Mary Magdalen Reading in the Wilderness* which was copied in prints and drawings in Prussia, France and Britain at the mid-century and beyond. See D' Oench, pp. 330–32, who points out that Diderot playfully associated the image with an enjoyable 'mortification of the senses'. These images evidently worked along similar lines to the sensationalism of pornographic reproductions (reputedly one of Sterne's interests).

48  Solkin, 'The Battle of the Ciceros', pp. 58–9.

49  Goldsmith, *The Vicar of Wakefield*, p. 127. The novel is explicit in its condemnation of the use of penal statutes to control the poor.

50  Hugh Kelly, *Memoirs of a Magdalen; Or, the History of Louisa Mildmay*, 2nd edn (London: W. Griffin, 1767), I, 58.

51  Hanway, *Virtue in Humble Life*, p. xxiii.

52  Kelly, *Memoirs of a Magdalen*, p. 49.

53  Markman Ellis argues that poor Maria's condition is framed within the controversy over the Lord Hardwicke's Marriage Act of 1753, which had aimed to prevent clandestine marriages but succeeded in increasing the number of invalid unions, making marriage expensive for the poor, and in preventing quick marriages. He also points out that in a French context Maria could not have married for love without the consent of the parish priest; if she had done so secretly, Sylvio would have been convicted of rape, and possibly executed. 'Being Sterne with Maria', Unpublished paper, pp. 3–6.

54  Kelly, *Memoirs of a Magdalen*, pp. 129, 191, 204.

55  See Ellis, *The Politics of Sensibility* on magdalen biographies, and specifically his discussion on pp. 180–84 of *The Histories of Some of the Penitents in the Magdalen House as Supposed to be Related by Themselves* (London: John Rivington and R. Dodsley, 1760) which he attributes to Lady Barbara Montague; a 'dangerous moral project' which was printed with the aid of Samuel Richardson.

56  D'Oench, 'Prodigal Sons and Fair Penitents'.

57  Kelly, *Memoirs of a Magdalen*, p. 118.

58  Ibid. p. 144.

59 See, for example, John Brown's sense of women's self-sufficiency, 'where the Women, scorning the timid and subordinate Character, affect a self-sufficient and haughty Independency; assert an unbounded Freedom of Thought and Action; and even pretend to guide the Principles of Taste and the Reins of Empire', in his *On the Female Character and Education*, p. 17.

60 Goldsmith, *The Vicar of Wakefield*, p. 135.

61 Thomas Warton, *The Pleasures of Melancholy: A Poem* (London: R. Dodsley and M. Cooper, 1747), pp. 14–15, ll.171–4.

62 Goldsmith, *The Vicar of Wakefield*, p. 136.

63 Ibid. 136.

64 John Milton, 'Il Penseroso', in Roy Flannagan (ed.), *The Riverside Milton* (Boston and New York: Houghton Mifflin Company, 1998), p. 75, l.198.

65 Hanway, *Virtue in Humble Life*, p. 183.

66 Ibid. p. 186.

67 Ibid. pp. 184–5.

68 Ibid. p. xvii.

69 William Alexander, *The History of Women, from the Earliest Antiquity to the Present Time, Giving Some Account of almost every interesting Particular concerning that Sex, among all Nations, ancient and modern* (London: W. Straham, T.Cadell, 1779), pp. 98, 59.

70 Hannah More, *Coelebs in Search of a Wife. Comprehending Observations on Domestic Habits and Manners, Religion and Morals*, 3rd edn, 2 vols (London: T. Cadell and W. Davies, 1809), I, 87.

71 John Clayton, *Friendly Advice to the Poor, Written and Publish'd At the Request of the late and present Officers of the Town of Manchester* (Manchester: J. Harrop, 1755), pp. 20, 31, 8, 13.

72 Ibid. pp. 37, 31.

73 Thompson, 'Time, Work-Discipline and Industrial Capitalism', pp. 352–403.

74 *The Clock-Makers' Outcry*, p. 42.

75 Ibid. pp. 43, 44.

76 There is some evidence to suggest the circulation of such a Shandean joke among women. See, for example, a letter to Immanuel Kant from Maria Charlotte Jacobi, wife of a friend, who writes teasingly in 1762: 'I make claim on your company tomorrow afternoon. I hear you say "Yes, yes I'll come." Well good, we shall await you and then my watch will get wound'. It is concluded from this reference to Sterne that the relationship was more than platonic. See Maria Charlotta Jacobi, née Schwink, to Immanuel Kant, 12 June 1762, in Immanuel Kant, *Correspondence*, ed. and trans. Arnulf Zweig (Cambridge: Cambridge University Press, 1999), p. 67.

77 Thompson, 'Time, Work-Discipline and Industrial Capitalism', p. 354.

78 Thomas Wedgwood to William Godwin, 31 July 1797, quoted in Thompson, 'Time, Work-Discipline and Industrial Capitalism', p. 403. As Thompson

relates, Wedgwood's plan of educational improvement had Wordsworth in mind as a superintendent: *The Prelude* was the response, with its attack on the instrumentalism and mechanistic control of these 'Stewards of our Labour'.

79 See his *Authority, Liberty and Automatic Machinery in Early Modern Europe* (Baltimore: Johns Hopkins University Press, 1986). Thanks to David Wootton for this reference. Mayr suggests that the metaphor of clockwork is central to early modern absolutist understanding of the order of the body, state and universe, but largely modified in the British political sphere by a more liberal understanding of the checks and balances at work in the state. It nonetheless contributed in more abstract form to a seventeenth-century mechanistic philosophy of nature which, as Francis C. Haber points out, continued to shape natural theology and secular cosmology long into the eighteenth century. See his 'The Clock as Intellectual Artifact' in Klaus Maurice and Otto Mayr (eds), *The Clockwork Universe: German Clocks and Automata 1550–1650* (New York: Neale Watson Publications/ Smithsonian Institution, 1980), p. 18.

80 Jean-Aimar Piganiol de la Force, *Nouveau voyage de France avec un itineraire, et des cartes fait exprès, qui marquent exactement les routes qu'il faut suivre pour voyager dans toutes les provinces de ce royaume*, 2 vols (Paris: Guillaume Desprez, 1755). Sterne's account of the Lyons visit is close to the original, including the information that the famous clock was out of order, and that the Tomb of the two lovers was subject to numerous possible explanations, which he embellishes in the story of Amandus in *Tristram Shandy*.

81 G. W. F. Hegel, *The Philosophy of History*, trans. J. Sibree and intro. C. J. Friedrich (New York: Dover Publications, 1956), p. 82.

82 Quoted in Klaus Maurice, 'Propagatio fidei per scientias: Jesuit Gifts of Clocks to the Chinese Court', in Klaus Maurice and Otto Mayr (eds), *The Clockwork Universe: German Clocks and Automata 1550–1650* (New York: Neale Watson Publications/ Smithsonian Institution, 1980), p. 29.

83 Smith, *The Theory of Moral Sentiments*, p. 87.

84 Ibid. p. 137. It is no accident that the sermon Sterne chooses to include in *Tristram Shandy* is 'The Abuses of Conscience Considered'.

85 Smith, *The Theory of Moral Sentiments*, p. 185.

86 Smith, *The Wealth of Nations*, pp. 19–20.

87 Thompson, 'Time, Work-Discipline and Industrial Capitalism', p. 354.

88 Alberto Moreiras, 'Ten Notes on Primitive Imperial Accumulation: Ginés de Sepúlveda, Las Casas, Fernández de Oviedo', *interventions* 2:3 (2000), 353–4.

89 Karl Marx, *Capital Volume I*, trans. Ben Fowkes (Harmondsworth: Pelican, 1975), p. 873.

90 Russell, II, 34. All further references are from the second volume and are cited by page number in the text.

91 Smith, *The Theory of Moral Sentiments*, p. 190.

92 Moishe Postone, *Time, Labor and Social Domination: A Reinterpretation of Marx's Critical Theory* (Cambridge: Cambridge University Press, 1996), p. 294. On Lukács see p. 215 n.109.

93 Ibid. p. 295.

94 I would read Sarah Scott's *Millenium Hall* in this light, and also those texts valorising what might be seen as a feminine 'gift economy'. On this latter point see Judith Still, *Feminine Economies: Thinking Against the Market in the Enlightenment and the Late Twentieth Century* (Manchester: Manchester University Press, 1997).

95 More, *Coelebs in Search of a Wife*, II, 176–7. Guest, *Small Change*, p. 326.

96 See my 'Time and the Working Mother: Kristeva's "Women's Time" Revisited', *Radical Philosophy* 91 (1998), 6–18.

97 Barrell, *Dark Side of the Landscape*, p. 76.

98 More, *Black Giles the Poacher* (1830), quoted in Barrell, *The Dark Side of the Landscape*, p. 76.

99 Brown, *On the Female Character and Education*, p. 10.

100 Dipesh Chakrabarty, *Provincializing Europe: Postcolonial Thought and Historical Difference* (Princeton and Oxford: Princeton University Press, 2000), p. 65.

101 Ibid. pp. 54, 70. 'The very category "capital"', writes Chakrabarty pertinently for my analysis, 'becomes a site where both the universal history of capital and the politics of human belonging are allowed to interrupt each other's narrative'.

102 Ibid. p. 54.

103 See the interview with Judith Butler in Peter Osborne (ed.), *A Critical Sense: Interviews with Intellectuals* (London and New York: Routledge, 1996), p. 118.

104 Guest, *Small Change*, pp. 322–3. Guest is exploring the complexities of such negativity as it is articulated in Jane West's poem, *The Mother* (1809) and Felicia Hemans's *The Domestic Affections* (1812).

105 Postone, *Time, Labor and Social Domination*, p. 295.

106 Mary Collier, *Poems on Several Occasions by Mary Collier, Author of the Washerwoman's Labour, with some Remarks on her Life* (Winchester: Mary Ayres for the Author, 1762). All further references to 'A Woman's Labour' from this edition cited by page and line number in my text.

107 Thompson, 'Time, Work-Discipline and Industrial Capitalism', p. 381.

108 Donna Landry, *The Muses of Resistance: Labouring-Class Women's Poetry in Britain 1739–1796* (Cambridge: Cambridge University Press, 1990), p. 57.

109 Barrell, *The Dark Side of the Landscape*, pp. 81–2. Barrell argues that Goldsmith's 'agrarian egalitarianism' may have disturbed readers in 1770, 'less as suggesting the possibility of a redistribution of proprety in land than as apparently hostile to the increasing discipline of labour' but that its pastoralism diffused such a threat. 'Only from about 1790 could *The Deserted Village* be read as a radical poem which pointed (by implication) to the future as well as to the past'. Collier's refusal of pastoralism is interesting in this context.

110 Henri Lefebvre, 'The Everyday and Everydayness', *Yale French Studies* 73 (1987), 10.

111 Thompson, 'Time, Work-Discipline and Industrial Capitalism', pp. 381–2.

112 Ibid. pp. 381–2.

113 Landry, *The Muses of Resistance*, p. 71.

114 The following short list of texts I discuss is not intended to be exhaustive. Most use material taken directly from Sterne, even, in the case of the anonymous (though attributed to Sterne) *Sterne's Maria; A Pathetic Story*, claiming to be a lost manuscript in the possession of his daughter Lydia Medalle. There are also narratives such as Elizabeth Blower's *Maria: A Novel in Two Volumes, by the Author of George Bateman* (London: T. Cadell, 1785); poems such as 'Maria. Taken from Sterne's *Tristam* [*sic*] *Shandy*' (London: np, ca.1785); numerous songs, such as Thomas Billington's 'Maria's Evening Service to the Virgin' (London: printed for the Author, 1786), and John Moulds' 'Sterne at the Tomb of Mouline's Maria' (London: S., A. and P. Thompson, ca.1785) and 'The Handkerchief or Sterne's Pledge to Maria' (London: T. Jones, ca. 1795), and the anonymous 'Maria's Urn' (London: H. Wright, ca.1790). Music was also written for the harpsichord: 'Maria. An Elegy. 'Maria, lovely Maid is Dead' (London: Catherine Fenton, for the Author, 1784). Other Marias surface at this time but are of rather more uncertain provenance, such as the anonymous *Memoirs of Maria, A Persian Slave* (London: np, 1790), which suggest perhaps that the literary celebrity of the name (imbricated with more conventional Mariological and magdalen associations perhaps) could be a convenient peg for plots of a radically different kind. Marias continue to emerge in nineteenth-century texts, such *as Maria; Or a Shandean Journey of a Young Lady During the Summer of 1822*, by Uncle Oddy (London: John Hatchard, 1823), whose unashamed borrowing from Sterne – particularly in the lifting of phrases and cadences from *A Sentimental Journey* – might appear to verge on pastiche.

115 [George Monk Berkeley], *Maria; Or the Generous Rustic* (London: T. Cadell; Edinburgh: C. Elliot, 1784), p. vii.

116 Anon., *Sterne's Maria; A Pathetic Story with an Account of her Death at the Castle of Valesine* (London: R. Rusted, ca.1800).

117 Anon., *The Letters of Maria; to which is added, An Account of her Death* (London: G. Kearsley, 1790), p. 75.

118 Anon., *Maria; Or, the Vicarage. A Novel in Two Volumes* (London: Hookham and Carpenter, 1796), I, 5–6.

119 Mary Wollstonecraft, *A Vindication of the Rights of Woman*, in *Political Writings*, ed. Janet Todd (Oxford: Oxford University Press, 1994), p. 143.

120 Ibid. p. 225.

121 Maria's 'indulged sorrow' causes her to alternate between psychological states: on the one hand 'the moping melancholy of indolence' and on the other 'the

restless activity of a disturbed imagination'. 'Was the world not a vast prison, and women born slaves?', she considers. Mary Wollstonecraft, *The Wrongs of Woman: Or, Maria, A Fragment*, ed. Gary Kelly (Oxford: Oxford World's Classics, 1998), p. 79.

122  Ibid. p. 106.

123  '*God tempers the wind*, said Maria, to the shorn lamb' (*SJ* 152). Sterne is translating the French proverb 'Dieu mesure le froid à la brebis tondue', which George Herbert had included in his *Outlandish Proverbs* as 'To a close-shorn sheep, God gives wind by measure'.

124  Wollstonecraft, *The Wrongs of Woman*, p. 155.

125  See John Whale's illuminating chapter 'Wollstonecraft, imagination and futurity' in his *Imagination Under Pressure, 1789–1832: Aesthetics, Politics, and Utility* (Cambridge: Cambridge University Press, 2000), p. 75.

126  Ibid. p. 82.

127  Wollstonecraft, *Vindication* p. 190. As she puts it: 'Mental as well as bodily exertion is, at first, irksome, so much so, that the many would fain let others both work and think for them' (p. 188).

128  Russell, *Essay*, II, 36.

129  Wollstonecraft, *Vindication*, p. 79.

130  Ibid. p. 190.

# CHAPTER

## 6

# 'BRAMIN, BRAMINE': STERNE, ELIZA DRAPER AND THE PASSAGE TO INDIA

How oft have I smarted at the Idea, of that last longing Look by w^ch thou badest adieu to all thy heart Sufferd at that dismal Crisis—twas the Separation of Soul & Body—& equal to nothing but what passes on that tremendous Moment.—& like it in one Consequence, that thou art in another World; where I w^d give a world, to follow thee

> Laurence Sterne, *Continuation of the Bramine's Journal*[1]

Gide's silliness: 'Just finished rereading *Werther*, not without irritation. I had forgotten how long it took him to die [which is not at all the case]. He keeps going on and on, until you want to give him a push, right into the grave. Four or five times, what you had hoped was his last breath is followed by another even more ultimate one . . . the extended leavetakings exasperate me.' Gide doesn't realize that in the novel of love, the hero is *real* (because he is created out of an absolutely projected substance in which every amorous subject collects himself) and that what he is looking for here is a man's death – is *my* death.

> Roland Barthes, *A Lover's Discourse*[2]

Laurence Sterne was never averse to turning his life and opinions into enterprise. This was also true of his death, parodically memorialised in *Tristram Shandy*'s black page, and personified in the later volumes of the novel pursuing him relentlessly across France. Consumption finally caught up with him in an anonymous London lodging house in 1768. In that year he published *A Sentimental Journey*, and also created his last work, *The Journal to Eliza*, the epistolary record of his love for Eliza Draper, altogether more helium-filled in its sentimental fantasy than his previous narratives. 'If I live not till your return to England, I will leave it you as a legacy' he wrote to the woman he had known for just three months.[3] It was an uncertain bequest, and came to haunt Eliza as she applied herself to life as the wife of an East India Company apparatchik, hosting 'the Shipping Gentry, that resort to us for traffic and Intelligence from all parts of India, China and Asia' at the Tellicherry Factory.[4] In 1769 she was already being blackmailed by Sterne's impecunious wife and daughter, who were in possession of Eliza's letters to Sterne. As Eliza wrote ruefully to her cousin, 'I have suffered so materially by giving a loose to my pen that I'm likely to repent as long as I live tho' there's nothing I ever wrote that I could not justify, if I might appeal to Truth & candour as my judges; – but I've been extremely faulty in putting it in any one's power to injure me, by transcribing & communicating what I ought not, the first at the Instigation of one I deemed all Benevolence & truth'.[5]

I want to explore the consequences of Eliza's 'giving a loose' to her pen – her injurious capture by writing – and to chart what might be seen as a particular choreography of intimacy staged by the letters and Sterne's memoir, one that leads from an intense projection of self into the scene of empire. Indeed it might be seen as testimony to how far the imperial suturing of subjectivity had succeeded, such that the very imagining of the self takes place seamlessly, almost unnoticed, within its territory. In particular, I want to explore what might might be seen as the universalising gesture contained in one trajectory of 'feeling beyond the nation',[6] testing what Étienne Balibar has called the 'scattered meaning of the universal' in the process.[7] In so doing, I will read the scandalous nature of the connection between Sterne and his 'belle Indian' in terms removed from the predilection for psychological biography that has mired it in portraits of what Roland Barthes terms the 'symptomal subject'.[8] And it is here, in finding a means of reading Sterne's text, that my chapter begins.

Critics have long resorted to assumptions about individual 'pathology' or moral dereliction to explain the curious narcissism of Sterne's *Journal*: the blend of sentimental feeling and the drive to write for fame and reward that makes it appear at once the most heartfelt and contrived of narratives. Opinions have been divided as to whether the journal was written with an eye to publication,[9] its very staginess seemingly enough of a sign of commercial intention to render the answer immaterial. Sterne had, after all, had a series of 'sentimental' friendships that were often conducted in the heat of epistolary passion.[10] Such was his fame (and need for income) that any act of writing was an opportunity for revenue. Whatever Sterne's feelings for his inamorata, there has been considerable critical investment in exposing evidence of his calculation in this case: from Thackeray's 'proof' of another dalliance at the same moment, to revelations about Sterne's recycling of earlier letters and writerly 'fibs' to Eliza about the timing of his wife's return from France that conveniently bring the narrative to the end. If Sterne's texts are, as Everett Zimmerman has argued, 'himself dying',[11] then the final lines of the *Journal* – left hanging without a full stop in impossible contemplation of eternal life with Eliza – dramatically invite the connection between the dying text and the natural life. How scandalous then, if it should prove a question of profit, or mortal imposture; if the dying proves not to be a death at all.

Eliza Draper becomes in this light an unwary victim of sentimental cynicism on Sterne's part, inadvertently trapped by the author's excessive compulsion to display: whether in his reading aloud of her impassioned letters in mixed company, or his showing off of her portrait, a gesture caught in John Hamilton Mortimer's *A Caricature Group* of 1767 which shows the author exposing his bare chest and heart-shaped locket to fellow *bons viveurs*.[12] There's no doubt that Sterne saw entrepreneurial possibilities in Eliza's letters even as he openly extolled her virtues to all who would listen.'When I am in want of ready cash, and ill health will permit my genius to exert itself', he wrote, 'I shall print your letters, as finished essays, "by an unfortunate Indian lady". The style is new; and would almost be sufficient recommendation for their selling well, without merit – but their sense, natural ease, and spirit, is not to be equalled, I believe, in this section of the globe'.[13] The very openness of the affair was framed by an unthinkable spectacle: writerly commerce, sensual passion, a trace of colonial otherness, and the ruination of age. It found partial expression in Richard Griffith's observation: 'There was nothing in the Affair worth making a Secret of. The World, that knew their Correspondence, knew the worst of it, which was merely a simple Folly. Any other Idea of the Matter would be more than the most abandoned Vice could render probable. To intrigue with a Vampire! To sink into the Arms of *Death alive!*'[14] It was either the most mundane and innocent of liaisons or so obscene that Griffith could only think of it in gothic and predatory terms: Eliza embraced by the undead. Whatever Eliza's rightful claims to 'Truth & candour', it was clear even in the sensationalism of Griffith's denial that her reputation was at stake.

It is of course possible to read these narrative fragments in ways that move beyond the biographical portrait. Harriet Guest's perceptive analysis of the exchange between Sterne and Eliza Draper accords Eliza herself some agency, as a woman who evidently derived pleasure and a limited power from her own gifts as a conductor of sensibility. Eliza had confided in her cousin that:

> One of my friends used to tell me, that Art had put me out of my Course, by rendering me the property of Mr. D., for that Nature designed me for an

> Actress, or the Wife of a very feeling Poet and Philosopher, rather than to a
> Gentleman of Independance [sic] and general Talents, and the reason he was
> pleased to assign for it was, the natural and supposed qualities of my Heart,
> together with an expressive Countenance, and a a manner capable of doing
> justice to the tender passions.[15]

The friend was probably Sterne, who styles Eliza his 'wife' in the *Journal*
(such that he felt it unwise to send the manuscript on to India and her
husband's perusal). As Guest explores, for Sterne and the Abbé Raynal after
him, Eliza functioned as just such an expressive touchstone and Muse: 'the
importance of Eliza Draper does not seem to focus on the subject–position
she represents, in the qualities that are perhaps intrinsic to her character, but
in her ability to elicit sentimental humanity, to provoke responses that reas-
sure us that what may seem merely impulsive, even lacking in propriety, is a
civilised capacity for tender fellow feeling, that "men of nice sensibility alone
can be touched with" '.[16] In this Eliza resembles the fictional figure of poor
Maria, who is also the occasion for the staging of exquisite feeling. Maria,
like Eliza, is described at the point of greatest moral ambiguity as a 'daughter' (at the very moment, incidentally, when Eliza is introduced into the text
of *A Sentimental Journey*), as if to play down the eroticism of the relation.
Though as an interlocutor Eliza is infinitely more socialised and equal – and
able to embrace Sterne's recognition in a complicated sense as a mark of her
own self-worth – there is nonetheless an erasure of individuality in Sterne's
representation of her, Guest suggests, which transforms her into a generalisable and ideal figure of feminine 'sociable humanity': 'She seems to square the
circle, to identify the sensuality of modern commercial taste with the modest
reserve and restraint that command respect.'[17] A vision of the sentimental
grail for a writer like Sterne; such a combination of sensual experience and
modesty was nonetheless much more difficult for a woman to live out, than
for a man to imagine, as Eliza's letters show. What is evident, as Guest reveals,
is that such an image becomes in Eliza's absence the means of Sterne's self-
fashioning. She is a 'second self' (*BJ* 191) who is 'blessd with such a certain
turn of Mind & reflection – that if Self love does not blind me – I resemble
no Being in the world so nearly as I do You – do you wonder that I have such
friendship for you?'(*BJ* 198).[18]

This account of the staging of Sterne's exchange with Eliza Draper usefully lifts an individualised pathology into the circuits of a broader discursive
terrain, so that seemingly local idiosyncrasies – Sterne's moral foibles and
scandalous desires – are shown to trace the self's insertion into universalising
categories of thought and feeling: here, that of 'humanity'. The continuous
boomerang effect in Sterne's work (the logic of an emergent Romanticism
perhaps) between sublime feeling and fleshly interest becomes part of a wider

philosophical and political dynamic, in which a particularised affective realm and its structures of belonging undergo extension beyond known boundaries. This is the tension in the Shandean construction of 'the world', as we saw earlier; at once provincial and representative. It offers a parallel narrative to the universalising ambition of English cosmopolitanism, as if 'humanity' is to be thought from the most vernacular (Shandy is a Yorkshire dialect word for crazy) and locally eccentric of places. Not just thought, but felt, because this is a dynamic, crucially, that has to be *lived*. What did it mean to *experience* the world as a subject of universal benevolence, to feel 'some generous joys and generous cares beyond myself' as the narrator of *A Sentimental Journey* puts it, reverberating in the 'great SENSORIUM of the world!'(*SJ* 155). What did it mean to 'feel beyond the nation'?[19] This was a political, as well as a metaphysical, question, one that the passage to India articulated in specific terms.

If Eliza represented the peculiarly feminine form of the 'amiable virtues', as Harriet Guest argues, she could not possess the self-command that would truly turn her into a citizen of the world in Adam Smith's universe, since that remained the stoic prerogative of men. If humanity is a feminine virtue, in his words, this is both its domestic potency and limitation, and Eliza is against her better nature no more than handmaiden, amanuensis, wife. Interestingly in her letters to her cousin Eliza reveals her own fantasies of becoming a moralist and law-giver, while recognising the inequality that defines her position: 'I have vanity enough to think I have understanding sufficient to give laws to my Family, but as that cannot be, if providence for wise purposes constituted the Male the Head I will endeavour to act an underpart with grace'.[20] The pressures of money that tied her to colonial life, and her sensibility – 'I cannot counteract my Nature'[21] – made this 'act' an increasingly arduous one: 'its very difficult for suffering Individuals to say "whatever is – is right"; at least I cannot till I have gain'd Wisdom which I'll endeavour to acquire in my Exile'.[22] As this chapter unfolds I want to discover in what ways such amiable humanity nevertheless positioned a woman as a subject of empire, despite the Smithian injunctions against it.

The difficulty of Sterne's identification with his 'second self' lies not only in a risky feminising of his position, but also in a potential destabilising of the hierarchies of reciprocal feeling that hold such inequalities in place. As we saw in chapter four, sympathy with another is predicated on that other's grateful and often silent recognition of his or her own subordination; sentiment, as Luc Boltanski explored, is 'not deployed within a metaphysics of justice'.[23] The case of poor Maria in Sterne's work revolves uneasily around this point, marked in *Tristram Shandy*, as we saw, by a textual embarrassment at the imbalance of power that the sentimental traveller erases. In his last work, however, the force of sentimental identification overrides the ordered equations of 'reciprocal commerce'. Eliza may be his 'friend', 'wife', even 'disciple', but she is also the occasion for the imagining of an 'unbounded' love; a liberation of a different order. The scandalousness associated with Sterne can begin to be read here, in the substance of his projection towards his 'suffering' double. Its key is the excessive language of love.

In his excellent account of the shifting sands of sociability at the mid-century, John Mullan describes an increasingly disciplinary emphasis on the control and scrutiny of sympathetic feeling. Unlike the young David Hume of *A Treatise of Human Nature*, who reads sympathy as a 'direct reproduction' of the feelings of others, Mullan suggests, Adam Smith understands the imagination to produce a 'copy' of the emotion, through a regulative process that involves observation and mediation.[24] As Mullan writes, quoting *The Theory of Moral Sentiments*:

> Not for Smith the natural society of responsive subjectivities described in the *Treatise*. A person may only obtain sympathy 'by lowering his passion to that pitch, in which the spectators are capable of going along within him. He must flatten, if I may be allowed to say so, the sharpness of its natural tone, in order to reduce it to harmony and concord with the emotion of those who are about him'. Only such an exercise in self-control can provide for a correspondence of 'sentiments' which 'is sufficient for the harmony of society'.[25]

It is possible to see from this vision of ordered harmony how much Sterne's work may have shocked through the passion and brio of its 'pitch'. As the French translator of his letters to Eliza explained:

> All sentiments of affection were confounded in his soul, and retained no fine distinctions there: friendship easily took the form of love, that is he felt for his friend as he would have for a lover, with the same effusions, the same excitements, and the same sorrows . . . Health, duties, reputation, all Eliza's interests became personal to him, her children were his, and he would have willingly sacrificed his country, his possessions, and his life for her, if this sacrifice could have contributed to her happiness.[26]

There is no measure in Sterne's vicarious identification with Eliza, which takes a sacrificial form; confusing the distinctions between different forms of affection – carefully distinguished in the taxonomies of the period – in its excess. Sterne might appear to be closer to the early Hume as Mullan describes him than to the abstraction of Smithian civility: to Hume's vision of a society reverberating with the flows of affection, in which 'morality . . . is more properly felt than judg'd of'.[27] Indeed in the *Treatise* Hume can only imagine 'love for mankind' in the terms of love between the sexes:

there is no such passion in human minds, as the love of mankind, merely as such, independent of personal qualities, of services, or of relation to ourself . . . An affection betwixt the sexes is a passion evidently implanted in human nature; and this passion not only appears in its peculiar symptoms, but also in inflaming every other principle of affection, and raising a stronger love from beauty, wit, kindness, than what wou'd otherwise flow from them. Were there an universal love among all human creatures, it wou'd appear after the same manner.[28]

From such 'peculiar symptoms', then, the extension of 'universal love' might be imagined. This is distinct from a benevolence that 'holds nothing of the self in view', as certain disinterested constructions would have it;[29] the view expressed in Henry Brooke's sentimental novel *Fool of Quality* 'that no soul was ever capable of any degree of virtue or happiness save so far as it is drawn away in its affections from self; save so far as it is engaged in wishing, contriving, endeavouring, promoting, and rejoicing in the welfare and happiness of others'.[30] In the eyes of the French translator, Sterne was willing to sacrifice himself to Eliza's interests, but his self was, indelibly, the crucible of that sympathy. Indeed the intense singularity of its identifications threatened to break through the reciprocal accommodations of sociability in the process.

It was a self-fashioning that could seem to some the height of selfishness, exacerbated by Sterne's position as a divine. His writings appeared to deface Christian values like so much graffiti.[31] Elizabeth Carter declared she would not read *A Sentimental Journey* on principle. 'Real benevolence would never . . . lead a clergyman to ramble about the world after objects with whom he has no particular connexion, when he might exercise the noblest duties of a benevolent heart in the regular discharge of his proper function, instead of neglecting it by indecent and buffoon writings'.[32] Yet 'real benevolence' was of course sorely stretched at home, as the sentimental novel shows, by social and economic exigencies that sympathy strained to assuage. In the thought of the later Hume, and in the 'stringent political conservatism' of Smith in particular, Mullan argues, that strain gives way to a moral calculus: sympathy is demoted, just one of a list of social virtues.[33] The natural mutuality underpinning the social bond gives way to a concept of utility, which takes on the work of community: 'Society may subsist among different men, as among different merchants, from a sense of its utility, without any mutual love or affection' Smith writes in *A Theory of Moral Sentiments*.[34] In the increasingly abstract universalism of the market, affective relations and the moral sense that arises from them are to be carefully regulated if they are to be trusted at all. Few have the capacity for fine sentimental feeling within a utilitarian world – 'as gold, though less serviceable than iron, acquires from its scarcity a value which is much superior', in Hume's words;[35] the problem is that what appears from one perspective a form of elevated connoisseurship looks deeply self-interested and pleasurably market-driven from another. If there was an obscene quality about Sterne's writings to certain of his contemporaries – a difficulty, too, in assessing their tone – it is perhaps because they expose the limits of affective regulation in riding out this double bind: marked by a *refusal* of disinterestedness and with it the ruse of a 'humanity' that rises *above* a realm of mutual passions as 'more generous and comprehensive'.[36] The intense idiosyncrasy of Sterne's work can thus be read as a reaction to disciplinary pressures (thus yoking it inextricably with the Smithian universe). Indeed, in parts, it is animated by a passional working through of a question of freedom. I want then to explore the amorous discourse of Sterne's *Continuation of the Bramine's Journal* in the light of such 'obscenity'.

## A Lover's Discourse

''Tis the Language of Love—& I can speak no other' (*BJ* 174). Sterne's *Journal* comprises fragments, and the banal repetitiveness of a love that must continually affirm itself in the absence of its object. Alongside the fort/da game with the image of Eliza, who is continually travelling towards India yet always in the room, the carriage, or about to sit down and eat at his table, is the rhythm of a body suffering: drawn to society yet sickened by it, rallying and relapsing, spitting blood into her India handkerchiefs, dosing with mercury, taking the waters at Harrogate Spa. 'The Want of thee is half my distemper', he writes (*BJ* 187). In the words of Roland Barthes, the lover is thus 'wedged between two tenses . . .: you have gone (which I lament), you are here (since I am addressing you). Whereupon I know what the present, that difficult tense, is: a pure portion of anxiety.'[37]

How then to grasp the nature and meaning of this 'anxiety', at this moment in time; this particular present? Barthes's *A Lover's Discourse* provides one approach, itself an extraordinary collage of fragments that captures what might be seen as the gestics of amorous discourse. There are genealogies that might connect Sterne's writing with Barthes's act of compilation, since Goethe's *Werther* provides much of his material, and it was Goethe after all who regarded Sterne 'in everything an indicator and an awakener'.[38] The dramatic method of Barthes's text unlocks the practice of Sterne's *Journal*: makes its 'anxiety' possible to read. In the staging of the speech of the lover, Barthes dramatises the discursive site in which, as my epigraph puts it, 'every amorous subject collects himself'(p. 219). In the very enunciative singularity of its 'I', this site can nevertheless be occupied by anyone who wants to pick up the refrain of amorous feeling. It is the 'joke' contained in the sentimental tale of the two lovers in *Tristram Shandy*, reduced formulaically to the loss, encounter and mutual death-in-love of Amandus ('he who is to be loved') and Amanda ('she who is to be loved') (*TS* 7.31.627–9). As Barthes adds in an aside of his own text, 'Ideally, the book would be a co-operative: "To the United Readers and Lovers" ' (p. 5). What Hume described as 'peculiar symptoms' are thus to be understood, as Sterne registered, in structural, not psychological, terms. Barthes's drama of a lover's discourse reveals Sterne's intense projection of self as at once intimate and impersonal: 'the site of someone speaking within himself, *amorously*, confronting the other (the loved object), who does not speak' (p. 3). It is for this reason I want to press the connection further, to trace the choreographies of the language of love traversing both texts.

Sterne's time is full of projects, in which a future life with Eliza is imprinted on his living in the present as if to transform it into the future anterior, what *will have been*:

> I continue writing, to do it to thee Eliza who art the *Woman of my heart*, & for whom I am ordering & planning this, & every thing else—be asured my Bramine that ere every thing is ripe for our Drama,—I shall work hard to fit out & decorate a little Theatre for us to act on—but not before a crouded house—no Eliza—it shall be as secluded as the elysian fields—retirement is the nurse of Love and kindness—& I will Woo & caress thee in it in such sort, that every thicket & grotto we pass by, *shall* sollicit the remembrance of the mutual pledges We have exchanged of Affection with one another—Oh! these expectations—make me sigh, as I recite them—& many a heart-felt Interjection! do they cost me, as I saunter alone in the tracks we are to tread together hereafter—still I think thy heart is with me—& whilst I think so, I prefer it to all the Society this world can offer—(*BJ* 214)

This passage suggests a lexicon ('Image–repertoire') of love's language: a vision of retirement, in which the landscape itself becomes memorialised through the future exchange of tokens and the uttering of sighs. It is a landscape caught in an unfinished state of subjunctive suspense, in which thickets, objects, rooms, become potential meeting places, or occasions (in a 'devouring metonomy' (p. 75)) for the merging of selves. Sterne has built an extension to his home, and in his imagining of the further construction of Eliza's 'Temple', a 'Sleeping room', practical plans give way to a metaphysical conceit reminiscent of Donne: 'Y$^r$ little Temple I have described—& what it will hold—but if it ever holds You & I, my Eliza—the Room will not be too little for us—but We shall be *too big* for the Room.—'(*BJ* 209). Despite the continual invocation of coupledom, the 'Theatre' described is really that of the self, here in a mode of construction (though equally prey to melancholic ruin and collapse). This is not a relation that can be inhabited 'discreetly, reasonably . . . one must either submit or cut loose' (p. 51), as Barthes puts it; it is subject to a 'hallucinatory manipulation' (p. 142) that can appear a form of madness:

> A man is mad if he is pure of all power.—But doesn't the lover experience any excitation of power? Subjection, though, is my business: subjected, seeking to subject the other, I experience in my fashion the will to power, the *libido dominandi*: do I not possess, like political systems, a strong, *articulated* discourse? Yet this is my singularity: my libido is entirely enclosed: I inhabit no other space but the amorous duel: not an atom outside, hence not an atom of gregarity: *I am crazy*, not because I am original (a crude ruse of uniformity), but because I am severed from all sociality. If other men are always, to various degrees, the militants of something, I am the soldier of nothing, not even of my own madness: *I do not socialize* (as it is said of someone that he doesn't symbolize). (p. 121)

'Remember You are mine—', writes Sterne, 'and stand answerable for all you say & do to me—I govern myself by the same Rule—& such a History of myself can I lay before you, as shall create no blushes, but those of pleasure' (*BJ* 219–20). There is undoubtedly a will to power in Sterne's amorousness that continually takes possession of Eliza, while recognising his own subjection; it is, moreover, woven through the weft of social life, in which the capture of his love object is both something repeatedly displayed in public gatherings and discovered in the secret passion of retreat: 'I have stole away to converse a few minutes with thee, and in thy own dressing room—for I make every thing thine & call it so, before hand, that thou art to be mistress of hereafter' (*BJ* 220). In this Sterne's text might appear much more comfortable with the embracing of sociality than Barthes's lover allows; indeed a major part of the fantasy is the insertion of Eliza into the comforting certainties of domestic life. Like Werther, who 'wants a place which is already taken' (p. 45), Sterne imagines himself as husband, even to the negotiation of Mr Draper's consent. 'To want to be pigeonholed is to want to obtain for life a docile reception', opines Barthes's lover (p. 46). The *Journal* seeks out the easing of its anxieties through just such a strategy, climaxing in the love story that will stand, Sterne suggests, as a footnote to *A Sentimental Journey*, and which I quote in full:

> I have brought y^r name *Eliza!* and Picture into my work—where they will remain—when You & I are at rest for ever—Some Annotator or explainer of my works in this place will take occasion, to speak of the Friendship w^ch Subsisted so long & faithfully betwixt Yorick & the Lady he speaks of—Her Name he will tell the world was Draper—a Native of India—married there

to a gentleman in the India Service of that Name—, who brought her over to England for the recovery of her health in the Year 65—where She continued to April the Year 1767. It was ab$^t$ three months before her Return to India, That our Author's acquaintance & hers began. M$^{rs}$ Draper had a great thirst for Knowledge—was handsome—genteel—engaging—and of such a gentle dispositions & so enlightend an understanding, That Yorick, (whether he made much opposition is not known) from an acquaintance—soon became her Admirer—they caught fire at each other at the same time—& they w$^d$ often say, without reserve to the world, & without any Idea of saying wrong in it, That their Affections for each other were *unbounded*— —M$^r$ Draper dying in the year *****—This Lady return'd to England & Yorick the year after becoming a Widower—They were married—& retiring to one of his Livings in Yorkshire, where was a most romantic Situation—they lived & died happily—and are spoke of with honour in the parish to this day——

(*BJ* 203)

If there is a craziness here it lies perhaps in the articulation of the most normative of social desires through an impossible bind, for both places – that of husband and wife – are already occupied, and it is only the brokerage of death that might liberate them. An ambiguous brokerage, at that, since the passage serves as an epitaph to lovers who are themselves 'at rest for ever'. Death becomes a part of a proleptic freedom. A craziness in the *articulation*, too, because Sterne's relation to Eliza is not a 'love story' – 'the tribute the lover must pay to the world in order to be reconciled with it' (p. 7) – in any narrative sense. While the critical reaction to Sterne's last work has at times endeavoured to turn it into one, the text is resistant to this narrative reconciliation. Not only is such a 'story' as Sterne presents it caught in a paradox, but his amorous language proves excessive, insistent in its acting out of 'the will to fulfillment' in Barthes's terms: 'By this will, I well up: I form within myself the utopia of a subject free from repression: I am this subject *already*. This subject is libertarian' (p. 55).

The notion of a libertarian subject clearly means something specific in the mid-eighteenth-century, where as we have seen the 'true born' Englishman's demand for liberty takes a number of forms, trammelled in the loves and antipathies of popular nationalism. In the Wilkite libidinal economy, the lifting of repression frees the independent subject to project himself rapaciously over the globe, in the process serving the instrumental needs of a society that preferred to avert its gaze from such a priapism. There is a consistent fascination in Sterne's writing with a release from repression, which sometimes resembles Wilkite libertinism, but also argues in moral terms for the expansion of human experience to acknowledge the passional realm that underpins it. 'Why the most natural actions of a man's life should be call'd his Non-Naturals' is a question posed in *Tristram Shandy* (*TS* 1.23.84); the point of its comic transgressions is precisely to bring the bourgeois order into contact with the realm it denies, for the physical 'health' of the body politic. This rewriting of the line between liberty and licentiousness suggests such transgression is intelligible, it 'symbolizes' in social terms, as Barthes puts it, in its epicurean refashioning of the mid-eighteenth-century good life. But I want to suggest the libertarian obscenity of Sterne's later work is of another order, one that does not 'socialize' in this sense. What is it that 'severs' this lover from sociality, in the terms of the late 1760s?

To begin to answer this question is to think about the particular field of desire articulated in *The Bramine's Journal*. The phallic adventurism celebrated by Wilkes suggested control, and economy: the correspondence of pleasure and calculation: 'Spend while we must, but keep it while we can'. The expenditure of Sterne's text by contrast appears to hold nothing back. Its unburdening of language works, like Scheherazade's tales, to keep death suspended, and Eliza in play:

> Indeed Indeed Eliza! my Life will be little better than a dream, till we approach nearer to each other—I live scarse conscious of my existence—or as if I wanted a vital part; & could not live above a few hours. & yet I live, & live, & live on, for thy Sake, and the sake of thy truth to me; which I measure by my own,—and I fight ag$^{st}$ every evil and every danger, that I may be able to support & shelter thee from danger and evil also.—upon my word, dear Girl, thou owest me much—but tis cruel to dun thee when thou art not in a condition to pay—I think Eliza has not run off in her Yoricks debt—(*BJ* 217)

The lover can 'live, & live, & live on' through writing, invoking and then refusing the language of bourgeois economy (owing, saving, paying, spending) to describe his relationship with the object of his love. Alongside this realm of exchange, occupied increasingly in the *Journal* by his wife, now returning from France, he works an alternative economy, one that invokes that other within a vision of total presence, imagined plenitude, which Eliza guarantees:

> Hail! Hail! My dear Eliza—I steal something every day from my sentimental Journey—to obey a more sentimental impulse in writing to you—& giving you the present Picture of myself—my wishes—my Love, my sincerity—my hopes—my fears—tell me, have I varied in any one Lineament, from the first Sitting—to this last—have I been less warm—less tender and affectionate than you expected or could have wish'd me in any one of 'em—or, however varied in the expressions of what I was & what I felt, have I not still presented the

same air and face towards thee?—take it as a Sample of what I ever shall be—
My dear Bramine—& that is—such as my honour, my Engagements &
promises & desires have fix'd me—I want You to be on the other side of my
little table, to hear how sweetly y$^r$ Voice will be in Unison to all this—I want
to hear what You have to say to Y$^r$ Yorick upon this Text.—what heavenly
Consolation w$^d$ drop from y$^r$ Lips & how pathetically you w$^d$ enforce y$^r$ Truth
& Love upon my heart to free it from every Aching doubt—Doubt! Did I
say—but I have none—(*BJ* 212)

Through the adulterous cliché of this statement – the conventionality of its
'hopes' and 'fears', its image of a mistress as ideal and self-confirming –
comes another dynamic, that marked by the 'fatality' of writing. The phrase
is Barthes's, but it already belongs to Sterne. On the one hand, the full and
stable presence claimed by the passage brings with it its own capture. As
Barthes explains, 'there is no benevolence within writing, rather a terror: it
smothers the other, who, far from perceiving the gift in it, reads there instead
an assertion of mastery, of power, of pleasure, of solitude' (pp. 78–9). Eliza's
letters register this fall from 'Benevolence and truth' in her own material
entrapment.[39] On the other hand terror also belongs to the writer. The
passage collapses almost immediately into insecurity, fear of Eliza's falsity
causing crisis: 'you are grieved when I talk thus; it implies what does not exist
in either of us—so cross it out, if thou wilt—or leave it as part of the picture
of a heart that *again* Languishes for Possession—and is disturbed at every
Idea of its Uncertainty.—So heaven bless thee—& ballance thy passions
better than I have the power to regulate mine' (*BJ* 213). This seesawing
movement, a continual negotiation of loss, wrecks equilibrium. Caught
between memory and impossible return, the writer experiences a form of
limbo: 'The Space between is a dismal Void' (*BJ* 210). As Barthes's lover
explains:

> The image of the other – to which I was glued, on which I lived – no longer
> exists; sometimes this is a (futile) catastrophe which seems to remove the
> image forever, sometimes it is an excessive happiness which enables me to
> unite with the image; in any case, severed or united, dissolved or discrete, I am
> nowhere *gathered together*; opposite, neither you nor me, nor death, nor any-
> thing else *to talk to*. (p. 11)

The lover strains to hear – 'I want to hear what You have to say to Y$^r$ Yorick
upon this Text' (*BJ* 212) – in this, Barthes suggests, he becomes 'a monstrous
receiver, reduced to an enormous auditive organ – as if listening itself
were to become a state of utterance: in me, it is the ear which speaks'
(p. 202). Yet what if there is no-one to talk to? 'I entrust myself, I transmit

myself (to whom? to God, to nature, to everything, except to the other)' (p. 11). It is perhaps the ear, rather than the phallus, which serves as an imperial signifier, broadcasting itself beyond known boundaries – 'I want to hear what You have to say' – or an auditive antenna, picking up vibrations, like a skin.

It is here that we might begin to understand the obscenity of Sterne's text, the way in which his lover's discourse fails to 'socialize'. It is not just in an inability to 'regulate', to bring its passional realm within the normative confines that would render it intelligible, and thus harmonious, in social terms. It is also in the nature of its self-transmission, the risk of its movement out, in which the intensity of affective identification with an other turns into the most impersonal of affirmations – 'I am the one who has the same place I have' (p. 129) – cutting through the careful mediations of eighteenth-century reciprocal commerce. There is something seemingly promiscuous about a relation to *an* other which through its very impossibility reveals itself to be structured curiously as a relation to *any* other; hence, perhaps, the amoral appearance of Sterne's recycling of earlier amatory letters to his wife or lovers.

Here there is also a larger question at stake: a drama that exposes the limits of subjectification. What is commonly held to mean the human, to count in normative terms as a person, is suddenly revealed in the process of 'unbounded' projection. There is disorientation in such a move, and also a glimpse of the fictional, constructed nature of what passes for the self. It is possible that this accounts in part for the tonality of Sterne's writing, the tendency for sensibility to be read as heartfelt, the springboard for a universalising benevolence, and yet cynically staged; and thus for the disappointment of readers who self-consciously found themselves acting out in their identifications, rather than feeling from the heart as they had intended; or caught in the tawdriness of a benevolent affection, that seemed, as Elizabeth Carter put it, to extend beyond the self no more than a 'fit of the gout'.[40] The intensely subjective individuation of this private selfhood is nonetheless a sign of a more impersonal demand. One in which the subject is distanciated from the customary practices of immediate community (like the Shandean family of his novel) into the 'freedom' of more abstract values and private convictions: a movement, in other words, performing what Étienne Balibar has termed the 'fictive universality' required by the hegemonising process of state formation. If the liberation of subjectivity is shaped by just such a demand at this point in the mid-eighteenth century, how obscene might it be to refuse the normative pressures attendant upon such a freedom, 'the standard price to be paid for the universalistic liberation of the individual'.[41] To discover what this might mean for Sterne's exchange with Eliza Draper, it becomes necessary to explore the pressures brought to bear on state imagining by the passage to India itself.

## Crossing the Line

Eliza's absence is experienced as a death. As she leaves for India, Sterne witnesses what he sees as a moment of disassociation: "twas the Separation of Soul & Body—& equal to nothing but what passes on that tremendous Moment.—& like it in one Consequence, that thou art in another World; where I w^d give a world, to follow thee' (*BJ* 215). The self thus projects itself towards an unknowable World, towards a space that is simultaneously the sublime and untranslatable realm of India, and the bourne from which no-one returns. 'Alas! you are as a dead Person' (*BJ* 219), the *Journal* declares.

The view that Sterne 'says nothing of India' in the *Journal* is an over-hasty conclusion in this context.[42] His styling of the exchange with Eliza Draper as the communication between a 'Bramin' and his 'Bramine'[43] is a rhetorical device, taken from the orientalist lexicon developing at this time. It leads directly to what Sara Suleri has called 'the tropological repository' of the subcontinent, one 'from which colonial and postcolonial imaginations have drawn – and continue to draw – their most basic figures for the anxiety of empire'.[44] The 'pure portion of anxiety' (p. 15) that I have explored in the *Journal* has other co-ordinates: of which the imagining of colonial absence as a kind of death – extreme negativity – is one instance. While the non-presence of India in the text would seem to be substantively true (though, as we will see, Eliza's letters to her family in England have more to say), this lack is a sign of the alterity conjured up by metropolitan imperial fantasy even as it points to the limits of Sterne's own experience. As Suleri puts it, 'the Indian sublime is at its most empty at the very point when it is most replete'. Eliza travels to a place that does not seem to locate itself within a horizon of interpretation, and it is to this that Sterne is partly responding. The pleasure and pain associated with imagining the passage to India in Sterne's text suggest a dimension of the 'psychic disempowerment signified by colonial encounter', in Suleri's words.[45] Sterne traces Eliza's journey:

> a Map of India coming in my Way—I begun to study the length & dangers of my Eliza's Voiage to it, and have been amusing & frightening myself by turns, as I traced the path-way of the Earl of Chatham, the whole Afternoon—good god! what a voiage for any one!—but for the poor relax'd frame of my tender Bramine to cross the Line twice! & be subject to the Intolerant heats, & the hazards w^ch must be the consequence of em to such an unsupported Being!— O Eliza! 'tis too much—& if thou conquerest these, and all the other difficulties of so tremendous an alienation from thy Country, thy Children, & thy friends, tis the hand of Providence w^ch watches over thee for most merciful purposes—(*BJ* 186–7)

The figuring of 'conquest' here concerns the mastery as survival of a self that is under threat, not the triumphal phallic entry into the 'unbounded sea' that is celebrated in Wilkite fantasy. It is an experience that is couched in feminine terms, but one that is thereby generalisable, registering the fear associated with the imperial project as a feminised reaction to a constituted sublime. At stake is the figuring of the domestic imperial subject, as I have been arguing throughout. What will become interesting is the way the encounter with 'another World' is both constitutive of that subject and yet, in this case, scandalously transformed and transforming: to what extent the subject of empire is, at this conjuncture, precisely, *feminine*.

'I cannot suffer you to be longer upon the Water—in 10 days time, You shall be at Madrass—the element rolls in my head as much as y^rs, & I am sick of the sight & smell of it' (*BJ* 217). The passage to India was often regarded as the crossing of a permeable, yet to some, insurmountable barrier, a metaphorics that aimed to contain the anxiety at newly subjected peoples who might choose to cross the sea in the other direction. It was a rhetorical vision truncating that movement articulated in Johnson's *Rasselas*, which I argued earlier was a form of imperial 'recoil': the fear that the happy valley might be broken into using the very means of technological expansion that had made empire possible. As Saree Makdisi explores in his work on the romantic figuring of Universal Empire, Edmund Burke used such rhetoric to define the nature of the imperial project at the trial of Warren Hastings, the former Governor of Bengal, in the late 1780s:

> The sea is between us. The mass of that element, which, by appearing to disconnect, unites mankind, is to them a forbidden road. It is a great gulf fixed between you and them, – not so much that elementary gulf, but that gulf which manners, opinions and laws have radicated in the very nature of the people. None of their high castes, without a great danger to his situation, religion, rank, and estimation, can ever pass the sea; and this forbids, forever, all direct communication between that country and this.[46]

Burke's vision of the sea as a literal and rhetorical gulf (a recurrent metaphor in his thinking about the governing of empire) plays down the fluidity of transmission of 'manners and opinions' across cultural barriers that trade and imperial conflict had encouraged, both within India and at home in Britain. Not only were Indian soldiers crucial to that expansion in India and further afield,[47] but large numbers of 'newly-acquired Asiatic subjects'[48] found themselves destitute at British ports, having been stranded by the Indiamen on which they had served.[49] While Burke's speeches tried to convey the inappropriateness of conventional political imagining in the administration of the subcontinent, in the projection of 'visions of stamp duties on *Perwanna's*, *Dusticks*, *Kistbundees*, and *Husbulhookums'* (and thus of American 'solutions' on another imperial territory),[50] the 'strange jargon'[51] of India found its way into the language of public culture and the street,[52] and Indian commodities into the realms of taste and popular forms of addiction.[53] Not only did the financial wellbeing of the nation increasingly appear to depend on the state of India, but the lives of those who worked in the production of British goods – the weavers in particular – were shaped by unseen (market) forces emanating from the subcontinent, invisible alliances and antipathies.

If there was on one level a Canute-like quality about Burke's rhetorical controlling of the tide, it nonetheless reworked widely circulated accounts of the subcontinent, in which he was well read. Travelling on the west coast of India in the early 1760s, one Danish visitor had admired the 'patience, probity and benevolence of the Hindoos', whose 'progressive improvement' was being retarded by the 'exorbitant power of the English'. The former were, he noted, 'at the same time the most unsocial people in the world'.[54] For the imperial power this notion of autonomy proved a way of distancing itself from the shock of extreme difference, the power of alternative systems of belief, while usefully naming them in singular terms. The historian Robert Orme, whose work Sterne takes up in the *Journal*, acknowledged the numerous different 'characters' that made categorisation of Indian identity almost impossible. Yet he described the resistance to assimilation on the part of those inhabitants of 'the richest empire of the globe' in terms similar to Burke: 'HIS religion forbids the Indian to quit his own shores: he wants nothing from abroad: he is so far from being sollicitous to convert the stranger to his own opinions, or from wishing him to assimilate with the nation, that if a foreigner were to sollicit the privilege of worshipping Vistnou, his proposal would be received with the utmost contempt'.[55] Behind the notion of autonomy ascribed to the Indian are a complex though familiar set of assumptions, not least a projection of self-sufficiency – 'he wants nothing from abroad' – that would have been seen as an ideal state to attain by those who regarded foreign trade as symptomatic of luxurious decline. As Alexander Dow described in his history, Bengal 'was always remarkable for its commerce', yet its people, 'from an inviolable prejudice of religion, abstemious, were averse to luxury themselves; and the wants of nature were supplied almost spontaneously by the soil and climate'.[56] For all his concern to avoid 'the ample field for fiction' opened up by Hindostan,[57] Dow's account dovetails in key respects with the utopias of abundance of the period, visions of societies who are feminised and rendered childlike in seeming indifference to their plenty, from the Tahitians of the South Seas to the realm of Voltaire's El Dorado, whose inhabitants agree never to leave in order to preserve their 'innocence and happiness'.[58]

The alterity of India thus undergoes a continuous and sometimes para-doxical translation within a prismatic imaginary that makes its difference recognisable to British eyes. What is figured as resistance, underlined by the 'impenetrable veil of mystery'[59] cast by priestly religion, becomes in another light a self-sufficiency that in turn reads as a feminine form of indolence and passivity. This condition could seem the height of vulnerability from one perspective – 'they are of all nations on earth the most easily conquered and governed'[60] – and was thus to be protected from the ravages of the unscrupulous, and the tyranny of the despot. Elsewhere however it resembles a stasis bordering on death that could do with a purgative:

> THESE people are of a mild, humane disposition, and are almost strangers to the passions that prevail among us. What motive of ambition can there be among men who are destined to continue always in the same state? They love peaceable labour and an indolent life, and often quote this passage of one of their favourite authors: *"Tis better to sit still than to walk; better to sleep than to awake; But death is best of all'.*[61]

Adaptation to such a realm held particular fears for Europeans who might themselves fall victim to what Dow saw as the 'slavery' which had in India become 'blended with human nature'; to an 'extreme sensibility', moreover, 'perhaps peculiar to natives of a hot climate, [which] carries pleasures to an excess which unmans the mind'.[62] As Robert Clive recorded in his account of British military success, 'we solaced ourselves with the pleasing reflection of having maintained the character of Britons in a Clime so remote from our own'.[63] In Burke's account the translations of such otherness and the fears they detonate become particularly generative. As both Suleri and Makdisi explore, India's distinctiveness means that its customs and laws had to be respected in its governance: in this, Burke's position is characteristic of a common strand of thinking. Indeed in his view it is the British who must adapt: 'all change on their part is absolutely impracticable. We have more ver-satility of character and manners, and it is we who must conform'. Yet a 'strict eye' needs to be kept on those who make the journey, lest the 'versatility' described becomes too virtuosic in its performance.[64] And India itself is stereotypically produced as a space of immovable composure – associated tropologically with the absolutes of death and love – unable ever to commu-nicate directly with a world whose energies and ambition work to 'drain' its riches, unable to be shaped, in Makdisi's terms, by the modernising impulses of the imperial project. India thus figures the limits of that project's own self-imagining (an antidote to the aleatory wandering of people and money that empire depends upon), even as it demands an even more intensive conjuring up of the same energies.

'During the decades of Burke's Indian engagement, the vocabulary that imperial England had developed in regard to the prospect of an Indian colony underwent some compelling changes: before the 1780s, India had largely functioned in the British imagination as an area beyond the scope of cartography, a space most inviting to European wills to plunder and to the flamboyant entrepreneurship of such a figure as Robert Clive'.[65] Horace Walpole's letters underline Sara Suleri's assessment. 'Lord Clive has been suddenly nominated by the East India Company to the empire of Bengal', he records in 1764, 'where Dupliex has taught all our merchants to affect to be king-making Earls of Warwick, and where the chief things they have made are blunders and confusion. It is amazing that our usurpations have not taught the Indians, union, discipline, and courage – we are governing nations to which it takes a year to send our orders'.[66] It is undoubtedly true that India posed particular problems for the cartographic imagination in this period, not just in terms of the limitations of geographical knowledge, but also as a failure of experiential comprehension that was reflected in expediency and governmental crisis. As one account explained, 'the several settlements being some as remote from others as England from Turky [sic] or Africa, the people on one coast have sometimes no more knowledge of what is doing on the other, than we have at home'.[67]

Yet between 1765 and the famine years of the early 1770s, the contradictions of this situation were newly evident. There was an increasing public awareness in Britain of the need to grasp Indian affairs, following the East India Company's assumption of tax collecting powers – the *Diwani* – and thus, with the taking on of the role of the state, a historiographic responsibility to understand the forms of property and law that governed its territory. However, as Ranajit Guha describes:

> They knew nothing of the agrarian system of India. For most of the English officers sent out to districts to manage the collection of revenues, it was a journey into the unknown in more than one sense. At every step they came up against quasi-feudal rights and obligations which defied any attempt at interpretation in familiar western terms. The hieroglyphics of Persian estate-accounts baffled them. It was only a part of the difficulty that they could not easily master the languages in which ancient and medieval texts relating to the laws of property were written; for tradition recorded in memory and customs embedded in a variety of local usages wielded an authority equal to that of any written code. It is therefore easy to understand why at this very early stage of its rule the Company did not succeed in evolving a coherent and uniform revenue policy for Bengal.[68]

If the imperial vocabulary of the later 1760s is marked by a certain interpretative failure, then, it also registers a reinforced drive to understand, and indeed reinscribe, this territory, impelled by political and economic necessity. Domestic interest had also heightened in the affairs of 'Nabob-land'. As Dow explained, 'THE affairs of India, though long of great importance to this kingdom, have only lately become objects of public attention . . . The current of public opinion has, at length, taken another direction. Men are rouzed into attention, with regard to a subject which concerns the welfare of the state. They begin to decide, in their own minds, upon affairs which stand in need of the interposition of the nation'.[69] The particular imbrication of the national and the imperial shifts at this moment, caught within a temporal lag: an empire whose sovereignty was not yet established, a colonial conquest that was not yet certain.

Although some accounts strained towards the tense that marks Laurence Sterne's *Journal*, the future anterior, as if to inhabit the security of later dominion, more often the present was seen as conflicted and incoherent, and thus difficult to navigate. It was a perception exacerbated by the mismanagement, violence and extortion that intensified in India after the deal of 1765. As Dow concluded, describing the battalions which had been consigned to tax collection duties, 'in place of those placid regulations, which render mankind useful to their lords, we substituted, with preposterous policy, force, the abrupt expedient of barbarous conquerors'.[70] By the early 1770s British atrocities were being detailed in the pages of the *Gentleman's Magazine*. William Bolts, a disaffected East India Company factor, was scathing in his *Considerations on India Affairs*: 'All branches of interior Indian commerce are, without exception, entirely monopolies of the most cruel and ruinous nature; and so totally corrupted, from every species of abuse, as to be in the last stages towards annihilation'.[71] The nemesis of Warren Hastings, Philip Francis, looked back on the five years from the Diwan as 'that period of delirium', 'the period of Darkness'. For Dow, writing his history at the height of the famine that killed a third of the population, India had been subjected to 'a monstrous and heterogeneous chaos of government' that had to be removed. 'It is an absolute conquest, and is so considered by the world', he declared, with olympian confidence; in such imperial reasoning the revisioning of India as a blank space that might be written over with the new property laws of a permanent plan functioned alongside the allowances made for cultural differences, those 'prejudices and usages which cannot be relinquished by the natives'. Property would 'bind them with stronger ties to our interest; and make them more our subjects; or if the British nation prefers the name – more our slaves'.[72]

This is a strategic blankness that suggests another, related, order of cultural labour than that producing the sublime and increasingly 'untouchable' spectacle of India that Suleri charts so revealingly in Burke's speeches; one indeed that instrumentally plays off different levels of proximity and abstraction, which is prepared to acknowledge what Dow sees as the 'domestic annals'[73] of Hindu history and yet obliterate them in the governmental interests of 'futurity'. One strategy is to posit this play as internal to the imperial history of the subcontinent before its continuance under the British. Thus the story of India under the Moghuls as Dow and others construct it reveals the prismatic nature of imperial reason: a byword for patriarchal despotism, 'Mahommedan' authority is in another light admirably vigorous, and founded in 'established forms and regulations' that make it possible to govern 'without the power of oppressing the body of the people'. In these histories the struggles with authority taking place within the British political realm – and in particular the weighing of force and sympathetic benevolence in the management of population – are almost continuously transculturated. Yet this was a careful rhetorical underwriting of state violence for all its protestations to the contrary, legitimated in Dow's constitution of the Indian native as someone who 'thinks the evils of despotism less severe than the labour of being free'. This, then, was the political meaning of 'indolence', and continually repeated in accounts which declared that political freedom was incompatible with life in the 'torrid zone'.[74]

The exchange between Laurence Sterne and Eliza Draper, 'Bramin' and 'Bramine', takes place within this 'period of delirium'. 'Talking of widows – pray Eliza, if you ever are such, do not think of giving yourself to some wealthy nabob – because I design to marry you myself,' Sterne wrote.[75] Eliza's reply from India acknowledges the violence underpinning the wealth:

> as to Nabobs, I despise them all – those who pretend to be Christians I mean. Have they not depopulated towns – laid waste villages, and desolated the plains of my native country? – Alas! they have fertilized the immense fields of India, with the blood of its inhabitants – they have sacrificed the lives of millions of my countrymen to their insatiable avarice – rivers of blood stream for vengeance against them – widows and orphans supplicate Heaven for revenge.[76]

Eliza's passage to India was of course a return to a world marked by the instability and adventurism of East India Company life. Her familial letters reveal the tenuousness of colonial control, which was at best virtual for all its formulation as an 'absolute conquest' after Plassey, and largely dependent on the complexities of the alliances built with local forces. 'We are deeply involved in Wars in almost every part of India', she records in 1769, 'how we shall make it out I know not'.[77] In particular she notes the threat of Hyder Ali, ruler of Mysore, 'a very clever & enterprising Man, accustomed to face, & Conquer Europeans', 'who has most of the Country powers about us, in total Subjection'; 'their's [sic] no leaving us now for Bombay, with any safety without a Convoy'.[78] 'I was within a hour once of being his Prisoner and cannot say but I thought it a piece of good fortune to escape that honor, tho' he has promised to treat all English Ladies well, that cheerfully submit to the Laws of his Seraglio.'[79] Eliza's family history already contained an abduction story (her grandmother's kidnap by the 'pirate' Angria[80]). The experience of East India settlement contained its own versions of frontier romance.

Eliza's writing from India assumes a range of positions and identifications, at once distanced from the often exoticised, sometimes threatening world of the 'natives' and yet, as the letter to Sterne shows, accusing those who have profited from her 'native country' of having 'waded through blood, to gain riches and power'. The forms of proximity and distance I have been describing work through as a rhetorical and affective anxiety in her own self-construction, accompanied at times by euphoria or disgust. Eliza's limited means, and the disappointments of her husband's employment in the Company, dislocate her from the wealthy world of the nabobs, and more importantly keep her in India. Increasingly, this appears a form of capture in which her husband colludes, an 'alienation' from the 'land of freedom and benevolence' that culminates in the breakdown of her marriage. Elsewhere she weighs what it means to be the 'belle Indian' she has been educated in England to be:

> As my reflection increases, I daily am more sensible of the loss I have sustained in not receiving those advantages which are the birthright of girls well born or by nature sociable, especially if their prospects are such as to give them the chance of being fixed in conspicuous life – such was my case – it is the case of all girls destined for India – No beings in the world are less indebted to education – None living require greater assistance from it – for the regulation of time in Eastern countries is such that every woman must naturally have a large portion of it; Leisure – this is either a blessing or a curse as our minds are disposed. The majority of us are extremely frivolous; this I grant. How should it be otherwise? . . . Climate, custom, and immediate examples induce to indolence – this betrays us into the practise of gallantry – that poisoner of all that's amiable and good.[81]

Eliza inhabits stereotypes that are seen in the common sense determinism of the mid-eighteenth century (heavily influenced by Montesquieu) as the inevitable result of climate and custom. 'Pray think generously of us Indian fair ones –', she writes to her cousin, 'and be our Advocate when you hear us traduced (which you often may) as a set of Ignorants, unknowing in every thing, but the Rites of Venus.–'[82] Her construction by both Sterne and the Abbé Raynal undoubtedly owes something to this stereotypification, and Eliza was clearly not averse to deploying such seductive connotations when it suited her. Yet Eliza's self-positioning is marked by ambivalence about these and related aspects of her formation as a girl 'destined for India', unable to find a place for herself as an intelligent yet dependent woman, frustrated by the limitations of colonial settlement yet clearly shaped, expanded, by its challenges. It is an experience that catches her between two cultures, seemingly equipped for neither:

> The Conveniences of Life in Abundance, together with Indolence and the habit of being careless as to Money Matters have spoiled me for an Economical English Manager – a ruined Constitution, and *grand Despise* for the Manners & Conversation of Indians, renders me equally unfit for all the Engagements of an Eastern Society.[83]

Yet despite her antipathy for India, which surfaces in the bitterness of her letters 'home' ('I wish you my dear Friend, all the Happiness, you can possibly wish yourself – and therefore I never wish to see you in India'[84]), Eliza does not only see her life as a 'belle Indian' as a form of ruination. It also involves a potential identification with what it means to be one among the 'Children of the Sun', and thus a particular vision of a realm of freedom. In order to assess this, I want to explore what it might mean for her to adopt the status of a 'Bramine'.

## Figuring the Brahmin

In her work on the 'metamorphic writing' that arises in the interstitial, transitional zones between cultures, Marina Warner argues that particular stories 'can act as powerful "congenors", materials through which one culture interacts and responds to another, even when unknown to each other; they conduct energies across barriers, though they may themselves dissolve from view in the resulting transformations'.[85] The stories Warner has in mind are those 'fantastic fictions' that often take a gothic and oriental form from the 1760s on, 'in chronological symbiosis, if not in actual engagement, with the ethnography of new territories and colonies, and within the material conflicts caused by French and English empire-building'. Thus the literature of the late eighteenth century begins to be haunted by the shape-shifting of captive genies, vampiric succubi and, in particular, the figure of the zombie: 'a spellbound person who has been robbed of will and feeling, a being who no longer enjoys choice, mobility and all the other freedoms that the era of revolutions invested in the individual, the citizen'.[86]

India provided one such contact zone. It had long been associated in English public culture with fantastical accounts of strange creatures and exotic practices, a fictionalising from which the mercantilist historiographers of the mid-century made a point of distancing themselves. Theirs was a much more instrumental sense of what the new rulers needed to know, and a practical crisis to diagnose; as Guha describes, writers like Alexander Dow, William Bolts and others aimed 'to equip the Company with a knowledge that would help it to extract the highest possible amount of revenue from the conquered territories and use it to finance its seaborne trade'.[87] Yet for all their frankness about the coercive ends of what Guha terms the 'collaboration between arms and researches',[88] their work shares with a wider cultural realm the need to register the very potent points of intercultural transmission, which might easily slip into the realm of the fantastical and otherworldly. To register, and also explain them, in ways that were to be eclipsed in the later utilitarian revision of Indian culture and history.

The figure of the Brahmin is one such point of dynamic transmission. The Brahmin has a powerful presence in forms of 'metamorphic writing' – in fables, moral stories, travel narratives and poetry – as well as in the British historiographical accounts of mid-eighteenth-century India. There were material reasons for this. As the highest, priestly caste, the Brahmins were seen to possess that precious, divinely ordained knowledge about the meaning of life in India that the British were only too eager to decipher. If the imperial ear assumed the force of an utterance, as we saw earlier, then the Brahmins, formed from Brahma's mouth, might offer the answers. They were often constructed as founts of philosophical revelation, such that paintings depicted East India officers in conversation with Brahminical figures,[89] and stories circulated about the dependency of particular British officials on their prophecies. If, as Philip Francis later declared in Parliament, 'History, in effect, is prophecy',[90] meaning that the teleological progress of history might be predicted whiggishly from the past, it could be argued that the phrase was at times literally the case in the British settlements of the India of the late 1760s. Certainly to the Governor of Bombay in Eliza Draper's time, it was, notoriously, Brahminical soothsaying, rather than any confident sense of projection from a then largely unknown historical past, that had an equal chance of unlocking the future.[91]

From one perspective this was evidently to collude with superstition, and to fall into the clutches of priests, those Enlightenment villains, who had darker interests in keeping their knowledge behind an 'impenetrable veil of mystery'.[92] The caste system, as a 'natural' and incontrovertible social ordering, underlined their sacerdotal power. This version of the Brahmin gradually assumes the whole regalia of imperial disgust and fascination, painted in increasingly lurid terms into the nineteenth century. Human sacrifice, female infanticide, the burning of widows (sati), and the brutal meting out of justice in ordeal trials (as Eliza Draper witnessed), were laid at the Brahmins' unfeeling door. As Amal Chatterjee has described, according to one 'degenerate' historical model, the Brahmins were in this guise held responsible for the decline of Indian civilisation from a more enlightened antiquity.[93] A historian like William Robertson, who attempted to rectify European prejudice in his celebration of the continuities of Indian civilisation, even arguing for the local appropriateness of 'artificial barriers of caste', nonetheless found the Brahmins guilty of 'deceit' in their promotion of superstition and false deities against what he saw as the enlightened theism of their own beliefs.[94]

Others saw their character as symptomatic of an Indian condition of continual 'caprice', evidence of 'a monstrous irrational imagination', and of the shifting truths and allegiances of an endless conflict and variety, that, lacking state form, could never yield a history of any kind. The words are Hegel's, from his discussion of the Indian 'dream-state' in *The Philosophy of History*, delivered as lectures in the 1820s. Hegel repeats the received terms of English accounts: the Brahmins are 'especially immoral', 'they do nothing but eat and sleep', moreover 'when they take any part in public life they show themselves as avaricious, deceitful, voluptuous. With those whom they have reason to fear, they are humble enough; for which they avenge themselves on their dependents. "I do not know an honest man among them," says an English authority.'[95] Life 'among the Hindoos' in India was thus characterised for Hegel by a form of enslavement, made more corrupt by its seemingly voluntary nature; an acquiescence in 'one unbroken superstition' that seemed the worst kind of self-abandonment:

> Annihilation – the abandonment of all reason, morality and subjectivity – can only come to a positive feeling and consciousness of itself, by extravagating in a boundlessly wild imagination; in which, like a desolate spirit, it finds no rest, no settled composure, though it can content itself in no other way; as a man who is quite reduced in body and spirit finds his existence altogether stupid and intolerable, and is driven to the creation of a dream-world and a delirious bliss in Opium.[96]

Like the figure of the zombie, then, the Brahmin's construction is marked by a particular form of slavery. Whereas the former's soul is stolen (often by a voodoo magic) and held captive – living labour become the living dead – the Brahmin is the culpable sign of a suicidal self-annihilation, of a reality 'bound fast in chains' and a wandering spirit unable to find rest. In the literature of a nascent empire at the more uncertain mid-eighteenth century, the seeds of such a thoroughgoing character assassination are already present: in the multiple meanings of 'indolence', and the generalised negativity suggested by the imaginative projections of an Indian love of death. Just as in the early writing of the new American republic, visions of freedom are dependent upon the imagined and actual subjection of others,[97] the 'slavery' of Indian life under-lined the seeming liberty and benevolence of British values; morever, it seemed to legitimate the case for moral action. Only Christian 'improvement' could save such 'lost' souls, as Wilberforce and others argued. At the same time this construction of the Brahmin captured aspects of modern experience in the metropolis itself. Such imagining was undoubtedly a means of self-reflection, with its vision of an enthralment to a world of external, incontrovertible will and inner distraction that, as we have seen, was already radically shaping British life in the latter decades of the eighteenth century.

Yet the Brahmin was a more complex shape-shifter than this in the texts of French and British writers and philosophers at the mid-eighteenth century, even before the work of orientalists like William Jones began to celebrate the wealth of Indian culture, and the *Bhagavad-Gita* was translated into English. The Hindu belief in metempsychosis, or the transmigration of souls, carried an optimistic, cosmopolitan, charge within the orientalist current of thought at this time. It appeared to link the Brahmin into a classical genealogy that had exponents in Greece and Rome, an influence, for some, on Pythagorean thought, and on Ovidian metamorphosis. There were debates about the par-ticular direction of this transmission, since it was important within certain historical accounts to establish the primary source, and thus Brahminical phi-losophy as a later, derivative copy of an imperial ur-thought. Alexander Dow argued that it had descended from the Druids and Homer, though he saw its belief in the extension of the soul through the bodies of animals as well as humans, as peculiar to the Brahmins.[98] Whatever its pedigree, in this form the Brahmin promised, not enslavement and revery, but transcendence: a meta-physical knowledge of transformation that enabled movement beyond mortal boundaries.

For writers like Voltaire, eastern philosophy offered the spectacle of a system of metaphysical reflection on the big questions of the day: optimism, happiness, and the nature of 'the best of all possible worlds'. Certain aspects of metempsychosis provided the occasion for humour, particularly the accompanying vegetarianism that appeared to take the view expounded in *Candide*, that 'sufferings give you rights',[99] to new extremes. In his 'Aventure indienne, traduite par l'ignorant'(1766), Voltaire has Pythagoras in the Indies learning that grass and oysters have their own complaint about ravaging bar-barians (sheep and humans respectively). In the widely translated 'Histoire d'un bon bramin'(1759), however, the Brahmin serves a more conventional purpose as a philosopher weighing the paradox that the preferred path of knowledge brings anguish and uncertainty, while his ignorant neighbour, who never reflects on the nature of her soul, lives in contentment: 'she believed in the metamorphoses of Vishnu with all her heart, and provided that she could wash herself in the pure water of the Ganges, believed herself to be the happiest of women'.[100] The particular dilemmas of slavery and freedom, the limits and mysteries of knowledge and belief, are here universalised; rather than relegating the Brahmin to a kind of primitive state of unreason, against which western freedom might be defined, he becomes a touchstone of the human condition.

The figures that emerge from the 'tales of metamorphosis' are thus not only shaped by the 'imperial gothic' that Marina Warner fascinatingly describes. While Brahminism takes on certain vampiric qualities in one mode, at the mid-century it is often a sign of universalising tendencies within the notion of sensibility, the acme of a sensitive philosophy. For Hegel in the 1820s the Hindu belief in reincarnation seemed the very reverse of the sentimental, in that its care for natural creatures was said to be at the expense of the human: 'The Hindoos will not tread upon ants, but they are perfectly indifferent when poor wanderers pine away from hunger'.[101] In the 1760s contrastingly it was a belief that resonated with Sterne's declaration 'are we not all relations?'(*SJ* 90), exemplified in uncle Toby's saving of the life of a fly in *Tristram Shandy*. As Orme had noted, 'all these casts acknowledge the Bramins for their priests, and with them admit the transmigration. In devotion to this opinion, some afflict themselves at the death of a fly, although occasion'd by inadvertence'.[102] The elevation of the Brahmin could thus be seen to echo the election of the sentimental philosopher and man of feeling. Eliza Draper's styling as 'Bramine' is of a piece with her construction as sentimental touchstone, her potential as 'the Wife of a very feeling Poet and Philosopher'.[103]

The power of such a figuring can be seen in numerous tracts from the period where its shapeshifting reveals the work of the imperial imaginary. In the poem *The Bramin: An Epilogue, to Edmund Nugent Esq.* (1751), seemingly written for a young man – Nugent's 'orient heir' – who has seen service in India (or is about to leave for it), the Brahmin is disengaged from its national roots to represent a universalised and nameless moral force or energy (which presumably guides and potentially animates the young man himself):

Hail, BRAMIN, hail, whatever name thy boast,
Increase of triumph to the British Coast!
Whatever climate for thy birth content,
All human kind acknowledge thee their friend.
Not Indian Titan, though his active rays
Ripen the mines, and give the gem to blaze,
Such warm emotions ever could inspire,

Mature the genius, or awake the fire:
We feel, we feel through each unlabour'd line
Religious rapture, energy divine![104]

The poem connects the Brahmin with sublimity and transcendence, linking conquest ('triumph') and friendship in an extraordinary wish fulfilment, as if to answer those (like Adam Ferguson, later) who saw the sheer extent of territorial gains in India rendering a wider political friendship, and thus the binding of imperial society by that means, impossible. The utopian horizon of an enlightened human order runs alongside the imperial project, appearing to reframe it in the terms of a vision of universal benevolence, even as it legitimates its rampant forms of accumulation (indicated by the 'ripening' mines):

The BRAMIN, all benevolence and love,
Comes forth, as if commission'd from above,
Like Noah's turtle, that with duteous haste
Skim'd her smooth voyage o'er the watery waste,
And to the just repairer of our race
Bore back the leaf of universal peace.
He comes, the cloud of ignorance to break,
The dim enlighten, and support the weak.
Behold him like that natal star arise,
Which to their Saviour led the raptur'd Wise:
Mark, how he soars above the sons of rhime,
Majestic, graceful, simple and sublime!

. . .

His breath is manna, and his words are balm,
And all the lessons, which he would impart
To human race, the transcript of his heart. (pp. 9–10)

The thematic stress here on peace and the 'balm' of words perhaps recalls the often expressed view of trade – the occupation of the young Nugent – as the healing of war and conquest, though the terms, appropriately enough for the 'Reverend' poet, are overwhelming, biblical and prophetic. The cosmopolitan delinking of the Brahmin – 'whatever name', 'whatever climate' – is interesting in this context. It refigures him via Christian appropriation into a broader vision of universal monarchy: 'The BRAMIN preaches, what had Athens mov'd,/ And Peter had rever'd, and Paul approv'd' (p. 8). As Dow also argued, against a polytheism attributed he said by European prejudice, Brahmins upheld that 'God is the *soul of the world*', and it was only 'the vulgar' who worshipped 'subaltern intelligences'.[105] It is evident that the Brahmin here functions as an ideological quilting point of the 'fictive universality' I discussed earlier: one site of identification at which religious and secular projections of the universal come together in globalised extension.[106]

The drama of the loss of caste for those daring to leave India's shores might thus be revisioned, as Elizabeth Hamilton's *Translations of the Letters of a Hindoo Rajah* (1796) confirms. As her Rajah contemplates his European voyage, in the light of 'the will of the omniscient spirit, the eternal Brahma', 'the loss of Cast' no longer frightens him: 'Can this Being, whose animating spirit is spread abroad over the whole universe! can he behold with displeasure, the attempt of any of his creatures, to explore the varied forms of being which partake of his essence?' If the Rajah is a citizen of the world, his perambulations have a purpose. He functions in this narrative as a conscience, reminding those Christians extolling the virtues of the eastern religions of 'their Musselman, and Hindoo friends' of the 'energetic eloquence of Paul, or the beautiful simplicity of the Gospels'. The universal toleration signified by Braminism becomes in this later form a check on orientalist identification, in a text whose celebration of Christian friendship and marriage is also an attack on the radical 'poojah of System' in the England of the 1790s. Hamilton nonetheless turns the stereotype of the 'lie-loving Bramin' on its head, in the ironic dismissal (and thus confirmation) of his assertion that it is the Christians who deal in slavery: 'the traffic of blood'.[107]

Such cultural co optation thus has particular meaning for the constitution of the national at different moments, even as it imagined such a projection in unbounded (and thus imperial) terms. The demands of the mid-century were distinct in this regard, and they required new forms of political and cultural imagining. As the author of *An Address to the Proprietors of India Stock* put it in 1769, 'unless the state views the transactions of that country [India] as that of the great body of the nation, there is wanting that harmony and universal bond of interest which secures the prosperity of national affairs'.[108] In a poem like *The Nabob; Or, Asiatic Plunderers*, it is possible to see this reconstitution of the national at work, in a dialogue between an Author and his Friend whose rhetoric is overtly Christian in tone. The Friend asks whether it is possible to feel with others: 'When ills are distant, are they then your own?' The Author replies:

. . . as man, I feel for man.
My country's honor has receiv'd a blot,
A mark of odium ne'er to be forgot:
A larger country still I boast: embrace

With a warm heart all *Adam's* wretched race
Not dipp'd in *Lethe*, I can feel all o'er,
Feel for the widow, orphan, stranger, poor.
Where'er oppression lifts its iron hand,
It strikes my brother in a distant land.
Clime, color, feature, in my bosom find
The friend to all; their stamp is still mankind,
And mankind too to noblest blood ally'd,
For he who bled for me, for them too dy'd.[109]

If the passage to India brought with it a sense of dislocation that some saw as a death, the very dissociation of soul and body, then Brahminical metamorphosis offered the analogous prospect of the dissolving of such boundaries. The deterritorialisations attendant on the figure of the Brahmin, loosed from name or climate, project beyond the limits of the 'great body of the nation' in the interests of generating a wider 'harmony' and 'universal bond', thereby consolidating (reterritorialising) that national body in the process.

It is in this densely worked and potent cultural space that Laurence Sterne and Eliza Draper style themselves as 'Bramin' and 'Bramine'. Theirs is of course a self-fashioning that can be read in the most literal of terms, picking up as it does on Sterne's status as a man of the Church and Eliza's 'Indian' identity in one. If Sterne is a priest, then Eliza is his 'disciple', 'treasure[ing] his instructions', like the 'transcript' of the poem, in her heart.[110] However, the self-association of Sterne in his *Journal* with the sensitive philosophy attributed to the Brahmins borrows more broadly from orientalist lexicon of the moment. One moral work (penned in part by Robert Dodsley, Sterne's first major publisher), entitled *The Oeconomy of Human Life*, translated, it claimed, 'from an Indian manuscript, written by an ancient BRAMIN', reveals the nuances of connection in literal detail.[111] Presenting itself as 'a small system of morality, written in the language and character of the gymnosophists, or bramins' (p. xii), it is a conduct text that contains the usual mid-century attack on idleness, and arguments for oeconomy, alongside exhortations to be a 'friend to mankind' (p. 71): 'Wouldst thou enjoy the good-will of all men? let thine own benevolence be universal', it declares (p. 135). The target of this tract is the management of affective feeling: the curbing of immoral desire, and careful monitoring of sentimental emotion: 'Tears may drop from thine eyes, though virtue falleth not from thine heart: be thou careful only that there is cause, and that they flow not too abundantly' (p. 162).

Here the ventriloquated wisdom of the Brahmin articulates the oeconomy of sensibility, the precise balance of tender feeling for humanity and its sensual expression, which Sterne's sentimentalism was seen both to exemplify and to trouble. The tract advocates love between the sexes, as an amorousness that has been purged of material excess: 'shut not thy bosom to the tenderness of love; the purity of its flame shall ennoble thine heart, and soften it to receive the fairest impressions' (p. 48). Moreover, it advises:

> When thou findest sensibility of heart, joined with softness of manners; an accomplished mind, with a form agreeable to thy fancy; take her home to thy house; she is worthy to be thy friend, thy companion in life, the wife of thy bosom. (p. 54)

Sterne fashions Eliza as a 'wife' in precisely this sense. Love here suggests an ideal reciprocity, pure communication; the body rendered docile, open to 'impressions' from the other. It is one route, as we discussed earlier, to the imagining of a generalised love for mankind, and certainly to a love for the nation. Yet if the feminine amiable virtues function like an affective adhesive within the social bond – at the same time, I want to argue, as *making safe the anxiety of empire as a form of love* – the tract has difficulty in maintaining such an equilibrium. The problem is that a dissociation between soul and body lies behind its oeconomy which sets off unexpected consequences and desires. 'The soul is the monarch of thy frame; suffer its subjects not to rebel against it' (p. 94), the tract declares, turning to political metaphor. If bodily desires make their demands known, like a mass revolt, the soul itself has a freedom that also has to be held in check:

> Guard her [the soul], for she is rash; restrain her, for she is irregular; correct her, for she is outrageous; more supple is she than water, more flexible than wax, more yielding than air. Is there ought that can bind her? (p. 100)

There is a latent vision of the mixed constitution of the British state in this Brahminical 'small system of morality', the balance of monarchical authority and restraint. Yet the soul, 'outrageous' and extravagant, is characterised by a mercurial shapeshifting that threatens to slip away from such containment. It is here, finally, that I want to locate the scandalousness of the exchange between Laurence Sterne and Eliza Draper, 'Bramin' and 'Bramine': at a point of insurrection within the oeconomy of imperial sensibility.

### The Scandalous Nature of Freedom

The 'Communion' Sterne imagines with his 'Bramine' is accompanied by metamorphosis. Unlike the realm of *Tristram Shandy*, where 'our minds shine not through the body' (*TS* 1.23.83), the ailing body of the *Journal* anticipates a state of transparency:

> I shall be sublimated to an etherial Substance by the time my Eliza sees me—
> she must be sublimated and uncorporated too, to be able to see me—but I was
> always transparent & a Being easy to be seen thro', or Eliza had never loved
> me nor had Eliza been of any other *Cast* herself, could her Bramine [112] have
> held *Communion* with her. (*BJ* 180)

There is ironic play with words here: Sterne's predilection for double
entendre that some readers found irreligious in itself. Thus this 'Communion'
has already, though not yet, taken place; is both a religious sacrament of
transcendence and yet another form of bodily congress. Sterne's words
reverberate with the associations of love, death, sex, redemption. 'The
*Hereafter*', the state of reunion which the text longs for – 'Thou shalt
lye down & rise up with me' (*BJ* 224) – carries a similar ambiguity. It 'is
but a melancholly term – but the Certainty of its coming to us, brightens
it up' (*BJ* 220). Another paradox: that the future 'hereafter' enigmatically
prophesied by Sterne in the pages of Eliza's 'Almanack' is already an
afterlife. It is a vision answered in more conventional Christian tones by
Eliza on board ship, contemplating her own mortality during a period of
illness:

> you are my adviser – my monitor – my better genius – may our reciprocal
> affections continue pure and unchanged, till the dissolution of our frail
> beings – and if an intercourse is allowed between the spirits of the departed,
> may we enjoy that exalted – that refined, etherial rapture – which the ardent
> seraphims know, while glowing with the emanations of their eternal
> Creator. [113]

The exchange between Sterne and Eliza (at this point, an exchange, for her
letter arrives as Sterne records weepily in the *Journal*) is a negotiation and
overcoming of mortal limits, most immediately those of the self. Yet it also
involves the mastery of the loss represented by the colonial passage to India,
through the figuring of a productive negativity, the generation of transformation. It is an anticipation that resembles a mourning in advance, for the
'tremendous moment' of that leaving for 'another World': a leaving that has
already, though not yet, taken place. In Roland Barthes's choreography,
amorous discourse at times articulates a love of death in precisely this
form, such that 'I might have the chance to abate my suffering without
yet having died': 'I conceive of death *beside me*: I conceive of it according
to an unthought logic, I drift outside of the fatal couple which links life and
death by opposing them to each other' (p. 12). Death becomes a territory,
marked by an 'unthought logic' of imperial projection. What might this
mean?

Montaigne wrote that 'to philosophize is to learn how to die', in that contemplative thought draws 'our souls somewhat outside ourselves, keeping
them occupied away from the body, a state which both resembles death and
which forms a kind of apprenticeship for it'.[114] Sterne (who knew his
Montaigne) makes his own contribution to the long tradition of *ars moriendi*,
one might argue, by moving outside the 'fatal couple' of life and death into
another state of 'apprenticeship'. This potentially ascetic move finds its echo
in the condition of sensibility, which attempts to establish a relation to the
other outside the confines of the self. And again in the British construction of
Brahminism, in which, according to Alexander Dow, the only desire to be
found in the realm of the 'Great Soul' is that of benevolence, rising above the
'selfish craving principle' of the 'vital soul'.[115] It is perhaps not surprising that
William Robertson saw a correlation between 'the manly active philosophy'
of Brahminism and stoicism, a stoicism that animated the universalising
thought of Adam Smith.[116] I want to suggest that imperial experience, the
literal fact of 'feeling beyond the nation', is marked by an analogous gesture
of (philosophico-aesthetic) removal, registered as a coexistence with a state
of negativity at this mid-century moment; an experience which put the 'self-
command' of Smith's philosophy under severe pressure and which, like the
game of fort/da, has continually to be reeled in, made safe, contained. In such
anxiety is also the disorientation and euphoria of unboundedness, in Sterne's
terms, of a world imagined without limits, loosed from the available narratives that might explain it. As Montaigne continues: 'To practice death is to
practice freedom. A man who has learned how to die has unlearned how to
be a slave. Knowing how to die gives us freedom from subjection and constraint.'[117]

Yet what kind of freedom, and for whom? It is perhaps Eliza Draper, and
not Laurence Sterne, who in her own way began to register the force of this,
in what Sterne saw as the 'fatal' world of Bombay, 'fatal', that is to 'thousands
of [her] Sex' (*BJ* 197). On Eliza's return from England in 1767 she had determined not to oppose her husband's will: 'Honour, prudence and the interest
of my beloved Children demand the necessary sacrifice and *I will make it*.'[118]
Writing 'sentimental Observations' from India to her cousin two years later,
the question of freedom from constraint feeds into a moment of rebellion,
which I quote in full:

We Children of the Sun, never hate or love coolly like some of the Northern
Insignificants. Nor do we cover a visit to the Frigid Zone by way of temper-
ing our passions. Away Apathy (another name for Hypocrasy [sic] and
Prudence) keep thy worldly Caution and boasted Equilibrium! I wish not a
participation of either! The honest African, whose wildness is term'd Savage
is far far dearer to me! Why have we an Imagination to conceive, and a Tongue

to give our conceptions their due force, unless to be sincere? Prudence! Decorum! forbids! Only so prudence and Decorum are to take the lead of sincerity and honesty! Mighty fine! because we must seem to court the World's approbation whether agreable to us or not. A simple Brahmin would despise such maxims, tho' they're approved in A Scool [sic] of politeness regulated by Europaeans [sic].

Upon my word most of your boasted English liberty does not amount to half the freedom the Slaves of Asiatic Slaves experience. Your persons are free, but Minds fettered, the worst and most ignominious destination of Slavery surely. Theirs vice versa; and a widow on the Ganges (the lowest of human reptiles because she's degraded for life and subject to the strikes of a hog feeder) will avow her sentiments more openly (tho' in declamation against the Laws of her Country) than a polish'd Europaean dare so do against the facination of Custom—and dishonest . . . of Hypocrisy or prudence because dirty interest or some other pitifully . . . makes him dread the ill will of fools in power or a Hydra Multitude, with whom sense and honesty rarely associate.[119]

Eliza's experience takes her to the limits of European oeconomy, for which she has been 'ruined' by life in India, and thus to the possibility of its critique. It does so because in following Sterne's dictum, to 'be true to thy self', in this other 'alienated' space, she comes to reflect on what makes her human, what qualifies her as a social being, the nature of her freedom. Her conclusion introduces its own equations: African and Asiatic slaves are shackled in body, but are free in mind, while for Europeans the constraints are reversed. She thus confronts the *quid pro quo* at the centre of Étienne Balibar's 'fictive universality':[120] liberation, in exchange for another kind of servitude, is freedom in the eyes of the enlightened values of the British state. A freedom from which she is dislocated, by her location, and her status as a woman. Such universal citizenship is predicated, as we have seen previously, on some persons and not others: not European women, not 'the honest African', not 'the widow on the Ganges', not this 'Bramine' (whose defence of the passions would itself have appeared a kind of slavery, and stereotypical at that). If the passage to India involved a travelling beyond the limits of self and nation – and thus a feminine openness to the other – it at all costs had to maintain its equilibrium, its amiable conformity to the virtues of English character. Life in India afforded her the imaginative opportunity to extend her sense of self, but it also clearly brought home to Eliza Draper the cost of her sociable 'consent' and the form of her inevitable exclusion. As William Russell reminded in his *Essay on the Character, Manners and Genius of Women*, in a description that has the force of an imperative: 'the tender sex do not love to set their souls so far a-wandering'. The 'universal love of mankind' was the business of men.[121]

There was nowhere to take the refusal voiced in Eliza's letter of 1769, beyond its passionate assertion of feminine subjecthood, which could only be imagined through negativity. Nowhere except her eventual flight from Daniel Draper. 'The D – l never intended a Severer Punishment', she later reflected, 'than that of a dependent Situation, for one of a free generous Spirit – it curbs every valuable Emotion of the Soul, and debases the Dignity of the Mind, by obliging it to pursue a course of action, only natural to the Illiberal & Illiterate!'[122]

If Eliza remonstrates with the subjection of those born to freedom (in Eurocentric terms), on the other side of her equation the condition of the 'honest African' and 'widow of the Ganges' does not concern her further. Yet her momentary identification with the 'Children of the Sun' reveals a glimpse, by default, of an emergent concept of universality – which Balibar names 'ideal' – an 'unconditional' form of claim then on the horizon in the 1760s, in which liberty could only be thought as inseparable from equality: a claim that found expression in the language of rights.[123] This is precisely one 'unthinkable logic' traced by the intense projection of self into the scene of empire, and it brings with it a sense of conflict, insurrection. The feminine subject of empire is generalisable, here, because her demand to transform the meaning of 'humanity' marks a wider *practice* of negativity to which others might also lay claim. For this eighteenth-century woman, sympathetic identification carries with it the unthinkable possibility of solidarity, continually disavowed. If sentiment is 'not deployed within a metaphysics of justice', it is undoubtedly haunted by it.[124] Just as Sterne's sentimental traveller incarcerates his captive to take his picture, unable to face a prospect of the millions of humanity 'born to no inheritance but slavery' (*SJ* 97), Eliza ultimately recoils from the logic of freedom, and in particular, its massification: the 'Hydra Multitude'. It brings the sentimental observer into too-close proximity to 'the irreducible "being there" of the dominated', in Balibar's terms.[125] The scandal of Sterne's writing perhaps lies here, in bringing the subject to the point where the Other does not 'socialize', a point not simply of embarrassment and ironic abandon, but of fear.

'The Brahmins are easy, plain, unaffected sons of simple nature – there's a something in their Conversation & Manners, that exceedingly touches me,' wrote Eliza Draper.[126] If such identifications produced comforting and detachable figures of reciprocity, they could also quickly transmute into more vampiric, and disconcertingly indifferent, forms, marking the insurrectionary point at which the Other might be encountered, as Slavoj Žižek describes, in the 'substantial weight of its *jouissance*'.[127] If the Brahmins had the 'ear' of their 'conquerors', they were also a potent sign of non-relation. 'There is not a more difficult subject for the understanding of men than to govern a Large Empire upon a plan of Liberty', Edmund Burke declared to Parliament in 1766.[128] The very projection of liberty on such a seemingly universal scale brought with it its own sense of trauma, projected onto the territories the British aimed to govern, and at the same time generated other subjects, of whom Eliza Draper was, despite herself, one. Sterne's memoir in her name demonstrates one particular, structural truth about the writing of imperial experience at such a moment. In the words of Roland Barthes: 'To know that one does not write for the other, to know that these things I am going to write will never cause me to be loved by the one I love (the other), to know that writing compensates for nothing, sublimates nothing, that is precisely *there where you are not* – this is the beginning of writing' (p. 100). And the death of Laurence Sterne.

## Notes

1 Laurence Sterne, *Continuation of the Bramine's Journal*, in *The Florida Edition of the Works of Laurence Sterne*, vol. 6, ed. Melvyn New and W. G. Day (Gainesville, FL: University Press of Florida, 2002), p. 215. All further references to the *Journal* will be cited as BJ and page number in the text.

2 Roland Barthes, *A Lover's Discourse. Fragments*, trans. Richard Howard (New York: Hill and Wang, 1979), p. 21.

3 Mrs Medalle (ed.), *Letters of the Late Rev. Laurence Sterne to his Most Intimate Friends on Various Occasions, as published by his Daughter Mrs Medalle and including the Letters between Yorick and Eliza*, 2 vols (Vienna: R. Sammer, 1797), II, 41. This edition of the text compiled by Lydia, Sterne's daughter, includes the later addition of the 'platonic' exchange between Sterne and Eliza Draper. It describes Eliza as 'wife of Daniel Draper, Esq.; Counsellor at Bombay, and at present Chief of the English factory at Surat; a gentleman very much respected in that quarter of the globe' (pp. 5–6). It appears Sterne sent the first part of his journal to Eliza, now lost; lodging the latter part with Anne James along with a letter to Daniel Draper: 'I fell in Love with yr Wife . . . but tis a Love, You would honour me for – for tis so like that I bear, my own daughter'. See Arthur H. Cash, *Laurence Sterne: the Later Years* (London and New York: Methuen, 1986), p. 285; and for an account of the discovery of the manuscript in the nineteenth century, p. 284 n68.

4 Eliza Draper to Thomas Limbrey Sclater, May 1769, in Arnold Wright and William Lutley Sclater, *Sterne's Eliza: Some Account of her Life in India, With Her Letters Written Between 1757 and 1774* (London: Heinemann, 1922), p. 96.

5 Eliza Draper to Thomas Limbrey Sclater, 10 April 1769, in Wright and Sclater, p. 86. Eliza writes that 'the Widow & Daughter of my best friend have occasioned my distress & Chagrine by threatening to do, what will render me, as the World may think, deservedly unhappy', and expresses fears in this letter that 'what I can do for them is very inadequate to what they may expect'.

6 I have borrowed this phrase from the title and substance of the *Social Text* col-

lection edited by Pheng Cheah and Bruce Robbins: *Cosmopolitics: Thinking and Feeling beyond the Nation* (Minneapolis and London: University of Minnesota Press, 1998).

7  Balibar, 'Ambiguous Universality', p. 146.

8  Barthes, *A Lover's Discourse*, p. 3.

9  Arthur Cash debates the Journal's status as a 'public document' in his biography, arguing against his own former position that Sterne had intended the text for publication, though suggesting the author nevertheless 'hoped it would become part of his image as a man of sensibility'. See Cash, *Laurence Sterne*, p. 285.

10 See Ian Campbell Ross, *Laurence Sterne: A Life* (Oxford: Oxford University Press, 2001) for the detailing of Sterne's infatuations and friendships with Catherine Fourmantel, Sarah Tuting, Lady Anne Warkwarth (daughter of the Earl of Bute), Eliza Draper, and anonymous others.

11 Everett Zimmerman, '*Tristram Shandy* and Narrative Representation', in Melvyn New (ed.), *Tristram Shandy: Contemporary Critical Essays* (London: Macmillan, 1992), p. 122. See also my analysis of the topography of death in Sterne's work in 'Mourning, Boundaries and the Strange Death of Laurence Sterne', in Habib Ajroud (ed.), *Across Boundaries* (Tunis: University of La Manouba, 1992), pp. 167–79.

12 Cash has a useful appendix on the caricature portrait by Mortimer in which he attempts to identify those present, surmising that they are drinking a toast to Eliza Draper (pp. 365–72).

13 Medalle, *Letters*, II, p. 75.

14 Quoted in Cash, *Laurence Sterne*, p. 279.

15 Eliza Draper to Thomas Limbrey Sclater, 10 April 1769, in Wright and Sclater, p. 82.

16 Harriet Guest, 'Sterne, Elizabeth Draper and Drapery', *The Shandean* 9 (1997), p. 27.

17 Ibid. p. 27.

18 Ibid, p. 28.

19 See Cheah and Robbins, *Cosmopolitics*, and note 6 above.

20 Eliza Draper to Thomas Limbrey Sclater, 29 November 1767, in Wright and Sclater, pp. 65–6.

21 Eliza Draper to Thomas Limbrey Sclater, 5 April 1771, Wright and Sclater, p. 120.

22 Eliza Draper to Elizabeth Sclater, 28 October 1768, in Wright and Sclater, p. 73.

23 Boltanski, *Distant Suffering*, p. 80.

24 John Mullan, *Sentiment and Sociability: The Language of Feeling in the Eighteenth Century* (Oxford: Clarendon Press, 1988), p. 44.

25 Ibid. p. 49.

26 *Lettres d'Yorick à Eliza, et d'Eliza à Yorick, traduits de l'anglois de Mr Sterne, augmentée de l'éloge d'Eliza par Mr L'Abbé Raynal* (Lausanne: Mourer, 1786),

pp. 6–7. The writer concludes that it can only be thought of as a platonic affection, adding 'j'aime à le voir exister, & que Sterne en soit le modele' (p. 7).

27 David Hume, *A Treatise of Human Nature*, ed. L. A. Selby-Bigge 2nd edn (Oxford: Clarendon Press, 1978), p. 470.

28 Ibid. p. 481.

29 See Abraham Tucker, discussed in Chapter 2. In his *Enquiries* Hume rethinks this scenario more carefully, as part of his concerted attempt to understand the limits of 'self-love', arguing that love between the sexes is a mark of a 'general benevolence in human nature' precisely because it is disinterested. See David Hume, *Enquiries Concerning Human Understanding and Concerning the Principles of Morals*, ed. L. A. Selby-Bigge and rev. P. H. Nidditch, 3rd edn (Oxford: Clarendon Press, 1975), p. 300.

30 Brooke, *The Fool of Quality* , p. 33.

31 Early reviewers were particularly concerned with Sterne's irreligion, though his later sentimental work changed views somewhat in that it was regarded as testimony to Christian benevolence. As Ralph Griffiths wrote in 1760 of the numerous pamphlets spawned by *Tristram Shandy*: 'Where he is obscene, they are filthy. In short, if this taste prevails, we need not wonder to see, in some future novel, the words which are chalked out on church walls, boldly printed in *Italicks*.' See his 'An Account of the Rev. Mr St****', and his Writings', *Grand Magazine* 3 (June 1760), 311.

32 Carter to Vesey, 19 April 1768, p. 166. Carter repeats the rumours about Sterne's financial neglect of his family, which had circulated long before firstly in relation to his mother, who had been imprisoned for debt.

33 Mullan, *Sentiment and Sociability*, p. 52.

34 Smith, *The Theory of Moral Sentiments*, p. 86; quoted in Mullan, p. 51.

35 Hume, *Enquiries*, p. 241.

36 Smith, *The Theory of Moral Sentiments*, p. 88.

37 Barthes, p. 15. All subsequent references will be cited by page number in the text.

38 J. W. von Goethe, quoted in Ross, p. 467 n74.

39 Eliza refers to her unwitting capture at the 'Instigation of one I deemed all Benevolence & truth' as we have seen in her letter to her cousin, quoted in Wright and Sclater, p. 86. As a later letter in March 1772 to their mutual friend Anne James suggests, Eliza gained some distance from her relationship – 'I was almost an idolator of his worth' – what concerned her was the wider circulation and interpretation of her letters: 'You knew not the content of these letters, and it was natural for you to form the worst judgement of them, when those who had seen 'em reported them unfavourably and were disposed to dislike me on that account'. It is precisely such *interpretation* that Barthes sees as the 'smothering' of the other, and which appears to cast doubt on Eliza's estimation of 'the mild, generous good Yorick we had so often thought him to be'. Wright and Sclater, *Sterne's Eliza*, p. 138.

40 Carter to Vesey, 19 April 1768, p. 167.

41 Balibar, 'Ambiguous Universality', pp. 161–3.

42 Cash, *Laurence Sterne*, p. 286.

43 In quotations, and in the title of this chapter, I have followed Sterne's text and retained the original (mis) spelling of Brahmin.

44 Sara Suleri, *The Rhetoric of English India* (Chicago and London: University of Chicago Press, 1992), pp. 4–5.

45 Ibid. p. 4.

46 Edmund Burke, 'Speech Opening the Impeachment, first day, Friday, February 15, 1788', quoted in Saree Makdisi, *Romantic Imperialism: Universal Empire and the Culture of Modernity* (Cambridge: Cambridge University Press, 1998), p. 100.

47 The short-lived conquest of Manila in the Philippines was launched from Madras in 1762 under the command of Colonel William Draper, bolstered by several hundred Asian recruits and two companies of French deserters. Anderson, pp. 515–17.

48 William Bolts, *Considerations on India Affairs; Particularly Respecting the Present State of Bengal and its Dependencies*, 3 vols (London: J. Almon et al, 1772), I, vi. Bolts here significantly defines 'British subjects' in India as both those 'newly-acquired Asiatic subjects' and 'British emigrants'.

49 See George, pp. 143–4. The East India Company would later house them in barracks, compelled by an Act of Parliament in 1814 to provide food, clothing and housing.

50 Edmund Burke, 'Observations on a Late State of the Nation', p. 174.

51 It provides humour in Foote's play, *The Nabob*, first performed in 1772: ' "Sir Matthew will settle upon Sir John and his Lady, for their joint lives, a jagghire." "A jagghire?" "The term is Indian, and means an annual income." "What strange jargon he deals in!".' Samuel Foote, *The Nabob; A Comedy in Three Acts* (London: T. Cadell, 1778), p. 9.

52 Peter Linebaugh notes the presence of Hindi words in the origins of thieves' cant in *The London Hanged*, p. 275.

53 I am thinking here not only of the predilection for tea (an addiction among working people which was questioned by some), but of the naming of other luxurious practices with their origins in the subcontinent, such as shampoo (derived from the Hindi word *champna*, to knead).

54 Niebuhr, II, 420, 423, 420. Niebuhr's account anecdotally conveys the diversity of people inhabiting the major centres of population, and also notes the sensitivity of the English to the control, viewing and mapping of space by competing European powers.

55 Robert Orme, *A History of the Military Transactions of the British Nation in Indostan, From the Year MDCCXLV. To Which is Prefixed a Dissertation on the Establishments made by Mahomedan Conquerors in Indostan*, 2nd edn, 3 vols

(London: John Nourse, 1773), I, 7. Orme had been born, like Eliza Draper, to an East India Company family in Anjengo, southern India.

56 Alexander Dow, *The History of Hindostan, from the Death of Akbar, to the Complete Settlement of the Empire Under Aurungzebe. To Which are Prefixed: 1. A Dissertation on the Origina and Nature of Despotism in Hindostan. 2. An Enquiry into the State of Bengal; with a Plan for Restoring that Kingdom to its Former Prosperity and Splendor* (London: T. Becket and P. A. De Hondt, 1772), p. lxii. Dow was an East India Company Lieutenant Colonel and strongly influenced by Scottish Enlightenment thought.

57 Alexander Dow, *The History of Hindostan; From the Earliest Account of Time, to the Death of Akbar; translated from the Persian of Mahummud Casim Ferisha of Delhi*, 2 vols (London: T. Becket and P. A. De Hondt, 1768), I, xxii.

58 Voltaire, *Candide*, p. 39.

59 Dow, *The History of Hindostan; From the Earliest Account of Time*, p. xxii.

60 Dow, *The History of Hindostan, from the Death of Akbar*, p. xxxv.

61 Abbé Raynal, *A Philosophical History of the Settlements and Trades of the Europeans in the East and West Indies*, trans. J. Justamond, 3rd edn (London: T. Cadell, 1777), I, 56. The quotation about the Indian love of death evidently had circulated from earlier accounts, such as Luke Scrafton's *Reflections on the Government &c of Indostan: With a Short Sketch of the History of Bengal, from the Year 1739–1756; And an Account of the English Affairs to 1758* (London: W. Richardson and S. Clark, 1763), p. 17.

62 Dow, *The History of Hindostan, from the Death of Akbar*, pp. xxi, xx.

63 Robert Clive, quoted in Amal Chatterjee, *Representations of India, 1740–1840: The Creation of India in the Colonial Imagination* (London: Macmillan, 1998), p. 52. Government policy in the 1760s actively prevented too much rapprochement with the ways of Indian life, inhibiting the learning of Persian and Hindi by East India Company writers, for example: 'In your public system you seem to entertain the idea that the Company are to adopt the eastern parade and dignity, but we are of the opinion that European simplicity is much more likely to engage the respect of the natives than an imitation of their manners'. A quotation from Fort William-India House correspondence, quoted in H. V. Bowen, *Revenue and Reform: the Indian Problem in British Politics 1757–1773* (Cambridge: Cambridge University Press, 1991), p. 11.

64 Quoted in Makdisi, *Romantic Imperialism*, p. 100.

65 Suleri, *The Rhetoric of English India*, p. 26.

66 Horace Walpole to Horace Mann, 22:6, 18 March 1764, p. 211.

67 Richard Owen Cambridge, *An Account of the War in India, Between the English and French, on the Coast of Coromandel, from the year 1750 to the Year 1760* (London: T. Jeffreys, 1761), p. ix.

68 Ranajit Guha, *A Rule of Property for Bengal: An Essay on the Idea of Permanent Settlement* (New Delhi: Orient Longman, 1981), p. 13. See P. J. Marshall, *The*

*Making and Unmaking of Empires: Britain, India and America 1750–1783* (Oxford: Oxford University Press, 2005), on the unevenness of the appropriation of political power in India, distinguishing between the take-over in Bengal where there was a functioning state apparatus, and the more precarious political conditions of the south.

69  Dow, *The History of Hindostan, from the Death of Akbar*, p. xxxix.

70  Ibid. p. cxii.

71  Bolts, I, viii.

72  Dow, *The History of Hindostan, from the Death of Akbar*, pp. cvi, cxvi, cxliii, cxx. The language of conquest represented a specific intervention in British politics in the late 1760s, since if the wars in India were not interpreted in mercantilist terms it meant that the Crown was the rightful beneficiary of the spoils. This was the debate, and its resolution in 1767 meant that the Treasury would receive £40,000 per annum, and the Company keep its territorial possessions. By 1772, when this volume was published, the argument had moved on, and the pressure for government control had intensified, as Dow's argument reveals. See Bowen, pp. 48–66, for the political manoeuvrings between Company and Government after 1765.

73  Dow, *The History of Hindostan; From the Earliest Account of Time*, p. vi.

74  Dow, *The History of Hindostan, from the Death of Akbar* pp. cl, xlii,vii, cxx.

75  Quoted in Wright and Sclater, p. 53.

76  Medalle, *Letters*, II, 69. Eliza's castigation of this bloodshed and corruption was not unusual within East India Company culture. It was shared by Robert Clive, who reviewed the excesses of his predecessors in his Select Committee after becoming Governor in 1765: 'Every spring of this government was smeared with corruption, that principles of rapacity and oppression universally prevailed, and that every spark of sentiment and public spirit was lost [or] extinguished in the ordinate lust of unmerited wealth'. Quoted in Bowen, p. 86. Clive was of course brought down by similar accusations.

77  Eliza Draper to Thomas Limbrey Sclater, May 1769, in Wright and Sclater, p. 99.

78  Eliza Draper to Commodore James, April 1769, in Wright and Sclater, pp. 106, 107. The successes of Hyder Ali in the west changed the political focus of East India Company policy, which had been locked on to Bengal; they also had material effects on the stock market at home, causing a severe crash. See Bowen, *Revenue and Reform*, pp. 23, 69.

79  Eliza Draper to Thomas Limbrey Sclater, May 1769, in Wright and Sclater, *Sterne's Eliza*, p. 95.

80  For a brief note on the kidnap and discussion of Angria's surrender to the British following the successes of Commodore James at Severndroog and (with Clive and Admiral Watson) Gheriah, see Wright and Sclater, *Sterne's Eliza*, pp. 7, 32–6. Angria retired as a pensioner of the East India Company.

81  Eliza Draper to Anne James, March 1772, in Wright and Sclater, p. 12. Though born in India, Eliza had been educated in England from the age of ten, and had

married Daniel Draper at fourteen, four months after returning to Bombay in 1758. He was thirty-four.

82  Eliza Draper to Thomas Limbrey Sclater, 5 April 1771, in Wright and Sclater, p. 121.

83  Eliza Draper to Thomas Limbrey Sclater, 4 March 1772, in Wright and Sclater, p. 131.

84  Eliza Draper to Anne James, 15 April 1772, in Wright and Sclater, p. 144.

85  Marina Warner, 'The Making of Imperial Gothic: *Omai*, *Aladdin* and the British Encounter with Zombies', *TLS*, 12 April 2002, 14. Warner takes the term 'congenor' from Peter Hulme's *Colonial Encounters*. The article is based on one of her Clarendon Lectures from 2001.

86  Ibid. pp. 14, 15.

87  Ranajit Guha, *Dominance without Hegemony: History and Power in Colonial India* (Cambridge, MA, and London: Harvard University Press, 1997), p. 74. Both Dow and Bolts attack the excesses of monopoly nonetheless, in Bolts' words, 'like the ideot-practice of killing the prolific hen to get her golden eggs all at once', Bolts, p. 192.

88  Ibid. p. 192

89  See for example George Colman's *An Officer Conversing with a Brahmin*, exhibited at the Society of Artists in 1771. This was based on experiences of India in the 1760s, recounted to Colman by an East India officer, Major Thomas Pearson. Only two pencil studies, and two fragments of the original, survive. See Alex Kidson, *George Romney 1734–1802* (London: National Portrait Gallery, 2002), p. 87. It seems that Sterne's response to the figure of the Brahmin may well have been influenced by art. In *A Sentimental Journey* he describes the head of a Franciscan monk Yorick encounters in terms of the paintings of Guido Reni: 'it would have suited a Bramin, and had I met it upon the plains of Indostan, I had reverenced it' (*SJ* 8).

90  Quoted in Guha, *A Rule of Property for Bengal*, p. 71.

91  Thomas Hodges was Governor of Bombay between 1767 and 1771. Both his accession to the Governorship and death were reputedly predicted by his close advisor, known as 'Hodges' Brahmin'. See Wright and Sclater, pp. 71, 111.

92  Dow, *The History of Hindostan; From the Earliest Account of Time*, p. xxii.

93  Chatterjee, *Representation of India*, p. 148.

94  William Robertson, *An Historical Disquisition Concerning the Knowledge which the Ancients had of India; and to the Progress of Trade with that Country Prior to the Discovery of the Passage to it by the Cape of Good Hope* (Basil: J. J. Tourneison, 1792), pp. 339–40.

95  Hegel, *The Philosophy of History*, pp. 166, 158–9.

96  Ibid., p. 167.

97  See Toni Morrison, *Playing in the Dark: Whiteness and the Literary Imagination* (London: Picador, 1992) on this point.

98 Dow, *The History of Hindostan; From the Earliest Account of Time*, p. l.

99 Voltaire, *Candide*, p. 27.

100 Voltaire, 'Histoire d'un bon bramin', in *Romans et contes*, ed. Frédéric Deloffre and Jacques Van Den Heuvel (Paris: Gallimard, 1979), p. 236.

101 Hegel, *The Philosophy of History*, p. 158.

102 Orme, *History*, I, 5.

103 Eliza Draper to Thomas Limbrey Sclater, 10 April 1769, in Wright and Sclater, p. 82.

104 Reverend Mr Dunkin, *The Bramin: An Epilogue, To Edmund Nugent Esq.* (London: R. Baldwyn, 1751), pp. 3, 6–7. All further references cited by page number in the text.

105 Dow, *The History of Hindostan; From the Earliest Account of Time*, p. lxix. See also Robertson, *An Historical Disquisition*, evidently informed by Dow.

106 Balibar traces via Hegel the way hegemony – 'fictive universality' – can be thought in terms of the 'analogies and incompatibilities, between *two conflicting realizations of universality*: the religious and the national–political'. Balibar, 'Ambiguous Universality', p. 156.

107 Elizabeth Hamilton, *Translations of the Letters of a Hindoo Rajah*, ed. Pamela Perkins and Shannon Russell (Peterborough, Ont.: Broadview Press, 1999), pp. 181, 306, 141.

108 Anon., *An Address to the Proprietors of East India Stock, Showing from the Political State of Indostan the Necessity of Sending Commissioners to Regulate Their Affairs Abroad* (London: np, 1769), quoted in Bowen, p. 21.

109 Anon., *The Nabob: Or, Asiatic Plunderers. A Satyrical Poem; in a Dialogue between a Friend and the Author* (London: printed for the Author, 1773), pp. 4–5.

110 Medalle, *Letters*, II, 18.

111 Anon., *The Oeconomy of Human Life. In Two Parts. Translated from an Indian Manuscript, Written by an Ancient Bramin* (London: np 1768). All page references will be cited in the text. Earlier English editions, attributed to both Dodsley and a John Hill MD, date from 1751, with a Dublin edition of 1750 carrying the latter name.

112 Sterne's orthography varies here, often referring to himself as Bramine.

113 Medalle, *Letters*, II, 34.

114 Michel de Montaigne, 'To philosophize is to learn how to die', in *The Complete Essays*, p. 89.

115 Dow, *The History of Hindostan; From the Earliest Account of Time*, pp. lviii–lix.

116 See Robertson, *An Historical Disquisition*, p. 299.

117 Montaigne, *The Complete Essays*, p. 96.

118 Eliza Draper to Thomas Limbrey Sclater, 29 November 1767, in Wright and Sclater, p. 65.

119 Eliza Draper to Thomas Limbrey Sclater, May 1769, in Wright and Sclater, pp. 92–3.

120 Balibar, 'Ambiguous Universality', p. 162.

121 William Russell, *An Essay on the Character, Manners and Genius of Women in Different Ages* (Philadelphia: R. Aitken, 1774), II, 36, 35.

122 Eliza Draper to Thomas Limbrey Sclater, 5 April 1771, in Wright and Sclater, p. 122.

123 See Balibar, 'Ambiguous Universality', pp. 163–70.

124 Boltanski, *Distant Suffering*, p. 80.

125 Balibar, 'Ambiguous Universality', p. 164.

126 Eliza Draper to Thomas Limbrey Sclater, May 1769, in Wright and Sclater, p. 98.

127 Slavoj Žižek, 'Afterword: Lenin's Choice', in V. I. Lenin, *Revolution at the Gates: A Selection of Writings from February to October 1917*, edited by Slavoj Žižek (London and New York: Verso Books, 2002), p. 174. Žižek is describing the limits of liberal multicultural tolerance in the face of traditional practices like the wife burning of Hinduism: 'Tolerance is "zero tolerance" for the real Other, the Other in the substantial weight of its *jouissance*'.

128 Edmund Burke, 'Speech on Declaratory Resolution', p. 47.

# 7

# CONCLUDING ALONG SHANDEAN LINES

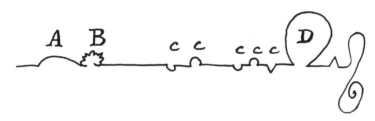

Figure 7.1. *Tristram Shandy* (6.40.571)

Figure 7.2. From *A Prospective Plan of the Battle fought near Lake George on 8th September 1755*[1]

Figure 7.3. *View of the Forts on the Hills of Veloor*, from Robert Orme, *A History of the Military Transactions of the British Nation in Indostan, From the Year MDCCXLV*[2]

'I defy the best cabbage planter that ever existed . . . to go on cooly and critically, and canonically, planting his cabbages one by one, in straight lines,
and stoical distances, especially if slits in petticoats are unsew'd up—
without ever and anon straddling out, or sidling into some bastardly digression——' (*TS* 8.1.655), writes the narrator of *Tristram Shandy*. The
wayward movement of Sterne's writing can sometimes present his reader,
like his embattled historiographer in volume one, with a prospect of 'endless
genealogies, which justice ever and anon calls him back to stay the reading
of' (*TS* 1.14.41–2). That those genealogies include the moment of the Seven
Years' War and its aftermath has been the contention of this book. Sterne's
serpentine lines, carefully notated on the page with their leaps and backslidings, their literal extra-vagance, mock the possibility of a *recta via*
through a world where 'things' appear to be 'crowded in so thick' (*TS*
4.32.400), lampooning the pretensions of a line of gravity 'drawn . . . by a
writing-master's ruler' (*TS* 6.40.571–2). What 'straddles out' in the attempt,
through slits in petticoats (or bursting through the hyphen in Thomas
Turner's journal, with which I began), is an aleatory means of charting and
grasping that world, pitching toward its mid-eighteenth-century complexity and reach. A formal wit, which in Sterne's writing registers the dynamics of a historical condition.

Sterne's 'bastardly' aesthetics are often associated with Hogarth's account
of the peculiar pleasures of the 'line of beauty', one that *'leads the eye a
wanton kind of chace'*.[3] His narratives might indeed seem to bear out a
Hogarthian logic (he had read his illustrator's *Analysis*), maintaining in their
twisting lines 'the continuity of its variety',[4] visually parodied above (Figure
7.1). Like Hogarth, Sterne resisted the 'stoical distances' of a classical order
in favour of the wandering lineaments of a natural world animated by an
erotics of discovery.[5] Yet for Hogarth the unravelling of the line promises
eventual satisfaction:

> It is a pleasing labour of the mind to solve the most difficult problems; alle-
> gories and riddles, trifling as they are, afford the mind amusement: and with
> what delight does it follow the well-connected thread of a play or novel, which
> ever in-creases as the plot thickens, and ends most pleas'd, when that is most
> distinctly unravell'd.[6]

Sterne's work, by contrast, whether (in the case of *Tristram Shandy*) playfully deemed a political allegory or a *'riddle*, without an *object'*,[7] seems to
withhold the cognitive pleasures of resolution and decipherment, and the
contentment Hogarth felt should follow. *Tristram Shandy* finally declares
itself the ultimate of cock-and-bull tales, *A Sentimental Journey* closes in a
hyphenated frisson of anticipation, while his memoir to Eliza concludes

in a death which is curiously proleptic, overwriting any simple notion of an ending. Decipherment is part of the game, but it doesn't definitively deliver; his serpentine lines and deferred conclusions are more like continual performances of encounter, with people, things, bodies, and words in passage.

I have speculated in this book that it is the climate of the Seven Years' War, shaped by a 'global' imperial conflict reaching tentacularly across continents, which is constitutive of the writerly dilemmas of Sterne's narratives; a crucible for the subjective universe they continuously unravel. The serpentine line, crazily idiosyncratic and 'Shandean' in its predilections, traces a self whose desires and imagination run across limits, stylistic individuation scripting its wayward tag against the grain of order and convention. A curious writerly liberation, in pursuit of a world whose extent and richness demand new forms, new cartographies, suggesting a *mimetic*, inventive grasp of experience in a world where limits (subjective, physical, territorial, commercial) have suddenly been expansively thrown open, boundaries redrawn. A form of cognition sometimes associated with children, who make sense of their environment through acting it out: the Shandean child, a historical bastard, journeys through the trajectories of desires and things as if animated by a new-found freedom: 'is a man to follow rules – or rules to follow him?' (*TS* 4.10.337).

Upended, that serpentine line resembles the gestural freedom of the arabesque, the projection of 'liberty' as a subjective sublimity in unbounded space, figured in the flourish of Trim's stick (Figure 7.4: *TS* 9.4.743). Such a gestics might indeed suggest (to adapt Peter Conrad's memorable phrase) a 'cardiograph of consciousness',[8] one that the German Romantics would later elevate into a vision of absolute freedom. Yet if Sterne's formal and ironic play anticipates what Schlegel saw as 'the freest of all licenses, for by its means one transcends oneself',[9] it also has specific co-ordinates. Such intensely individuated expression arrives in a time when it is simultaneously located in the most impersonal of spaces, not only as the effect of a writing (in which you discover yourself to occupy, despite your own best efforts to realise your Life and Opinions, a place where you are not) but also as an effect produced in the process of subjectivation itself, which calls (interpellates) you into social being. It is a process which takes an imperial form in the world of the 1760s. It involves what I have explored as the *quid pro quo* between freedom and subjection, described by Balibar as 'the price for the universalistic liberation of the individual'.[10] A price weighed and reimagined in the public culture of mid-century Britain.

In the wavy trajectories and friskiness of Sterne's lines it is possible to trace other silent lineaments: the cartographies of rivers sketched by military surveyors and engravers, the printed topologies of hillsides and fortifications.

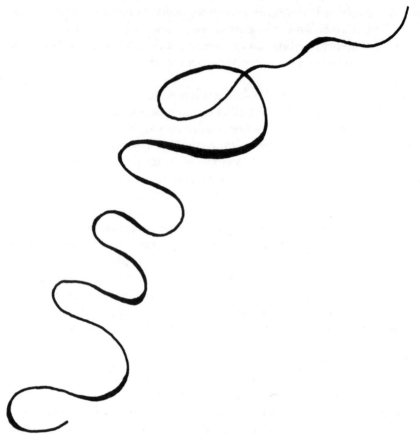

Figure 7.4. Arabesque from *Tristram Shandy* (*TS* 9.4.743)

Serpentine lines wind their way through the popular maps and vistas of distant territories reproduced in engravings and geographical essays, pored over by Thomas Turner and his like on quiet evenings, which were not only sources of information but forms of imaginative possession for those who would never venture beyond their four miles' diameter. The juxtaposition opening my conclusion, of Sterne's wandering line with images drawn arbitrarily from the mapmakers of America (Figure 7.2) and India (Figure 7.3), borrows from the method of Sternean wit. Wit, understood in eighteenth-century terms, involves the discovery of 'similitudes'. As Burke puts it in his *Enquiry*, in the process of 'making resemblances we produce *new images*, we unite, we create, we enlarge our stock'.[11] There is a resemblance between the crazy lines and alphabetical denotations of *Tristram Shandy* and the cartographic prints of the period, invited by the novel's graphical references: 'inv. T. S.' (Tristram Shandy created this), 'Scul. T. S.' (Tristram Shandy engraved this). It is here, if we extrapolate from the mimetic and associational method of Sterne's writing, that a principle of montage – the juxtaposition of previously unconnected or incongruous materials – liberates new historical images. In other words, the formal play of his works, often read in terms of a proto-modernist reflexivity, sparks a historical counter-memory specific to its time. What it reveals is not just the instrumental presence of an imperial reason, which the narratives both mimic and resist. But also a glimpse of a critical truth: that at its most intensely self-creating and singular, the 'modern' subjective self emerging from their pages discovers itself to be spoken from elsewhere.

What was the cost of this discovery? Management of such a 'liberation', and the exacting of its 'price', were central to what I have been exploring as the cultural work of empire. It involved a state imagining that could take the most lunatic and Shandean of forms even as it projected new visions of authority on its domestic population and over distant territories. It is part of the irony of the age (an irony we continue to experience) that the response to such an administration, and indeed the resistance to 'the strange absurdity'[12] of its equations in which bodies and lives are exchanged for things, became part of its instrumental armoury. The reaction to the calculus of empire – in the name of universal humanity, civilisation (a word coined in the 1760s), or liberty – could as easily become its means.

Sterne's rejection of the *recta via* had more than rhetorical force, if the weight of straight lines across the empire could be grasped as more than a question of aesthetic play, and certain of his readers knew it. Not only did the instrumental rationality of territorial imposition have devastating consequences on those already inhabiting newly 'discovered' lands, but the working of straight lines, their very 'cultivation' (to pick up Sterne's metaphor of husbandry with the cabbage planter), was more than a metaphorical discipline in the tropology of empire. From one perspective Sterne's wayward lines trouble the ordered economy built on an imperial *recta via* and its careful calibration of the nonfreedom of others. An aesthetic economy revealed in the words of James Grainger's 'West-India Georgic' of 1764, *The Sugar Cane*:

> As art transforms the savage face of things,
> And order captivates the harmonious mind;
> Let not thy blacks irregularly hoe;
> But, aided by the line, consult the site
> Of thy demesnes, and beautify the whole.[13]

There was in such aesthetic irregularity the potential for critique, which others would appropriate (Ignatius Sancho and Karl Marx among them). Yet the nature of such Shandean 'trouble' stems in part from its aesthetic inhabiting of autonomy, in which even as human experience and community appear obstinately *resistant* to the operations of power – in the free 'bastardly' play of everyday life – they are subject to another order of autonomy that rebounds in a more devastating and instrumental form.[14] The cultural work of the state, a making of community as an administrative 'work' of love and death, is testimony to this rebound, in which those affective values drawn from the haven of private life – familial feeling, sentimental affinities with others, moral duties and responsibilities – which might vociferously protest the harshness of the way of the world and its inequalities, could be brought into service.

The toleration for the eccentricities of the Shandy men suggests a recognition of their hobbyhorsical games for the coping mechanisms they are: 'so long as a man rides his HOBBY-HORSE peaceably and quietly along the King's highway, and neither compels you or me to get up behind him,—
—pray, Sir, what have either you or I to do with it?' (*TS* 1.7.12). And in this idiosyncratic play is a 'lesson to the world "*to let people tell their stories their own way*"' (*TS* 9.25.785) that might seem an antidote to a realm increasingly ordered in disciplinary terms, a mark of the capriciousness of multiple flows of human experience in the face of the cultural work I have been charting. A kind of freedom often laid at Sterne's door: ordinary life, the physical world, will have its sway. Yet however much the crazy vagaries of thought and desire challenge, sometimes despite their best efforts, the *recta via* – a life of 'straight lines, and stoical distances' – they are also haunted by an instrumentality that can break heads, necks and hearts in turn. The philosophy of Walter Shandy will stop at nothing: 'never man crucified TRUTH at the rate he did' (*TS* 9.32.804). Uncle Toby's innocent war games lead to an apology for the violence which has 'unmanned' him, and to the castration-cum-circumcision of his hapless nephew. And if Tristram Shandy's attempt to 'ride' rather than control the vicissitudes of life appears a new kind of solution, then even his flexible associationism risks becoming captured by the instrumentalism of a realm of 'things'; by the appetites and gratifications of the market which for some commentators were synonymous with a 'reigning Shandean taste'.[15]

I mentioned at the outset of this book that what presents itself in my analysis of Sterne's works might appear something like a story of incorporation. Accommodation to the challenge of imperial expansion entailed a reassessment of the legacy of the past (and its continual reinvention), and it also required an imaginative projection – sometimes beyond the familiar boundaries of the nation, forms of inherited tradition, or outside well-trodden trajectories of trade – and a corresponding formulation of a selfhood adequate to such circumstances. This was a necessary form of disorientation, the imagining of a self who could break from the 'tutelage' of the past, as in Kant's enlightenment dictum, who might nonetheless find it difficult, once set loose in the world, like the narrator of *Tristram Shandy*, 'to achieve a steady pace'.[16]A self, like the Yorick of *A Sentimental Journey* perhaps, who could ideally travel and translate at the same time, finding in the tingling of his nerve endings – the cheerful serendipity of unexpected encounters – the measure of a wider human sensorium in which all are seemingly the same under the skin. Like Swift and Defoe before him, Sterne acknowledges that the 'expatriated adventurer' wanders across the barriers set by nature (though not, now, by providence): 'nature has set up by her own unquestionable authority certain boundaries and fences to circumscribe the discontent of man . . . laying him under almost insuperable obligations to work out his ease, and to sustain his sufferings at home' (*SJ*, 13). But once oriented and extended outside his or herself, in literal or indeed phenomenological ways, that adventurer is faced with a different kind of economy, one of almost impossible communication 'out of our own sphere'.

In Yorick's sentimental optimism is a strong current of universalising thought which promises to bridge this gap. Its ethical method involves a kind of deviation, wandering off the beaten track in search of a more intimate gestics:

> I count little of the many things I see pass at broad noon day, in large and open streets.—Nature is shy, and hates to act before spectators; but in such an unobserved corner, you sometimes see a single short scene of her's worth all the sentiments of a dozen French plays compounded together—and yet they are *absolutely* fine;—and whenever I have a more brilliant affair upon my hands than common, as they suit a preacher just as well as a hero, I generally make my sermon out of 'em—and for the text—'Capadocia, Pontus and Asia, Phrygia and Pamphilia'—is as good as any one in the Bible.
> (*SJ*, 141)

The biblical text that makes sense of this natural theatre is a vision of speaking in tongues – the moment when the holy ghost translates among a community of strangers: 'how hear we every man in our own tongue, wherein we were born?'[17] It is possible to find a means of communicating beyond nature's limits, armed with uncle Toby's lesson on the saving of a fly: 'this world surely is wide enough to hold both thee and me' (*TS* 2.12.131). Here was a fantasy of communicative friendship, mutual understanding in the very acknowledgement of difference, central to the binding of the nation at home as well as in its global reach.

Yet if there is a utopian kernel to this sentimental travelling, present in the cosmopolitan vistas of European streets, eulogies to wordless friendship, or in the humanitarian equivalences that had Sterne write of his brothers and sisters burdened by the yoke of slavery, it is quickly brokered by a Christian universalism that could also 'explain' the inequity and violence of imperial experience and keep it in place. The lesson of Job, at the mercy of an inexplicable divine decisionism, offered a caution (as we saw in Chapter 4) to those tempted to rail against 'my case', like Job's wife, who recommends that he 'curse God and die'; also setting limits to a sentimental reciprocity that might seem to imply intervention rather than sympathy, the demand for justice, rather than pity. It was a 'work' that accompanied such universalising projections, in which questioning of the inequity of circumstances was tantamount to criticising the mysteries of providential law, the hidden scaffolding of humanitarian friendship. Mysteries which would be recast once more in Adam Smith's machinic aestheticising of utility, central to both *The Theory of Moral Sentiments* and *The Wealth of Nations*.

If Sterne could seem 'all Benevolence' to many, in the words of Eliza Draper,[18] it is perhaps because his work in key respects offered a vision of selfhood founded on the sympathetic management of these contradictions. 'The writings of Sterne', wrote Thomas Jefferson, 'form the best course of morality that ever was written', a 'course' that had its influence in the early years of the American Republic, whose emergence the events of the Seven Years' War had set in train.[19] In William Hill Brown's *The Power of Sympathy*, which characteristically exhibits the dramatic style and breathlessness of Sterne's sentimental writing, 'the suffrage of the virtuous and the good' is registered for women in particular as an aestheticised mode of affective experience underlined by quotation from the original: ' "Was I in a desart", says *Sterne*, "I would find wherewith in it to call forth my affections—If I could do no better, I would fasten them on some sweet myrtle, or seek some melancholy cypress to connect myself to—I would court their shade and greet them kindly for their protection—If their leaves withered, I would teach myself to mourn, and when they rejoiced, I would rejoice along with them".'[20] Such an affective pedagogy, in which the self teaches itself to discover moral connections with others, with nature, even in a 'desart', is part of the attraction of Sterne's benevolence; underwritten by a tolerance for human appetites and desires, and the owning of their prejudicial sway within the self. It is a pedagogy that shapes Sterne's Anglican humanism (and perhaps accounts for the popularity of his religious writing), which argues for making the best – passing beyond melancholy and mourning – of the way things are.

In Sterne's sermons the propensity to wander beyond established limits is permitted, and pleasurable, as in 'The House of Feasting and the House of Mourning Described':

we are travellers, and, in the most affecting sense of that idea . . . like travellers, though upon business of the last and nearest concern to us, may surely be allowed to amuse ourselves with the natural or artificial beauties of the country we are passing through, without reproach of forgetting the main errand we are sent upon; and if we can so order it, as not to be led out of the way, by the variety of prospects, edifices, and ruins which sollicit us, it would be a nonsensical piece of saint errantry to shut our eyes. (*Sermons*, 2.13)

The temptation 'to be led out of the way', framed here in aesthetic terms, is constantly present, its limits not always certain. To pursue the allegory, it takes the self beyond 'the true temperate climate fitted for us by nature, and in which every wise man would wish to live', as this Anglican vicar writes in his sermon on 'Job's expostulation with his wife': 'God knows, we are perpetually straying out of it, and by giving wings to our imaginations in the transports we dream of, from such or such a situation in life, we are carried away alternately into all the extremes of hot and cold, for which we are neither fitted by nature, or prepared by expectation, we feel them with all their violence, and with all their danger too' (*Sermons*, 15. 148–9). These were dreams about the straying nature of the imagination that cashed out in the material trajectories of empire, both in its energies and cost. For those transported, like the captain of the *Rippon*, into a 'Climate more fatal than the Enemy',[21] which had ended Sterne's father's life in an earlier campaign, there was a literal truth to these dangers. Like the testing of Robinson Crusoe, these were experiences that might lend themselves to more secularised kinds of parable. At the same time these were dreams and thrills of self-projection that could sometimes seem in their unboundedness to offer the most sublime risk to that self, the 'death' imagined in the voyage out of his *Journal*.

Daring to travel, called out beyond limits 'fitted to us by nature', the imperial self risked shipwreck. But risk it had to, not least because this was the precondition of the making of community at home as well as abroad. The opening page of Smith's *The Theory of Moral Sentiments* argued that the imagination alone could 'carry us beyond our own person' to understand the embodied experience of others.[22] This was true of relations with family members and neighbours as well as those with distant strangers inhabiting a 'world in the moon'. If the imagination was acknowledged as fundamental to the social bond, it was also notoriously difficult to 'command', sometimes 'forceably' pressganging its victim 'sometimes whither he would not' or whipping up a 'riot of the mind and senses' (*Sermons*, 2.16). Sterne's sermon on feasting and mourning suggests a certain sanguinity about the wild zone of the imagination (somewhat against the grain of the lesson from Ecclesiastes), suggesting that a man or woman might learn through 'exercise and custom' how to manage its temptations:

> no doubt, numbers of all ages escape unhurt, and get off this dangerous sea without shipwreck. Yet, are they not to be reckoned among the more fortunate adventurers?—and though one would not absolutely prohibit the attempt, or be so cynical as to condemn every one who tries it, since there are so many I suppose who cannot well do otherwise, and whose condition and situation in life unavoidably force them upon it—yet we may be allowed to describe this fair and flattering coast—we may point out the unexpected dangers of it, and warn the unwary passenger, where they lay. We may shew him what hazards his youth and inexperience will run, how little he can gain by the venture, and how much wider and better it would be [as is implied in the text] to seek occasions rather to improve his little stock of virtue than incautiously expose it to so unequal a chance, where the best he can hope is to return safe with what treasure he carried out—but where probably, he may be so unfortunate as to lose it all—be lost himself, and undone forever. (*Sermons*, 2.17)

The pedagogies at work in this passage hint at the need to manage the experience of the 'expatriated adventurer'. At their centre is a vision of accumulation that we have met before. Like Johnson's *Rasselas* the lesson is ultimately about the vanity of human desires, and while journeying is not prohibited, the hope is that the adventurer returns with his books balanced, his stock intact, his eye on more metaphysical certainties. One element in the metaphorics of empire, I've suggested, is a fantasy that the traveller maintains his integrity (and it is particularly a question of masculine identity) even when encountering change. Sterne's biblical lesson keeps faith with an 'empire of reason and religion' (*Sermons*, 2.20) that anchors such integrity in a specific economy of the self: one in which independence is concomitant with a discipline and restraint. Within these metaphorics the feminine is both feared and necessary: a sign of unbounded excess, which a man must risk; and the rescuing domestic affinities that bind him to home.

This offers more than a moral essay about the 'duty of setting bounds to our desires', as one sermon expounded (*Sermons*, 12.123). It sets out, indeed, 'the price for the universalistic liberation of the individual'.[23] It was a price exacted in the forging of new kinds of social subjectivity for new conditions: the cultural work demanded by the state imagining of empire. To be a member of a free state, we remember, was to consent to the rules of the club. Even as Sterne's 'licentious' writing continued to threaten the foundations of

Church and State in the eyes of some late-century jeremiahs,[24] he would find his place as moralist in William Godwin's *Enquiry Concerning Political Justice*, countering Montesquieu's vision that 'in a free state, every man will be his own legislator'. Godwin quotes from the 'Abuses of Conscience' sermon, embedded in *Tristram Shandy*: 'It is the office of conscience to determine, "not like an Asiatic cadi, according to the ebbs and flows of his own passions, but like a British judge, who makes no new law, but faithfully declares that law which he finds already written"'.[25] In this sermonical answer to the Shandean question – 'is a man to follow rules – or rules to follow him?' (*TS* 4.10.337) – was the internalisation of authority essential to political being.

Yet such a cultural work does not have the last word. If there is a key to the Shandean riddle, it involves the passage in his writing from the comic humour of his great novel to the ironic saturation of the later narratives, the dynamic which made his writing incomprehensible, even obscene, to many of his contemporaries. '*Humour*', argued Kant, 'means the talent for being able to put oneself at will into a certain frame of mind in which everything is estimated on lines that go quite off the beaten track (a topsy-turvy view of things) and yet on lines that follow certain principles'.[26] Kant would have agreed with Sterne (whose jokes he enjoyed) that laughter had a medicinal property; and that even if humour took a wayward path, its aim was ultimately normative – a form of bodily equilibrium summed up in the lines from *Tristram Shandy*: 'True *Shandeism*, think what you will against it, opens the heart and lungs, and like all those affections which partake of its nature, it forces the blood and other vital fluids of the body to run freely thro' its channels, and makes the wheel of life run long and chearfully round' (*TS* 4.32.401). In this cheerful physiology of accommodation was the aesthetic vindication of a form of life, actively achieved in the riding out of serpentine vicissitudes of pain and pleasure; a condition which one sermon describes as 'contented, and if not happy, at least resigned' (*Sermons*, 15. 149).

Despite the outrage of some critics, Sterne's manual of benevolence included his comic method, which was seen to provide a 'counterbalance'[27] to the existential presence of hardship, that seemingly universal condition ('without distinction of climate, country or religion' (*Sermons*, 3.28)) – measured in poverty, war, death, illness, disappointment – lived out in ordinary, local time, one that is brought into a certain geopolitical relief during the Seven Years' War and its aftermath. As *Tristram Shandy*'s dedication to William Pitt, architect of the war, suggested, he hoped 'to fence against the infirmities of ill health, and other evils of life, by mirth', a laughter that had ambitions beyond the life of the 'poor Wight of a Dedicator' to the health of the body politic itself. Yet if 'True Shandeism' offers the vision of a healthy equilibrium of self and world, an ideal plenitude (like that of true friendship) where nothing, ultimately, is lost or exchanged, it also threatens to collapse at every turn. In the Author's Preface, that plenitude is revealed as a masturbatory wish-fulfilment, or as a dialectic of wit and judgement which operates under conditions of scarcity: 'one would wonder how it holds out, or could be sufficient for the wants and emergencies of so many great states, and populous empires' (*TS* 3.20.230). Elsewhere the calculus is brutal. Like the '*Mortgager* and the *Mortgageé*', 'the *Jester* and the *Jesteé*' are caught in a transaction whose obligations they had better come to understand (*TS* 1.12.30).

'L—d! said my mother, what is all this story about?——' (*TS* 9.33.809). How then to 'read, read, read, read' (*TS* 3.36.268) the play of Sterne's writing, its ironic negotiation of the 'wants and emergencies' of the age? What of the difficulty of deciphering it, the *non-knowledge* registered by Thomas Turner's hyphen? In the nonsense of Sterne's writing, whether in the cock-and-bull reduction of the end of *Tristram Shandy*, or the sexual treaty-breaking of the last page of *A Sentimental Journey*, we are brought up against its method, if not its meaning. These are dynamics which seemingly come to nothing, offering a diminution in tension, like the wry deflation in waiting for a punchline that never arrives. Jest, like music, offers a play of 'aesthetic ideas, or even . . . representations of the understanding, by which, all said and done, nothing is thought', writes Kant in his *Critique of Judgement*. 'The understanding, missing what it expected, suddenly lets go its hold, with the result that the effect of this slackening is felt in the body by the oscillation of the organs'. Such health-producing 'oscillation' continues to resonate; its absurdity raises 'a hearty, convulsive laugh'.[28]

Kant illustrates the working of nonsense with a famous joke, set in Eliza Draper's Surat. There's an Indian man at an Englishman's table who watches a bottle of beer being opened, and all the beer frothing out. 'The repeated exclamations of the Indian showed his great astonishment. "Well, what is so wonderful in that?" asked the Englishman. "Oh, I'm not surprised myself", said the Indian, "at its getting out, but at how you ever managed to get it all in".' For Kant, this story produces laughter not because it assumes a witty superiority over the 'ignorant Indian', nor because it reveals any further understanding in the exchange that we might enjoy, but because 'the bubble of our expectation was extended to the full and suddenly went off into nothing'.[29]

The story from Surat is not a particularly funny one to modern ears, drawing as it does on that racist repository of stereotypes which were often called in to explain cultural difference along genetic lines. Like John Locke's King of Siam who refuses to believe that ice can exist, Kant's Indian is not to know about the manufacture of beer, the Englishman's national tipple – and there is something posited as naïve and childlike about such 'ignorance' despite its empirical explanation – but whereas experience and probability excuse the King, in Kant's joke they are apparently beside the point. It is difficult to name what the laughter marks except the performance of a moment of misrecognition, the nonsensical reversal of froth in space and time. How would you put froth in a bottle? Perhaps the Indian had, in the fundamental absurdity of his question, a point to make. Yet as with most jokes killed by explanation, conjecture is superfluous. The joke does not provide material for reflection, in Kant's way of telling it, it is what it does. The frothing release of beer anticipates the release of expectation, and thus what Kant describes as the physical slackening at work in the organs of a laughing body: like froth, like nonsense, it all comes pleasurably to nothing.

What might it *mean* however to imagine this encounter, in an imperial space, as productive of a 'free and absolute nothing', as Winfried Menninghaus describes, a nothing, moreover, that 'continues to resonate in itself'? [30] It carries something of a wish-fulfilment, the vision of an encounter in which nothing is thought, nothing transformed: a fantasy of empire without repercussions, from Surat to Boston to 'the world in the moon'. With absurdity comes the release of tension. It may be, wrote Friedrich Schlegel on irony, that 'the salvation of families and nations rests' upon such non-knowledge: 'it would fare badly with you if, as you demand, the whole world were ever to become wholly comprehensible in earnest'.[31] This is Yorick's lesson in *Tristram Shandy*, punished for exposing the truth as he finds it; it is also the disturbance resonating in Sterne's ironies, in which the implication of such a journey – its fascination with encounter and its necessary misrecognitions – may rebound, like the plangent seriousness of a last laugh, on you.

The nonsensical gesture of the cock-and-bull tale, in which meaning vanishes, its writerly expenditure turning out to be 'about' no more than the frothy pretensions of its performance, might seem to confirm the suspicions of those who would want to resist such a strong reading of Sterne's mercurial ironies; or to see style as the man, no more extending beyond his tawdry predilections, as Elizabeth Carter opined, 'than a fit of the gout'.[32] But it is a gesture in the 1760s that has meaning in itself, precisely because of such a self-projection and reduction, meanings generated in the movement from the literal to the metaphorical, from jest to seriousness and back again. As Karl Marx will later put it in Shandean terms, in his struggle with the Prussian censor, 'I treat the ludicrous seriously when I treat it ludicrously, and the most serious immodesty of the mind is to be modest in the face of immodesty'.[33] If laughter is normative, or read as a sign of ignorance, like that of Adam Smith's laughing artizans, who unlike the philosopher of trade cannot understand the wondrous lunacy of the universal machine they serve,[34] in Shandean form it mocks the pretensions of universalising thought, pretensions that have a human cost.

In the final pages of *Tristram Shandy* the story of the cock and the bull emerges from an exchange about the making and unmaking of a man, the euphemistic, sexualised flows of language connecting procreation and the 'killing and destroying' made glorious in battle. It picks up perhaps on Christopher Smart's poem at the outset of the Seven Years' War, in which the Cock and the Bull are disaffected veterans of the battlefield and the home front, put out to market, waiting for justice to recoil on their human masters who have not valued their sacrifice:

> Yes – we excel in arts and arms,
> In learning's lore, and beauty's charms;
> The sea's wide empire we engross,
> All nations hail the British cross;
> The land of liberty we tread,
> And woe to his devoted head,
> Who dares the contrary advance,
> One Englishman's worth ten of France.
> These, these are truths what man won't write for,
> Won't swear, won't bully, and won't fight for?
> Yet (tho' perhaps I speak thro' vanity)
> Would we'd a little more humanity?
> Too far, I fear, I've drove the jest,
> So leave to Cock and Bull the rest.[35]

In Sternean wit – and in the irony that increasingly marks his writing – is an exposure, and a weighing of the cost, of being birthed into this cultural work of love and death. And a glimpse too of what it began to mean for others to negotiate – and refuse – the price exacted for the self's 'liberation' in the imperial calculus of the 1760s. A deeper, unconditional gravity at the heart of Shandean wit, played out in its 'lesson to the world, "*to let people tell their stories their own way*" '(TS 9.25.785).

## Notes

1   *A Prospective Plan of the Battle fought near Lake George on 8th September 1755, between 200 English with 250 Mohawks under the Command of General Johnson and 2500 French and Indians under the Command of General Dieskau in which the English were Victorious, Captivating the French General with a Number of his Men, Killing 700 and Putting the Rest to Flight*, dr. Samuel Blodget, engr. Thomas Johnston (Boston, 1755). Courtesy of the Massachusetts Historical Society.

2   'View of the Forts on the Hills of Veloor As Seen From the Pettah', in Orme, II, 602–3. Permission British Library 1572/942.

3 William Hogarth, *The Analysis of Beauty* (Menston Yorks: The Scholar Press, 1973), p. 25.

4 Ibid. p. 38.

5 One animated, as Frédéric Ogée has written, by 'suggestiveness (a combination of actual and imaginary discovery) and potentiality (a combination of progress and suspension)'. See his 'The Flesh of Theory: The Erotics of Hogarth's Lines' in Bernadette Fort and Angela Rosenthal (eds), *The Other Hogarth: Aesthetics of Difference* (Princeton and Oxford: Princeton University Press, 2001), p. 64.

6 Hogarth, *The Analysis of Beauty*, pp. 24–5.

7 A review of a French account of the then most recent volumes of *Tristram Shandy*, *London Chronicle* (16 April 1765), p. 373.

8 Peter Conrad, *Shandyism: The Character of Romantic Irony* (Oxford: Blackwell, 1978), p. 102.

9 Friedrich Schlegel, 'On Incomprehensibility', in *Friedrich Schlegel's Lucinde and the Fragments*, trans. Peter Firchow (Minneapolis: University of Minnesota Press, 1971), p. 265.

10 Balibar, 'Ambiguous Universality', p. 162.

11 Burke, *A Philosophical Enquiry*, p. 17.

12 Goldsmith, Letter XVII, *The Citizen of the World*, p. 75.

13 Grainger, p. 22, ll.267–70. The 'order' Grainger is imagining is a military one, for his poem continues with a vision of the art which transforms the frontier into a 'tented field' where 'Brigade and Squadron, whiten on the sight; and fill spectators with an awful joy' (p. 23)

14 There are two notions of autonomy at work here: the understanding of art's autonomy as a 'form of life', in which collective life is posited as self-sufficient and untouched by a cultural modernity dividing art, life and politics into separate spheres, and a notion of autonomy marked by that division. My thinking is informed by Jacques Rancière's 'The Aesthetic Revolution and its Outcomes: Emplotments of Autonomy and Heteronomy', *NLR* 14 (2002), 133–51.

15 Philanthropos, p. 27.

16 Immanuel Kant, 'An Answer to the Question: What is Enlightenment?', in D. Simpson (ed.), *German Aesthetic and Literary Criticism: Kant, Fichte, Schelling, Schopenhauer, Hegel* (Cambridge: Cambridge University Press, 1984), p. 30.

17 Acts 2: 8. The reference made in Sterne's passage is to 2:9–10.

18 Eliza Draper to Thomas Limbrey Sclater, 10 April 1769, in Wright and Sclater, p. 86

19 Thomas Jefferson to Peter Carr, 10 August 1787, in *Writings*, p. 902.

20 William Hill Brown, *The Power of Sympathy* (1789) collected with Hannah Webster Foster, *The Coquette*, ed. Carla Mulford (Harmondsworth: Penguin

Books, 1996), pp. 15–16. The quotation is from *SJ* 51 and its context – on the richness of life's experiences offered 'him who interests his heart in everything' – is a swipe at Smollett's disgruntled travel writing.

21  Gardiner, *An Account of the Expedition to the West Indies*, p. 73.

22  'Though our brother is upon the rack, as long as we ourselves are at our ease, our senses will never inform us of what he suffers. They never did, and never can, carry us beyond our own person, and it is by the imagination only that we can form any conception of what are his sensations'. Smith, *Theory of Moral Sentiments*, p. 9. This is a scenario dramatised in Corporal Trim's reading of the 'Abuses of Conscience' sermon in *Tristram Shandy*, when he responds to a story about the Inquisition as if his own brother is on the rack.

23  Balibar, 'Ambiguous Universality', p. 162.

24  See D.Whyte, *The Fallacy of French Freedom and the Dangerous Tendency of Sterne's Writings, Or An Essay Shewing that Irreligion and Immorality Pave the Way for Tyranny, and Anarchy: and that Sterne's Writings are both Irreligious and Immoral: Concluding with Some Observations on the Present State of France* (London: np, 1799).

25  Godwin, *Enquiry Concerning Political Justice*, p. 236.

26  Kant, *Critique of Judgement*, p. 203.

27  The mechanistic metaphor of the 'counterbalance' (linking back to the clockwork analogy for the universe) surfaces in *TS* 4.8.334. It is suggested in Kant's compensatory notion of laughter in the third *Critique*: 'Voltaire said that heaven has given us two things to compensate us for the many miseries in life, *hope* and *sleep*. He might have added *laughter* to the list – if only the means of exciting it in men of intelligence were as ready to hand, and the wit or originality of humour which it requires were not just as rare as the talent is common for inventing stuff *that splits the head*, as mystical speculators do, or *that breaks your neck*, as the genius does, or that *harrows the heart* as sentimental novelists do (aye, and moralists of the same type)'. Kant, *Critique of Judgement*, pp. 201–2. Notably philosophical, aesthetic and moral writings bring about their own catastrophe, something that Kant discussed in the 1760s, and Sterne dramatised with comic effect.

28  Kant, *Critique of Judgement*, pp. 198, 199.

29  Ibid. pp. 199–200.

30  Winfried Menninghaus, *In Praise of Nonsense: Kant and Bluebeard*, trans. Henry Pickford (Stanford, CA: Stanford University Press, 1999), pp. 24, 25.

31  Schlegel, 'On Incomprehensibility', p. 268.

32  Carter to Vesey, 19 April 1768, p. 167. 'Froth' was exactly how Samuel Johnson regarded Sterne's sermons, as Ross reports, p. 329.

33  Karl Marx, 'Comments on the Latest Prussian Censorship Instruction', in Karl Marx and Friedrich Engels, *Collected Works* (London: Lawrence and Wishart, 1975), I, 113. This quotation follows a direct reference to *Tristram Shandy*, which had been the model for Marx's early attempt at writing a comic novel.

34 For discussion of the 'laughing artizan' see the chapter on Smith in Wendy Motooka, *The Age of Reasons: Quixotism, Sentimentalism and Political Economy in Eighteenth-Century Britain* (London and New York: Routledge, 1998), pp. 198–230.

35 Christopher Smart, 'A Story of a Cock and a Bull', in *Selected Poems*, ed. Karina Williamson and Marcus Walsh (Harmondsworth: Penguin Books, 1990), p. 14, ll. 1–14. The poem was first printed at the outset of war in the *Literary Magazine* (May/June, 1756). See on this connection with Smart, Mark Loveridge, 'Stories of COCKS and BULLS: The Ending of *Tristram Shandy*', *Eighteenth-Century Fiction*, 5 (1992), 35–54. The Seven Years' War also weaves through Smart's extraordinary *Jubilate Agno*, written during his incarceration in an insane asylum between 1758 and 1763.

# BIBLIOGRAPHY

Adorno, Theodor, 'Culture and Administration', in his *The Culture Industry: Selected Essays on Mass Culture*, ed. Jay Bernstein, trans. Wes Blomster (London: Routledge, 1991), pp. 93–113.

Al Dahnak, Jumana, 'Women's Conceptualisation of Selfhood in Relation to Marriage: A Study of Selected Fiction by Women Writers of the 1770s' (Unpublished Ph.D. Thesis, University of Leeds, 2002).

Alexander, David, *Affecting Moments: Prints of English Literature Made in the Age of Romantic Sensibility 1775–1800* (York: University of York, 1993).

Alexander, William, *The History of Women, from the Earliest Antiquity to the Present Time, Giving Some Account of almost every interesting Particular concerning that Sex, among all Nations, ancient and modern*, 2 vols (London: W. Straham, T. Cadell, 1779).

Allen, Brian, *Francis Hayman* (New Haven and London: Yale University Press, 1987).

Alliez, Éric, *Capital Times: Tales from the Critique of Time* (Minneapolis: University of Minnesota Press, 1996).

Althusser, Louis, and Étienne Balibar, *Reading Capital*, trans. Ben Brewster (London: Verso, 1979).

Anderson, Benedict, *Imagined Communities: Reflections on the Origin and Spread of Nationalism* (London: Verso, 1991).

Anderson, Fred, *Crucible of War: The Seven Years' War and the Fate of Empire in British North America 1754–1766* (London: Faber and Faber, 2000).

Andrew, Donna T., 'Popular Culture and Public Debate: London, 1780', *The Historical Journal* 39:2 (1996), 405–23.

Anon., *An Address to the Proprietors of East India Stock, Showing from the Political State of Indostan the Necessity of Sending Commissioners to Regulate Their Affairs Abroad* (London: np, 1769).

Anon., 'The Birth of Shandy; *A new* Ballad', *The Imperial Magazine, or, Complete Monthly Intelligencer* (October 1760), 551.

Anon., *Characterism, or the Modern Age display'd: being an Attempt to expose the Pretended Virtues of both Sexes; with a Poetical Essay on each Character* (London: printed for the Author, 1750).

Anon., *The Clockmakers' Outcry Against the Author of the Life and Opinions of* Tristram Shandy. *Dedicated to the Most Humble of Christian Prelates* (London: J. Burd, 1760).

Anon., *A Description Of Vauxhall-Gardens Being A Proper Companion and Guide for All Who Visit That Place* (London: S. Hooper, 1762).

Anon., *England's Constitutional Test for the Year 1763* (London: J. Morgan, 1763).

Anon., *An Essay on Woman. A Poem*, by J. W. Senator (London: printed for the Editor, 1763).

Anon., *An Essay on Woman*, by Pego Borewell, Esq. (London: printed for the Author, 1763).

Anon., *Explanatory Remarks Upon the Life and Opinions of Tristram Shandy, Wherein the Morals and Politics of this Piece are clearly laid open*, by Jeremiah Kunastrokius MD (London: E. Cabe, 1760).

Anon., *The Invasion, A Farce* (London: L. Davis and C. Reymers, 1759).

Anon., *A Letter on the Nature and State of Curiosity* (London: J. Roberts, 1736).

Anon., *A Letter to the Right Honorable The Earl of B\*\*\* on a Late Important Resignation, and its Probable Consequences* (London: J. Coote, 1761).

Anon., *The Letters of Maria; to which is added, An Account of her Death* (London: G. Kearsley, 1790).

Anon., *Lettres d'Yorick à Eliza, et d'Eliza à Yorick, traduits de l'anglois de Mr Sterne, augmentée de l'éloge d'Eliza par Mr L'Abbé Raynal* (Lausanne: Mourer, 1786).

Anon., *The Life and Memoirs of Mr Ephraim Tristram Bates, Commonly Called Corporal Bates, A Broken-hearted Soldier* (London: Malachi \*\*\*\*, for Edith Bates, Relict of the aforesaid Mr Bates, and sold by W. Owen, 1756).

Anon., *Maria; Or a Shandean Journey of a Young Lady During the Summer of 1822*, by Uncle Oddy (London: John Hatchard, 1823).

Anon., *Maria; Or, the Vicarage. A Novel in Two Volumes*, 2 vols (London: Hookham and Carpenter, 1796).

Anon., 'Maria's Urn' (London: H. Wright, ca.1790).

Anon., *Memoirs of Maria, A Persian Slave* (London: np, 1790).

Anon., *The Nabob: Or, Asiatic Plunderers. A Satyrical Poem; in a Dialogue between a Friend and the Author* (London: printed for the Author, 1773).

Anon., [Robert Dodsley?] *The Oeconomy of Human Life. In Two Parts. Translated from an Indian Manuscript, Written by an Ancient Bramin* (London: np, 1768).

Anon., *Sterne's Maria; A Pathetic Story with an Account of her Death at the Castle of Valesine* (London: R. Rusted, ca. 1800).

Anon., *The Ten Plagues of Great Britain of Worse Consequences than those of Egypt, Described Under the Following Heads: I. Disregard to our own Productions II. Luxury and Waste in Great Families III. Effeminacy IV. Gaming V. Love of Novelty VI. Hypocrisy VII. Drunkenness VIII. Avarice and Usury IX. Pride X. Idleness. The Whole intended to show, That Whatever Crimes or Foibles infect the Minds of a People, are far more injurious to a Nation than bodily Plagues. By a Well-wisher to Great-Britain* (London: R. Withy, 1757).

Anon., *Two Dialogues on the Man-Trade* (London: J. Waugh, 1760).

Anon., *The Vocal Miscellany: A Collection of above Four Hundred celebrated Songs; Many of which were Never before Printed with The Names of the Tunes prefixed to each Song, Volume Second and Last* (London: A. Bettesworth and C. Hitch et al., 1738).

Arrighi, Giovanni, *The Long Twentieth Century: Money, Power, and the Origins of Our Times* (London: Verso, 1994).

Baillie, John, *An Essay on the Sublime* (London: R. Dodsley, 1747).

Baird, Theodore, 'The Time Scheme in *Tristram Shandy* and a Source', *PMLA* 51 (1936), 803–20.

Bakhtin, Mikhail, *The Dialogic Imagination*, ed. Michael Holquist, trans. Caryl Emerson and Michael Holquist (Austin, TX: University of Texas Press, 1981).

Balibar, Étienne, 'Ambiguous Universality', in his *Politics and the Other Scene* (London and New York: Verso Books, 2002), pp. 56–74.

—— 'Citizen Subject', in Eduardo Cadava, Peter Connor and Jean-Luc Nancy (eds), *Who Comes After the Subject?* (London and New York: Routledge, 1991), pp. 33–57.

Barrell, John, *The Dark Side of the Landscape: The Rural Poor in English Painting 1730–1840* (Cambridge: Cambridge University Press, 1980).

—— *English Literature in History 1730–80: An Equal Wide Survey* (London: Hutchinson, 1983).

—— 'Sir Joshua Reynolds and the Englishness of English Art', in Homi K. Bhabha (ed.), *Nation and Narration* (London: Routledge, 1990), pp. 154–76.

Barthes, Roland, *A Lover's Discourse. Fragments*, trans. Richard Howard (New York: Hill and Wang, 1979).

Bayle, Pierre, *The Dictionary Historical and Critical of Mr. Peter Bayle*, trans. P. Desmaizeaux, 2nd edn (5 vols, 1734; reprinted New York and London: Garland, 1984).

Bentham, Jeremy, 'A Table of the Springs of Action', in J. Bowring (ed.), *The Works of Jeremy Bentham*, 11 vols (Edinburgh: W. Tait, 1843), II.

Berg, Maxine, 'Women's Work, Mechanization and the Early Phases of Industrialization in England', in R. E. Pahl (ed.), *On Work: Historical, Comparative and Theoretical Approaches* (Oxford: Basil Blackwell, 1988), pp. 61–94.

[Berkeley, George Monk], *Maria; Or the Generous Rustic* (London: T. Cadell; Edinburgh: C. Elliot, 1784).

Bhabha, Homi, 'DissemiNation: time, narrative, and the margins of the modern nation', in Homi K. Bhabha (ed.), *Nation and Narration* (London and New York: Routledge, 1990), pp. 291–322.

Billington, Thomas, 'Maria's Evening Service to the Virgin' (London: printed for the Author, 1786).

Blackburn, Robin, *The Overthrow of Colonial Slavery 1776–1848* (London: Verso, 1988).

Blackstone, William, *Commentaries on the Laws of England*, 4 vols (Oxford: Clarendon Press, 1765–9).

Blower, Elizabeth, *Maria: A Novel in Two Volumes, by the Author of George Bateman*, 2 vols (London: T. Cadell, 1785).

Boltanski, Luc, *Distant Suffering: Morality, Media and Politics* (Cambridge: Cambridge University Press, 1999).

Bolts, William, *Considerations on India Affairs; Particularly Respecting the Present State of Bengal and its Dependencies*, 3 vols (London: J. Almon et al., 1772).

Bond, Donald F. (ed.), *The Spectator*, 5 vols (Oxford: Clarendon Press, 1965).

Boswell, James, *Life of Samuel Johnson* (London: Everyman, 1992).

Bowen, H. V., *Revenue and Reform: the Indian Problem in British Politics 1757–1773* (Cambridge: Cambridge University Press, 1991).

Brewer, John, Neil McKendrick and J. H. Plumb, *The Birth of a Consumer Society: The Commercialization of Eighteenth-Century England* (London: Europa, 1982).

Brewer, John, 'The Eighteenth-Century British State: Contexts and Issues', in Lawrence Stone (ed.), *An Imperial State at War: Britain from 1689 to 1815* (London and New York: Routledge, 1994), pp. 52–71.

—— *Party Ideology and Popular Politics at the Accession of George III* (Cambridge: Cambridge University Press, 1976).

—— *The Sinews of Power: War, Money and the English State* (London: Unwin Hyman, 1989).

Brooke, Frances, *The History of Emily Montague* (Toronto: McClelland and Stewart, 1983).

Brooke, Henry, *The Fool of Quality* (London: George Routledge, 1906).

Brooks, Peter, 'Melodrama Body Revolution', in Jacky Bratton, Jim Cook and Christine Gledhill (eds), *Melodrama: Stage Picture Screen* (London: British Film Institute, 1994), pp. 11–24.

Brown, John, *An Estimate of the Manners and Principles of the Times* (London: L. Davis and C. Reymers, 1757).

—— *An Explanatory Defence of the Estimate* (London: L. Davis and C. Reymers, 1758).

—— *On the Female Character and Education: A Sermon Preached on Thursday the 16th of May, 1765, at the Anniversary Meeting of the Guardians of the Asylum for Deserted Female Orphans* (London: L. Davis and C. Reymers, 1765).

Brown, William Hill, *The Power of Sympathy*, with Hannah Webster Foster, *The Coquette*, ed. Carla Mulford (Harmondsworth: Penguin Books, 1996).

Buchanan, James, *The British Grammar: Or, an Essay in Four Parts towards Speaking and Writing the English Language Grammatically and Inditing Elegantly for the Use of the Schools of Great Britain and Ireland, and of Private Young Gentlemen and Ladies* (London: A. Millar, 1762).

[Burke, Edmund], 'History of the War', *Annual Register* 1(1758), pp. v–77.

—— *A Philosophical Enquiry into the Origin of our Ideas of the Sublime and the Beautiful*, ed. Adam Phillips (Oxford: Oxford University Press, 1990).

—— *The Writings and Speeches of Edmund Burke, Volume II: Party, Parliament, and the American Crisis 1766–1774*, ed. Paul Langford (Oxford: Clarendon Press, 1981).

Butler, Judith, *Bodies That Matter: On the Discursive Limits of 'Sex'* (New York and London: Routledge, 1993).

Cambridge, Richard Owen, *An Account of the War in India, Between the English and French, on the Coast of Coromandel, from the year 1750 to the Year 1760* (London: T. Jeffreys, 1761).

Cash, Arthur H., 'The Birth of Tristram Shandy: Sterne and Dr Burton', in Paul-Gabriel Boucé (ed.), *Sexuality in Eighteenth-Century Britain* (Manchester: Manchester University Press, 1982), pp. 198–224.

—— *Laurence Sterne: the Later Years* (London and New York: Methuen, 1986).

'Cato', *Thoughts on a Question of Importance Proposed to the Public, whether is it probable that the Immense Extent of Territory acquired by this Nation at the late Peace, will operate towards the Prosperity or the Ruin of the Island of Great Britain?* (London: J. Dixwell, 1765).

Chakrabarty, Dipesh, *Provincializing Europe: Postcolonial Thought and Historical Difference* (Princeton and Oxford: Princeton University Press, 2000).

Chatterjee, Amal, *Representations of India, 1740–1840: The Creation of India in the Colonial Imagination* (London: Macmillan, 1998).

Cheah, Pheng, and Bruce Robbins (eds), *Cosmopolitics: Thinking and Feeling beyond the Nation* (Minneapolis and London: University of Minnesota Press, 1998).

Cheah, Pheng, *Spectral Nationality: Passages of Freedom from Kant to Postcolonial Literatures of Liberation* (New York: Columbia University Press, 2003).

Churchill, Charles, *Gotham: A Poem Book I* (London: Printed for the Author, 1764).

—— *The Prophecy Of Famine. A Scots Pastoral* (London: Printed for the Author, 1763).

—— *The Times, A Poem* (London: Printed for the Author, 1764).

Clark, Anna, 'The Chevalier d'Eon and Wilkes: Masculinity and Politics in the Eighteenth Century', *Eighteenth-Century Studies* 32 (1998), pp. 19–48.

Clark, Ewan, *Miscellaneous Poems* (Whitehaven: J. Ware, 1779).

Clark, J. C. D., *The Dynamics of Change: the Crisis of the 1750s and English Party Systems* (Cambridge: Cambridge University Press, 1982).

Clarkson, Thomas, *An Essay on the Slavery and Commerce of the Human Species Particularly the African, Translated from a Latin Dissertation which was Honoured with the First Prize in the University of Cambridge for the Year 1785* (London: J. Phillips, 1786).

Clayton, John, *Friendly Advice to the Poor, Written and Publish'd At the Request of the late and present Officers of the Town of Manchester* (Manchester: J. Harrop, 1755).

Cohen, Murray, *Sensible Words: Linguistic Practice in England 1640–1785* (Baltimore: Johns Hopkins University Press, 1977).

Colley, Linda, *Captives: Britain, Empire and the World 1600–1850* (London: Jonathan Cape, 2002).

Collier, Mary, *Poems on Several Occasions by Mary Collier, Author of the Washerwoman's Labour, with some Remarks on her Life* (Winchester: Mary Ayres for the Author, 1762).

Conrad, Peter, *Shandyism: The Character of Romantic Irony* (Oxford: Blackwell, 1978).

Cooper, Anthony Ashley, Lord Shaftesbury, 'Sensus Communis: An Essay on the Freedom of Wit and Humour in a Letter to a Friend' (1709), in *Characteristicks of Men, Manners, Opinions, Times*, ed. Philip Ayres, 2 vols (Oxford: Clarendon Press, 1999).

Corrigan, Philip and Derek Sayer, *The Great Arch: English State Formation as Cultural Revolution* (Oxford: Basil Blackwell, 1985).

Daly, James, *Sir Robert Filmer and English Political Thought* (Toronto and Buffalo: University of Toronto Press, 1979).

Davenant, Charles, *The Political and Commercial Works of that Celebrated Writer Charles D'avenant LLD, Relating to the Trade and Revenue of England, the Plantation Trade, the East-India Trade, and African Trade, collected and revised by Sir Charles Whitworth*, 5 vols (London: printed for R. Horsfield et al., 1771).

Dayan, Joan, 'Legal Slaves and Civil Bodies', *Nepantla: Views from South* 2:1(2001), 3–39.

De Bolla, Peter, *The Discourse of the Sublime: Readings in History, Aesthetics and the Subject* (Oxford: Blackwell, 1989).

Defoe, Daniel, *The Consolidator: Or, Memoirs of Sundry Transactions from the World in the Moon. Translated from the Lunar Language. By the Author of the True-Born English Man* (London: Benjamin Bragg, 1705).

—— *An Essay at Removing National Prejudices Against a Union with Scotland, Part III* (1706: no place nor publisher).

—— *The History and Remarkable Life of the Truly Honourable Col. Jacque, Commonly Call'd Col. Jack*, 2nd edn (London: J. Brotherton et al., 1723).

Derrida, Jacques, *The Politics of Friendship*, trans. George Collins (London and New York: Verso Books, 1997).

D'Oench, Ellen, 'Prodigal Sons and Fair Penitents: Transformations in Eighteenth-Century Popular Prints', *Art History* 13: 3 (1990), 318–43.

Dollimore, Jonathan, *Sexual Dissidence: Augustine to Wilde, Freud to Foucault* (Oxford: Clarendon Press, 1991).

Dow, Alexander, *The History of Hindostan; From the Earliest Account of Time, to the Death of Akbar; translated from the Persian of Mahummud Casim Ferisha of Delhi*, 2 vols (London: T. Becket and P. A. De Hondt, 1768).

—— *The History of Hindostan, from the Death of Akbar, to the Complete Settlement of the Empire Under Aurungzebe. To Which are Prefixed: 1. A Dissertation on the Origina and Nature of Despotism in Hindostan. 2. An Enquiry into the State of Bengal; with a Plan for Restoring that Kingdom to its Former Prosperity and Splendor* (London: T. Becket and P. A. De Hondt, 1772).

Dunkin, Reverend Mr, *The Bramin: An Eclogue, To Edmund Nugent Esq.* (London: R. Baldwyn, 1751).

During, Simon, 'Transports of the Imagination: Some Relations between Globalization and Literature', *ARENA journal* 20 (2002–3), 123–39.

Dwyer, John, 'The Civic World of Adam Smith', in Peter Jones and Andrew S. Skinner (eds), *Adam Smith Reviewed* (Edinburgh: Edinburgh University Press, 1992), pp. 190–213.

Dyer, John, *The Fleece: A Poem in Four Books* (London: R. and J. Dodsley, 1757).

Eagleton, Terry, 'The Good-Natured Gael', in his *Crazy John and the Bishop and other Essays on Irish Culture* (Cork: Cork University Press/Field Day, 1998), pp. 68–139.

Egerton, Judy, *Wright of Derby* (London: Tate Gallery, 1990).

Eisenstein, Sergei, 'Dickens, Griffith and the Film Today', in his *Film Form: Essays in Film Theory*, ed. and trans. Jay Leyda (London: Dennis Dobson, 1951), pp. 195–255.

Eliot, George, *Middlemarch* (Harmondsworth: Penguin Books, 1965).

Ellis, Markman, 'Being Sterne with Maria' (unpublished paper).

—— *The History of Gothic Fiction* (Edinburgh: Edinburgh University Press, 2000).

—— *The Politics of Sensibility: Race, Gender and Commerce in the Sentimental Novel* (Cambridge: Cambridge University Press, 1996).

Escott, Angela, 'Generic Diversity in the Plays Of Hannah Cowley' (unpublished PhD thesis, University of London, 2005).

Ferguson, Adam, *An Essay on the History of Civil Society* (Edinburgh: A. Kincaid and J. Bell; London: A. Millar and T. Caddel, 1767).

Ferguson, Frances, 'The Sublime of Edmund Burke, or the Bathos of Experience', *Glyph* 8 (1981), 62–78.

Ferguson, Moira, *Subject to Others: British Women Writers and Colonial Slavery, 1670–1834* (New York and London: Routledge, 1992).

Filmer, Sir Robert, *Patriarcha and Other Political Works*, ed. Peter Laslett (Oxford: Blackwell, 1979).

Flavell, Julie M., 'The "School for Modesty and Humility": Colonial American Youth in London and Their Parents, 1755–1775', *The Historical Journal* 42:2 (1999), 377–404.

Fleetwood, W., *The Relative Duties Of Parents and Children, Husbands and Wives, and Masters and Servants, Consider'd in Sixteen Sermons* (London: Charles Harper, 1705.

Foote, Samuel, *The Nabob; A Comedy in Three Acts* (London: T. Cadell, 1778).

Fort, Bernadette, and Angela Rosenthal (eds), *The Other Hogarth: Aesthetics of Difference* (Princeton and Oxford: Princeton University Press, 2001).

Foucault, Michel, 'Governmentality', in G. Burchell, C. Gordon, and P. Miller (eds), *The Foucault Effect: Studies in Governmentality* (London: Harvester Wheatsheaf, 1991), pp. 87–104.

—— 'The Political Technology of Individuals', in Luther H. Martin, Huck Gutman, Patrick H. Hutton (eds), *Technologies of the Self: A Seminar with Michel Foucault* (London: Tavistock Press, 1988), pp. 145–62.

Furniss, Tom, *Edmund Burke's Aesthetic Ideology: Language, Gender and Political Economy in Revolution* (Cambridge: Cambridge University Press, 1993).

Gardiner, Richard, *An Account of the Expedition to the West Indies, Against Martinico, Guadelupe, and other the Leeward Islands; Subject to the French King, 1759* (London: Zech Stuart, 1760).

Garrick, David, *Harlequin's Invasion; or, A Christmas Gambol* (1759), in *The Plays of David Garrick*, ed. by Harry William Pedicord and Frederick Louis Bergmann (Carbondale and Edwardsville: Southern Illinois University Press, 1980), I, 199–225.

George, M. Dorothy, *London Life in the Eighteenth Century* (Harmondsworth: Penguin (Peregrine) Books, 1966).

Gilmore, Ian, *Riot, Risings and Revolution: Governance and Violence in Eighteenth-Century England* (London: Pimlico, 1993).

Godwin, William, *Enquiry Concerning Political Justice and Its Influence on Modern Morals and Happiness*, ed. Isaac Kramnick (Harmondsworth: Penguin Books, 1985).

Goldsmith, Oliver, *The Citizen of the World*, in Arthur Friedman (ed.), *Collected Works of Oliver Goldsmith* (Oxford: Clarendon, 1966), II.

—— 'The Deserted Village', in Arthur Friedman (ed.), *The Collected Works of Oliver Goldsmith* (Oxford: Clarendon Press, 1966), IV, 287–304.

—— 'On Public Rejoicings for Victory', in Arthur Friedman (ed.), *Collected Works of Oliver Goldsmith* (Oxford: Clarendon Press, 1966), III, 16–21.

—— 'The Revolution in Low Life', in Arthur Friedman (ed.), *The Collected Works of Oliver Goldsmith* (Oxford: Clarendon Press, 1966), III, 195–8.

—— 'Threnodia Augustalis', in Arthur Friedman (ed.), *The Collected Works of Oliver Goldsmith* (Oxford: Clarendon Press, 1966), IV, 326–40.

—— 'The Traveller; Or a Prospect of Society', in Arthur Friedman (ed.), *The Collected Works of Oliver Goldsmith* (Oxford: Clarendon Press, 1966), IV, 248–69.

—— *The Vicar of Wakefield*, in Arthur Friedman (ed.), *The Collected Works of Oliver Goldsmith* (Oxford: Clarendon Press, 1966), IV, 13–184.

Gordon, Catherine M., *British Paintings of Subjects from the English Novel 1740–1870* (New York and London: Garland, 1988).

Gough, James, *A Practical Grammar of the English Tongue* (Dublin: Isaac Jackson, 1754).

Grainger, James, *The Sugar-Cane. A Poem in Four Books* (London: R. & J. Dodsley, 1764).

[Griffith, Richard], Biographer Triglyph, *The Triumvirate: or, the Authentic Memoirs of A (ndrews) B (eville) and C(arewe)*, 2 vols (London: W. Johnston, 1764).

Griffith, Richard and Elizabeth Griffith, *A Series of Genuine Letters Between Henry and Frances*, 6 vols (London: J. Bew, 1786).

Griffiths, Ralph, 'An Account of the Rev. Mr St****, and his Writings', *Grand Magazine* 3 (June 1760), 311.

Grosley, Pierre, *Londres* (Neuchatel: Aux dépends de la Société Typographique, 1770).

Guest, Harriet, 'A Double Lustre: Femininity and Sociable Commerce, 1730–60', *Eighteenth-Century Studies* 23 (1989–90), 479–501.

—— *Small Change: Women, Learning, Patriotism* (Chicago: Chicago University Press, 2000).

—— 'Sterne, Elizabeth Draper and Drapery', *The Shandean* 9 (1997), 8–33.

Guha, Ranajit, *Dominance without Hegemony: History and Power in Colonial India* (Cambridge, MA and London: Harvard University Press, 1997).

—— *A Rule of Property for Bengal: An Essay on the Idea of Permanent Settlement* (New Delhi: Orient Longman, 1981).

Gunn, J. A. (ed.), *Factions No More: Attitudes to Party in Government and Opposition in Eighteenth-Century England* (London: Cass., 1972).

Gunning, Tom, 'The Horror of Opacity: The Melodrama of Sensation in the Plays of Audré de Lorde', Jacky Bratton, Jim Cook and Christine Gledhill (eds), *Melodrama: Stage Picture Screen* (London: British Film Institute, 1994), pp. 50–61.

Haber, Francis C., 'The Clock as Intellectual Artifact', in Klaus Maurice and Otto Mayr (eds), *The Clockwork Universe: German Clocks and Automata 1550–1650* (New York: Neale Watson Publications/ Smithsonian Institution, 1980), pp. 9–18.

Hamilton, Adrian, *The Infamous Essay on Woman or John Wilkes Seated Between Vice and Virtue* (London: André Deutsch, 1972).

Hamilton, Elizabeth, *Translations of the Letters of a Hindoo Rajah*, ed. Pamela Perkins and Shannon Russell (Peterborough, Ont.: Broadview Press, 1999).

[Hanway, Jonas], *A Letter from a Member of the Marine Society Shewing the Piety, Generosity and Utility of their Design, with respect to the Sea-Service, at this Important Crisis*, 4th edn (London: J.Waugh; W. Fenner; C. Say, 1757).

—— *Virtue in Humble Life: containing Reflections on the Reciprocal Duties of the Wealthy and Indigent, the Master and the Servant: Thoughts on the Various Situations, Passions, Prejudices, and Virtues of Mankind, Drawn from Real Characters: Fables Applicable to the Subjects: Anecdotes of the Living and the Dead: the Result of Long Experience and Observation. In a Dialogue between a Father and his Daughter, in Rural Scenes. A Manual of Devotion, comprehending extracts from Eminent Poets*, 2 vols (London: J. Dodsley, 1774).

Harris, James, *Hermes: Or, A Philosophical Inquiry Concerning Language and Universal Grammar* (London: H. Woodfall for J. Nourse and P. Vaillant, 1751).

Hazeland, William, *A Sermon Preached in the Chapel of the Asylum, Near Westminster-Bridge, on the Sunday before Christmas-Day, 1760* (London: J. Beecroft, 1761).

Hegel, G. W. F., *The Philosophy of History*, trans. J. Sibree (New York: Dover Publications, 1956).

Hobbes, Thomas, *Leviathan*, ed. C. B. Macpherson (Harmondsworth: Penguin Books, 1968).

Hogarth, William, *The Analysis of Beauty* (Menston Yorks: The Scholar Press, 1973).

Howes, Alan B. (ed.), *Sterne: The Critical Heritage* (London and Boston: Routledge and Kegan Paul, 1974).

Hughes, Helen Sard, 'A Precursor of Tristram Shandy', *JEGP* 17(1918), 227–51.

Hume, David, *Enquiries Concerning Human Understanding and Concerning the Principles of Morals*, ed. L. A. Selby-Bigge, rev. P. H. Nidditch, 3rd edn (Oxford: Clarendon Press, 1975).

—— 'On the First Principles of Government', in his *Essays and Treatises on Several Subjects* (London: A. Millar; Edinburgh: A. Kincaid and A. Donaldson, 1758), pp. 20–22.

—— *A Treatise of Human Nature*, ed. L. A. Selby-Bigge, 2nd edn (Oxford: Clarendon Press, 1978).

Jefferson, Thomas, *Writings*, ed. Merrill D. Peterson (New York: The Library of America, 1984).

Jenyns, Soame, *A Free Inquiry into the Nature and Origin of Evil*, 4th edn (Dublin: G. and A. Ewing, 1758).

Johnson, Samuel, *An Account of the Life of Mr. Richard Savage, Son of the Earl Rivers* (London: J. Roberts, 1744).

—— *Diaries, Prayers and Annals, The Yale Edition of the Works of Samuel Johnson*, ed. E. L. McAdam, Jr., with Donald and Mary Hyde (New Haven and London: Yale University Press, 1958), I.

—— *The History of Rasselas, Prince of Abissinia* ed., D. J. Enright (Harmondsworth: Penguin Books, 1985).—

—— *The Idler and The Adventurer, The Yale Edition of the Works of Samuel Johnson*, ed. W. J. Bate, John M. Bullitt, and L. F. Powell (New Haven and London: Yale University Press, 1963), II.

—— 'Observations on a Letter from a French Refugee in America to his Friend a Gentleman in England', in *Political Writings, The Yale Edition of the Works of Samuel Johnson*, ed. Donald J. Greene (New Haven and London: Yale University Press, 1977), X, 167–76.

—— 'Review of Lewis Evans, *Analysis of a General Map of the Middle British Colonies in America*', in *Political Writings, The Yale Edition of the Works of Samuel Johnson*, ed. Donald J. Greene (New Haven and London: Yale University Press, 1977), X, 197–212.

—— 'Taxation no Tyranny: An Answer to the Resolutions and Address of the American Congress', in *Political Writings, The Yale Edition of the Works of Samuel Johnson*, ed. Donald J. Greene (New Haven and London: Yale University Press, 1977), X, 401–55.

—— 'The Vanity of Human Wishes', in *Juvenal in English*, ed. Martin M. Winkler (Harmondsworth: Penguin, 2001), pp. 220–31.

Jones, Vivien (ed.), *Women in the Eighteenth Century: Constructions of Femininity* (London: Routledge, 1990).

Jones, Sir William, *The Principles of Government; In a Dialogue Between a Scholar and a Peasant, Written by a Member of the Society for Constitutional Information* (London: printed and distributed gratis by the Society for Constitutional Information, 1783).

Kant, Immanuel, 'An Answer to the Question: What is Enlightenment?', in D. Simpson (ed.), *German Aesthetic and Literary Criticism: Kant, Fichte, Schelling, Schopenhauer, Hegel* (Cambridge: Cambridge University Press, 1984), pp. 29–34.

—— *Conclusion of the Elements of Ethics* in *Doctrine of Virtue, Metaphysics of Morals*, trans. Mary Gregor (Cambridge: Cambridge University Press, 1991).

—— *Correspondence*, ed. and trans. Arnulf Zweig (Cambridge: Cambridge University Press, 1999).

—— *The Critique of Judgement*, trans. James Creed Meredith (Oxford: Clarendon Press, 1986).

—— 'On the miscarriage of all philosophical trials in theodicy', in his *Religion and Rational Theology*, trans. and ed. Allen W. Wood and George di Giovanni (Cambridge: Cambridge University Press, 1996), pp. 24–37.

—— *Perpetual Peace and Other Essays*, trans. Ted Humphrey (Indianapolis and Cambridge: Hackett Publishing Company, 1983).

Kelly, Hugh, *Memoirs of a Magdalen; Or, the History of Louisa Mildmay*, 2nd edn, 2 vols (London: W. Griffin, 1767).

Kendrick, Robert, 'Re-membering America: Phillis Wheatley's Intertextual Epic', *African American Review* 30:1 (1996), 71–88.

Keymer, Thomas (ed.), *The Cambridge Companion to Sterne* (Cambridge: Cambridge University Press, forthcoming 2008).

—— *Sterne, The Moderns, and the Novel* (Oxford: Oxford University Press, 2002).

Kidson, Alex, *George Romney 1734–1802* (London: National Portrait Gallery, 2002).

King, Reyahn, Sukhdev Sandhu, James Walvin and Jane Girdham, *Ignatius Sancho: An African Man of Letters* (London: National Portrait Gallery, 1997).

Lamb, Jonathan, 'Sterne and Irregular Oratory', in John Richetti (ed.), *The Cambridge Companion to the Eighteenth-Century Novel* (Cambridge: Cambridge University Press, 1996), pp. 153–74.

Landry, Donna, *The Muses of Resistance: Labouring-Class Women's Poetry in Britain 1739–1796* (Cambridge: Cambridge University Press, 1990).

Langdon, Samuel, *Joy and Gratitude to God For the Long Life of a Good King and the Conquest of Quebec* (Portsmouth, NH: Daniel Fowle, 1760).

Lefebvre, Henri, 'The Everyday and Everydayness', *Yale French Studies* 73 (1987), 7–11.

Linebaugh, Peter, *The London Hanged* (Harmondsworth: Penguin, 1993).

Linebaugh, Peter, and Marcus Rediker, *The Many-Headed Hydra: Sailors, Slaves, Commoners and the Hidden History of the Revolutionary Atlantic* (New York and London: Verso Books, 2000).

Lloyd, David and Paul Thomas, *Culture and the State* (New York and London: Routledge, 1998).

Locke, John, *An Essay Concerning Human Understanding*, ed. Peter H. Nidditch (Oxford: Clarendon Press, 1975).

—— *Essays on the Law of Nature*, ed. W. von Leyden (Oxford: Clarendon, 1970).

—— *Two Treatises of Government*, ed. Peter Laslett, 2nd edn (Cambridge: Cambridge University Press, 1967).

Long, Edward, *The Anti-Gallican; Or, the History and Adventures of Harry Cobham Esquire* (London: T. Lownds, 1757).

[Long, Edward], *Candid Reflections upon the Judgement lately awarded by the Court of King's Bench in Westminster-Hall on what is commonly called the Negroe-Cause, by a Planter* (London: T. Lowndes, 1772).

Lonsdale, Roger (ed.), *The New Oxford Book of Eighteenth-Century Verse* (Oxford: Oxford University Press, 1984).

Loveridge, Mark, 'Stories of COCKS and BULLS: The Ending of *Tristram Shandy*', *Eighteenth-Century Fiction*, 5 (1992), 35–54.

Lukács, Georg, *The Historical Novel*, trans. Hannah and Stanley Mitchell (Harmondsworth: Pelican Books, 1981).

Machiavelli, Niccolò, *The Prince*, trans. George Bull (Harmondsworth: Penguin Books, 1961).

Mackenzie, Henry, *The Man of Feeling*, ed. Brian Vickers (Oxford: Oxford University Press, 1967).

Makdisi, Saree, *Romantic Imperialism: Universal Empire and the Culture of Modernity* (Cambridge: Cambridge University Press, 1998).

Mann, Michael, *The Sources of Social Power Volume II: The Rise of Classes and Nation-States 1760–1914* (Cambridge: Cambridge University Press, 1993).

Markley, Robert, 'Sentimentality as Performance: Shaftesbury, Sterne, and the Theatrics of Bourgeois Virtue', in Felicity Nussbaum and Laura Brown (eds), *The New Eighteenth Century* (New York and London, 1987), pp. 210–30.

Marshall, P. J., *The Making and Unmaking of Empires: Britain, India and America 1750–1783* (Oxford: Oxford University Press, 2005).

Marx, Karl, *Capital Volume One*, trans. Ben Fowkes (Harmondsworth: Pelican, 1975).

—— 'Comments on the Latest Prussian Censorship Instruction', in Karl Marx and Friedrich Engels, *Collected Works* (London: Lawrence and Wishart, 1975), I, 109–31.

—— *Grundrisse*, trans. Martin Nicolaus (Harmondsworth: Penguin Books, 1973).

—— 'Labour Rent', *Capital Volume Three*, trans. David Fernbach (Harmondsworth: Penguin Books, 1991), 925–30.

Maurice, Klaus, 'Propagatio fidei per scientias: Jesuit Gifts of Clocks to the Chinese Court', in Klaus Maurice and Otto Mayr (eds), *The Clockwork Universe: German Clocks and Automata 1550–1650* (New York: Neale Watson Publications/ Smithsonian Institution, 1980), pp. 27–36.

Mayr, Otto, *Authority, Liberty and Automatic Machinery in Early Modern Europe* (Baltimore: Johns Hopkins University Press, 1986).

McFarlane, Cameron, *The Sodomite in Fiction and Satire 1660–1750* (New York: Columbia University Press, 1997).

McKeon, Michael, *The Origins of the English Novel 1600–1740* (Baltimore and London: Johns Hopkins University Press, 1987).

McLynn, Frank, *1759: The Year that Britain Became Master of the World* (London: Jonathan Cape, 2004).

McNeil, David, *The Grotesque Depiction of War and the Military in 18th Century English Fiction* (Newark, DE: University of Delaware Press; London: Associated University Presses, 1990).

Medalle, Mrs (ed.), *Letters of the Late Rev. Laurence Sterne to his Most Intimate Friends on Various Occasions, as published by his Daughter Mrs Medalle and including the Letters between Yorick and Eliza*, 2 vols (Vienna: R.Sammer, 1797).

Menninghaus, Winfried, *In Praise of Nonsense: Kant and Bluebeard*, trans. Henry Pickford (Stanford, CA: Stanford University Press, 1999).

Merwe, Pieter van der, 'The Life and Theatrical Career of Clarkson Stanfield 1793–1867' (unpublished PhD thesis, University of Bristol, 1979).

Middleton, Richard, *Bells of Victory* (Cambridge: Cambridge University Press, 1986).

Moglen, Helene, *The Philosophical Irony of Laurence Sterne* (Gainesville, FL: The University Presses of Florida, 1975).

Monk, Samuel H., *The Sublime: A Study of Critical Theories in Eighteenth-Century England* (Ann Arbor: University of Michigan Press, 1960).

Monkman, Kenneth, 'More of Sterne's Politicks 1741–1742', *The Shandean* 1 (1989), 53–108.

Montaigne, Michel de, *The Complete Essays*, trans. M. A. Screech (Harmondsworth: Penguin Books, 1991).

Montesquieu, C. L. de S. Baron de, *The Spirit of the Laws*, trans. T. Nugent (New York: Hafner Publishing Company, 1949).

More, Hannah *Coelebs in Search of a Wife. Comprehending Observations on Domestic Habits and Manners, Religion and Morals*, 3rd edn, 2 vols (London: T. Cadell and W. Davies, 1809).

—— *Sacred Dramas: Chiefly Intended For Young Persons: The Subjects Taken from the Bible to which is added Sensibility. A Poem* (London: T. Cadell, 1782).

Moreiras, Alberto, 'Ten Notes on Primitive Imperial Accumulation: Ginés de Sepúlveda, Las Casas, Fernández de Oviedo', *interventions* 2:3 (2000), 343–63.

Meaghan Morris, *The Pirate's Fiancée* (London: Verso Books, 1988).

Morrison, Toni, *Playing in the Dark: Whiteness and the Literary Imagination* (London: Picador, 1992).

[Mortimer, Thomas], Philanthropos, *Every Man His Own Broker., Or A Guide to Exchange Alley* (London: S. Hooper, 1761).

Motooka, Wendy, *The Age of Reasons: Quixotism, Sentimentalism and Political Economy in Eighteenth-Century Britain* (London and New York: Routledge, 1998).

Mullan, John, *Sentiment and Sociability: The Language of Feeling in the Eighteenth Century* (Oxford: Clarendon Press, 1988).

Nancy, Jean-Luc, *The Inoperative Community*, trans. Peter Connor et al. (Minneapolis and Oxford: Minnesota University Press, 1991).

New, Melvyn (ed.), *The Sermons of Laurence Sterne: The Notes* (Gainesville: University Presses of Florida, 1996).

—— 'Sterne and the Narrative of Determinateness', *Eighteenth-Century Fiction* 4:4 (1992), 315–29.

—— *Tristram Shandy: Contemporary Critical Essays* (London: Macmillan, 1992).

Niebuhr, Carsten, *Travels Through Arabia, and Other Countries in the East. Performed by M. Niebuhr, now a Captain of Engineers in the Service of the King of Denmark*, trans. Robert Heron, 2 vols (Edinburgh: R. Morison, G. Mudie, T. Vernor, 1792).

Nisbet, Richard, *The Capacity of Negroes for Religious and Moral Improvement Considered: With Cursory Hints, to Proprietors and to Government, for the Immediate Melioration of the Condition of Slaves in the Sugar Colonies: to which are subjoined Short and Practical Discourses to Negroes on the Plain and Obvious Principles of Religion and Morality* (1789) (Westport, CT: Negro Universities Press, 1970).

Nussbaum, Felicity A., *The Autobiographical Subject: Gender and Ideology in Eighteenth-Century England* (Baltimore and London: Johns Hopkins University Press, 1989).

O'Neale, Sondra A., *Jupiter Hammon and the Biblical Beginnings of African-American Literature* (Metuchen, NJ and London: Scarecrow Press, 1993).

Orme, Robert, *A History of the Military Transactions of the British Nation in Indostan, From the Year MDCCXLV. To Which is Prefixed a Dissertation on the Establishments made by Mahomedan Conquerors in Indostan*, 2nd edn, 3 vols (London: John Nourse, 1773).

Osborne, Peter (ed.), *A Critical Sense: Interviews with Intellectuals* (London and New York: Routledge, 1996).

Otis, James, *The Rights of the British Colonies Asserted and Proved* (Boston, MA; London: J. Almon, 1764).

Paine, Thomas, *The Rights of Man* (Harmondsworth: Penguin, 1985).

Pares, Richard, *War and Trade in the West Indies 1739–1763* (London: Frank Cass & Co, 1963).

Pateman, Carol, *The Sexual Contract* (Cambridge: Polity Press, 1988).

Patterson, Orlando, *Slavery and Social Death: A Comparative Study* (Cambridge, MA; London: Harvard University Press, 1982).

Pennington, Montagu (ed.), *A Series of Letters between Mrs. Elizabeth Carter and Miss Catherine Talbot, from the year 1741 to 1770. To which are added, Letters from Mrs. Carter to Mrs. Vesey, between the years 1763 and 1787; published from the original manuscripts*, 2 vols (London: F. C. and J. Rivington, 1808).

Perelman, Michael, *The Invention of Capitalism: Classical Political Economy and the Secret History of Primitive Accumulation* (Durham and London: Duke University Press, 2000).

Perkins, Merle L., 'European Politics', *Studies on Voltaire and the Eighteenth Century* 36 (1965), 43–72.

—— 'Peace Projects of Saint-Pierre and Rousseau', *Studies on Voltaire and the Eighteenth Century* 36 (1965), 92–111.

—— 'Voltaire and the Abbe de Saint-Pierre on World Peace', *Studies on Voltaire and the Eighteenth Century* 18 (1961), 9–34.

Pierce, David and Peter de Voogd (eds), *Laurence Sterne in Modernism and Postmodernism* (Amsterdam: Rodopi, 1996).

Piganiol de la Force, Jean-Aimar, *Nouveau voyage de France avec un itineraire, et des cartes fait exprès, qui marquent exactement les routes qu'il faut suivre pour voyager dans toutes les provinces de ce royaume*, 2 vols (Paris: Guillaume Desprez, 1755).

Piozzi, Hester, *The Intimate Letters of Hester Piozzi and Penelope Pennington 1788–1822*, ed. Oswald G. Knapp (London: John Lane, 1914).

Pittock, Murray G. H., 'The Aeneid in the Age of Burlington: A Jacobite Text?' in Toby Barnard and Jane Clark (eds), *Lord Burlington: Architecture, Art and Life* (London and Rio Grande, OH: The Hambleden Press, 1995), pp. 231–49.

—— *Celtic Identity and the British Image* (Manchester: Manchester University Press, 1999).

—— *Inventing and Resisting Britain: Cultural Identities in Britain and Ireland 1685–1789* (London: Macmillan, 1997).

Pocock, J. G. A., *Barbarism and Religion Volume One: The Enlightenments of Edward Gibbon 1737–1764* (Cambridge: Cambridge University Press, 1999).

—— *Virtue, Commerce and History* (Cambridge: Cambridge University Press, 1985).

Pollack, Sheldon, 'Cosmopolitan and Vernacular in History', *Public Culture* 12:3 (2000), 591–625.

Pope, Alexander 'Epistle to a Lady', in F. W. Bateson (ed.), *The Twickenham Edition of the Poems of Alexander Pope*, 2nd edn (London and New York: Methuen and Yale University Press, 1961), III. ii, 46–74.

—— *Essay on Man*, in Maynard Mack (ed.), *The Twickenham Edition of the Poems of Alexander Pope* (London and New Haven: Methuen and Yale University Press, 1950), III.i.

—— *The Iliad of Homer*, in Maynard Mack (ed.), *The Twickenham Edition of The Poems of Alexander Pope* (London and New Haven: Methuen and Yale University Press, 1967), VII–VIII.

—— *Windsor-Forest*, in E. Audra and Aubrey Williams (eds), *The Twickenham Edition of the Poems of Alexander Pope* (London and New York: Methuen and Yale University Press, 1961), I, 123–94.

Postone, Moishe, *Time, Labor and Social Domination: A Reinterpretation of Marx's Critical Theory* (Cambridge: Cambridge University Press, 1996).

Pringle, Sir James, *The Life of General James Wolfe, the Conqueror of Canada: Or the Elogium of that Renowned Hero, Attempted According to the Rules of Eloquence. With a Monumental Inscription, Latin and English, to Perpetuate His Memory* (London: for J. Kearsly, 1760).

Rancière, Jacques, 'The Aesthetic Revolution and its Outcomes: Emplotments of Autonomy and Heteronomy', *NLR* 14 (2002), 133–51.

—— *On the Shores of Politics*, trans. Liz Heron (London and New York: Verso Books).

Raynal, Guillaume-Thomas, Abbé de, *A Philosophical History of the Settlements and Trades of the Europeans in the East and West Indies*, trans. J. Justamond, 3rd edn, 5 vols (London: T. Cadell, 1777).

Renan, Ernest, 'What is a Nation?, in Bhabha, Homi (ed.), *Nation and Narration* (London: Routledge, 1990), pp. 8–22.

Reynolds, Joshua, *Discourses on Art*, ed. Robert R. Wark (New Haven and London: Yale University Press, 1997).

Robbins, Caroline, *The Eighteenth-Century Commonwealthman: Studies in the Transmission, Development and Circumstance of English Liberal Thought from the Restoration of Charles II until the War with the Thirteen Colonies* (Cambridge, MA: Harvard University Press, 1959).

Robertson, William, *An Historical Disquisition Concerning the Knowledge which the Ancients had of India; and to the Progress of Trade with that Country Prior to the Discovery of the Passage to it by the Cape of Good Hope* (Basil: J. J. Tourneison, 1792).

Rose, Jacqueline, 'Margaret Thatcher and Ruth Ellis', in *Why War? – Psychoanalysis, Politics, and the Return to Melanie Klein* (Oxford: Blackwell, 1993), pp. 41–86.

Ross, Ian Campbell, *Laurence Sterne: A Life* (Oxford: Oxford University Press, 2001).

Rousseau, Jean-Jacques, *Émile*, trans. Barbara Foxley (London: J. M. Dent, 1993).

—— *The Social Contract and Discourses*, trans. G. D. H. Cole, rev. J. H. Brumfitt and John C. Hall (London: Dent Everyman, 1993).

Roworth, Wendy Wassyng (ed.), *Angelica Kauffman: A Continental Artist in Georgian England* (Brighton: Reaktion Books, in association with The Royal Pavilion Art Gallery and Museum, 1992).

Rudé, George, *Wilkes and Liberty. A Social Study of 1763 to 1774* (Oxford: Clarendon Press, 1962).

Russell, William, *Essay on the Character, Manners and Genius of Women in Different Ages. Enlarged from the French of M. Thomas*, 2 vols (Philadelphia: R. Aitken, 1774).

Sancho, Ignatius, *The Letters of Ignatius Sancho*, ed. Paul Edwards and Polly Rewt (Edinburgh University Press, 1994).

Savage, Richard, *The Bastard: A Poem* (Dublin: S. Harding, 1728).

Schlegel, Friedrich, 'On Incomprehensibility', in *Friedrich Schlegel's Lucinde and the Fragments*, trans. Peter Firchow (Minneapolis: University of Minnesota Press, 1971), pp. 257–71.

Schmitt, Carl, *The Nomos of the Earth in the International Law of the Jus Publicum Europaeum* trans. G. L. Ulmen (New York: Telos, 2003).

Schochet, Gordon J., *Patriarchalism in Political Thought. The Authoritarian Family and Political Speculation and Attitudes, Especially in Seventeenth-Century England* (Oxford: Blackwell, 1975).

Scott, Sarah, *A Description of Millenium Hall* ed. Gary Kelly (Peterborough, Ont.: Broadview Press, 1995).

—— *The History of Mecklenburgh, From the First Settlement of the Vandals in that Country to the Present Time* (London: J. Newbury, 1762).

—— *The History of Sir George Ellison*, 2 vols (London: A. Millar, 1766).

—— *The Life of Theodore Agrippa D'Aubigné* (London: Edward and Charles Dilly, 1772).

Scrafton, Luke, *Reflections on the Government &c of Indostan: With a Short Sketch of the History of Bengal, from the Year 1739–1756; And an Account of the English Affairs to 1758* (London: W. Richardson and S. Clark, 1763).

Sedgwick, Eve Kosofsky, *Between Men: English Literature and Male Homosocial Desire* (New York: Columbia University Press, 1985).

Sekora, John, *Luxury: The Concept in Western Thought, Eden to Smollett* (Baltimore and London: Johns Hopkins University Press, 1977).

Sharp, Granville, *The Just Limitation of Slavery in the Laws of God, Compared With the Unbounded Claims of the African Traders and British American Slaveholders* (London: B. White, E & C. Dilly, 1776).

—— *The Law of Liberty, Or Royal Law, by which All Mankind Will Certainly Be Judged! Earnestly Recommended to the Serious Consideration of all Slaveholders and Slave-Dealers* (London: B. White, E. & C. Dilly, 1776).

Sheridan, Thomas, *A Course of Lectures on Elocution* (London: np, 1762).

Smart, Christopher, *Selected Poems*, ed. Karina Williamson and Marcus Walsh (Harmondsworth: Penguin Books, 1990).

Smith, Adam, *An Inquiry into the Nature and Causes of the Wealth of Nations*, ed. R. H. Campbell, A. S. Skinner and W. B. Todd, 2 vols (Oxford: Clarendon Press, 1976).

—— *Lectures on Jurisprudence*, ed. R. L. Meek, D. D. Raphael, P. G. Stein (Oxford: Clarendon Press, 1978).

—— *The Theory of Moral Sentiments*, ed. D. D. Raphael and A. L. Macfie (Oxford: Clarendon Press, 1976).

Smollett, Tobias, *Continuation of the Complete History of England to 1765*, 5 vols (London: Richard Baldwin, 1763–68).

—— *Humphry Clinker*, ed. Angus Ross (Harmondsworth: Penguin Books, 1967).

Solkin, David H., 'The Battle of the Ciceros: Richard Wilson and the politics of landscape in the age of John Wilkes', in Simon Pugh (ed.), *Reading Landscape: Country – City – Capital* (Manchester: MUP, 1990), pp. 41–65.

—— *Painting for Money: The Visual Arts and the Public Sphere in Eighteenth-Century England* (New Haven and London: Yale University Press, 1992).

Starr, G. A., 'Sentimental De-Education', in Douglas Lane Patey and Timothy Keegan (eds), *Augustan Studies: Essays in Honour of Irvin Ehrenpreis* (Newark, DE: University of Delaware Press; London: Associated University Presses, 1985), pp. 253–62.

Sterne, Laurence, *The Life and Opinions of Tristram Shandy, Gentleman: The Text*, The Florida Edition of the Works of Laurence Sterne, vols 1–2, ed. Melvyn New and Joan New (Gainesville, FL: University Presses of Florida, 1984).

—— *The Letters of Laurence Sterne*, ed. Lewis Perry Curtis (Oxford: Clarendon Press, 1935).

—— *A Sentimental Journey through France and Italy and Continuation of the Bramine's Journal: The Text and Notes*, The Florida Edition of the Works of Laurence Sterne, vol. 6, ed. Melvyn New and W. G. Day (Gainesville, FL: University Presses of Florida, 2002).

—— *The Sermons of Laurence Sterne*, The Florida Edition of the Works of Laurence Sterne, vols 4–5; ed. Melvyn New (Gainesville, FL: University Presses of Florida, 1996).

Still, Judith, *Feminine Economies: Thinking Against the Market in the Enlightenment and the Late Twentieth Century* (Manchester: Manchester University Press, 1997).

Stone, Lawrence, *The Family, Sex and Marriage in England 1500–1800* (Harmondsworth: Penguin Books, 1979).

Suleri, Sara, *The Rhetoric of English India* (Chicago and London: University of Chicago Press, 1992).

Swenson, James, *On Jean-Jacques Rousseau* (Stanford, CA: Stanford University Press, 2000).

Swift, Jonathan, *Gulliver's Travels* (Harmondsworth: Penguin Books, 2003).

Teschke, Benno, *The Myth of 1648: Class, Geopolitics and the Making of Modern International Relations* (London: Verso, 2003).

Thompson, E. P., 'Time, Work-Discipline and Industrial Capitalism', in his *Customs in Common* (Harmondsworth: Penguin, 1991), pp. 352–403.

Todd, Janet, *Sensibility* (London: Routledge, 1986), p. 97.

Trumbach, Randolph, *The Rise of the Egalitarian Family: Aristocratic Kinship and Domestic Relations in Eighteenth-Century England* (New York and London: Academic Press, 1978).

Trumpener, Katie, *Bardic Nationalism: The Romantic Novel and the British Empire* (Princeton: Princeton University Press).

Tucker, Abraham, *The Light of Nature Pursued* (1768–77), 4 vols (Bristol: Thoemmes Press, 2003).

[Tucker, Josiah], *The Case of Going to War, For the Sake of Procuring, Enlarging, or Securing of Trade, Considered in a New Light, Being a Fragment of a Greater Work* (London: R. and J. Dodsley, 1763).

Turner, James Grantham, ' "A Wanton Kind of Chace": Display as Procurement in *A Harlot's Progress* and Its Reception', in *The Other Hogarth: Aesthetics of Difference*, ed. by Bernadette Fort and Angela Rosenthal (Princeton and Oxford: Princeton University Press, 2001), pp. 38–61.

Turner, Thomas, *The Diary of Thomas Turner 1754–1765*, ed. David Vaisey (Oxford: Oxford University Press, 1984).

Voltaire, 'Aventure Indienne traduite par l'ignorant', in *Romans et contes*, ed. Frédéric Deloffre and Jacques van den Heuvel (Paris: Gallimard, 1979), pp. 281–3.

—— *Candide and Related Texts*, trans. David Wootton (Indianapolis/Cambridge: Hackett Publishing Co., 2000).

—— 'Histoire d'un bon Bramin', in *Romans et contes*, ed. Frédéric Deloffre and Jacques van den Heuvel (Paris: Gallimard, 1979), pp. 235–7.

—— *Political Writings*, ed. and trans. by David Williams (Cambridge: Cambridge University Press, 2000).

—— *Treatise on Tolerance and Other Writings*, ed. and trans. Simon Harvey, (Cambridge: Cambridge University Press, 2000).

Wallace, Robert, *Various Prospects of Mankind, Nature and Providence* (London: np, 1761).

Walpole, Horace, *The Castle of Otranto*, ed. Emma Clery (Oxford: Oxford University Press, 1994).

—— *The Yale Edition of Horace Walpole's Correspondence*, ed. W. S. Lewis (London and New Haven: Yale and Oxford University Presses, 1974).

Warburton, William, *The Divine Legation of Moses Demonstrated, on the Principles of a Religious Deist, From the Omission of the Doctrine of a Future State of Rewards and Punishments in the Jewish Dispensation* (London: Fletcher Gyles, 1738).

Warner, Marina, 'The Making of Imperial Gothic: *Omai, Aladdin* and the British Encounter with Zombies', *TLS*, 12 April 2002.

Warton, Thomas, *The Pleasures of Melancholy: A Poem* (London: R. Dodsley and M. Cooper, 1747).

Watts, Carol, 'A Comedy of Terrors: *Candide* and the Jus Publicum Europaeum', *South Atlantic Quarterly* 104:2 (2005), 337–47.

—— 'The Modernity of Sterne', in David Pierce and Peter de Voogd (eds), *Laurence Sterne in Modernism and Postmodernism* (Amsterdam: Rodopi, 1996), pp. 19–38.

—— 'Sterne's Politicks, Ireland and the Nature of Evil-Speaking', in Thomas Keymer (ed.), *The Cambridge Companion to Sterne* (Cambridge: Cambridge University Press, forthcoming 2008).

—— 'Time and the Working Mother: Kristeva's "Women's Time" Revisited', *Radical Philosophy* 91 (1998), 6–18.

Weiskel, Thomas, *The Romantic Sublime: Studies in the Structure and Psychology of Transcendence* (Baltimore and London: Johns Hopkins University Press, 1976).

Whale, John, *Imagination Under Pressure, 1789–1832: Aesthetics, Politics, and Utility* (Cambridge: Cambridge University Press, 2000).

Wheatley, Phillis, *The Collected Works of Phillis Wheatley*, ed. John C. Shields (New York and Oxford: Oxford University Press).

Whitehead, W., 'Verses to the People of England', *Annual Register* 1(1758), 398.

Whyte, D., *The Fallacy of French Freedom and the Dangerous Tendency of Sterne's Writings, Or An Essay Shewing that Irreligion and Immorality Pave the Way for Tyranny, and Anarchy: and that Sterne's Writings are both Irreligious and Immoral: Concluding with Some Observations on the Present State of France* (London: np, 1799).

Wilkes, John, *The History of England from the Revolution to the Accession of the Brunswick Line* (London: S. Almon, 1768).

—— *The North Briton Revised and Corrected by the Author*, 2 vols (Dublin: John Mitchell, 1764).

Williams, Raymond, *Marxism and Literature* (Oxford: Oxford University Press, 1977).

Wilson, Kathleen, 'Empire of Virtue: The Imperial Project and Hanoverian Culture 1720–1785', in Lawrence Stone (ed.), *An Imperial State at War: Britain from 1689 to 1815* (London and New York: Routledge, 1994), pp. 124–62.

—— *The Island Race: Englishness, Empire and Gender in the Eighteenth Century* (London and New York: Routledge, 2003).

—— *The Sense of the People: Politics, Culture and Imperialism, 1715–1785* (Cambridge: Cambridge University Press, 1995).

Wollstonecraft, Mary, 'Letters Written in Sweden, Norway and Denmark', in Marilyn Butler and Janet Todd (eds), *The Works of Mary Wollstonecraft* (London: Pickering and Chatto, 1989), IV.

—— *A Vindication of the Rights of Woman*, in *Political Writings*, ed. Janet Todd (Oxford: Oxford University Press, 1994).

—— *The Wrongs of Woman: Or, Maria, A Fragment*, ed. Gary Kelly (Oxford: Oxford World's Classics, 1998).

Wood, Allen W., 'Kant's Project for Perpetual Peace', in *Cosmopolitics: Thinking and Feeling beyond the Nation*, ed. Pheng Cheah and Bruce Robbins (Minneapolis: University of Minnesota Press, 1998), pp. 59–76.

Wright, Arnold, and William Lutley Sclater (eds), *Sterne's Eliza: Some Account of her Life in India, With Her Letters Written Between 1757 and 1774* (London: Heinemann, 1922).

Young, Arthur, *The Farmer's Letter to the People of England*, 2nd edn (London: np, 1771).

Zafar, Rafia, *We Wear the Mask: African Americans Write American Literature 1760–1870* (New York: Columbia University Press, 1997).

Zimmerman, Everett, '*Tristram Shandy* and Narrative Representation', in Melvyn New (ed.), *Tristram Shandy: Contemporary Critical Essays* (London: Macmillan, 1992).

Žižek, Slavoj, 'Afterword: Lenin's Choice', in V. I. Lenin, *Revolution at the Gates: A Selection of Writings from February to October 1917*, ed. Slavoj Žižek (London and New York: Verso Books, 2002).

# INDEX